Strategic Integrated Marketing Communications

This book provides a disciplined, systematic look at what is necessary to the planning and implementation of an effective Integrated Marketing Communications (IMC) programme.

Throughout, attention is paid to balancing theory with practical application, how to successfully implement theory for effective communication. Step-by-step, knowledge and understanding builds through the book, starting by laying a foundation to provide context, looking at the role of IMC in building brands and strengthening companies. The book then considers what goes into developing and executing effective messages, and how to ensure that they are consistent and consistently delivered, regardless of media. A detailed, practical overview of the strategic planning process is provided, illustrated by numerous examples and cases, along with 'desktop' tools and worksheets for developing and implementing an IMC plan.

The 4th edition of this classic textbook has been fully updated throughout, and includes:

- Updated and expanded coverage of digital media, including issues relating to privacy and media strategy.
- New sections on setting campaign budgets, brand architecture, target audience action objectives, social marketing communication, and such practices as gamification and experiential marketing.
- Extended content on international advertising and shared cultural values.
- The introduction of a channels-based typology of marketing communication.
- Updated international examples and case studies throughout.

A comprehensive and accessible guide to the steps of planning and developing an effective IMC campaign, this book should be core reading for students studying Integrated Marketing Communications, Strategic Communications, Principles of Advertising, Media Planning and Brand Management.

Larry Percy is a marketing and communications expert and consultant with more than 40 years' experience. He previously held posts at Copenhagen Business School, University of Pittsburgh's Katz Graduate School of Business, the University of Oxford, Luiss Business School in Rome, and the Stockholm School of Economics. He has more than 90 publications to his name, including 12 books, and has served on the editorial board of a number of academic journals.

Strategic Integrated Marketing Communications

Fourth Edition

Larry Percy

Routledge
Taylor & Francis Group

LONDON AND NEW YORK

Designed cover image: artvea

Fourth edition published 2023
by Routledge
4 Park Square, Milton Park, Abingdon, Oxon, OX14 4RN

and by Routledge
605 Third Avenue, New York, NY 10158

Routledge is an imprint of the Taylor & Francis Group, an informa business

First edition published by Butterworth Heinemann/Elsevier 2008
Third edition published by Routledge 2018

British Library Cataloguing-in-Publication Data
A catalogue record for this book is available from the British Library

ISBN: 978-0-367-77061-7 (hbk)
ISBN: 978-0-367-77062-4 (pbk)
ISBN: 978-1-003-16963-5 (ebk)

DOI: 10.4324/9781003169635

Typeset in Bembo
by MPS Limited, Dehradun

Access the Support Material: www.routledge.com/978-0-367-77062-4

Contents

Figures

Tables

Adverts

Preface

Integrated Marketing Communication (IMC) as it is generally understood today has been around now for some 35 years. It was back then that academics and marketers began to take the various ideas associated with effective marketing communication and put them together in a consistent and systematic way. Of course, many of these principles had been around for a long time, but it was the idea of integrating all aspects of communication that took hold.

Yet, as we have been pointing out since the first edition of this book, IMC is honoured more on paper than in reality. Even though managers continue to agree that IMC is important to their marketing communication efforts, and many will say they do indeed practice it, the sad truth is that it is rarely the case. There are many reasons for this, and we will be dealing with some of them in the first chapter.

Nevertheless, IMC does provide the best possible approach to building an effective communication program for a brand or company. Why? It is because at its heart IMC is all about planning and consistency of message and execution. A disciplined strategic planning process will help ensure that the right message reaches the correct target audience at the right time in order to maximize the likelihood of effectively processing the message, leading to the desired communication effect. It is also what ensures that each execution no matter how it is delivered, has the same message and a consistent look and feel. This means for messages in everything from traditional media to digital media, business cards, trade shows, packaging, the sides of delivery trucks, sales kits; *anything* at all where a potential consumer may be exposed to the brand or company. It is this consistency across media, and within campaign as well, that optimizes the likelihood of a brand's message getting through, even in a world full of distractions.

This planning process and how to execute it is what this book is all about. Throughout, we are paying attention to what is all too often a contentious relationship between academic theory and practical application. It is essential to understand the theory underlying effective communication, but that theory must be applied. In the book we present the essential theory, and we show how it is used to plan and execute an effective IMC campaign.

The book begins with an overview of IMC to provide context, looking at its origins as a marketing discipline and its importance to brands and companies. With this as a foundation we examine the building blocks of IMC, beginning with a look at its major components, with a special emphasis on digital media, and then looking more deeply at what is required to develop and execute an effective message. In the last section of the book all of this comes together in a detailed consideration of the strategic planning process, what goes into it, the process itself, and how it is implemented. Along the way numerous cases and examples are provided, plus a number of 'desktop' tools and worksheets that help summarize what goes into effective IMC planning and implementation.

New to this edition is a much expanded look at media and media planning concepts such as reach and effective frequency. Throughout, more attention is given to digital media, including an expanded section in the media chapter. A general model of positioning is now included that underscores the important relationship between positioning and brand awareness and brand attitude strategy. Also new is a look at the role the preconscious plays in message processing, and a section has been added on content marketing.

Many people have been involved in bringing this new edition to publication, and I want to thank them all. I would especially like to thank Laura Hussey at Routledge who has helped with the many details needed. And as with everything I write, my grateful thanks to Kristie Hutto. She continues to manage typing it all from my not always easy to read hand-written pages. Beyond those directly involved with the book, I want to again acknowledge and thank my long-time colleague and friend John Rossiter, who continues to provide intellectual stimulation and challenges, making all of my work better. There is no one better in our field. And as always, thanks to my wife Mary Walton for her continuing support and encouragement.

Larry Percy

Part I

Introduction to IMC

In the first part of the book we introduce the notion of integrated marketing communication (IMC) and look at its overall role in building strong brands and strengthening companies. IMC as a marketing discipline emerged in the1980s. This is not to say that marketers did not do many of the things implied by IMC before this time, only that it was not until then that the idea was formalized as it is understood today. There were many definitions of IMC in those early days, and even today the term is used in a variety of ways when discussing marketing communication activities. IMC is *planning* in a systematic way in order to determine the most effective and consistent message for the appropriate target audience.

Despite most marketers believing IMC is important and should be practised, the reality is that it is rarely successfully implemented. There are several reasons for this, largely concerned with the way companies are organized, their culture, and how those likely to be involved in a truly *integrated* marketing communication effort are compensated. If managers' salaries, promotions, and bonuses are linked to the size of their budgets, their primary concern will likely be to optimize their share of the IMC pie rather than consider what might be best for the brand overall.

To be effective, IMC must follow a thorough strategic planning process; one will be briefly introduced in Chapter 1. It will outline what is involved in providing a firm foundation for gaining an understanding of the various aspects and elements of IMC that will be discussed in subsequent chapters, leading up to the final part of the book, which deals with IMC strategic planning in depth. With this foundation in place, Chapter 2 will consider the role of IMC in building brands and Chapter 3 how IMC strengthens companies. The two are interrelated, as we will see.

The key to building effective brands is first finding the correct positioning, and then successfully creating a strong, positive brand attitude. IMC is critical to ensuring that all aspects of a brand's marketing communication are delivering a consistent message towards that end. It also plays an important role in managing the communication strategies associated with a company's branding strategy within its overall product and brand portfolio.

All the marketing communication efforts for a company's brands will also contribute to its overall corporate identity, image, and reputation. Although *marketing* communication is not the only communication affecting corporate identity, image, and reputation, it plays a significant role. IMC programmes must therefore also be consistent with, and be a part of, the management and delivery of all other aspects of a company's communication. Corporate meaning, which is comprised of all those elements, will inform a corporate brand, and this *corporate* brand must be compatible with all the brands the company markets.

DOI: 10.4324/9781003169635-1

1   Overview of IMC

In the world of marketing and communication, much changes. There is no question that over the past several years we have seen a surge in e-marketing and a seemingly endless stream of digital media introductions, especially with social media. This has led many to suggest that the role of advertising and other marketing communication options, and how they work, is also changing. It is *not*. The mind still processes information in the same way, and the *role* of advertising and other marketing communication continues to be what it has always been: to move more of a branded product or service or to obtain a higher price point than would have been possible without it. Rossiter and Percy (2013) have provided a number of examples of how both practitioners and academics are encouraging this false notion with the use of what they call 'masking jargon'. In effect, using new terms for old concepts; providing an illusion of change.

Why do we bring this up at the beginning of a book on integrated marketing communication? When the idea of IMC emerged in the mid- to late 1980s it was something new, not just a new name for the practice of including various types of marketing communication options in a campaign; that is, it was new if correctly understood and implemented. Unfortunately, few companies seem able to truly implement effective IMC. We will touch on several of the key reasons for this later in this chapter. First, however, we need to understand just what is meant by integrated marketing communication (IMC).

What is IMC?

We might briefly define IMC as the planning and execution of all types of advertising-like and promotion-like messages selected for a brand, service, or company, in order to meet a common set of communication objectives or, more particularly, to support a single 'positioning'. We believe strongly that the key to IMC is *planning*, and the aim is to deliver a *consistent* message, something that has become more and more difficult in the age of digital media, where the content of advertising for a brand may change frequently, even daily.

Original definitions of IMC

In 1989, the American Association of Advertising Agencies (known as the 4As) formed a task force on integration that was to define IMC from the viewpoint of the 4As agencies. The task force came up with this definition of IMC:

DOI: 10.4324/9781003169635-2

A concept of marketing communications planning that recognizes the added value of a comprehensive plan that evaluates the strategic roles of a variety of communication disciplines (e.g., general advertising, direct response, sales promotion, and public relations) and combines these disciplines to provide clarity, consistency, and maximum communication impact.

In the same year, the investment firm Shearson Lehman Hutton (1989) issued a detailed report on consumer advertising, with special emphasis on diversification into areas that would lead to integration. They concluded that a number of changes happening in the marketplace would force traditional packaged goods marketers to take a much more integrated approach to marketing. They noted that high-involvement, non-service products (for example, cars or cruise holidays), where the selling task is more complicated, were at that time more apt to use integrated strategies. The report concluded that the dynamics were in place for a surge in demand for integrated communication from all kinds of advertisers.

In their 1993 book *Integrated Marketing Communication* (perhaps the first book to really deal with the subject), Don Schultz and his colleagues talked about IMC as a new way of looking at the whole, where once we only saw parts such as advertising, public relations, sales promotions, purchasing, employee communication, and so on (Schultz et al., 1993). They saw IMC as realigning communication to look at the way the consumer sees it, as a flow of information from indistinguishable sources. They observed that professional communicators have always been condescendingly amused that consumers call everything advertising or public relations.

They recognize with concern, if not chagrin, that that is exactly the point. It is all one 'thing' to the consumer who sees or hears it. They go on to say that IMC means talking to people who buy or don't buy based on what *they* see, hear, feel, and so on; it is not just about a product or service. It also means delivering a return on investment, not just spending a budget. This definition 'looks back' at the goals of IMC. We will be looking largely from a strategic perspective for *planning and implementing* IMC.

More recent definitions of IMC

The emphasis in those early days was certainly on *planning*, and to our mind this must remain at the heart of any definition of IMC. But today, 20 years on, IMC is considered more from a customer relationship point of view. Tom Duncan, at the University of Colorado, who like Don Schultz and his colleagues at Northwestern, was one of the early academics to restructure their advertising programmes in terms of IMC, saw it as *simply put* (our emphasis) a 'process for managing customer relationships that drive brand value' (Duncan, 2002). Nothing 'simple' at all we would argue. He goes on to say that what this means is that IMC is a 'cross-functional process for creating and nourishing profitable relationships with customers and other stakeholders by strategically controlling or influencing all messages sent to these groups and encouraging data-driven, purposeful dialogue with them'.

There is a lot here in this definition. Of course, marketing is (or should be) about satisfying consumer demand. But we would suggest that the real key here, in terms of IMC, is 'strategically controlling or influencing all messages sent', and to do that requires strategic planning. Duncan goes on to 'define' the major elements within his definition. The idea of a cross-functional process refers to a need for all parts of a company and vendors working on a particular brand to work together to 'plan and merge all messages a company sends to its target audiences'. We totally agree, but, as we will see, getting everyone involved in a brand's marketing communication to cooperate is very difficult. Creating and nourishing stakeholder relationships and profitable customer relationships refers to IMC identifying those target audiences most likely to contribute to long-term profit, including both consumers and others with links to a brand (for example, Government regulatory agencies and investors). Strategically controlling or influencing all messages means that every contact with the market must be consistent, and encouraging purposeful dialogue implies that people want the ability to interact with a company.

As we said, there is a lot here in this definition but, in the end, IMC is really all about *planning* in order to deliver a *consistent message*. Effective IMC should certainly encourage strong customer relationships, but it does that through effective planning in order to develop an integrated communication programme that will optimize specific communication objectives that lead to a desired behaviour on the part of a target audience. Many of the original concepts associated with IMC have changed or evolved over the years (Kitchen and Schultz, 2009), but again we would argue that the key to IMC remains understanding it strategically, as a *planning* function.

Strategies for building strong profitable relationships with customers and other stakeholders are part of the marketing plan, and effective marketing communication should support that plan. This is perhaps a good place to say something about what should be involved in setting objectives for long-term profit in IMC planning. Rossiter et al. (2018) have made an important point about market share and profit. While building market share is of course desirable, they suggest it is widely misunderstood. The ultimate objective for every company is *profit*. But if you cannot easily change your price or the cost of production, the only way to increase profit is by increasing *unit sales,* or more specifically the rate of unit sales. It therefore follows that unit sales should always be the primary operational marketing objective for an IMC programme, and *not* market share.

A *strategic* understanding of IMC must be based on a rigorous planning process that will identify appropriate target audiences, set specific communication objectives for these target audiences, develop marketing communication that will accomplish those objectives in a consistent way, and find the best ways of delivering the message. That is what IMC, and this book, is all about.

Managing IMC

In the early years of IMC thinking, despite the feelings of many marketing managers that advertising agencies may not have been the best planning catalyst for IMC, they did play a major role in providing and managing these initial attempts at integrating marketing communication. A number of very large advertising agencies and agency groups were quite active in this new area of IMC. They were all selling themselves as being able to provide all the services and disciplines a marketer could want for marketing communication. But even at the time, what they were offering as IMC was not what their clients either wanted or what they were willing to pay for. Although 85 percent of advertisers said they wanted IMC services, only a fraction felt their advertising agency would provide it. Major agencies tried to deal with this issue in different ways. Many agencies set up programmes to educate their executives in IMC. Major advertising agencies may have had a slow or even wrong start, but there is no doubt that they seemed committed to delivering IMC for their clients. In today's world, however, very little, if any, of this early zeal remains.

Even though the marketing communication industry has always been comprised of a variety of speciality groups, almost by default traditional advertising agencies took the lead in the IMC planning for their clients' brands. The reason was simple: the vast majority of a company's communication budget was usually with an advertising agency. But today, there has been a virtual explosion in the number of new agencies devoted to specific aspects of marketing communication, fuelled in a large part by an (unfortunate) trend toward an ever-increasing emphasis on promotion, as well as a surge in digital media. There are now 'digital' agencies, for example, that deal only in advertising for digital media. Unfortunately, this only complicates the ability to develop and manage sound strategies for IMC. Let us consider for a moment just some of the many groups that could play a role in the creation and delivery of marketing communication.

To begin with, there are all the traditional sources of marketing communication messages such as advertising agencies (everything from full-service agencies to boutiques), sales promotion or collateral agencies, public relations firms, and specialty agencies (for example, those dealing with trade shows or event marketing). Add to them corporate identity groups, packaging specialists, branding companies, the increasing number of direct response agencies, and telemarketers. Then there are internet agencies, digital and social media agencies, and media buying groups (who themselves are playing a greater role in overall communication strategy).

Distribution channels can also have an impact, and not only with trade communications. Retailers certainly play an influencing role through co-op programmes or channels marketing. All franchise organizations have participation from franchises in their marketing communication. Soft drink and beer companies have bottlers and distributor networks that frequently have a strong voice in the direction of their brand's marketing communication.

Then there is the company's organization itself, which could include any number of departments with some responsibility for marketing communication, and unfortunately, in most cases these departments have their own managers and operate independently of each other. Too many companies still practise vertical rather than horizontal management, which means departments are often unlikely to even talk to each other, let alone work together. Even in large companies where a single group has been created to oversee all marketing communication, and to coordinate the efforts of all outside agencies and suppliers (something essential for effective IMC, we would argue), it is often difficult to wrest control from brand management. There is also a long history of tension between the sales force and marketing teams.

Now, multiply all of this by the number of countries where a company markets its brands. While it is not unusual for many marketing communication suppliers to have global networks, it is still a management nightmare. Global IMC must take into account local differences, while still maintaining a consistent overall positioning for the brand. One way international marketers try to deal with this is by consolidating all their global marketing communication efforts in one agency with the capacity of handling most of its marketing communication needs, either within the agency itself or through its network of sister organizations. An example of this, Reebok's problems with managing its social media globally, is discussed in the box below.

All of this potential input into a company's marketing communication must be controlled and managed in order to ensure a consistent strategy and message. This is not easy, and even with the best of intentions it is difficult to implement effectively. But, if there is to be effective IMC, this problem must be solved. There must be a central source that has *real* responsibility, not only for coordinating the efforts of all those involved in the process, but also for the authority to make decisions. Perhaps the most important decision they must have the authority to make is how the marketing communication budget is to be allocated.

The role of advertising and promotion in IMC

We mentioned earlier that one of the main reasons traditional advertising agencies originally took the lead in managing IMC was because that was where most of the money for marketing communication was to be found. But all of this has changed. With the increasing short-term focus on the bottom line, promotion-oriented marketing communication is playing an ever-larger role, and, along with the increasing growth in digital media, many companies are questioning the role of advertising today. They shouldn't. The role of advertising in IMC is now, as it has always been, to sell more of a branded product or service, or to achieve a higher price that consumers are willing to pay than they would otherwise be willing to in the absence of advertising (Rossiter and Percy, 2013).

Too much social media?

Can you have too much social media? For many multinational companies, the answer is 'yes'. Reebok was one such company. Marketing managers around the world were establishing several media campaigns with Facebook and Twitter, and showed content on numerous YouTube channels. Management knew this was a problem and an audit was initiated to identify company-created and fan-created accounts using Reebok trademarks. The results uncovered 232 Facebook pages, 30 Twitter accounts, and some 100 YouTube channels. Based on this, individual markets were asked to eliminate local accounts in favour of global Reebok accounts. For some markets, for example Hong Kong, this made a lot of sense. For others, such as India, where their Facebook page had nearly 1.8 million fans, it did not make sense. After their audit, Reebok's overall social media presence was cut roughly in half, and management reported that the effect paid off.

Source: *Advertising Age*, 10 December 2012

Where exactly does advertising fit in IMC? As we have tried to make clear, IMC is a *planning* concept, so the easy answer is that advertising 'fits' when and where it makes sense in most effectively communicating with the target audience. But this easy answer will not be satisfactory to many managers.

In today's world, where does advertising end and promotion begin? If a commercial includes a direct response 0800 numbers or asks consumers to print a coupon, is this advertising or is it promotion? In the past, advertising has been traditionally delivered through measured media: television, radio, newspaper, magazines, outdoor, and more and more today, digital media. But advertising messages are also delivered through direct marketing and channels marketing (for example, trade-oriented marketing such as co-op programmes), areas where in the past one only found promotional messages. As we shall see later, different from advertising only in the sense that the communication objective requires immediate action.

The consumer certainly does not know (or, we suspect, care) what constitutes 'advertising', as we mentioned earlier. In an interesting study conducted in the USA by the Leo Burnett Company, 1,000 consumers were called at random and asked what they would call a wide variety of marketing communication forms (Schultz, 1995). They found that consumers answered 'advertising' to more than 100 different forms of marketing communication. Many of the answers indeed would fit most advertising executives' definitions of advertising. But what about such things as sweepstakes/contests/games, product catalogues, information brochures, window displays in stores, coupons, bill inserts, and such? They sound more like traditional promotion, but well over 90 percent of the consumers interviewed called them 'advertising'. In fact, 92 percent said product packaging is advertising! Perhaps not surprisingly, consumers seem to see almost every form of marketing communication as advertising.

Rossiter et al. (2018) make two interesting points about the role of traditional advertising compared with promotion in today's marketing communication. Addressing the swing to promotion in marketing communication budgets, they point out that in spite of this swing: (a) there had been an *increase*, not a decrease in the use of general advertising media, especially digital, and (b) most of the growth in promotion, apart from all-but-required trade promotions, had been *additional* – and most of this in advertising-like promotions.

Nevertheless, in traditional terms the rate of advertising growth has followed the pace of media inflation, while other areas of non-traditional advertising, as well as promotion, have experienced real growth. This second point about advertising-like promotions is very important. It is not traditional forms of incentive promotion that are growing, but promotion-oriented messages that are very advertising-like. For example, as Rossiter and Percy (1997) point out, direct mail and telemarketing are thought of as promotion rather than advertising. When properly used, they are as much advertising, in the sense of building brand awareness and brand equity, as they are promotion in the sense of meeting some short-term sales objective. The same may be said of free-standing inserts (FSIs), by far the most widely-used way of delivering coupons. In the strictest sense these are promotion-oriented media, and we treat them as such in this book, but they are also very *advertising-like* in their ability to help build awareness and equity for a brand.

This blurring of the old distinctions between advertising and promotion is yet another reason for the importance of IMC, because what one might think of as traditional advertising skills now have such a critical role in every form of marketing communication. As we will see, planning an effective IMC programme requires the manager to address strategic creative and media questions that have always been addressed in traditional advertising. These principles are simply being applied to a wider range of options. In IMC, one is setting communication objectives and selecting media to maximize their ability to effectively reach the target market. But rather than only considering certain ways of using advertising, or independently considering some form of promotion, the planning and execution of all marketing communication should be *integrated*. The point is that in the end one may consider any marketing communication that deals with brand-building as delivering an advertising message, and any marketing communication that is looking for short-term action on the part of the target audience as delivering a promotion message. Promotions should include advertising messages.

As we shall see in later chapters, it does not matter what form a marketing communication message takes or how it is delivered, the strategic foundation for the development and execution of the message remains the same.

The brain will process the words and images the same way regardless, of how they are delivered. Sound is sound, words are words and pictures are pictures to the brain, regardless of where the sense organs find them. As Bavelier and Green (2011) put it, technological changes do not change the way the brain works, and the principles of brain organization have not changed since the advent of language thousands of years ago. This is especially important to keep in mind when using digital media. It will be processed in the same way as a message delivered in any other medium.

Barriers to effective IMC

Despite the fact that most marketers seem to agree that IMC makes sense, after 30 years there is little evidence that it is being practised by many companies. Where it is being used, it is probably most likely to be found among fast-moving consumer goods (fmcg) companies operating globally as they look for ways to coordinate their international marketing communication needs.

It should not be assumed by marketing managers that if they are not practising IMC they are simply not enjoying the potential benefits of it. Without IMC, a brand's marketing communication could be significantly *less* effective; the more complex the market, the less effective it will be. The lack of IMC, the lack of coordinated communications planning and the delivery of a consistent message could lead to multiple portrayals of a brand in the market. Even if the positioning is the same, if there is a lack of a consistent look and feel to all a brand's marketing communication there will be no synergy or 'lift' from the overall programme.

With a consistent look and feel (something we deal with in Chapter 10), the overall impact of a campaign is much greater than the sum of its parts because the *processing* of each piece of marketing communication is facilitated by the prior processing of other messages in the campaign. When the individual messages being delivered lack this consistency, the processing of each different piece of marketing communication must begin from scratch. A promotion that contains the same general look and feel as the brand's advertising, which is carried over with the packaging and reflected in in-store merchandising, means that prior exposure to any of these pieces of marketing communication will aid in the processing of the others. If each of these pieces has its own unique look, there will be no prior learning or foundation available when someone sees it. They must process the message on its own. As we see in later chapters, getting someone to process marketing communication at all is difficult. Effective IMC helps.

Research has shown that there is a link between IMC and an increase in sales, market share, and profit (Marketing Week, 2002), so why hasn't IMC been more widely adopted? We like the reason offered by Pickton and Broderick (2005): it is 'partly due to ignorance, unwillingness and inertia, and partly due to the sheer difficulties of achieving the integration'. Indeed!

Perhaps the single biggest problem revolves around the decision-making structure of most marketing organizations. The structure or organizational make-up of a company or agency, and the way managers think about or approach marketing questions frequently pose problems in trying to implement IMC programmes. We will be looking at this in terms of specific organizational barriers to IMC and an organization's character. Additionally, the issue of compensation is often a serious roadblock to effectively implementing IMC.

Organizational barriers

While effective IMC requires coordination among all of a brand's 'voices', most organizations spend their time developing vertical communications programmes. This results in a need for *horizontal* relationships struggling within *vertical* organizations. This leads to problems at the organizational level, where parallel structures, multiple departments and functional specialties discourage the kind of communication *between* specialities required for IMC planning. This type of problem is epitomized by the brand management concept, and moves by some large packaged goods companies to category or channel management are only likely to make the problem worse. IMC requires a central planning expertise in marketing communication. With diffused resources, individual manager relationships with marketing communication agencies and vendors, and (critically) a lack of incentive to cooperate, it is no wonder there are problems when it comes to effectively developing and implementing IMC programmes.

Organizational structure

Although there is a broad agreement among marketing managers over the need for IMC, the very organizational structure of many marketing companies stands in the way of it being effectively implemented. At the core of this problem is an organization's ability to manage the interrelationships of information and materials among the various agencies and vendors involved in supplying marketing communication services. There are a number of specific structural factors that can make this difficult.

The low standing of marketing communication in an organization

Unfortunately, for too many marketers, their marketing communication has a very low priority within the organization. For many in top management, spending money on marketing communication is a luxury that can only be afforded when all else is going well. One of the fastest ways for someone concerned with the financial statement to send large chunks of cash to the bottom line is to not spend budgeted marketing communication money. With this sort of attitude, it is not surprising that those most responsible for marketing communication occupy lower-level positions within the organization.

Adding to this problem is the trend toward decentralized decision-making. With more people empowered to make decisions at increasingly lower levels, it becomes very difficult, if not impossible, to ensure an IMC programme. This is compounded by the tendency to look to specialists when confronted with large or complicated projects.

Specialization

To effectively manage IMC, ideally those in charge will be marketing communication generalists. Where do you find such a person in today's marketing organizations? What one is most likely to find in companies are people specializing in a particular area, and these specialists rarely talk to each other. They have their own budgets, their own suppliers and jealously guard the areas they control. The problem becomes even more complex when one considers the marketing communication suppliers these specialists use. Each being a specialist in a particular area (for example, advertising, direct mail, merchandising), they naturally advocate their own solutions for marketing communication programmes.

By their very nature, whether intraorganizational or between suppliers, these specialists will want to keep communications programmes separate.

Given the narrow focus and understanding of these specialists, it is very difficult to bring them together in the first place, let alone expect them to have the broad understanding of many marketing communication options necessary for effective IMC planning. But even if they did have this understanding, getting them to give up control, especially when it is unlikely to be financially advantageous (which we will discuss more specifically later), is a lot to ask, yet this is precisely what is necessary for IMC to work within an organization.

Organizational character

In addition to the problems inherent in the way most marketing organizations are structured, there are more intangible aspects of an organization's thinking and behaviour that also pose problems for implementing IMC. We have just seen how traditional organizational structure can impede the flow of information and ideas within the organization. Because of this type of structural barrier, it is very difficult for an entire company to share a common understanding of that company's marketing communication.

It is important for everyone working in a company to understand and communicate the appropriate 'image' in any marketing communication. Anyone who has contact with customers must reflect the image projected by the company's marketing communications. This means store clerks, sales force, telephone operators, and receptionists; all are part of a company's marketing communication, and hence in many ways are IMC 'media'. Too often, only those directly involved with the marketing communication programme are familiar with it and this can be a serious problem.

Culture of the organization

How managers think is conditioned both by their own background and the culture of the company. This potential problem is then compounded in the IMC case when the culture of the marketer must interact with the culture of marketing communication agencies and vendors. A great deal of literature on management addresses the idea that an organization will have its own defining culture, and that employees of the firm will absorb that culture. Although that culture will not completely determine an individual manager's way of doing things, it will certainly have a significant impact on its development (Prensky et al., 1996). This leads inevitably to such organizational feelings as 'This is the way we do it'; 'We've always done it this way'; 'It works for us'. Attitudes such as these can get in the way of integrated thinking and planning, both within an organization and working with outside agencies and vendors.

Management perceptions

How managers perceive IMC can often impede the implementation of effective IMC. When managers come from different backgrounds or different marketing communication specialities, either within the marketing organization or at marketing communications agencies or vendors, they are likely to have different perceptions of what constitutes IMC and the roles various people should play in IMC planning and implementation. Additionally, there are strong proprietary feelings among managers toward the 'superiority' of their own specialty within the communication mix.

Because of this, it is not surprising to find that there are any number of notions about how best to go about implementing IMC. We, of course, argue that while the marketer must take the lead in IMC planning, strategy should be worked out among all relevant parties, who then execute creative work guided by the common creative brief(s), coordinated through the marketer.

Resistance to change

Different perceptions of IMC will certainly mediate effective implementation. But much more troubling is the natural resistance to change that the idea of IMC is likely to trigger, making it difficult to implement despite general acceptance of the benefits. The most serious concern is probably a fear that the manager responsible for IMC planning will not fully appreciate someone else's area of expertise. This problem is especially compounded when advertising takes the lead (which it should in most cases) because of long-held feelings that advertising managers simply do not understand or even consider other means of marketing communications (which, unfortunately, is too often the case). This is aggravated by the short-term tactical experience, for example, of those working in promotion compared with the more long-term thinking of advertising managers. If employees feel the IMC manager does not fully appreciate their worth, they are certain to worry about where their specialties will fit in department budgeting, and fear their jobs will become less important or even redundant. Such feelings could easily cause resistance to the implementation of IMC planning.

Another way of looking at some of these issues of resistance to change is in terms of both intraorganizational and interorganizational politics. It doesn't matter if the motivation is individual self-interest or actual belief in the superiority of one's way of doing things, the result is the same. People, departments, and organizations want power and the rewards that go with it. Too often, managers and their staff believe they will be giving up too much if they implement effective IMC planning. Compensation is only one aspect of this problem, as discussed below. There are feelings of prestige and position that have, in many cases, been hard-won, and the combining of responsibilities required by IMC seem to threaten. This can be a very difficult problem.

Financial emphasis

Another important aspect of the character of an organization that bears on IMC implementation is the misguided emphasis on financial rather than consumer considerations in the development of marketing strategy. The attitude of many managers is to let financial considerations drive their thinking when setting marketing objectives, rather than consumer wants or needs. But the consumer should be at the centre of IMC planning. IMC requires an understanding of how consumers make decisions and behave, as we discuss later in the book. When a marketer's attention is more financially focused than consumer-focused, the planning environment will be less likely to successfully nurture IMC.

Compensation

Compensation issues are less of a direct problem within a marketing organization than with agencies and vendors, but even there it is a problem. We have already referred to several circumstances where marketing communication specialists within a company are likely to be concerned about the importance of their position in a realigned, IMC-oriented marketing communication group. Such concerns lead quite naturally to worries about salaries and promotion and dampen enthusiasm for IMC.

The real concern over compensation lies with those agencies and vendors that serve the marketing communication needs of the marketer. This has certainly proved to be a stumbling block to many large advertising agencies that have tried to offer their clients a full range of marketing communication services, as well as within even smaller agencies where there are groups dedicated to different areas of the business, especially for digital media advertising. Group managers at these agencies are traditionally rewarded based on their total billings and income. That being the case, how likely is it that the management of the traditional advertising group will suggest to their client that perhaps they would be better off spending more of their money on social media or direct marketing, even if there is a digital or direct marketing group at the agency, let alone if the work would need to be done elsewhere?

Somehow these managers (at least within an agency or vendor offering multiple communication services) must be compensated without regard to how much is spent on their particular specialty, but in terms of the overall business. Without such a scheme, IMC is impossible because those in charge of a particular type of marketing communication will be more concerned with 'selling' their specialty, not with how their specialty will best contribute to an overall IMC programme. This problem is aggravated when a number of competing agencies or vendors are asked to work together.

It should not be surprising that any company will want to maintain its profitability in a changing world. Likewise, it should not be surprising that they will be more interested in their own financial well-being than in providing the best overall IMC programme for their clients. This underscores the need for tight control of planning by the marketer.

Overcoming the barriers

Although the need for IMC is widely understood and accepted, as the previous discussion makes clear, the path to implementation is hampered by many potential barriers. We have summarized these potential barriers in Table 1.1. These barriers are not insurmountable, and the rewards from effective IMC make the effort worthwhile. By becoming aware of these potential problems, and identifying them within their own organization, managers are on the way toward overcoming them.

We do not pretend that dealing with these problems is easy, after all, they go to the heart of how companies function day to day. The way decisions are made and the way an organization is structured, are part of the operational lifeblood of a company. Change requires trust, and this trust comes from a total understanding of what is involved and the long-term potential.

Identifying IMC opportunities

It could be said that every opportunity to use marketing communication is an IMC opportunity because all marketing communication should be based on careful strategic

Table 1.1 Barriers to effective IMC

Organizational barriers
- Vertical organizational structures where cooperation is needed between functions
- Structure makes it difficult to manage information from various agencies and vendors
- Low standing of marketing communication function
- Specialization gets in the way of integration

Organizational character
- Rigid organizational culture
- No common understanding of what constitutes IMC
- Resistance to change and fear over who will be in charge
- Financial considerations placed ahead of consumer considerations

Compensation issues
- Without budget control, communication specialists fear they will lose position and financial reward
- Rewards are linked to budget size or billings, not the overall programme

---

planning in order to ensure a consistent message, and in almost any case more than one way will be required to deliver that message. Remember that *any* communication between a brand and its market is part of its marketing communication. So even if all that is used is a direct mail programme, there must be consistency between the content of the mailing and the envelope it is mailed in, and if there is a package involved, that package should reflect the benefit and imagery contained in the direct mail piece.

If you own a small business in a small town, say a dress shop, and you want to place an advertisement in the local newspaper announcing a sale, the imagery presented in that advertisement should be consistent with the image of the shop itself: the type of merchandise, the signage, and the general 'feeling' the customer will experience when visiting the shop.

But more often when one is thinking about IMC one is concerned with larger marketing communication programmes. Perhaps the key to identifying a need for an IMC programme is the complexity of the market with which one is dealing. The more complex, the more likely it will be that multiple or novel solutions will be required. Many things can contribute to the complexity of a communication problem. The most obvious is multiple communication objectives, but there are others that involve the target audience, the product or service itself, and the distribution of the product or service, as outlined in Table 1.2.

Table 1.2 Market complexity

	Indications of complexity
Target audience	• multiple people involved in decision • audiences with conflicting interests • different media habits
Product or service	• highly technical or innovative • variety of models • multiple attributes
Distribution	• highly influential in decision • limited or specialized

Target audience complexity: There are a number of target audience considerations that lead to complexity in planning and delivering marketing communication. To begin with, the more people involved in the decision process, the more difficult the communication task. In a simple case, where one person plays all the roles in a decision, such as someone looking for a snack in the afternoon for an energy boost, a straightforward message to a single individual is all that is needed. But as more people become involved in the decision, the potential need for multiple messages through a variety of media or delivery systems increases. This can happen in situations as varied as a family, where children are lobbying parents for a special treat, to a large company planning to update its IT.

Product or service complexity: If the product or service is highly technical or innovative, the communication task can be more complex. For example, when a new consumer electronics product is introduced, people need to be made aware of it, and interest stimulated. But they will also want a high level of information to complete what is usually a high-involvement decision. If several models are available, again the information requirements will be greater. Even with seemingly less complex consumer needs, this opens opportunities for IMC. For example, dehydrated soups can be marketed as soup or as cooking ingredients, as great for lunch or to take on a camping trip.

Distribution complexity: An often-overlooked opportunity for IMC can be found in the distribution for a product or service. This goes beyond simple trade promotions. Many delivery systems have a great deal of influence on a brand being chosen.

Understanding consumer decision making

The more complex the market, as we have just seen, the more likely it is that an IMC programme will be needed. But even in seemingly uncomplicated situations a more extensive IMC programme may be needed than is apparent at first glance. In Chapter 12 we talk further about consumer decision-making, and something called a behavioural sequence model (BSM), which helps a manager better understand how their target audience makes purchase decisions in the brand's product category. It provides a detailed and dynamic picture of the target audience in terms of the overall decision process and enables a manager to recognize potential IMC opportunities.

A good understanding of how a target audience makes decisions will alert a manager to the many possible marketing communications options that might be required, and help pinpoint:

- complexity of the target audience;
- complexity of the distribution;
- complexity of the purchase decision;
- short- versus long-term communication objectives;
- need to isolate segments;
- need for multiple messages;
- opportunities for unique message delivery;
- opportunities for trade incentives;
- likely importance of retail messages.

We have seen how complexity in the market implies a need for IMC. Understanding consumer decision-making helps alert the manager to subtle complexities that are more a function of how consumers make decisions than of actual market conditions. For example, the roles played by various members of the target audience may add a complexity not otherwise easily noticed, and the ways in which information is gathered may signal *consumer-perceived* complexity within distribution that might otherwise be overlooked.

The most important insight into the need for IMC and the guidance for strategic IMC planning provided by an understanding of consumer decision-making is related to message needs. As one looks at how people go about making decisions in a category, the more complex the process, the greater the need for multiple options to deal with that complexity. If the decision is one that builds over time, such as the decision to buy a new car, it will help identify short- and long-term communication objectives. Continuing with the car example, over the long term, one must nurture an image for a vehicle that will help bring it into the consumers' considered set when they begin to think about a new car, but also provide detailed information and incentives for the short term when the final choice is being made. The need for an IMC programme under these circumstances would be obvious from an understanding of how decisions are made for a new car.

IMC strategic planning

In Part IV we take a close look at the strategic planning process and how it leads to effective IMC. At this point, however, a brief introduction to the steps involved in IMC strategic planning is in order. This will provide a framework for better understanding the importance of the material in the chapters leading up to the specific discussion of IMC strategic planning in the development of effective IMC.

The strategic planning process itself begins with consideration of the marketing plan. Although the ultimate consumer is at the heart of any communication programme, with IMC there is much more. Are we looking at local or regional markets, or globally? The marketing plan will detail this. It will also identify whom we wish to reach as ultimate purchaser or user. For example, it will indicate whether a trial or repeat-purchase strategy is to be pursued. Is the brand looking primarily to attract new users (a trial action objective) or to increase business from existing customers (a repeat-purchase action objective)? But the marketing plan does not deal with others who may play an important role in the decision process. The manager needs to know as much as possible about all the influences in the market that are likely to contribute to a positive response to the brand. The ultimate purchasers or users, along with anyone who may influence their decisions, are potential targets for communication. This could include other people who may have an influence on the ultimate consumer, the trade, or even the image and reputation of the company (as we will see in Chapter 3). Gaining this additional insight will be part of the strategic planning process.

Additionally, the marketing plan will provide a *general* positioning for the brand. It will identify the brand's major competition and such things as whether it will be marketed as a 'value' brand or 'luxury' brand. While this will set the overall parameter for the brand's positioning in the market, how the brand will be positioned within its marketing communication is part of the strategic planning process.

In order to develop effective marketing communication for a brand, it is important for managers to organize their thinking in terms of how an IMC programme will help meet the brand's marketing objectives. Reviewing the marketing plan provides the necessary background on how the brand is to be marketed and identifies the target market and overall positioning for the brand. With this background, the manager is ready to begin the strategic planning process that will lead to an IMC plan, that will in turn support the marketing objectives for the brand.

Table 1.3 The five-step IMC strategic planning process

Step one	Identify and select the appropriate target audience
Step two	Determine how that target audience makes product and brand decisions
Step three	Establish how the brand will be positioned within its marketing communication and select a benefit to support that position
Step four	Set communication objectives
Step five	Identify appropriate media options consistent with the communication objectives to optimize message delivery and the processing of the message

The five-step strategic planning process

Strategic planning for IMC involves a five-step process. First, one must identify and select the appropriate target audience; second, determine how they make brand decisions; third, establish how the brand will be positioned within its marketing communication, and select a benefit to support that position; fourth, set the communication strategy; and finally, match the appropriate media options to that strategy to optimize delivery and processing of the message. Table 1.3 provides an overview of the IMC strategic planning process, which will be discussed in detail in Chapter 12.

During this process, the manager must begin to consider the advantages and disadvantages of various advertising and promotion options for satisfying the communication objectives. Advertising and specific promotions have particular strengths, and these must be matched to the communication tasks. It will not be at all unusual at this stage to consider many more potential communication options than the brand has the resources to execute. But this is part of the strategic planning process, and one of the real strengths of IMC. *Everything* is considered, then the best choices are made within strategic and budget parameters.

Consider this example. Suppose a company is introducing a new cereal aimed at children. If we want mothers to purchase the new cereal for their children, we will probably need to make both mother and children *aware of the brand* and form a positive *brand attitude*, and we will certainly want the mother to form a positive *brand purchase intention*. One can advertise to both mothers and children to make them aware of the brand, but probably in different media. For example, one might use television advertising in children's programming and print advertising in women's magazines. These same vehicles could also be used for messages aimed at creating a positive brand attitude. In fact, the same advertisements would no doubt do both jobs. But would this be enough? Perhaps a premium could be offered to children to stimulate heightened interest, especially if there is heavy and popular competition. Where is a mother likely to make up her mind to buy the new cereal? Probably at home, at the insistence of the child. But if the child is not with the mother when she is shopping, will she remember? To help, some in-store merchandising might work.

You can see that even with this rather simple example, a number of alternative communication tasks are suggested, using both advertising and promotion, and delivered in various ways. It may be that in the end only a single commercial is produced and run in early evening family programming. That would still constitute IMC, even though only television advertising was used. IMC is the strategic planning *process*, not whether multiple marketing communication voices are used. Strategic IMC planning is used to arrive at the optimum solution within strategic and budget constraints, whatever the eventual execution. Although this would be highly unusual, it underscores the important point that IMC is the result of a planning process that leads to the optimum communication programme for a brand, whatever that might be.

This strategic planning process may seem simple enough, and managers may think, 'We do this already, or near enough'. We agree that the logic is rather straightforward, but the implementation requires a great deal of attention and understanding. That is what this book is all about.

Summary

In this chapter, a number of IMC definitions were introduced. From the beginning, definitions of IMC have built around two key elements: the role of multiple communication vehicles and the need for consistency in message delivery. At the heart of these definitions is the idea of *planning*. Even though later definitions have considered IMC in terms of 'customer relationships' (reflecting the late 1990s marketing interest in the subject), we have argued that at its core IMC is about *planning* in order to deliver a *consistent message*.

There is no really settled way in which IMC is managed and delivered. Early on, large advertising agencies and their holding companies began to offer a variety of marketing communication services to clients, drawing on their wide base of operations. But in the end, this did not work out well, even though it tends to remain the best option for ensuring central planning (especially for global marketers).

To effectively implement IMC, it is critical to understand the roles of advertising and promotion in the marketing communication mix. In today's world, it is often difficult to decide whether something is an advertisement or promotion offer. From a strategic standpoint, the only important consideration is how the message fits within the overall IMC programme. As we see in later chapters, advertising is used for longer-term strategic efforts to build brand awareness and attitude, while promotions are designed for shorter-term tactical needs to stimulate immediate action.

While most marketers believe that IMC is important for their brands, there are a number of barriers that stand in the way of effective implementation. In fact, true IMC is the exception, not the rule. The difficulty comes from the ways in which most companies are structured, the character of most organizations that militate against change, and compensation issues. Overcoming such deeply rooted organizational practices is very difficult, and requires the commitment of top management to succeed.

Almost any marketing communication task is an opportunity for IMC, and identifying the important points for communication comes from an understanding of how consumers make brand decisions in the category. This is a key part of the strategic planning process. It begins with a review of the marketing plan, leading to target audience selection, modelling the brand decision process, identifying the optimum positioning for the brand, establishing the communications strategy, and then selecting media consistent with that strategy to effectively deliver the message.

Review questions

1 How would you define IMC?
2 Discuss why you feel recent definitions of IMC are or are not an improvement on earlier definitions?
3 What is required for effective management of IMC?

4 How is trade involved in a brand's IMC?
5 What are the unique roles of advertising and promotion in IMC strategy?
6 Why is it so difficult to implement effective IMC?
7 How can the barriers to IMC be overcome?
8 Identify companies you believe practise IMC, based on their marketing communication, and discuss what it is about their marketing communication that makes you choose them.
9 What are the important keys to identifying IMC opportunities for a brand?
10 Is IMC appropriate for all brands?

References

Bavelier, D. and Green, C.S. (2011) Neuroscience: Browsing and the brain. *Nature*, 3 February, *470*(7332), 37–38.

Duncan, T.R. (2002) *Principles of Advertising and IMC*. New York: McGraw-Hill.

Kitchen, P.J. and Schultz, D.E. (2009) IMC: New horizon/fake dawn for a marketplace in turmoil? *Journal of Marketing Communication*, *15*(2–3), 197–204.

Marketing Week (2002) Everyone wins integration game, 18 April.

Pickton, D. and Broderick, A. (2005) *Integrated Marketing Communication*, 2nd edition. Harlow, England: Prentice-Hall, p. 25.

Prensky, D., McCarty, J.A. and Lucas, J. (1996) Integrated marketing communication: Examining planning and executional considerations. In E. Thorson and J. Moore (eds.), *Integrated Communication*. Mahwah, NJ: Lawrence Erlbaum Associates, pp. 67–184.

Rossiter, J.R. and Percy, L. (1997) *Advertising Communications and Promotion Management*. New York: McGraw-Hill.

Rossiter, J.R. and Percy, L. (2013) How the roles of advertising merely appear to have changed. *International Journal of Advertising*, 32(3), 391–398.

Rossiter, J.R. and Percy, L., and Bergkist, L. (2018) *Marketing Communications: Objectives, Strategy, Tactics*. London: Sage.

Schultz, D.E. (1995) What is direct marketing. *Journal of Direct Marketing*, 9(2), 5–9.

Schultz, D.E., Tannebaum, S.I. and Lauterbuin, R.F. (1993) *Integrated Marketing Communications*. Lincolnwood, IL: NTC Business Books.

Shearson Lehman Hutton (1989) *Report titled* Diversification Begets Integration.

2   Brands and IMC

The key to building a brand, beyond the obvious marketing considerations such as a viable product, effective pricing strategy, and distribution, is to correctly position the brand, and build a positive brand attitude that will lead to strong brand equity. This is what gives a brand meaning, and it is marketing communication that *drives* the meaning of a brand. One could argue (and we do) that without marketing communication, and especially advertising, it would be difficult, if not impossible, to have what we understand as a brand.

Effective IMC assumes a consistent positioning and communication strategy across every contact with the market, building a strong positive brand attitude. Without it, different messages and images can lead to confusion in the minds of the consumer as to exactly what the meaning of a brand is. In this chapter, we will be introducing how one goes about positioning a brand (we will go into more detail in Chapter 9), how building a strong brand attitude leads to brand equity, and what all of this means for brand portfolio decisions.

The role of IMC in building brands

While brand-like seals and labels have been around since the Bronze Age (Wengrow, 2008), brands, as we understand them today, began with the Industrial Revolution in around 1760. As economies and demand for goods grow, competition for customers grows as well. To help retain customers and build loyalty for their products, manufacturers need a way for their customers to easily identify their products as different from competitors. Up until then, most products were sold in bulk to retailers who then packaged them and sold them on, often in unmarked packages. But by the mid-18th century manufacturers began to place their own unique mark on their products, and branding as we have come to know it had begun.

The original meaning of the word 'brand' is thought to have come from an old Norse word *brandr*, meaning 'to burn'. We recognize this meaning, which is in fact, the second meaning offered in the *Oxford English Dictionary* (OED). What is the first? If you look up the word brand in the OED you will find the following definition: 'goods of particular name or trademark'. This may be literally what is meant by a brand, something that identifies a particular product or service, but it is a long way from what we understand a brand to be. That 'particular name or trademark' does a lot more than distinguish one good from another. Brands have specific *meanings* to consumers, and these meanings derive in part from experience, but in the main from how a brand has been positioned and presented to people through marketing communication; ideally, through IMC.

DOI: 10.4324/9781003169635-3

Before going further, let us pause to be certain of what we mean when we are talking about marketing communication. Marketing communication is *every* contact between the brand and the market. This means much more than the usual notion of advertising and promotion. It means everything: packaging, the outside of the truck that transports the company's products, sales kits for the trade, business cards, sponsorships, store signs, collateral, retail store layout (if the brand is sold at retail, or is in fact a retail store), newsletters – you get the point. This is why IMC is so critical in building successful brands. Management of a brand must coordinate all these aspects of the brand's communication, ensuring a consistent message.

Returning to what is meant by a brand, we see it in terms of a *label*, again following the OED: something that is 'attached to an object to give information about it'. The concept of a brand transcends its 'particular name or trademark', providing information about itself, *meaning*. This meaning develops over time, as a result of the brand's marketing communication. Effective IMC ensures control over this meaning.

If we take the idea of a brand and extend it to politicians or celebrities (a frequent metaphor), the point remains. A politician or celebrity becomes a 'brand' when people learn things about them through various forms of mass communication, and it is communication in one form or another that sustains them as a 'brand' in their market. Without it, that person is merely someone working in government (or wanting to), or an unknown. Just as with a product or service, successful politicians and celebrities want their name to mean something specific to their market. They want their 'brand' to carry with it a particular meaning. Just like other brands, they accomplish this through effective positioning and building a strong favourable attitude.

Social meaning

The role of IMC in building social meaning parallels what we have just been discussing. Within a social context, among other things, brands can be a catalyst for social differentiation or integration, and for brand communities. This follows from the personal meaning brands can have.

The communication value of brands may be thought of as fundamentally integrative. This follows from work in social differentiation and social integration. Basically, this involves something that dates to the end of the 19th century with Veblen (1899) and the idea of conspicuous consumption. Researchers working in this area today are concerned with the importance of brand meaning as a function of both the product itself and the consumer (Vargo and Lusch, 2004). In other words, the consumer will help contribute to the meaning and understanding of a brand, something often referred to as social meaning. A good overview of this may be found in Rosenbaum-Elliott et al. (2018). Our reason for bringing it up is to remind us that how a brand is positioned and marketed with IMC will contribute to how some people will adopt that imagery in how they see themselves. This can then itself contribute to a brand's identity, and managers must be aware.

People often think about brands in terms of human characteristics. This can occur as a direct result of how they perceive users of a particular brand, or perhaps owing to a celebrity endorser. It may also follow indirectly from marketing communication, everything from advertising or symbols associated with a brand to the brand name itself (Aaker, 1997). Another key factor in personalizing brand meaning comes from the emotional associations people have with brands (Percy et al., 2004).

There is a great deal of evidence that men and women understand the same advertising execution in very different ways (Elliott et al., 1995). Much of this no doubt follows from a difference in the motivation that often drives male and female decisions to use a particular product, but there is no question that marketing communication can inform social differentiation. This offers the potential for the effective use of IMC to reflect gender identity in creating a social differentiation brand strategy, or, on the other hand, to implement different creative strategies to minimize differentiation. An effective IMC programme is essential to a social differentiation strategy for a brand, because such a strategy requires even more coordination and control.

The idea of social integration and brands, on the other hand, reflects the notion that in the everyday use of brands, their meaning can help create and maintain social relationships (Douglas and Isherwood, 1979). Kates (2000) has even suggested that brand meaning can be used as a social integration strategy for non-heterosexuals. This follows from the idea that brands are involved in the building and nurturing of groups as a result of a common or shared brand meaning, leading to 'brand communities'. Brand communities were defined in a well-regarded study by Muniz and O'Guinn (2001) as 'non-geographic' communities based on a clearly structured set of relationships among brand admirers. A part of this idea of brand community results from a shared feeling that competitive brands do not measure up. It is taking the idea of brand loyalty beyond the individual brand user, suggesting there is a certain communal sense that they are different, more legitimate uses of the brand, than others who merely purchase it.

IMC can certainly play a key role in the development of brand communities. It is the coordinated effectiveness of IMC that ensures a correct, consistent message. But beyond that, as part of an IMC programme a brand can encourage brand communities through such activities as 'brandfests'. Daimler Chrysler's Jeep brand, for example, hosted events for owners, and found that it significantly increased the likelihood of repurchase among those who attended (McAlexander et al., 2002).

It is the same two pillars of marketing communication that also drive social meaning for a brand: positioning and brand attitude. Of course, for both product and social brand meaning, there is much more involved. If one is not aware of a brand, one will not know how it is positioned; if one does not correctly process messages about a brand, it is unlikely that one will come to the desired meaning or build a positive brand attitude. But positioning and brand attitude provide the foundation for building a strong brand equity, and are at the heart of brand-building with strategic IMC.

Cultural values and brand perceptions

Cultural values will not only be an important consideration in the planning process for IMC, as we shall see in Chapter 11, but this will also inform how a brand is perceived. As you might imagine, the social meaning of a brand is likely to vary across cultures. Also, Aaker (1997) identified five traits consumers seem to attribute to a wide range of brands: sincerity, excitement, competence, sophistication, and ruggedness. But when these traits are applied across different cultures, there are significant differences in which traits are attributed to a particular brand.

Culture also plays an important role in whether or not a brand is perceived as being either local or global, and this becomes a factor in the positioning strategy for a brand within IMC. Positioning a brand as 'global' obviously differentiates it from a local or regional positioning, creating a certain cultural tension that will impact both perception and consumer behaviour. On the other hand, a brand's perceived 'localness' will likely provide a cultural value for consumers because it reflects a relevance and acceptability to local markets. A perceived 'localness' for a brand can provide leverage against global brands. The equity of local brands across major European countries has been found to be generally higher than international or global brands (Schuiling and Kapferer, 2004).

Positioning

Positioning is the first step in laying the foundation for building a strong brand with IMC. When thinking about positioning a brand with marketing communication, one talks about something different from what is seen as 'positioning' in a marketing sense. A marketing plan will have established a general positioning for a brand in terms of such things as pricing strategy and product features, and in relation to specific segments of a market.

Positioning in marketing communication involves how a brand is to be positioned to the target audience within message executions. There are two fundamental questions that must be answered in order to ensure an effective positioning: To what need, from the consumer perspective, should the brand be linked? The answer to this question helps position the brand to optimize brand awareness. The second question is, what benefits should be emphasized in order to best communicate what the brand offers? The answer to this question will help position the brand to build a strong, positive brand attitude.

Before these questions are addressed, however, it is necessary to understand the difference between two basic types of brand positioning: central and differentiated. A brand that is *centrally* positioned must be seen to deliver all the basic benefits associated with the product category. The market regards centrally positioned brands as among the best brands, if not the best, in a category. Because of this, their marketing communication does not need to continually remind people of their benefits. They are assumed. It is enough to remind people that the brand is 'the best'. The ultimate central positioning is when the brand name becomes a generic term for the category. This would include such brands as Xerox, Kleenex, and Hoover.

With all other brands, a *differentiated* positioning should be used. As the term implies, a differentiated positioning looks for a way to differentiate the brand from its competitors. This is accomplished by looking for a specific benefit (or a small set of benefits in some cases where there is a high-involvement purchase decision) that is important to the target audience, and that they believe, or can be persuaded to believe, the brand will deliver better than any of its competitors.

The only exception to this is when a brand is believed to be just as good as the category leader, especially if it is lower priced. In that case, the manager could choose to use a central positioning because the brand, like the centrally positioned category leader, will be seen to deliver on all the main category benefits.

Once the basic positioning structure is established, whether the brand should be centrally or differentially positioned, it is time to deal with the questions introduced earlier. The first step in answering those fundamental questions is to gain an understanding of how *consumers* look at a category.

Understanding how markets are defined

In the beginning of this section on positioning, we pointed out how the term 'positioning' is used in marketing differs from how it is used in marketing communications.

Nevertheless, the *marketing* positioning will inform the positioning strategy for a brand's marketing communication. The bridge between the two is how the market is understood and defined by the consumer.

Among other things, a brand manager will look at how competitors are positioned within the market, and along what benefit dimensions. Decisions must be made about whether to position a brand in 'gaps' (if they exist) or to attack the position of a specific competitor. Earlier, we suggested that two of the criteria often used in market positioning are pricing strategy and product features. If there are no lower-priced high-quality brands in a market, and a brand's margins can sustain it, a manager might decide to reposition the brand at a lower price point.

This would have a direct effect on how that brand would need to be positioned in its marketing communication. But it need not suggest that the communication positioning must be based specifically on the lower price. It would probably make more sense to reinforce the quality image in light of the lower pricing strategy to reassure users that the product quality was not being sacrificed for the lower price. The key is how the consumer sees the market. Do they believe, or can they be persuaded to believe, that a high-quality product in this category can be sold at a lower price?

Let us consider another example. In mid-2005, the British soft drink marketer Britvic decided to reposition its Tango brand after a five-year slide in sales, and increasing competition from leading brands like Coca-Cola (Advertising Age, 2005). With the introduction of Coke's 'Z' range of zero-added sugar soft drinks, they decided to reposition Tango, in marketing terms, by introducing a clear, low-sugar product as Tango Clear. This obviously required a change in how the brand was positioned within its marketing communications, leading to a variation of the brand's long-running campaign that featured some unlucky person being unexpectedly accosted, followed by the tagline 'You know when you've been Tango'd'. The new positioning within its advertising followed the product change, focusing on the benefit of a 'clear' soft drink, and with a new tagline, changed slightly from the original, 'It's clear when you've been Tango'd'. This consistency with earlier advertising reflects good IMC, as we discussed in the first chapter, and will deal with at length later in this book.

In this case, the brand was following a shift in consumer demand from heavily sugared fizzy soft drinks to more healthy alternatives. But it still begs an important question for positioning. What exactly is the market in which Tango competes? The obvious answer is the soft drink market, but there is much more to it than that. Of course, Tango is a soft drink, and the new Tango Clear had no colour and was low in calories. So, should Tango be positioned in the fizzy drink market? Should it be positioned in the fruit drink market or the clear drink market or the low-calorie market? As you can see, the answer is really not that obvious.

Positioning and brand awareness

From an IMC positioning standpoint, getting the right answer here is critical to effective positioning. If we do not fully understand how Tango's customers define the market, we will not be able to optimize the positioning for brand awareness. It is essential to understand what Tango is associated with in its target market's memory so that when customers think about Tango, it is linked to the correct category need.

One of the ways to look at how consumers 'see' a market is with something called hierarchical partitioning. The thinking behind this approach is that there is a particular

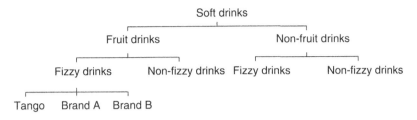

Figure 2.1 Hypothetical hierarchical partitioning of the soft drink market.

set of product attributes that a consumer will consider when defining a market and that they use that set of attributes to sub-divide the market into successively smaller segments. The smaller the segment, the more alike the products and brands in that set will be seen by the consumer, and it will be from that hierarchically defined set that an actual choice will be made.

As we have just seen, Tango might be seen as competing in any of a number of markets. Figure 2.1 illustrates one way the market might be defined by the consumer. If this was indeed the case, Tango's marketing communication must seek to link the brand in the consumer's mind with fizzy fruit soft drinks so that when the 'need' for a fizzy fruit soft drink occurs, Tango will come to mind. Notice that this partitioning of the market ignores the fact that Tango is colourless and low in calories. But if this is how consumers see the market, those attributes are unnecessary for building brand awareness.

But this does *not* mean that either 'colourless' or 'low in calories' should not be used as benefits in the brand's marketing communication. It only means that they do not figure out how the consumer *defines* the market. It could be very effective to select the 'colourless' attribute to focus on in the IMC campaign (as the brand did) in order to help build a positive brand attitude.

On the other hand, perhaps the soft drink market is defined by consumers as shown in Figure 2.2. If Figure 2.2a was correct, it would mean that Tango was seen by consumers as a clear fizzy drink, competing with other clear carbonated soft drinks like Pepsi Clear. If Figure 2.2b reflected how consumers see the market, they would see Tango as a low-calorie fruit drink, competing with both fizzy and non-fizzy products. The way consumers define a market identifies a brand's competitors.

What we have been discussing is the most common way markets are defined by consumers in terms of product attributes. But it is also possible for markets to be partitioned by consumers in terms of things such as end benefits or usage situations. Continuing with our Tango example, the soft drink market might be seen in terms of end-benefit such as 'healthy' or 'refreshing'. If this were the case, the essential positioning link for brand awareness would seek to associate Tango in the consumers' minds as either a 'healthy' or 'refreshing' drink, so that when they wanted either a healthy or refreshing drink they would think of Tango. Similarly, the soft drink market might be seen in terms of usage situations like 'after exercise' or 'watching weight'.

It should now be clear why it is so important to get this correct. The first job of positioning is to establish the link between the brand and the category need in the mind of the consumer so that when the need occurs, the brand comes to mind. This is what brand awareness is all about.

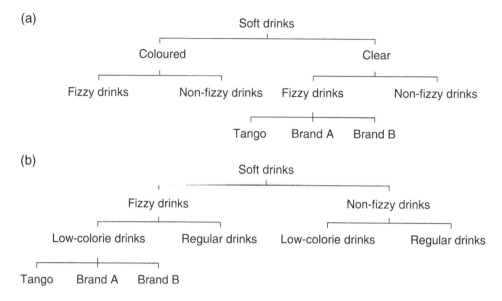

Figure 2.2 Hypothetical alternative hierarchical partitioning of the soft drink market.

Positioning and brand attitude

The second issue that must be considered in positioning a brand in marketing communications is how it will be presented within the message and execution. One is looking for the best way to communicate what the brand offers so that it will be seen to be not only different from competitive brands, but better. This reflects the positioning decision for optimizing brand attitude. Later, in Chapter 12, we will look more closely at how to go about selecting the benefit to talk about, and how to best focus on the benefit in the execution to reflect the underlying motivation driving behaviour in the category.

What we want to focus on at this point is the initial positioning decision a manager must make about how to position what the brand offers; the decision as to whether the message should be about specific characteristics of the brand or product, or about the user of the brand. In addressing the question of what a brand offers, there are two basic options for positioning. The brand may be positioned towards the user or towards a specific benefit of the brand (or in some cases a set of benefits). These are referred to as user-oriented versus product-oriented positioning.

It is not often that a user-oriented positioning should be used in IMC, but it can be an option when a brand is being marketed to a particular segment, and the strategy is to specifically address them in the message. This might be the case, for example, if one were advertising a high-end music system and wanted to target a small segment of 'knowledgeable' buyers. A user-oriented position here might use a message that talked about the brand as being for 'sophisticated' or discerning buyers.

Another case where user-oriented positioning might be considered is where social approval is the primary motivation driving the behaviour of a brand's target audience. Social approval is one of the two positive motivations that can drive purchase behaviour (the other positive motive is sensory gratification). Motivation is one of the foundations of brand attitude strategy, along with involvement, and will be covered in depth in Chapter 4. When social approval is motivating the target audience, it means they are buying the product in search of an opportunity for social reward through personal recognition. An example here would be when a man buys the woman in his life an expensive piece of jewellery. It is unlikely that he is buying it for personal enjoyment, but rather for positive response from the woman. Advertising messages here might talk about the brand as ensuring the man will be rewarded by the woman when he buys it.

These are the two principal situations where the manager has the option of a user-oriented positioning. In one case the brand is positioned to 'flatter' a specific segment of the market being targeted, and in the other, it offers the personal recognition the target audience is seeking in buying the product. One may also use a product-oriented positioning in these cases, but in all other cases, a product-oriented positioning is required.

With a product-oriented positioning, the benefits of a product are the message. While the execution may feature users, the focus of the message will be on the benefit and the brand's performance. Using benefits that are important to the target audience and that the brand is seen as delivering (or can be persuaded it delivers), a product-oriented positioning will seek to present what the brand offers in a way that will be seen as not only different from the competitive brands, but better.

Positioning is the first pillar in the foundation for building strong brands. In this brief overview, we have seen how positioning in marketing communication is not necessarily the same as the positioning of the brand in a marketing plan, but it will always be in support of the brand's overall positioning in the market. A brand will be either centrally or differentially positioned and assume either a user- or product-oriented positioning as appropriate. The positioning provides the link between a need and the brand for brand awareness, and a link between the brand and its benefit for building brand attitude. There is more to it of course, as we see in later chapters. Establishing the correct positioning is critical to building brand awareness and a strong brand attitude. In the next section, we take a look at brand attitude, and we will continue to re-visit it throughout the book.

Brand attitude

Brand attitude is the second pillar in the foundation for building strong brands with IMC. What exactly is brand attitude? Everyone has brands that they like and brands that they don't like. That preference *reflects* their brand attitude. But where does it come from? People who study consumer behaviour like to use something called an expectancy-value model to explain how people form attitudes (Fishbein and Ajzen, 1975).

In its simple form, the expectancy-value model of attitude suggests that someone's attitude towards an object (A_o), a brand in our case, is a function of everything they know or believe about that object (b_i) weighted by how important each of those beliefs is to them (a_i):

$$A_o = \sum_{i=1}^{n} a_i b_i \qquad (2.1)$$

where A_o = attitudes towards the object
a_i = importance of belief
b_i = belief about the object

Let us consider an example. Think about a product like toothpaste. What are some of the things you 'know' or believe about toothpaste? Perhaps that it has fluoride, helps whiten teeth, freshens breath, helps prevent tooth decay, etc. How important is it to you that toothpaste has fluoride, helps whiten teeth, etc.? Now consider a brand of toothpaste like Crest. Do you believe Crest has fluoride, helps whiten teeth, etc.? Does it have a lot of fluoride? Does it really whiten teeth or only do an average job?

In the end, your attitude towards Crest will be the result of how many of the things that are important to you in toothpaste are delivered by Crest. The more benefits, important to you, that you feel Crest offers, the more positive your brand attitude for Crest will be. If it offers many benefits important to you, you will probably really like it. If it doesn't, or perhaps more importantly if you do not think that it does, you will not have as favourable an opinion or attitude towards it. If you feel it does a really bad job on an important benefit, you may not like it at all.

Of course, you have probably never really thought about toothpaste in this much detail before. Nevertheless, perceptions of benefits like these have made their way into your memory, and associations of brands with these benefits have gone into forming your overall summary judgements about them. You do not need to 'think through' why you hold the attitude you do for different brands, you need only to recall the summary judgement. You simply 'like' Crest better than Colgate. In effect, the brand name and its meaning free you from making extensive evaluations of brand alternatives every time you make a purchase decision.

Where does most of the brand knowledge come from that informs brand attitude? Marketing communication, and how the brand is positioned in the message. Experience plays a role, but for most people, for most brands, they simply 'know' something about them. Think about two very different product categories, like beer and automobiles. You are probably aware of many more brands in each category than those with which you have had personal experience, but you probably have 'attitudes' about them. You think some brands are better than others; this is a strong lager; that is a luxury motor. Each brand in the category with which you are aware has taken on a meaning that reflects your experience, knowledge, beliefs, and feelings about it: brand attitude. The primary source of that information comes from the positioning of the brand and what is said about it in marketing communication. Effective IMC ensures strong and consistent support for building and nurturing a positive brand attitude.

Another way of building brand attitude is to associate the brand with a public service message. But, as we shall see in Chapter 7 when we talk about sponsorships and events, the message should have a link to the product. While a certain amount of 'goodwill' for a brand may initially result from an association with a public service message when there is an obvious connection between the message and the brand, the positive feeling toward the brand will be stronger and reinforced. The Ariel advert shown in Advert 2.1 does just that. There is a clear link between the brand and its package, and the message: store it out of reach of children. And the execution provides a stronger visual reinforcement of the message.

How IMC is used to effectively build a positive brand attitude will be dealt with in Chapter 4, when we look at the role of traditional advertising in IMC. What we want to talk about here is how a positive brand attitude leads to strong brand equity.

Advert 2.1 Ariel.

Source: © Procter & Gamble UK.

Building brand equity

We have already mentioned that a positive brand attitude leads to a strong brand equity. But what exactly is brand equity? There are almost as many definitions of brand equity as there are people talking about it, but almost all will have in common the idea that brand equity represents an *added value* to a product, a value that goes well beyond the objective characteristics of the product itself (Rosenbaum-Elliott et al., 2018). This added value makes the brand name itself a strong financial asset to the company marketing it. It does this because a strong brand equity means that a brand is well known, is positively associated in the minds of consumers, is seen as 'better' than other brands, and is likely to have a strong core of loyal users (Aaker, 1991). This in turn ensures better distributors and strong demand.

How does this manifest itself? Moran (1994) long ago offered a good way to both understand and measure brand equity by looking at it in terms of *price elasticity of demand,* which reflects how a brand will respond to price cuts and price increases. He referred to this as 'upside elasticity' and 'downside elasticity', and they provide an indication of both a 'value equity' and 'uniqueness equity'. A high-value equity follows from a high upside elasticity, where sales go up quickly as a result of even a small price cut because the brand is now seen as a better value at a lower price. Uniqueness equity follows from downside elasticity, where low downside elasticity would indicate high uniqueness because sales do not fall, or fall much, when the brand raises its price, or when competitors lower theirs. Both value equity and uniqueness equity contribute to the key marketing objective at the brand level, increasing unit sales leading to long-term profit.

Think of some of the products you buy, especially fast-moving consumer goods or other low-involvement products. Is there really that much of a difference between brands of washing powder, mouth rinse, toilet tissue, underwear, or tinned tomatoes? Why do most people prefer to buy a branded aspirin rather than a generic one when both are nothing but aspirin? Why do some people not only prefer Coke to Pepsi (or Pepsi to Coke), but *passionately* prefer it to the point of not even wanting to drink the other? This is in spite of the fact that these passionately loyal drinkers cannot tell the difference between the two in blind taste tests. Obviously, something is going on here that goes well beyond the sensory characteristics of the product.

So, what is it about certain brands that lead people to feel they are better than others, even when they may use the same basic ingredients, get the job done equally well, or even taste the same? The answer is brand equity. For these people, there is just something 'better' about it, and there is no arguing with them. Ask the people at Coke who tried to introduce New Coke in the mid-1990s. Managers at Coke felt they were losing out to Pepsi among the younger demographic, and thought the reason was that Pepsi's formulation was somewhat sweeter. They decided to introduce a re-formulated product that people, Coke drinkers, and Pepsi drinkers, preferred to both their current products. When they developed a product that was indeed preferred by everyone, it was introduced as New Coke, with the intention of replacing the original product.

But there was an almost violent reaction in the market among loyal Coke drinkers. They were incensed that the company was considering phasing out their beloved product! The company quickly backtracked, and it was New Coke that retired. How could they have made such a mistake? They completely ignored the strong brand equity Coke had built with more than 100 years of advertising, reminding drinkers that 'all the world loves a Coke' and 'Coke is it'. All the many taste tests conducted to find the perfect formulation were conducted 'blind'. No one knew what product they were drinking. You can bet that had they tested the 'preferred' formulation with original Coke when Coke drinkers knew what they were drinking, original Coke would have been preferred.

This entrenched power of brand equity was illustrated in an interesting neuroimaging study. As we will see in Chapter 8, emotional associations with brands are an important part of how people process information about them, and these emotional memories (stored in the amygdala) interact with knowledge and assumptions about brands that come from the hippocampus when we make judgements. A group of neurobiologists used functional magnetic resources imagery (fMRI), a process that measures brain activity, to determine what parts of the brain are energized when taste preferences are made (McClure et al., 2004). The test was conducted in both labelled and blind conditions and among loyal and non-loyal drinkers of the brands Coke and Pepsi.

What they found was that when people did not know what they were drinking, only that part of the brain dealing with sensory evaluations (the ventromedial prefrontal cortex) was active, and preference was basically random. Regular drinkers were no more likely to pick their 'favourite' than the one they did not drink. But when there was brand knowledge, for loyal Coke drinkers the hippocampus, dorsolateral prefrontal cortex, and midbrain were also active. These are the areas of the brain known to be involved in influencing behaviour based on emotion and affect (i.e., 'liking'). No surprise, they preferred Coke. In effect, they were showing the influence of brand equity. The positive feelings associated with the brand were activated by the knowledge that they were drinking their favourite brand.

In a very real sense, a brand only exists in the mind of the consumer, in the meaning that has been built over time through marketing communication. To the extent that this marketing communication, in all its aspects, has been consistent in positioning the brand effectively and building a positive brand attitude, a strong brand equity will evolve leading to loyalty that goes well beyond any rational consideration of the product. This is what results from truly effective IMC. Of course, even the best IMC programmes will not lead to complete loyalty to a brand among everyone. But they will encourage a positive brand attitude that does energize positive brand equity, and this will help maximize brand loyalty.

Again, think of your own feelings for different brands. You may be fiercely loyal to a particular brand in a category, but still feel that one or two other brands in that category are also quite good. You may feel that some brands have strong brand equity, indeed stronger and more positive than the brand you buy, yet you do not buy them. Examples here might include brands such as Rolls-Royce or Learjet. You just 'know' they are good brands, and not because of your experience with them. You know they are good brands because over time the marketing communication for those brands has built a positive brand attitude in your mind, leading to strong brand equity.

In these examples, you may not even be aware of much exposure to their marketing communication. After all, you are unlikely to be in their target audience. But you will have been exposed to them indirectly through such things as product placement in movies and through general word of mouth. All of this is an important part of effective IMC in building a brand.

Product portfolio

	Product Type A	Product Type B	Product Type C	Etc.
Brand portfolio	Brand 1 Brand 2	Brand 1 Brand 2 Brand 3 Brand 4	Brand 1	

Figure 2.3 Product and brand portfolio grid.

Brand portfolio considerations

Most marketers, even relatively small ones, offer more than one product or brand. This may take the form of something as simple as a line of items under a single brand name to multiple products and brands offered by large multinational companies. For any marketer offering more than a single product, it is important that the marketing strategies for their brands be coordinated in order to optimize the overall profitability of the company. This coordination is generally thought of as product portfolio management and within it, brand portfolio management.

One might think about this in terms of a grid, as illustrated in Figure 2.3. Here, all the products a company markets would be shown along the top, with the brands offered beneath each product. We are not going to discuss this in depth because it is covered properly in strategic brand management texts (for example, Rosenbaum-Elliott et al., 2018); it is nonetheless important to have a general idea of what is involved in product and brand portfolio management because it informs IMC strategy.

A *product portfolio* describes the various products a company markets, within a category: both individual products as well as product lines. A *product line* is a group of products within a particular product category that are closely related to each other, often because they are seen as being used for the same thing. As an example, Levi-Strauss markets a line of trousers under the Levi's, Dockers, Signature, and Denizen brands. A *brand portfolio* describes all of the brands a company markets within a category, and it too may contain individual brands as well as brand lines. A *brand line* will include all of the products that are marketed under a single brand name. looking again at Levi-Strauss, their Levi's brand line includes Levi's, Levi's 501, Levi's 511, and Levi's 721.

Product and brand portfolio management looks at everything a company now markets, as well as future plans for acquisitions, product line extensions, and brand extensions, in order to optimize the contribution of each product and brand for the overall health of the company. Issues such as the core competencies and equity of the parent company and individual brands must be considered; also, the market segments to be served, and competitive positioning within those markets. The implementation of such planning relies fundamentally on branding strategy, and the implementation of branding strategy is the job of IMC.

Branding strategy

Branding strategy involves something Kapferer (1997) has called 'brand hierarchy', which reflects the level at which a brand name is used. The basic question is: should a product be uniquely branded or encompass some combination of an existing brand name (or the parent brand) with a new one, generally known as sub-branding? Sub-branding has many permutations, but comes down to adding a new brand name to an existing brand name in order to borrow the already existing strength and equity of that brand, while at the same time creating a specific brand identity for the new brand. The advantage of sub-branding is that it permits the creation of brand-specific beliefs, but without the necessity of starting from scratch.

In Kapferer's discussion of branding strategy, he introduces a useful distinction. He looks at alternative branding strategies in terms of the extent to which a brand will function as an indicator of product origin versus differentiation of the product. A stand-alone or uniquely branded product seeks to differentiate the brand. It implies that the company behind the brand is unknown. This provides greater latitude for brand extensions, but requires a heavy initial investment in marketing, especially marketing communication.

Sub-branding strategies seek to provide an indicator of the product's origin. The two most commonly understood types of sub-branding are known as *source* branding and *endorser* branding. With a source branding strategy, the parent company or brand is supporting the quality of the product, and the brand must be positioned to reflect the equity of the parent. If a source branding strategy is used, either the company or an appropriate brand name from the company's brand portfolio is used to *introduce* the new brand. Examples here would be IBM ThinkPad and Nestlé's Crunch.

An endorser branding strategy implies that the parent brand has given its 'approval' and support to the product, while assuming a secondary position, encouraging the brand to develop its own image with the cross-potential of nurturing the parent. With an endorser branding strategy, the brand name comes first, with the parent brand second, and often with a significantly reduced presence. Examples here would be Philadelphia cream cheese from Kraft and Kira St Johns Wart from Lichtwer Pharma.

Stand-alone brands

The advantage of a unique, or stand-alone, brand is that it enables a brand to create its own identity independent of a parent brand. As mentioned, this usually requires more of an investment, but it permits the brand to develop more in directions that may not be compatible with a parent brand's core competency or equity. It also avoids the possibility of negative associations with the parent informing the image of the brand or even the possibility of a negative response to the brand reflecting on the parent.

Just such a possibility influenced (then) Anheuser-Busch's branding strategy when they first introduced a reduced-calorie beer. They were not willing to risk the equity of their existing brands, especially their flagship brand Budweiser, by initially introducing a sub-brand like Bud Light. They were concerned that potentially negative associations with 'light' beers among their core market could reflect badly on their brands. As a result, they created a new brand that, while it used the parent company as a source, avoided the use of existing brand names: Anheuser-Busch Natural Light.

This case provides a good example of how IMC is involved in brand portfolio strategy. The marketing communication for the new brand needed to link Natural Light to Anheuser-Busch, but without associating it in memory with existing Anheuser-Busch brands. It required its own, distinct, identity. The initial advertising and other marketing communication treated the new brand specifically as a source brand, always prefacing Natural Light with Anheuser-Busch. Unfortunately, the research discovered that when people ordered it they asked for a Bud Light or Busch Light (what the industry refers to as the 'bar call'). They quickly changed the advertising, dropping the reference to Anheuser-Busch and focusing attention on 'Natural', spending much of each execution establishing the beer call as 'give me a Natural'.

Over time as the market for lower-calorie beers established itself, Natural Light eventually became a price brand without marketing support, and the brewery introduced a lower-calorie version of each of their key brands at the time: Bud Light, Busch Light, and Michelob Light. In branding strategy terms, this represents a brand extension where the branding strategy was a 'brand source' strategy, with the brand endorsing the quality of the beer and acting as a seal of approval. The product was not meant to seem autonomous. Today, Bud Light has itself become a part of a source branding strategy with the entry into the hard seltzer category with Bud Light Seltzer.

A good example of a stand-alone brand being created specifically to avoid negative carryover from the parent company is the case of O_2. In 2002, BT Cellnet was a brand in real trouble, losing shares to competitors such as Orange and Vodafone in the UK. A decision was made to de-merge parent BT Wireless from BT, and reintroduce the brand as O_2, distancing itself completely from its antecedent. While this required a significant marketing investment, coupled with the need to supply an ongoing revenue stream to support what was in many ways an existing brand, the new brand enjoyed strong initial support, quickly reaching, and surpassing the old levels of its predecessor brand, BT Cellnet. The company attributed much of this success to the benefits of an IMC campaign addressing consumers, trade, and staff.

Sub-brands

As discussed earlier, sub-branding generally follows either a source or endorser branding strategy. These sub-branding strategies may operate at either a corporate or brand level. Nestlé's Crunch is an example of a *corporate* source branding strategy, with the parent company supporting the quality of the product. Nescafé Gold Blend is an example of a *brand* source strategy, where the brand Nescafé supports the quality of the product. Nescafé, of course, is a Nestlé brand, but it is a stand-alone brand. While there is an obvious alliterative reference to the parent company, it is not explicitly a part of the branding strategy. This same corporate or brand-level distinction operates with endorser branding strategies as well (for example, Norwich Union, an AVIVA company).

Product and brand portfolio strategies inform a company's branding strategy, and how IMC will be used to establish the brands in their markets. To illustrate, consider AB InBev, the world's largest brewer, yet there is no 'AB InBev' beer brand. Are you familiar with what brands they do market? Following the acquisition of Anheuser-Busch by Interbrew in 2008 and the creation of the new name, perhaps you do know (or might guess) that AB stands for Anheuser-Busch, and that they brew Budweiser, but their brand portfolio contains more than 400 brands. Their strategy is to focus on three global brands (Stella Artois, Corona, and Budweiser), a few key multi-country brands (such as Leffe and Hoegaarden), with the remaining brands in specific local markets. According to their website, all their brands have 'clearly defined and consistently communicated

Product portfolio

	Global brands	Multi-country brands	Local brands
Brand portfolio	Budweiser Corona Stella Artois	Becks Hoegaarden Leffe	Carling Black Label Fosters Harbin Modelo Especial Patagonias Others

Figure 2.4 Partial AB InBev product and brand portfolio grid.

values, making them "Value Based Brands"'. The brand AB InBev only exists, in reality, for the *financial* community, but bear in mind that this too must be considered as part of their overall IMC campaign.

Let us look more closely at this. Figure 2.4 presents a partial product and brand portfolio grid for AB InBev. Are you surprised at the brands in their portfolio? In addition to the many brands in their portfolio, this does not even begin to account for the extent of their brand lines. Budweiser alone, for example, includes Budweiser, Budweiser Nitro Gold, Budweiser Select, Budweiser 55, Budweiser Chelada, and Budweiser Zero.

It is part of their branding strategy to *not* link their individual brands with the parent company. With the exception of the international premium and specialty brands, whose channel costs are already paid and thus return a higher profit, the heart of their portfolio strategy is local brands representing in most markets either the number one or number two selling brand in that market.

IMC strategic planning for AB InBev, among other things, would need to take into account the fact that the overall corporate positioning is to look at most of their brands as 'local'. This certainly fits with their positioning of Modelo Especial in 2017 as 'Mexico's premium beer'. Contrast that with their positioning of Stella Artois as the 'world's number one Belgium beer'. They are letting you know that Stella Artois is a global brand, number one *worldwide*. Several of their local brands capitalize on where they are brewed, tapping into something Kroeber-Riel (1993) has talked about as 'cultural schema', those memories or feelings that are reflected as cultural values, which we talked about earlier in the chapter. Fosters, for example, use the line 'Australia's Favourite Beer Brand' on their cans, and start with their advertising built around the tagline, 'good call'. However, most of their brands, regardless of type, do not use a geographic reference, allowing for greater flexibility in distribution: for example.

AB InBev offers an example of where the parent company itself is not a brand or a part of the branding strategy. Volkswagen offers a much different example of product and brand portfolio strategy. Everyone knows that Volkswagen is a 'brand' with a number of sub-brands such as Polo and Passat. Many people may also know that they are the parent company for other car 'brands', such as Audi and Porsche. But not many people know that they are also the parent company of Bugatti and Bentley.

Think about this in terms of IMC strategy. If you are marketing Bentley, would you want people to know that you are a Volkswagen company? VW's brand equity may be positive in many respects, but it is unlikely to favourably transfer to Bentley, let alone to the over €3 million Bugatti! On the other hand, while it might seem that the perceived high quality and luxury associated with Bentley could help boost the perception of the VW brand, the problem is that the two brands are not compatible. They satisfy different category needs and market segments.

People would be unlikely to believe that a Volkswagen, priced at €30,000, could deliver the same high quality as a Bentley, priced at €350,000. In positioning, this reflects the need to correctly link the appropriate need with a brand. Effective IMC will help ensure that when a need for a particular type of car occurs, the advertised brand comes to mind. This requires building the appropriate links in memory, as discussed earlier.

Volkswagen itself basically uses a source branding strategy. Recall that a source branding strategy is where the parent company is supporting the quality of its sub-brands, and the sub-brands reflect the equity of the parent brand. In terms of IMC strategy, an umbrella family spirit should be present, even though the sub-brands have their own individual names and specific communications strategy. In the early 2000s, for example, regardless of whether it was advertising for a Golf, Passat, or other VW sub-brand, while each sub-brand's advertising was unique, it was all tied together with the tagline 'Drivers Wanted' under the VW logo.

In this section, we have taken only a brief look at how product and brand portfolio strategy informs branding strategy, which in turn establishes the foundation for IMC strategy. The point is that a manager cannot approach the development of an IMC programme for a brand without an understanding of the company's overall branding strategy within its portfolio management. The hard work of developing an effective IMC strategy for a brand is, of course, specifically brand centred, but it must be consistent with the overall marketing strategy for a firm's portfolio of brands, as reflected by its branding strategy.

Summary

In this chapter, we have looked at how IMC helps build brands. Brands have meaning, and that meaning builds over time largely as a function of marketing communication. An important part of a brand's meaning will also include social meaning, the product of both the brand and the consumer, and this too is informed by marketing communication. We looked at the important role of cultural values, and whether a brand is perceived as global or local.

It might even be argued that one could not have a brand without marketing communication. This is because marketing communication should be seen as *every* contact between a brand and its market. This means everything from advertising and promotion in its traditional sense to such things as store presentation, packaging, events, and product placement in movies. In other words, any representation of the brand. It is IMC that offers the manager the ability to ensure consistency of meaning over all contact with the market.

This begins with establishing the optimum positioning for the brand. The general positioning will have been provided by the marketing plan, but a specific positioning must be established for marketing communication. This requires correctly identifying the link between the brand and category need in order to effectively build awareness for the brand and selecting the correct benefit for increasing positive brand attitude. Brand attitude is critical in building strong brands because it is a positive brand attitude that leads to a strong brand equity, and the important difference between value equity and uniqueness equity.

IMC must also take into account product and brand portfolio considerations, especially branding strategies. To the extent that a company offers different brands within a category or brand extensions, the branding strategies will inform how the communications strategy for those brands or extensions will be developed. Stand-alone brands provide an opportunity for unique identification, independent of a parent brand (where one exists). Sub-brands will reflect the identity of the parent brand, either as a source or endorser. With a source branding strategy, the parent is supporting the quality of the product. Any endorser branding strategy implies that the parent brand approves and supports the brand while assuming a secondary position.

Review questions

1   How does IMC help build brands?
2   Why is it important to consider cultural values in the planning process?
3   In what way is a celebrity or politician a brand?
4   How is IMC involved in creating social meaning for a brand?
5   Identify brands that you feel have created social meaning and discuss how IMC is likely to have contributed.
6   Why is positioning so critical to effective IMC in building brands?
7   Identify competing brands that are clearly positioned differently and discuss which position is likely to be more effective.
8   Is there likely to be a centrally positioned brand in the beer category? What about household cleaners, computers, and designer fashions?
9   Identify brands that use a user-oriented positioning and discuss its appropriateness.
10   What is the relationship between positioning and brand awareness and brand attitude?
11   How would you define brand attitude?
12   What is the role of IMC in establishing and building brand attitude?
13   Explain the relationship between brand equity and the price elasticity of demand.
14   Select a brand that you feel has strong brand equity and discuss the role of brand attitude in building and sustaining it.
15   How does a brand's portfolio management impact on IMC strategy?
16   Identify examples of stand-alone, source, and endorser brands, and discuss how IMC should be used to support their brand strategy.

References

Aaker, D.A. (1991) *Managing Brand Equity*. New York: Free Press.

Aaker, J. (1997) Dimensions of brand personality. *Journal of Marketing Research, 34*(3), 347–356.

Advertising Age (2005) 13 June, 18.

Douglas, M. and Isherwood, B. (1979) *The World of Goods: Towards an Anthropology of Consumption.* London: Alter Lane.

Elliott, R., Jones, A., Benefield, A. and Barlow, M. (1995) Overt sexuality in advertising: A discourse analysis of gendered responses. *Journal of Consumer Policy, 18*(2), 71–92.

Fishbein, M. and Ajzen, I. (1975) *Belief, Attitude, Intention, and Behaviour: An Introduction to Theory and Research*. Reading, Massachusetts, MA: Addison-Wesley Publishing Company.

Kapferer, J.N. (1997) *Strategic Brand Management*, 2nd edition. London: Kogan Page.

Kates, S. (2000) Out of the closet and into the streets: Gay men and their brand relationships. *Psychology and Marketing*, 17(6), 493–504.

Kroeber-Riel, W. (1993) *Buldkommunikation*. Munich: Verlag-Vahlenn; see also an introduction to his work available in English, J. Olson and W.K. Sentis (eds), Advertising and Consumer Psychology, Volume 3, New York: Praeger, 1986.

McAlexander, J., Schouten, J. and Koenig, H. (2002) Building brand community. *Journal of Marketing*, 66(1), 38–54.

McClure, S.M., Li, J., Tomlin, D., Cypert, K.S., Mantague, L.M. and Montague, P.R. (2004) Neural correlates of behavioural preference for culturally familiar drinks. *Neuron*, 44(2), 379–387.

Moran, W.T. (1994) Marketplace measurement of brand equity. *Journal of Brand Management*, 1(5), 272–282.

Muniz, A. and O'Guinn, T. (2001) Brand community. *Journal of Consumer Research*, 27(4), 412–432.

Percy, L., Hansen, F. and Randrup, R. (2004) *Emotional response to brands and product categories*, Proceedings from ESOMAR, Lisben.

Rosenbaum-Elliott, R., Percy, L. and Pervan, S. (2018) *Strategic Brand Management*, 2nd edition. Oxford: Oxford University Press.

Schuiling, I. and Kapferer, J. (2004) Real differences between local and international brand's strategic implications for international marketers. *Journal of International Marketing*, 12/4, 97–112.

Vargo, S.L. and Lusch, R.F. (2004) Evolving to a new dominant logic for marketing. *Journal of Marketing*, 68(1), 1–7.

Veblen, T. (1899/1979) *The Theory of the Leisured Class*. New York: Kelly.

Wengrow, D. (2008) Prehistory of commodity branding. *Current Anthropology'*, February 1, 49(1), 7–34.

3 Companies and IMC

In the last chapter, we saw how a company's name may be used as a brand, or as a source or endorser within its branding strategy. In this chapter, we look at the *company itself* as a 'brand', not as the name of a product. There is a vast literature on corporate and organizational identity and imagery, and we examine this area along with reputation. However, our primary concern is with the role IMC plays in these areas and the development and nurturing of a company as a brand, just as we were concerned with the role of IMC in building and sustaining product brands in the last chapter.

What we will see is that there is a great deal of similarity, at least on the surface: companies, like brands, are also positioned, but their positioning is usually referred to as a 'vision'. They work to establish positive attitudes towards the company among their various publics and stakeholders in order to build a strong corporate brand equity.

The role of IMC in strengthening companies

People who work in the field of corporate imagery and identity are generally concerned with the idea of the company as either an organization or corporate entity, and how it is represented and communicated to its various audiences and stakeholders (Hatch and Schultz, 2000). Corporate identity is usually thought of as being different from organizational identity, although there is some overlap (Hatch and Schultz, 2000). The principal distinction between these two views of a company reflects an internal versus external perspective.

When considering *organizational* identity and imagery, one is looking *within* the company at employees or other internal stakeholders. When considering *corporate* identity and imagery, one is usually concerned with looking outside of the company to external audiences (Table 3.1). IMC should and must play a role in the establishment and maintenance of a company's identity, but within the area of corporate, not organizational, imagery and identity.

This is a broad statement, of course. The image of a company that is projected to the outside world must find consonance within the organization. This is especially true of service industries, and, to a lesser degree, business-to-business firms, where employee contact with the consumer plays a significant role in building both corporate and brand attitude. But researchers in organizational identity like to think about it in terms of (among other things) the perspective from which identity is defined.

As Hatch and Schultz (2000) have described, corporate identity will reflect the thinking and direction of top management, even if they take into account the opinions of other members of the organization. Organizational identity, however, will reflect the

DOI: 10.4324/9781003169635-4

Table 3.1 Corporate versus organizational identity and imagery

Corporate	**External**, looking at the company's outside target audiences
Organizational	**Internal**, looking at employees and other stakeholders within the company

many ways everyone within an organization thinks about themselves as an organization. As they put it, 'corporate identity requires taking a managerial perspective, while appreciation of organizational identity requires an organizational perspective' (Hatch and Schultz, 2000). While acknowledging a potential overlap between corporate and organizational identity, and the fact that IMC's direct role in building corporate identity will inform organizational identity, we look at IMC's role in strengthening a company in terms of corporate identity.

It should be obvious that corporate communication in all its forms (press releases, annual reports, sponsorships, etc.), but especially corporate advertising, must be consistent with its general marketing communication. The arguments for consistency in the delivery of a brand's message (as outlined in Chapter 1) hold for corporate communication. Such consistency creates a recognizable picture of a company, regardless of the channel of communication (van Riel, 2000).

Consider this example: if a company presented itself as modern and innovative, yet marketed 'traditional' products, would that make any sense? In terms of our discussion in the last chapter on branding strategy, what if they were using a source or endorser branding strategy? Even though the corporate message would be separate from the brand messages, the corporate brand equity that is being relied upon to 'guarantee' the brand would be at odds with the image the brand has established. The two images would simply not be compatible.

Even if our hypothetical company used only a stand-alone branding strategy for the products they market, this would still not be a good idea. While the brand images would not be connected with the parent, the parent would be connected to the brands. It would be hard to imagine a company like Proctor & Gamble, which does not incorporate the corporate name as part of their branding strategy, not including their brands in some fashion within their corporate communication. Recall our discussion of AB InBev. Their corporate communication is all about their brands, but AB InBev does not appear as a part of their brand marketing communication. Not only must brand messages be consistent across all channels of communication, and corporate messages be consistent in all their media, but brand and corporate messages must be consistent.

Christensen and Cheney (2000) have made the interesting observation that corporate existence can no longer be separate from the question of communication. In their view, companies have convinced themselves that success will depend very much upon their ability to not only differentiate their products or services from competitors, but to actually justify their existence through the corporate image they project. To quote them: 'identity is the issue, and communication seems to be the answer'.

This is reminiscent of how, back in the 1970s, Mobil Corporation (now ExxonMobil) was perhaps the first company to integrate advertising, public relations, and policy statements from the company into an explicit 'corporate advocacy' campaign (Crable and Vibbert, 1983). They became proactive in the face of public and government concerns over oil prices and supply. One of their efforts in trying to better manage their overall image was to publish a series of 'advertorials' on a number of socio-political issues. What this did was move the overall positioning of Mobil as a company beyond the image of their products. But as we have discussed, that must still be consistent with the image of their products.

With increased scrutiny of companies from a wide range of sources ranging from advocacy groups to government, to say nothing of the '24/7' media news cycle, companies today are more and more concerned with their general image and identity. Many are following what Dahler-Larsen (1997) has called 'moralized discourses', using corporate communication to gain what the company sees as 'responsibility'. IMC must play a central role in coordinating the image of the corporation with that of its products. BP (British Petroleum) offers a good example of what we have been talking about. For several years, their corporate communication has been trying to change its image and identity from petroleum to a more broadly based energy company, paying attention to environmental concerns. This effort, unfortunately, suffered from the 2010 oil spill in the Gulf of Mexico. They tried again in 2019, but were challenged, and dropped the campaign (see Box below).

Corporate reputation communication

In 2019, BP (British Petroleum) launched a campaign in an effort to raise their profile as a good corporate citizen. It was their first such campaign since the Deepwater Horizon oil spill in 2010, and it highlighted their efforts to embrace clean energy. Unfortunately for BP, it was challenged by lawyers for the activist group Client Earth as 'misleading'. The global campaign, centred around the message "We see possibilities everywhere" that talked about efforts to embrace clean energy, was withdrawn in February 2020. BP's CEO Bernard Looney said at the time they would not replace it, and introduced a new policy promising to end corporate reputation advertising.

Source: theoligist.org, 22 June 2020

Corporate identity, image, and reputation

The terms corporate identity, corporate image, and corporate reputation are often used interchangeably, but there are important differences between them that a manager should understand because they inform strategy. These differences are often painfully detailed by academics, but this should not deter us from appreciating the strategic implications associated with each of the concepts.

Grahame Dowling (2001) has offered a set of rather clear and helpful definitions for each of these concepts that identify the principal differences between them. He describes *corporate identity* as: 'the symbols and nomenclature an organization uses to identify itself to people (such as the corporate name, logo, advertising, slogan, livery, etc.)'. Following this definition, examples of corporate identity would include such things as IBM, the Nike 'swoosh', and the Macintosh apple. But corporate identity begins with the company name, and getting that right is critical and not an easy task.

Corporate image is regarded as 'the global evaluation (comprised of a set of beliefs and feelings) a person has about an organization'. The important point here is that an 'image' is in the eye of the beholder. To the extent that a company has succeeded in creating a consistent image over time, there should be general consensus within its target markets as to what that image is. Volvo is concerned with making 'safe' cars; Rolls-Royce with making high-quality, luxurious cars. Regardless of the nameplate (the word the car industry likes to use for the brand), if you know it was made by Volvo, because of the company's image, you would expect it to be 'safe'.

But as Dowling (2001) points out, not everyone is likely to hold the same beliefs and feelings about a company. This means it is unlikely that any company has a *single* image. The job of IMC is to build and nurture as consistent an image as possible among the largest number of a company's various audiences. The fact that a company has many different audiences to address (for example, government regulators, shareholders, employees, and consumers) complicates the job, and underscores the need for effective IMC; a centrally managed communication effort to project a consistent image.

Dowling (2001) defines *corporate reputation* as: 'the attributed values (such as authenticity, honesty, responsibility, and integrity) evoked from the person's corporate image'. Again, this means there is the potential for a wide-ranging understanding of a company's reputation owing to the potential differences in value assessment among different people, and among various target audiences. What is important to one person or group may not be to another, and certain values may carry different weights among different people and groups. This potential problem increases for multinational companies because of the ways in which values can be culturally driven.

With this introduction to corporate identity, image, and reputation as a foundation, let us now take a closer look at each concept.

Corporate identity

The idea of corporate identity as defined by Dowling (2001) is rather straightforward: the words and symbols a company uses to set itself apart from other companies so people will recognize it. Originally, the study of corporate identity tended to be centred on a rather narrow, graphic design perspective. One of the earliest models of corporate identity was proposed by the German corporate design firm of Birkigt and Stadler (1986). There is no doubt that visual imagery via graphic design can play a significant part in corporate identity (just think of the 'golden arches'). There is much more to it, as we will see. In fact, there is a good deal more to it, but the field of identity studies is well beyond the scope of this book. Nevertheless, some appreciation of the scope of corporate identity studies is in order if we are to understand the role of IMC in the development and sustaining of corporate identity.

In introducing a collection of articles on corporate identity in their book, John Balmer and Stephen Greyser (2003) offer a useful way of looking at the field of identity studies. They suggest regarding it as inhabiting three different 'worlds', a *triquadri orbis* in their words. It begins with the narrow world of graphic design, and what they call *visual identification*. Graphic presentation is an important consideration in developing an IMC programme. As an example, from its earliest years IBM has been informally known as 'Big Blue'. In the early 2000s, IBM's advertising reflected this visually by framing graphically all their advertisements, even television commercials, with horizontal blue bars on the top and bottom of the page and screen. With consistent use of this graphic device, soon one immediately identified these messages with IBM, even before exposure to the corporate tag.

The second 'world' of identity is what Balmer and Greyser (2003) called *organizational identity*. As they put it, this reflects the use of corporate identity in answering the question,

'Who are we?' This aspect of corporate identity addresses the internal audience of the organization and is of less interest to us given our focus on a company's external audiences. But we cannot ignore it. How employees see the company they work for is critical to overall communication efforts in service industries, and in any business where employees have significant contact with customers (e.g., banks and retail stores). This is where such things as company newsletters and other internal corporate communications must be consistent with the overall image being projected to the population at large, and as a result, part of IMC.

The third 'world' of identity studies is *corporate identity*. It seeks to answer the questions, 'What are we?' as well as 'Who are we?' This is the world of identity studies with which we are most concerned, and the one addressed by the marketing literature. But it is important to keep in mind that both the visual identification and organizational identification worlds will play their part in the overall perception of a company's identity. The role of corporate identity is critical to any discussion of corporate strategy, and this includes image, reputation, and, importantly, communication.

As Dowling (2001) has suggested, while managers generally have a pretty good understanding of corporate image and reputation, they often confuse corporate image with corporate identity. This can, and often does, result in wasting a great deal of a company's communication budget. Part of the responsibility of IMC is to ensure that there is no confusion between identity and image in a company's corporate communication. It is also the job of IMC to ensure that there is no confusion *within* corporate identity.

Corporate identity types

According to Balmer and Greyser (2003), corporate identity should not be viewed as a monolithic phenomenon, but one comprised of multiple types of identity. They argue that companies have more than one identity and that they can coexist without problems when well managed. Five identity types are proposed: actual identity, communicated identity, conceived identity, ideal identity, and desired identity (Table 3.2).

The *actual identity* of a corporation reflects its various realities – everything from management style to market performance, structure to performance. *Communicated identity* is driven by corporate communication, as well as more informal and non-controlled communication such as word-of-mouth and media commentary. The *conceived identity* of a company is the perception of it held by its various audiences. The *ideal identity* reflects what would be the optimum positioning for a company, and is subject to change over time in relation to the correct environment. *Desired identity* is what top management sees as their vision for the company. It differs from the ideal identity in being more likely to reflect the CEO's ego than the strategic realities of the day.

Table 3.2 Multiple corporate identities

Identity	Description
Actual	Reflects reality
Communicated	Driven by corporate communication
Conceived	Perception held by target audiences
Ideal	Optimum positioning for corporation
Desired	Top management vision

Source: Adapted from Balmer and Greyser (2003).

As you can see, these various identities devolve from both internal and external sources. Beyond the obvious, this will also include such things as the internal response to company culture and values, as well as the external influence of industry culture and socio-cultural influences generally. Corporate communication, as part of an IMC programme, is likely to drive communicated identity and inform conceived and actual identity. A company's ideal identity should be a goal of corporate communication, to the extent that a corporation's vision is strategically based and will be reflected in its corporate communication.

IMC should serve as a mediating factor for all aspects of corporate identity. One of the concerns voiced by Balmer and Greyser (2003) in discussing multiple corporate identities is that all too often there is a 'misalignment' of the identities, which leads to identity problems. They suggest that it is the responsibility of corporate leadership groups to manage identities to ensure broad consensus, and we see IMC as the key to implementing their effort.

Corporate image

In concept, corporate image parallels brand image. Both are in the 'eye of the beholder', the result of an overall evaluation of the brand or company in terms of a 'set of beliefs and feelings' as Dowling (2001) put it in his definition. This has been the traditional way of looking at image, and from a consumer behavioural- or psychological perspective has been studied within the context of information processing. Compounded with corporate identity, this is an important point that reflects a critical difference between the two concepts. Corporate identity is usually studied from a management perspective, looking at how a company wishes to be seen by its various public. Corporate image, on the other hand, is the result of how those various publics have processed the information they have about a company.

Corporate image will inform how people make decisions and form attitudes towards companies. There is discussion among scholars in the area as to how all this occurs (Christensen and Askegaard, 2001), but we need not get into that discussion here. The important point about an 'image' (whether a company, brand, or anything else) is that it is the result of processing information. This information is then consolidated in memory. Image in the sense we are concerned with is not 'imagination'. It is the result of associations in memory that are reviewed and updated when new information about a company is received. This means that corporate image is always subject to change.

One of the key differences between corporate identity and image is the *source*. Christensen and Askegaard (2001) consider this a very important point. In reviewing the literature on corporate identity and image, they found that, generally speaking, the idea of corporate identity is associated with the *sender* of communication messages (i.e., internal, the source is the company). A company chooses how to 'identify' itself, as we saw in the last section.

On the other hand, corporate image is more commonly related to the *receiver* of communication messages (i.e., external, the audience is the source). In a very real sense, a company's image is 'created' in the minds of its various audiences as they process communications about the company. The resulting image will of course be significantly mediated by the content of the message sent, but that message will always be filtered through each individual's existing knowledge and assumption about the company, and what is said about it (Table 3.3).

Table 3.3 Corporate image versus corporate identity

Corporate image	Associated with the **sender** of corporate communication and reflecting how the company wishes to be perceived
Corporate identity	Related to the **receiver** of corporate communication and reflecting how they perceive the company based on everything they know about it

Perhaps it is because the corporate image is constructed externally, by individuals rather than organizationally driven, that it seems to attract less attention from those involved in the study of corporate identity, image, and reputation. A suggestion of this might be found in the 'problems' with corporate image identified by Balmer (1998): multiple meanings, negative associations, the difficulty or impossibility of control, its multiplicity, and the different effects on various audiences.

Looking at these difficulties, they seem to imply that a company does not have *direct* control over its image, and this is seen to be a problem. But we would argue that where corporate image communication is an integral part of a company's IMC programme, they will be exercising a significant level of control over the resulting image. When all of a company's communication about itself and its brands are coordinated and addresses a consistent, viable strategy the perception of the company, its corporate image, will reflect that communication. People will be processing a consistent message, one projecting a specific image. Successful processing of that message will result in the desired corporate image. How to accomplish this is what this book is all about, at both the brand and corporate levels.

According to Balmer and Greyser (2003), when considering corporate image academics look at image from one of four perspectives: the transmitter of images, receiver-end image categories, the focus of images, and construed images. Within each perspective there are a number of ways to look at an image. Each reflects various ways corporate image might be treated strategically within an overall communication plan.

The first category focuses upon the company as the transmitter of images. This is similar to the general perspective taken of corporate identity, but here refers to image management. Corporate image is being looked at in terms of its communication strategy and objectives. Here we find such things as the creation and delivery of a single image to all a company's audiences and the notion that corporate image is principally a function of the company's overall visual identity (which you will remember is a key element of how corporate identity is defined).

The remaining three perspectives are from the perspective of the market, not the company. With receiver-end image, one is looking at the corporate image in terms of the *immediate* processing of a message from the corporation (transient image). This reflects everything from advertisements, to packaging to logos. It also is concerned with the congruence of the projected image of the company and how customers see themselves. The key is that the focus is on the receiver of the message, not the sender. What Balmer and Greyser (2003) called focus-of-image looks at corporate image in terms of the various brand and category images. Finally, the corporate image may be looked at in terms of what one group, such as the company's employees, *think* another group, such as their customers, believes about the company.

This gives some idea of the complexity involved in dealing with corporate image. There are many ways of looking at it, with a corresponding potential for multiple interpretations. One of the tasks for IMC is to minimize the chance of multiple interpretations. From a communication standpoint, in the end a manager is concerned with creating a corporate image that is understood by the target audiences in the way in which it was intended. IMC ensures that all a company's communication, both corporate and brand, consistently reinforces the desired image.

Corporate reputation

Dowling's (2001) definition of corporate reputation is based upon the values a person associates with their understanding of a company's image. As he puts it, it is a *value-based* construct. When looking at corporate reputation this way, it is important to understand that it is enduring values that are being considered (or at least values that are likely to be held over the long term by most people, and unlikely to change in the short term). These values would include such things as integrity, honesty, and responsibility. When a company is seen to be holding values important to its target audiences, it will enjoy a positive corporate reputation. This in turn, *because* of the perception of shared values, will lead to feelings of trust and confidence in that company.

Many people look at corporate image and corporate reputation as overlapping constructs, but as Dowling reminds us, it is important to keep them separate. In fact, he suggests that the way to a strong corporate reputation is through a strong corporate image. Companies seek a strong corporate image built on positive beliefs and feelings about the company, consistent with an overall corporate positioning strategy. As we have seen, it is one of the tasks of IMC to build and nurture that image.

Once a corporate image is established, it should be linked to values important to its stakeholders. This is because values do not change, at least not in the short term. But it is possible to change or alter perceptions about a company. The role of IMC here is critical. Everything communicated about a company and its brands must be consistent with the establishment of the desired corporate image, and with the association in memory to the appropriate values. In this case, values operate very much like emotions in framing an understanding of brands and companies. Companies, like brands, are linked in memory with specific emotional associations. These emotions are present in working memory whenever someone is thinking about that company or processing new information about it. We deal with the role of emotion in processing messages in much more detail in Chapter 8.

In the same way, the effective linking of a company in memory with positive values should ensure the presence of the resulting reputation in working memory when a person is thinking about that company, and there when processing communications about it. This is the result of something neuropsychologists call top-down processing, where one's knowledge and assumptions about a thing (in this case, the company) will be present in working memory whenever one is consciously processing information about it.

Because corporate reputation is value-based, it enjoys a strategic advantage over the corporate image. Both are dependent on individual perceptions, and the strength of a positive reputation will be greater than a positive image. Part of the reason is that an image is less permanent and more variable because it is based upon beliefs and feelings, while reputation, based on values, is less subject to short-term change. Another is that a company's reputation will be more stable in the presence of negative publicity. Because it is value-based and not belief-based, negative information about the company will have a much more difficult time altering the association in memory. And in today's world of social media and the incredible speed with which negative messages about a company can spread, a strong corporate reputation is critical.

Imagine a pharmaceutical company that enjoys a corporate image for high-quality products, but no well-formed reputation. Imagine another with a corporate reputation for trustworthiness. Now suppose that a question is raised in the press about the efficacy of a drug they both market. Each company launches a campaign affirming the quality of their product, but which is most likely to be believed by more people? It is more likely to be the company with a reputation for trustworthiness. Why? An image for quality products could have been built on many things, for example, a long history in the business. But the beliefs upon which that image was built are unlikely to include 'truthfulness'. It is unlikely to come into most people's minds when building an image of a company's products. On the other hand, a reputation for trustworthiness reflects an association with individual values. If a person believes a company is trustworthy, they will believe they tell the truth. This follows from something known as inoculation theory (McGuire, 1969), where the build-up of positive affect, a company's reputation in this case, will help 'inoculate' you, leading to resistance to negative information about the company.

Building corporate identity, image, and reputation

Now that we have an overview of what constitutes corporate identity, image, and reputation, it is time to examine what is involved in successfully developing and communicating each. Before beginning, however, it will be important to look at the interrelationships among them. As should already be clear, there is a certain overlap between these constructs, and each is somewhat dependent upon the others.

In fact, you may be thinking that a great deal is being made of very little in crafting such specific differences in these constructs. In many ways this is true, but for academics these differences are important. They permit looking at aspects of corporate strategy and how both the internal and external audiences and stakeholders of a company 'see' that company. From a manager's perspective, understanding that their company may be seen in different lights by different people, and for different reasons, should help in developing an effective overall communications programme to position the company in the minds of its audiences. Each of these three ways of 'seeing' a company must be accounted for in a firm's IMC.

The study of corporate meaning that led to the constructs we have been talking about began in the 1950s with a focus on corporate image. This was joined in the 1970s by the idea of corporate identity. Then, in the late 1980s, the study of corporate reputation was added to the mix. With the addition of each new perspective, offering a different way of looking at companies, more was understood about corporate meaning. Now, there is a new focus on corporate meaning, *corporate brands* (which we address in due course).

Balmer and Greyser (2003) have suggested that there are six critical questions that characterize the study of corporate meaning, and five of the six bear upon our discussions. Three of these questions relate directly to the constructs we have been talking about, and two others indirectly. Five of the six questions and their related construct are detailed in Table 3.4. Taken together, they provide insight into the areas that must be addressed in effectively building a positive corporate identity, image, and reputation.

Table 3.4 Keys to corporate meaning

Corporate identity	What are the company's distinct attributes?
Corporate image	How is the company currently perceived?
Corporate reputation	How is the company perceived over time?
Corporate communication	What does the company communicate and to whom?
Corporate branding	What is the corporate covenant?

Source: Adapted from Balmer and Greyser (2003).

The first question, 'What are the company's distinct attributes?' relates to corporate identity. The second, 'How is the company currently perceived?' relates to corporate image, and the third, 'How is the company perceived over time?' to corporate reputation. In answering these questions, the manager will have addressed the fundamental issues driving corporate communication strategy. They also outline the underlying relationship between the constructs. Corporate identity sets out the character of the company that set it apart from competitors, which when successfully communicated to the appropriate target audience will inform how it is perceived at any one time: the corporate image. How it is perceived over time will result in its corporate reputation.

Dowling (2001) addresses this issue of corporate meaning directly. He suggests that a good corporate identity (especially in terms of corporate symbols) will enable people to more easily recognize a company. Symbols and other features of corporate identity act as triggers in memory for helping to recall and elaborate its image. When you see Apple's trademark logo or McDonald's 'golden arches' it will quickly activate the beliefs and emotions in memory associated with the brand, but also the company, its corporate image. When these are positive and consistent with someone's values in terms of corporate behaviour, it will lead to a positive corporate reputation.

Perhaps the most important question this raises is: 'To whom and what do we communicate?' This, of course, defines communication, and in terms of IMC we would add 'and how?' Getting this correct is what will ensure the desired corporate meaning among a company's target audiences and key stakeholders. Of the remaining questions raised by Balmer and Geyser, we briefly look at the idea of corporate branding next. The issue of organizational identity, because of its internal company orientation, is generally unrelated to the fundamental development of IMC strategy, which looks primarily at external consistencies. As a result, that aspect of corporate meaning is of less interest to us in this book (although it will not be totally ignored).

Corporate brand

In a sense, a corporate brand is the reflection of corporate meaning as we have been discussing it. As shown in Figure 3.1, the key concepts of corporate identity, image, and reputation are related as suggested by Dowling (2001), and, as each is communicated to the company's target audience, they contribute to building a corporate brand. It is a summary image that acts as an umbrella over all the firm's marketing activity, as well as its communication with all its stakeholders. There are all types of associations outside of product or brand considerations that may become linked to corporate brands, as Brown (1998) and his colleagues remind us. In effect, the dimensions of corporate meaning reflect this, and their fusion provides the foundation for corporate brand equity.

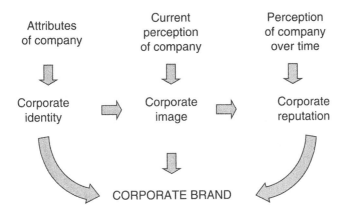

Figure 3.1 Corporate brand as a function of corporate meaning.

Developing corporate names

Coming up with a new corporate name seems to be becoming more difficult and expensive. In the past, it was a simple process: name the company after the founder. That is where Proctor & Gamble came from, the founder's names. When candle maker William Proctor and soap maker James Gamble got together back in 1837, the corporate name followed naturally. But in today's world of global marketing, where names must make sense across any number of languages and cultures, as well as survive the scrutiny of social media comment, a great deal of attention must be paid to a new corporate name.

Kraft Foods, when spinning off its snack business, is reported to have vetted names for the new company in focus groups representing 28 languages. Nevertheless, the new name chosen faced a storm of criticism. It was derived from combining 'monde', from the Latin word for 'world', and 'delez', which was supposed to represent 'delicious'. But when the name is said in Russian it sounds like an expression they have for oral sex. The company said that only happens when the name is mispronounced, and that they were quite happy with it because, as a corporate spokesperson put it: 'It builds on our higher purpose, which is "make today delicious" and captures the idea of a delicious world, which is great for a global snack company'. Does this new name Mondelez (pronounced Mohn-dah-*leez*) convey this idea to you?

When Fortune Brands spun off some of its business, the new stand-alone division was called Beam Global Spirits and Wine. But this was quickly shortened to Beam, Inc. after its well-known bourbon brand, Jim Beam. As a spokeswoman for the company put it: 'Everybody knows what Jim Beam is, so we we're like, "Let's not overthink it", and let's just keep it real and keep it authentic and tie back to our roots'.

Source: *Advertising Age*, 4 April 2012

Much of the effort in creating a corporate brand is in response to a realization that among consumers such things as how a company treats its employees, addresses environmental concerns, and other issues related to its role in society, is being factored into their brand purchase decisions. This has led to more and more companies building corporate brands as a strategic marketing tool in order to improve overall financial performance (Roberts and Dowling, 1998; Hatch and Schultz, 2001).

There is much more to a corporate brand than a single unifying tagline, slogan, or logo. According to Hatch and Schultz (2001), there are three critical interdependent elements that go into making an effective corporate brand: culture, vision, and image. The job is difficult because different groups drive each element. Culture reflects the internal organization's values and behaviour and how employees feel about the company. Corporate culture plays an important role in the corporate brand, especially with symbolic management. What might it mean, for example, to be an employee or customer of a designated Certified B Corporation assuming they knew what that was? A Certified B Corporation is a designation assigned by Blab, a global non-profit, that 'grades' companies on a set of rigorous standards of social and environmental performance, accountability, and transparency. Those designated are for-profit businesses dedicated to social and environmental issues and include the Brazilian cosmetic company Natura, Unilever's Ben & Jerry's, and Patagonia. According to Larsen (2000), such companies create emotional bonds and messages that attract and maintain both employees and other stakeholders.

Vision will come from top management, usually the CEO. Image (used here in its broad meaning) is how the rest of the world sees the company. The core of corporate branding is the alignment between these three elements (Schultz, 2005).

It is critical to a successful corporate brand that a consensual image (again in its broadest sense) be built among its various target audiences, one that is both an accurate representation of the company as well as being consistent with overall corporate strategy. This requires the consistency in communication that results from an effective IMC programme, one that is informed by corporate communication strategy.

In addition to effectively communicating with its external audiences, the corporate brand must be internalized by the organization, and communicated through all its personal contacts with those outside the organization; everyone from vendors to the trade to consumers to stakeholders. The involvement of employees is considered important to the development of a corporate brand. In building a corporate brand, a company must pay particular attention to its employees. They must buy-in, and especially for retail, this must inform their behaviour with customers. As with all IMC, internal communication with employees must be consistent with what is being communicated elsewhere. Czarniawska (1997) has suggested that it is necessary to understand how employees work, make sense of their role within the company, and how symbols and corporate stories (which we will discuss below) inform their perceptions to effectively manage a corporate brand. In other words, a company's employees' experience with their brand must be consistent with what their consumers are hearing. Internal communication should always be a significant part of any IMC program.

Corporate brand equity

In the last chapter, we introduced the idea of brand equity. Since in a very real sense companies and corporations are also 'brands'. They will have their own equity, independent of their brand's equity. Corporate brand equity is a result of how it has been represented and communicated to its various audiences and stakeholders; and this follows from the relationship between corporate identity, corporate image, and corporate reputation that we have been discussing (Dowling, 2001).

According to Keller (2000), this 'occurs when relevant constituents hold strong, favourable, and unique associations about the corporate brand in memory'. While this is generally true, recent research has shown that in some cases it may actually be to the advantage of a corporation to be seen by certain stakeholders as similar to others in their specific industry, depending upon their expectations regarding overall corporate behaviour in a particular industry (Brammer and Pavelin, 2006). One way this may occur is that a corporation is seen as more legitimate or socially acceptable to the extent that it is seen as similar to others in terms of what is expected of such companies (Deephouse and Carter, 2005).

With a strong corporate brand equity, just as with product brand equity, relevant target audiences will feel more favourably toward the company, leading to a more favourable response to all of its corporate communication, beyond any purely objective reading of the message. Just as with marketing communication for brands, in building corporate brand equity there are several possible objectives for corporate communication (Biehal and Shenin, 1998). But just as for brands, awareness and attitude will *always* be objectives. Keller has suggested that it is important to link beliefs to the company that can be leveraged by marketing communications for brands. Strong corporate brand equity results from achieving awareness and salience for the company, and the establishment of attitudes towards the company that reflect a positive corporate reputation.

This means ensuring that beliefs about the company, learned and nurtured through its communication, must be linked in memory to appropriate values held by target audiences. This is a step beyond what is necessary for building a positive brand attitude, but it is the beliefs associated with the company's brands through marketing communication that will help reinforce the corporate image, and hence corporate brand equity. The role of IMC in assuring consistency and continuity between marketing communication and corporate communication in driving both product brand equity and corporate brand equity is critical.

One remaining point should be considered here. Corporate brand equity is not the same as the equity for its products, even when the brand name for the product is the company name, or is the company name used as a source or endorser. The equity associated with a company through its branding strategy will of course help inform the corporate image and corporate brand equity. But as we have seen, corporate meaning extends well beyond product or brand perception. A good example of this is Benetton. Benetton as a clothing retailer has one image: as a corporation taking strong stands on social issues, another. You may like the products found at Benetton, while not agreeing with the positions the company takes, or for that matter, even know about them. On the other hand, you may disagree so strongly with the company's social positions that even though you find their merchandise stylish and attractive, you will not buy them. Or you may shop there simply to show your support for their social positions, even though you find their clothing rather like that found at other stores.

Corporate communication

Now that we have an idea of what is involved with corporate meaning and corporate brands, it is time to look at corporate communication. As we saw in comparing brand equity with product brand equity, the essence of corporate communication versus marketing communication is that corporate communication is much broader. Where marketing communication is focused on the consumer or potential consumer and relies (primarily) on specific paid media for delivering the message, corporate communication must deal with a wide range of different audiences, including an important emphasis on communicating with employees, and is not limited to paid media. Public relations, for example, can play a significant role here.

Van Riel (2003) has characterized corporate communication as a fusion of marketing, management, and organizational communication. But Balmer and Gray (2003) take a much broader view – something they call 'total corporate communication', consisting of primary, secondary, and tertiary communication. What they define as primary communication is really indirect communication, the result of such things as product or service performance, company policy, and employee behaviour. These do 'communicate' something about that company and effect corporate image, but we would not include them directly within strategic IMC planning.

Secondary communication, on the other hand, is directly related to IMC. Balmer and Gray (2003) see it as 'planned, "formal" communication policies of organizations' involving such things as advertising and other forms of marketing communication, including public relations. They define tertiary communication in terms of the *effect* of third-party communication. This would include communication about the company from such sources as word-of-mouth, and even what competitors say about them. This type of communication about a company is not directly controlled by the company, but it must still be carefully nurtured as a part of any effective IMC plan. Together, all of this may indeed account for 'total corporate communication', and it will all be important in defining corporate meaning. But from a managerial and not academic standpoint, our concern must be with strategically planned and controlled corporate communication.

One way of appreciating the complexity of corporate communication is to consider Berstein's (1984) idea of a corporate communication wheel, or more particularly Balmer and Greyser's (2003) adaptation of it (Figure 3.2). It begins by asking corporate management to identify all the important audiences with whom they need to communicate. These groups form the outer ring of the wheel. Then it requires a list of all the available channels of communication for delivering the message. These become a circle within the circle of potential target audiences. In the Balmer and Greyser modification, they include 11 potential target audience groups and 11 possible communication channels. As they explain, that alone results in 121 considerations!

But that is not all. A number of other considerations are contained within the two outer circles of the wheel. These include such things as country of origin, business partnerships, and category or industry image, among others. All these must be considered for each target audience group – communications channel combination. Within each target group, there could be segments, and various channels of communication themselves are comprised of multiple delivery vehicles (think of just the alternatives available with mass media alone, which is only a single communication channel).

In reality management must set priorities, but that itself requires careful planning. Then in addition to optimizing with whom you wish to communicate and to most effectively deliver the message, there is the task of developing a *consistent* message. A recent suggestion has been something called the *sustainable corporate story*.

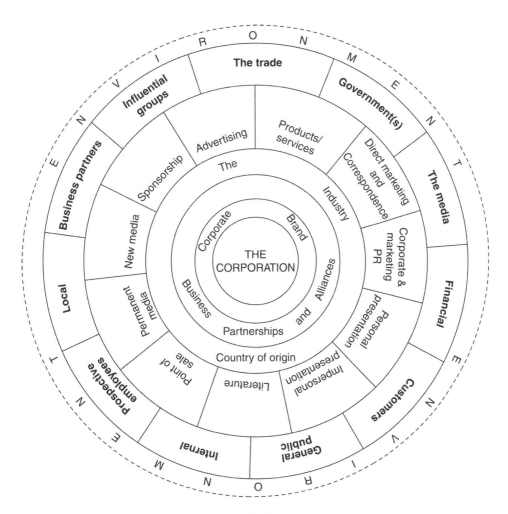

Figure 3.2 The new corporate communications wheel.

Source: Adapted from Balmer and Greyser (2003).

Corporate story

In developing a corporate brand strategy, there are two basic routes: functional versus symbolic, depending upon the stakeholder groups involved. Consumers are more likely to respond to a functional strategy, whereas employees and outside groups may be more interested in a company's socially responsible behaviour and be more responsive to a symbolic strategy. A functional strategy is simply one that is benefit-oriented; one that differentiates the corporate brand in some way, as with brands, from other corporations.

There are a number of potential symbolic strategies, one of which is the use of sponsorships. While there seems to be little evidence that sponsoring cultural events or sports actually has a long-term effect upon the corporate brand (a point we shall make for brands as well in Chapter 7), there is evidence that it can build positive perceptions of the company among consumers and employees (Madvijal, 2000). But, perhaps the strongest symbolic corporate brand strategy would be to develop an emotional link to the appropriate stakeholder group through corporate stories.

The risky business of sponsorships

The 2012 Winter Olympic games pose a dilemma for potential sponsors: risk being associated with an authoritarian regime where horrifying human-rights abuses have been documented, or miss out on the opportunity to market your brands on one of the biggest global stages. The 2022 Olympics may potentially bring a climax to the many years of work by activist groups and some Western governments who have been highly critical of what they see as serious human-rights issues in China. But in a number of recent cases, the Chinese government has been swift to enact severe economic punishment on those who express even the slightest criticism.

Airbnb highlights this dilemma. They are one of the 'Olympic Partners' for the 2022 Winter games, the highest level of sponsorship available. Even before Airbnb became an Olympic sponsor, human rights advocates had been challenging them over why its lodgings are made available in a country where Uighurs in the province of Xinjiang are housed in concentration camps and subjected to forced labour and other abuses. Airbnb is one of many companies that taut their commitment to social responsibility, something that an increasing number of consumers are taking into account when making brand decisions. But activists point out that when it comes to China, they don't seem to be that concerned.

It is a catch-22. Risk alienating consumers who deplore companies doing business with a country of such horrifying human-rights abuses; or risk the Chinese government's wrath and inevitable economic consequences, including the loss of its 1.4 billion consumers.

Source: The Wall Street Journal, 13–14 February 2021

Just as with their brands, a company wants to maintain a strong presence in their market and to build a strong positive attitude toward the company and its products. But it will also want to build more emotional connections with all of its various stakeholders, and corporate stories provide a good way of doing that. When building a corporate story, the question of 'authenticity' becomes an important factor. It must be based on real past experiences. Corporate stories are thought by organizational theorists, for example, to be an effective way to motivate employees by providing both novelty and credibility (Barry and Elmes, 1997). Interestingly, there is evidence from a wide range of companies in a number of different markets that credibility can be enhanced through emotional perceptions of *openness* (Maathuis, et al., 2003), which should follow from a corporate story's authenticity.

Many people have written about the sustainable corporate story, describing it as a comprehensive narrative about the entire company, including things like its history and mission statement (van Riel, 2000). Because it is unique to each company and goes beyond corporate image to include more descriptive elements, it offers an opportunity for creating a consistent, believable impression. Van Riel (2003) has identified four criteria that he feels are necessary to the development of an effective corporate story: it

Table 3.5 Keys to an effective corporate story

Relevant	Important to company's target audience
Responsive	Permits interaction between company and target audiences
Realistic	Focuses upon company's unique characteristics
Sustainable	Satisfies needs and desires of target audiences while meeting company objectives

Source: Adapted from van Riel (2003).

should be *relevant* with regard to the company's various target audiences; *responsive* in that it allows for an interaction between the audience members and the company; *realistic* in focusing upon the company's unique and enduring characteristics; and *sustainable*, satisfying the needs and desires of relevant audiences while meeting its own objectives (Table 3.5).

The story itself should only be a few pages in length (Larsen, 2000), and use a rich narrative to deliver the message (Shaw, 2000). The key is that the corporate story must inform *all* of a company's corporate communication, including spontaneous day-to-day interactions among employees and between any company representative and its external audiences. It is the sustainable corporate story that helps align all of a company's messages, regardless of the audience. Larsen (2000) has argued that a corporate story can be a powerful tool for differentiating a company and its products from competitors, and even suggests that it may become the primary vehicle for differentiation.

The sustainable corporate story provides a way of ensuring consistency in everything the company communicates, planned and unplanned. When there is a corporate story in place, it will set the parameters for the strategic development of all corporate and brand communications. The corporate story acts as a starting point (in the words of van Riel, (2000)), and provides the umbrella under which all the company's communication falls. IMC provides a way of *managing* the strategic development and delivery of all of a company's *planned* communication.

Corporate advertising

We have spent most of this chapter looking at corporate communication from the perspective of academics who study organizational or corporate communication. This provides an important insight into the complexity of the issue and the various ways in which a company may communicate with its internal and external audiences, whether planned or not. Dowling (2001), a respected academic in the field, offers a more traditional view of corporate communication, at least from the manager's perspective, focusing upon corporate advertising. He uses the term advertising in its broadest sense to include all forms of corporate communication. This is consistent with our definition, following from the Latin root of the word *advertere*, roughly translated as 'to turn toward'.

The job of advertising in this sense is to build positive attitudes towards the company, leading to a strong corporate brand equity, and this regardless of the communication channel involved. An advertising message can be delivered through channels well outside traditional media: communication channels such as the annual report, employee newsletters, the chairman's speech to a financial group, websites, etc.

Table 3.6 When to use corporate advertising to advertise to stakeholders who are not often exposed to the company's brand advertising

---

- If the corporate name contributes additional value equity to its otherwise branded products
- When the purchase cycle is longer than a year
- When there is a need for 'issue management'
- To occasionally thank their employees

Source: Adopted from Dowling (2001).

An important issue for managers is the role corporate advertising should play in the overall communication mix. This, of course, will depend upon the overall strategic corporate and marketing objectives. But corporate advertising should play a role, and be consistent with the brand message. Dowling (2001) sees corporate advertising as either 'image-' or 'issue-' oriented. In this traditional view of things, corporate 'image' advertising deals with such issues as communicating with financial markets, employees, creating goodwill, and addressing special interest groups. Corporate 'issue' advertising deals with positioning the company on social or industry issues and countering adverse publicity. In effect, these traditional views of corporate advertising cover the areas addressed by the academic views of corporate communication, only more generally.

Advert 3.1 for Garniger provides a good example of corporate issue-oriented advertising. They are committing to a number of sustainability goals by 2025, which are clearly presented. This execution is very well done. The headline will be processed at a glance, letting the reader immediately know that Garniger 'Commits to Green Beauty'. The eye will then quickly pick up and process the four goals. Then, for the interested reader, details are provided for each goal. Additionally, the message is reinforced by the use of a green background.

Dowling identified five circumstances where it makes sense to use corporate advertising. It should be used to advertise directly to stakeholders who are not often exposed to a brand's advertising; if the corporate name contributes additional value equity to its otherwise branded products; if the purchase cycle is longer than a year; when there is a need for 'issue management'; and simply to occasionally thank their employees (Table 3.6).

Dowling also makes the point about the quality of most corporate advertising, with which we agree (and imagine you may also). He feels that too often corporate advertising is simply 'awful' and invites the reader to look through worldwide business magazines like *Business Week, The Economist, Forbes,* and *Bloomberg Businessweek* as proof. As he puts it, much corporate advertising is self-important and both long-winded and dull or short and vague about what the company does; it is basically uninteresting and uninspiring. As a result, many managers (especially top management) feel that corporate advertising is always ineffective, whether for companies or brands.

There are exceptions, of course, and creatively executed advertising can and will be effective. One of the goals of this book is to provide the insight and tools necessary to ensure that happens.

Also, under the umbrella of corporate advertising is advertising by trade groups and associations. An example of image-oriented advertising from a number of years ago in the U.S. was a campaign over two years by the National Potato Promotion Board. Research indicated that people had a number of misconceptions about potatoes, leading to negative attitudes. The NPPB ran a campaign using a refutational strategy to correct these misconceptions, especially that potatoes were fattening. After two years consumption of potatoes not only stopped declining, but increased by over 17 percent due largely to the advertising.

Advert 3.1 Garniger.

A good example today of issue-oriented advertising by an association may be seen in Advert 3.2 from the Confederation of European Paper Industry, a group that represents the paper industry. The CEPI advert is letting you know that you should 'love paper' because '60 percent of the energy used to produce paper and paper packaging in Europe comes from renewable sources', a point of which most people are unlikely to be aware.

Advert 3.2 CEPI.

Summary

In this chapter, we have looked at the role of IMC in strengthening companies, and specifically *companies as brands*. We saw that this primarily involves a company's identity and image, along with reputation. A distinction was made between companies as organizations versus corporations, where organizational identity and imagery are concerned with internal audiences and corporate identity and imagery with external target audiences. IMC's role is primarily with companies as corporations, not organizations.

Corporate identity has been described as those symbols and words used to identify a company to its target audience, and corporate image as how that target audience 'sees' the company; the beliefs and feelings they have about the company. On the surface this seems a rather straightforward distinction, but much more is involved. Corporate identity includes graphic associations with the company; it also includes how employees see the company (especially important when those employees interact with customers). But from an IMC standpoint, it is a broad range of identities projected by the company that is of interest: active identity, communicated identity, conceived identity, ideal identity, and desired identity. IMC helps mediate all these various aspects of corporate identity.

Corporate image reflects how a company's target audiences evaluate it in terms of their collective beliefs and feelings (i.e., their attitudes towards the company). As a result, corporate image informs the decisions people make about that company and is subject to change as new information is processed about the company (from IMC sources as well as other external communications; for example, press accounts). A company does not have direct control over its image, in the sense that it cannot literally dictate what people should think about it; clearly effective IMC will mediate that image.

Corporate reputation reflects the values its various target audiences associate with their understanding of its image. In this sense, reputation and image are related, but it is important to consider them separately. One of the jobs of IMC is to ensure that the image of a company is positively associated in people's minds with appropriate values. These values that people hold will act very much like emotions in 'framing' how new information about the company will be received and processed. Corporate identity helps drive corporate image, which in its turn informs corporate reputation.

All of this is part of corporate meaning, and corporate meaning is now drawn together into something thought of as a corporate brand. This idea of creating a corporate brand has been a response to heightened awareness on the part of senior corporate management that such things as how the company is perceived on important social issues can have a direct bearing on brand decisions. This means building corporate brand equity as well as individual brand equities. It is the job of corporate communication to accomplish all of this, and one way of dealing with it is with what is now known as a sustainable corporate story. IMC provides a way of managing both the strategic development and delivery of all the company's planned communication: corporate and brand.

Review questions

1 What is the role of IMC in strengthening companies as opposed to brands?
2 Discuss the difference between a company's image and its identity. How does this differ from a company's reputation?
3 Identify examples of corporate identity.
4 Find examples of corporate communication that address the company's identity.
5 Discuss the problems associated with establishing corporate image.
6 Identify companies that you feel share your values and companies that do not.
7 In what ways does a company's reputation have a strategic advantage over its image?

8   What is corporate meaning and what role does IMC play in it?

9   How is a corporate brand different from a product brand and in what ways are they alike?

10   Discuss the interrelationships between a company's corporate brand equity and the brand equity of its products.

11   Under what circumstances would a company want to be seen as similar to other companies in their industry?

12   How does corporate communication differ from brand communication?

13   What is the role of IMC in corporate communication?

14   What are the key strengths of corporate stories?

15   Create a corporate story for a company with which you are familiar.

16   Find examples of good corporate advertising.

References

Balmer, J.M.T. (1998) Corporate identity and the advent of corporate marketing. *Journal of Marketing Management, 14(8)*, 963–996.

Balmer, J.M.T. and Gray, E.R. (2003) Corporate Identity and Corporate Communications: Creating a Competitive Advantage. In J.M.T. Balmer and S.A. Greyser (eds.), *Revealing the Corporation*. London: Routledge, pp. 124–136.

Balmer, J.M.T. and Greyser, S.A. (2003) *Revealing the Corporation*. London: Routledge.

Barry, D. and Elmes, M. (1997) Strategy retold: Toward a narrative view of strategic discourse. *Academy of Managerial Review, 22(2)*, 429–452.

Berstein, D. (1984) *Company Image and Reality: A Critique of Corporate Communications*. Eastbourne, UK: Holt, Reinhart, and Winston.

Biehal, G.J. and Shenin, D.A. (1998) Managing the brand in a corporate advertising environment. *Journal of Advertising, 28(2)*, 99–110.

Birkigt, K. and Stadler, M. (1986) *Corporate Identity: Grundlagen, Funktronen and Beispielen*. Landsberg an Lech: Vetog Moderne Industrie.

Brammer, S.J. and Pavelin, S. (2006) Corporate reputation and social performance: The importance of 'fit'. *Journal of Management Studies, 43(3)*, 435–455.

Brown, T.J. (1998) Corporate associations in marketing: Anecdotes and consequences. *Corporate Reputation Review, 1(3)*, 215–233.

Christensen, L.T. and Askegaard, S. (2001) Corporate identity and corporate image revisited: A semiotic perspective. *European Journal of Marketing, 35(3/4)*, 292–315.

Christensen, L.T. and Cheney, G. (2000) Self-Absorption and Self-Seduction in the Corporate Identity Game. In M. Schultz, M.J. Hatch, and M.H. Larsen (eds.), *The Expressive Organization*. Oxford: Oxford University Press, pp. 246–270.

Crable, R.E. and Vibbert, S.L. (1983) Mobil's epideictic advocacy: Observations of prometheus-bound. *Communication Monographs, 50(4)*, 380–394.

Czarniawska, B. (1997) *Narrating the Organization*. Chicago: University of Chicago Press.

Dahler-Larsen, P. (1997) Moral Functionality and Organizational Identity: A Perspective on the New 'Moralized Discourses' Discourses' in Organizations. In M.A. Rahim and R.T. Golembiewsky (eds.), *Current Topics in Management, Vol. 2*. Greenwich, CN: JAI Press, pp. 305–326.

Deephouse, D.L. and Carter, S.M. (2005) An examination of difference between legitimacy and organizational reputation. *Journal of Management Studies, 42(2)*, 329–360.

Dowling, G. (2001) *Creating Corporate Reputations*. Oxford: Oxford University Press.

Hatch, M.J. and Schultz, M. (2000) Scaling the Tower of Babel: Relational Differences between Identity, Image, and Culture in Organizations. In M. Schultz, M.J. Hatch, and M.H. Larsen (eds.), *The Expressive Organization*. Oxford: Oxford University Press, pp. 11–31.

Hatch, M.J. and Schultz, M. (2001) Are the strategic stars aligned for your corporate brand? *Harvard Business Review*, https://hbr.org/2001/02/are-the-strategic-stars-aligned-for-your-corporate-brand. Accessed on 8 March 2018.

Keller, K.L. (2000) Building and Managing Corporate Brand Equity. In M. Schultz, M.J. Hatch, and M.H. Larsen (eds.), *The Expressive Organization*. Oxford: Oxford University Press, pp. 115–137.

Larsen, M.H. (2000) Managing the Corporate Story. In M. Schultz, M.J. Hatch, and M.H. Larsen (eds.), *The Expressive Organization*. Oxford: Oxford University Press, pp. 196–207.

Maathuis, O., Rodenberg, I., and Sikkel, D. (2003) Credibility, emotion or reason? *Corporate Reputation Review*, 6(4), 333–345.

Madvijal, R. (2000) The influence of social alliances with sports teams on intention to purchase corporate sponsor's products. *Journal of Advertising Research*, XXIX(4), 13–24.

McGuire, W.J. (1969) The Nature of Attitude and Attitude Change. In G. Lindsey and E. Pronson (eds.), *Handbook of Social Psychology*, *Vol. 3*. Reading, MA: Addison-Wesley Publishing Company, pp. 263–265.

Roberts, P.W. and Dowling, G. (1998) The value of enhancing the firm's corporate reputation: How corporate reputation helps attain and sustain superior profitability, working paper, Australian Graduate School of Management, University of New South Wales.

Rosenbaum-Elliott, R., Percy, L. and Pervan, S. (2018) *Strategic Brand Management*, 2nd edition. Oxford: Oxford University Press.

Schultz, M. (2005) A Cross-Disciplinary Perspective on Corporate Branding. In M. Schultz, Y.M. Antorini, and F.F. Cgaba (eds.), *Corporate Branding: Purpose/People/Process*. Copenhagen: Copenhagen Business School Press, pp. 23–55.

Shaw, G.G. (2000) Planning and Communicating Using Stories. In M. Schultz, M.J. Hatch, and M.H. Larsen (eds.), *The Expressive Organization*. Oxford: Oxford University Press, pp. 182–195.

van Riel, C.B.M. (2000) Corporate Communication Orchestrated by a Sustainable Corporate Story. In M. Schultz, M.J. Hatch, and M.H. Larsen (eds.), *The Expressive Organization*. Oxford: Oxford University Press, pp. 157–181.

van Riel, C.B.M. (2003) The Management of Corporate Communication. In J.M.T. Balmer and S.A. Greyser (eds.), *Revealing the Corporation*. London: Routledge, pp. 161–170.

Part II

Components of IMC

In the first part of this book we looked at integrated marketing communication(IMC), its definition and a broad introduction. IMC's role in building brands and strengthening companies was discussed. In this part we begin to examine the fundamental building blocks of IMC, the basic elements that go into building brands and strengthening companies, and how messages are delivered. In Chapters 4 and 5 we look at the meaning of traditional advertising and promotion, noting that they represent a fundamental *strategic* difference in communication objectives. Marketing communication that is primarily directed towards building brand equity through a strong brand attitude over time is what is traditionally understood as advertising. When the primary objective of marketing communication is to generate an immediate brand purchase intention, that is what is traditionally understood as a promotion. *All* marketing communication, regardless of how the message is delivered, will be either advertising or promotion, depending upon its strategic intent.

Advertising tends to be associated in most people's minds with mass media like television, newspapers, magazines, and increasingly digital media, and promotion with print media, direct mail, and now digital as well. In Chapter 6 we look at some basic media concepts, and because of its growing importance, a general discussion of digital media. But there are many other ways of delivering an advertising or promotion message. In fact, any contact between a brand and its target audience occurs through media of some kind. In addition to mass media and digital, this would include such things as sponsorships, product placement, digital marketing, public relations, and even the package itself. Many of these have been around for a long time, but too often are simply not considered as part of an IMC marketing communication campaign. We shall be looking at these alternative ways of delivering IMC messages in Chapter 7.

Strategic IMC planning must look at every available option for delivering both advertising and promotion messages, and for reaching both a brand's and a company's target audience. Although certain media tend to be associated with advertising or promotion, there is no reason to exclude any option that makes sense given the IMC plan and, critically, is compatible with the processing requirements associated with the communication objective (something that will be covered in Chapter 12).

DOI: 10.4324/9781003169635-5

4 Advertising

We begin Part II by looking at advertising and how it is used in a marketing communication (IMC) campaign. But first, it is important to understand a fundamental strategic difference between traditional ideas of advertising compared to traditional ideas of promotion. A good way of looking at this goes back to the Latin roots of the two words, advertising and promotion. Daniel Starch (1926), one of the pioneers in advertising theory and measurement, was perhaps the first to use these Latin roots in defining them, back in the 1920s. The Latin root of advertising is *advertere*, which translates roughly as 'to turn towards', and this is the strategic role of advertising in IMC. The Latin root of promotion is *promivere,* which roughly translates to 'move ahead', which reflects its primary strategic role in IMC.

One of the more troublesome issues associated with IMC is the 'role' of advertising and promotion. This has become a problem because of the blurring of the traditional distinction between them, as we saw in Chapter 1. In the past, advertising was delivered using what was known as 'measured media', so called because independent services 'measured' the size of the audience for such things as television, radio, newspapers, magazines, and outdoors. But in today's world of 'digital media', measurement is posing a real problem; one made even more difficult with the proliferation of rogue 'advertisements' that are not produced by the brand. Advertising messages are also delivered through direct marketing and channels marketing (for example, through trade-oriented marketing such as co-op programmes), areas where in the past one only found promotional messages.

The point here is that whether something is an advertisement or a promotion is not a factor of how the message is delivered, but the strategic intent of the message. With advertising, the primary intent is to build brand awareness and brand attitude; with promotion, it is to drive short-term sales or product usage. These are strategic concerns that reflect the desired communication objective for a particular message in an IMC campaign and follow from their Latin meanings. How that message is delivered will be a factor in terms of an appropriate fit with the communication objective (as we shall see in Chapter 12), and then optimizing a media strategy within an overall IMC plan.

The old way of looking at advertising versus promotion in terms of how they are delivered no longer holds. In fact, what has been thought of as advertising skills now play a critical role in all forms of marketing communication, including promotion. In this chapter, we begin to look at advertising issues and in the next chapter, promotion. But as they are discussed, remember that these same principles will apply regardless of how the message is delivered, whether by direct marketing, sponsorship, event marketing, or traditional and digital media. Brand awareness and brand attitude are always message objectives, even with a promotion where the primary communication objective is brand purchase intention.

DOI: 10.4324/9781003169635-6

The role of advertising in IMC

Advertising in IMC is to 'turn' the consumer's mind towards the advertised brand, as we have just seen. It does this by raising awareness of the brand among the target audience and by building positive attitudes towards the brand. This positive brand attitude then helps build a strong brand equity.

All marketing communication should help build brand awareness and contribute to a positive feeling for the brand. But when this is the primary communication objective, it is specifically advertising. Because brand awareness and brand attitude take time to build, compared with promotion, advertising plays a more long-term strategic role in IMC. Over time, effective advertising will successfully seed the brand in memory as satisfying an appropriate need and will associate the brand with positive attitudes that are linked to positive motivations to buy and use it when that need occurs.

As we discussed in Chapter 2, both brand awareness and brand attitude are important in positioning a brand, so it follows that a critical role for advertising in IMC is to effectively position a brand relative to its competition, and we talked about how this is done. We also saw in Chapter 2 that brand attitude is arguably the key component in building and sustaining brand equity. Within an IMC programme, it is advertising that is critical to the process of building and maintaining a brand's equity.

In summary, advertising's role in IMC is to raise awareness of a brand, linking it to an appropriate category need. At the same time, advertising will build positive brand associations in memory that lead to a positive attitude towards the brand. As a part of this, advertising will be optimally positioning the brand within its category, uniquely differentiating it from competitors on benefits important to the consumer and what they believe (or can be persuaded to believe) the brand delivers. This, in its turn, will lead to strong brand equity.

Types of advertising

Different authors discuss 'types' of advertising in different ways. Pickton and Broderick (2005), for example, take a narrow, detailed view of what constitutes different types of advertising. For print advertising alone they talk about such things as full-display advertising, ROP (or run-of-paper), double-page spreads, specially positioned with no other advertisements around them, prime positioning, semi-display advertisements, classified advertising, and advertorials.

Most of these distinctions are understood in terms of the creative freedom involved in the execution, or where the advertising is placed within a newspaper or magazine. Classified advertisements and advertorials are distinguished by their content. They also make distinctions as a function of media, for example, infomercials being the television equivalent to advertorials in the press, or infomercials being the internet equivalent to television commercials. While these terms are a bit dated now, the idea is sound. And, the notion of advertorials is certainly still relevant, now generally known as branded content. content, as discussed in the box below. In effect, Pickton and Broderick are illustrating the great variety of ways advertising may be created and delivered. This notion is echoed by many others writing about IMC, who talk about different types of advertising in terms of creative tactics: humour, hard sell, testimonial corrective, advocacy, fear appeal, etc.

Rossiter et al. (2018), on the other hand, take a much broader view of what constitutes different types of advertising. For them, the main types of advertising are brand-building advertising, by which they mean advertising placed in mass media; direct-response advertising; and corporate image advertising and other company-oriented advertising (for example, sponsorships) that is not advertising specific brands. They are making a primary distinction between a brand focus and company focus, as well as singling out direct-response advertising, which has as its goal the creation of an immediate positive brand attitude in order to elicit an immediate response to the message. And note here that this applies regardless of the media used to deliver that message to the target audience.

Our own view is more along the lines of Rossiter et al., looking at a broader classification of advertising. From our perspective, in considering different types of advertising within an IMC framework, it makes sense to look at the task objective for the advertising; the contribution the advertising is making to overall IMC strategy. Fundamentally, we see this as directly related to the type of message and its target audience because the creative approach will be different depending on the general target audience.

Even though all advertising within an IMC campaign must have a consistent 'look and feel', brand advertising to consumers will be different from retail advertising to consumers; advertisements for one business advertising to another will look different from corporate image advertising. The approaches are different even when the same people are part of the target audience. Looked at in this way, the main types of advertising would include: consumer brand advertising, retail advertising, business-to-business (B2B), and corporate image advertising.

Branded content

In looking beyond traditional display advertising for digital marketing, many brands have turned to something called collaborative content. As the chief media officer at Razorfish, a digital advertising agency, has put it: 'The enthusiasm for content marketing is partially an acknowledgement by the industry that banner ads can't be our best and only answer.' Collaborative content, along with similar alternatives such as 'branded content', native advertising, and 'sponsored content', are all in response to the fact that web and social media users are much more likely to respond to a message that does not look like advertising than to one that does. You can expect better results if the message takes on some of the same form as the rest of the content in the medium. On Facebook that could mean more sponsored stories, on Twitter, prompted accounts and tweets, and with other new media it means content that looks very much like the editorial content on the site.

Some companies are using brand-sponsored articles to help drive a better response to display advertisements on the same page. The *Atlantic* magazine has found that click-through rates are more than one and a half times higher when an advertisement is placed next to custom content from the advertiser. One example involved placing a lead banner advertisement for Mercedes above the masthead as a series of Mercedes-sponsored posts that contained video interviews with innovators from a wide variety of businesses.

However, not everyone agrees that the idea of content marketing is 'new'. It has been argued that this is nothing more than a digital version of the old idea of *advertorials*. The Interactive Advertising Bureau feels that customer content will prove to be too labour-intensive and cost-heavy to displace traditional advertising units. The US media director of Intel acknowledged that customer content does require a tremendous amount of work to develop individual content programmes for partner sites.

Source: *Advertising Age*, 29 October 2012

Table 4.1 Four basic types of advertising

Consumer advertising	Brand-focused advertising directed towards individual consumers, delivered via a wide range of possible media
Retail advertising	Involves store image as well as products or services offered, and generally uses local media
B2B advertising	Addresses both customers and the trade, and uses specialty media directed to target segments
Corporate advertising	Promotes the company rather than the product or service offered, and addresses all important target audiences

A brand, store or company, will be positioned differently within each of these types of advertising, and the creative executions are likely to differ. In fact, one can usually easily recognize each of these different types of advertising by simply looking at them illustrated. In each case, because it is advertising, the primary communication objectives are brand awareness and brand attitude. When different types of advertising are part of an IMC campaign, even though the approach may be different, effective executions will nonetheless have a consistent 'look and feel'. Anyone looking at them will understand them to be messages from the same company. In summary, then, we can think of messages in terms of the four types shown in Table 4.1.

- *Consumer advertising*: This is what most people think of when they are thinking about advertising. It is brand-focused, seeking to make consumers more aware of a brand and to form positive attitudes towards it, 'turning' the mind of the consumer towards a positive consideration of the brand.
- *Retail advertising*: The unique aspect of retail advertising is that it generally involves two brands: the store itself and the products or services it offers. Retail advertising may be 'image'-oriented, raising awareness of the store and creating a positive attitude towards the store, or it may be used to raise awareness of the products it sells, nurturing a positive brand attitude for those brands in order to indirectly enhance awareness and favourable attitudes for the store itself.
- *B2B advertising*: The difference here is that B2B advertising need not specifically address the end-user. B2B advertising may seek to build awareness and positive brand attitudes not only among a company's customer base, but also among the trade and other aspects of the distribution system with which they deal.
- *Corporate image advertising*: Traditionally, this is advertising that promotes a company itself rather than the products or services it markets. It seeks to positively raise the salience of the company, and create a favourable attitude towards it, among particular target audiences that can range from consumer markets, to the financial community to government regulatory agencies., as we saw in the last chapter.

We now take a closer look at these four types of advertising.

Consumer advertising

The job of consumer advertising is the building and nurturing of brands. In Chapter 2 we discussed the idea of brands and their relationship with IMC in some detail, and pointed out that in many ways, without marketing communication, and especially advertising, there would not be brands. Roderick White (1999) suggests that because consumer advertising is the most intense and visible form of marketing communication, it has a key role to play in the successful marketing of a brand. As he puts it 'Advertising cannot turn a sow's ear into a silk purse, but, given a good or – ideally – superior product, it can help to build it into a strong brand'. Or, as John Phillip Jones (1999) put it, 'Advertising's greatest single contribution to the business is its ability to build brands'.

White (1999) has also suggested that the role of advertising has traditionally been viewed as aiding sales, and does this by creating awareness of a brand, providing essential information about the brand, helping to build a relevant brand image, and, once the brand is established, by reminding the consumer to try, buy or use the brand. Or, as we have put it, the primary communication objective for advertising is to build brand awareness and a positive brand attitude.

The advertisement for Billington's in Advert 4.1 offers a good example. As we see later in the chapter, this represents a low-involvement, transformational brand attitude strategy. Advertising for food 'ingredient' products like sugar must appeal to the positive motivation driving the desire for the finished product. It does an excellent job of creating a positive feeling, which itself becomes a benefit for the brand. Just thinking about that gingerbread cookie makes you feel good. When the brand is seen in the store, it will be this good feeling from the advertisement that is remembered, and the reason to purchase.

Consumer advertising should be the dominant form of marketing communication in any IMC campaign for a *brand*. The primary means of delivering the advertising message in almost all cases should be television or digital media because of their intrusive and dynamic nature and their unique ability to reach large audiences and sustain attention. Other mass media, as well as other non-traditional means, may also be used where appropriate.

Retail advertising

Retail advertising, as already pointed out, may focus on either the image of the store itself, or on the products or services it offers. But even when the advertising features products or services, it will influence the image of the store. Anything connected with a retail store will be part of how that store is perceived, because those things will be part of the associations in memory linked to it. So, while retail image advertising has a direct effect on building brand attitude for a store, advertisements for the products it sells will have an indirect effect on attitudes towards the store.

If you were to see advertising for a new women's clothing store and it was featuring expensive designer labels in the advertisements, you would have knowledge and assumptions about such clothing in memory, and this would be associated with the new store as you form a perception of the store's image and initial attitudes towards it. This would be part of top-down processing, which we will be dealing with in Chapter 8. On the other hand, if the new store featured mass-market brands of women's sportswear, your initial attitudes would be very different. A retail store's image will clearly be affected by the products it sells.

In every sense, retail advertising is *brand* advertising, whether featuring brands on offer or the store itself. Advert 4.2 for The House of Bruar is a very good example of this. It is creating a strong positive image for Bruar as a high-quality brand with both the visual and the copy. While it does feature a product, it is in support of the image of Bruar as the 'Home of Country Clothing'. The advert's copy reinforces the visual and the image of high quality, as well as the invitation to 'Experience the very best in contemporary country clothing'. But it should be pointed out that most retail 'advertising' is not traditional advertising as we are defining it. Most of it is promotion. In other words, for most of the 'advertising' run by retailers the

Advert 4.1 Billington's.

Source: © 2013 ABF Plc Associated British Foods plc.

Advert 4.2 House of Bruar.

primary communication objective is immediate brand purchase intention, not building brand attitude for the store. The retailer wants you to come and visit the store. Even though most people, including marketing managers, call this 'advertising', it is important to understand that strategically unless the primary communication objective is brand awareness and brand attitude, it is not advertising. Building positive awareness and attitude is the role traditional advertising performs in IMC.

Most retail advertising is local in nature because the target audience for any particular retail store will be drawn from its immediate geographic area. This means media selection will be oriented to local and digital media. However, retailers with stores in many cities or even countries (for example, large franchise operations like Benetton or McDonald's, or large retailers such as H&M) will, of course, use media with broader reach. Regardless, the appropriate must reflect the advertising's strategic and communication objectives.

Thus, retail advertisements are reinforcing brand awareness, and alerting the consumer to where the brand may be purchased. Remember that we are talking about retail *advertising* here, not retail promotion where the emphasis will be on price. However, with steadily falling circulation various forms of digital media are playing a greater role.

For most retailers, when they are advertising their own product or service, local television and targeted digital media, with print support, will likely be the best options. In all cases, the media chosen must be appropriate for the specific brand awareness and brand attitude strategies (which we discuss later in the chapter). In all cases, the media chosen must be appropriate for the specific brand awareness and brand attitude strategies.

The role of channels marketing in IMC

This is a good place to introduce the idea of channels marketing because it involves the use of advertising (as well as promotion) by a marketer in conjunction with retailers and other areas of the trade.

Channels marketing is a term that refers to marketing communications geared to assisting the marketer at all levels of trade. The term 'channels marketing' evolved out of the importance of trade-oriented promotions. The two principal components of channels marketing are co-op advertising and tactical marketing. While co-operative or co-op advertising has been around for a long time, tactical marketing is relatively new. Co-op advertising is an arrangement between a marketer and a retailer to co-operate when selling the marketer's brand or service. It consists of advertising programmes that are nothing more than extensions of the marketer's basic marketing communication plan, funded in whole or part by the advertiser and designed to assist the retailer in selling the brand or service. Unfortunately, marketers lack control over co-op and cannot be sure it will be used as planned.

Tactical marketing, however, is a channel-oriented marketing communication system that is designed to alter the terms of marketing in favour of the marketer and leverage incremental support from the retailers, and other areas of the trade, by offering them specific advertising and promotion paid for by the advertiser on an *earned* basis. Simply put, the concept is to offer the retailer comprehensive, customized advertising and promotional support in exchange for incremental sales features, distribution, and/or store space.

Co-op advertising and tactical marketing may appear quite similar, as they should; tactical marketing is an outgrowth of basic co-op principles, but the difference lies in how these techniques are applied.

Co-op advertising

Co-op programmes are usually broad in scope and passive in nature. In a typical co-op arrangement, a brand's entire retailer base is eligible to participate, with retailers earning a certain budget for advertising or promotion based on sales volume. The marketer provides set material for use by the retailer, and then reimburses the retailer for its use on a periodic basis up to the limits of an established budget.

Generally, the retailer takes advantage of the money and marketing communication as they see fit. To counter this, marketers should make a special attempt to encourage greater retailer participation or a particular strategic shift in retailer activity by manipulating allowances or methods of allocating funds. For the most part, however, traditional co-op programmes are straightforward.

Tactical marketing

Tactical marketing is always a *proactive* effort. When tactical marketing is considered, a brand is looking for specific and incremental support from a given retailer. In return for this support, the marketer will create a specific programme tailored to the needs of that retailer and will fund and implement the programme. With tactical marketing the *marketer* controls the entire process from beginning to end.

Tactical marketing concepts grew out of the need for brands to provide a more individualized execution than was possible with most co-op programmes. In traditional co-op advertising, the marketer reimburses the retailer or pays them all or part of the cost of the advertising or promotion. As retailers became more and more powerful through consolidation and the formation of buying groups, and with the expansion of national chains through mergers, they began using co-op advertising as a profit centre to offset their operating costs. Frequently, funds went to increasing store margins and other non-advertising functions. With an increasing power advantage, retailers began forcing marketers to participate in retailer-initiated programmes which may or may not have been to the advantage of the marketer or its brands. In effect, the marketer had lost control of co-op programmes to the retailer.

As a result of this situation, the tactical marketing concept was developed as an alternative retailer marketing system that could provide the marketer with a means of extending brand support at the retail level with control flexibility, while providing complete coordination and production services to the retailer. This means that a retailer could take advantage of marketing communication provided by the marketer, but also work in more of a partnership. Tactical marketing also enlarges on the more traditional print orientation of co-op programmes by providing the retailer with access to television and radio commercials, direct marketing, sponsorships, outdoor and other IMC options. But perhaps most importantly in terms of IMC, a specific marketing communication plan customized to particular retailers is used – one consistent with the overall IMC strategy.

Overall, co-op advertising programmes tend to be general, passive, and standardized, whereas tactical marketing is specific, proactive, individualized, and highly participatory.

B2B advertising

B2B advertising is targeted at those who are part of the decision-making process for purchasing products or services for a company, who may or may not be the end-user. This is especially true for advertising targeted to the trade (for example, wholesalers or distributors).

In such cases, B2B advertising is concerned with maintaining awareness and a positive brand attitude for a company's products so that the trade will stock and sell them.

Given the nature of the market for B2B products, the target audience for advertising tends to be much smaller than the target audience for most consumer advertising. While the target audience is likely to be small (relatively), the composition of that target audience tends to be more complex. IMC programmes with B2B advertising will be targeted not only in terms of the decision-makers involved, but also the type of product or service being offered. The first step is to identify target companies, then the right people in those companies involved in the decision process.

For most B2B purchase decisions, there will be more than one person involved in the process. But while many people may be involved, it is important to remember that advertising must be directed to *individuals*; individuals in their role within the decision process. This is the case, of course, for all advertising. But the likelihood of a number of different people playing important yet different roles in the purchase decision process is much greater in B2B marketing.

Consider Rolls-Royce jet engines. Their target market is obviously quite small, comprised of only a handful of jet aircraft manufacturers. But within that select market, they must maintain a high brand salience (when the need for jet aircraft engines arises, they want Rolls-Royce to come to mind), and they need to build and nurture a positive brand attitude among all of those in the target companies likely to be involved in the selection of a jet engine supplier. This is likely to be a group decision at the target companies, but the advertising must be strategically targeted to every individual and the role they play in the decision process. There will be technical experts and engineers who help influence the selection, there will be senior management involved and there may also be outside consultants advising the company. The message to each group must reflect its role, yet be consistent in terms of the overall approach.

IMC plays a key role in keeping images consistent over different messages to different target audiences. It may make strategic sense to focus on different benefit sets for each target, requiring different executions; however, the 'look and feel' must be the same, projecting a consistent overall image for the company and brand. This is especially important for something that has been called *dual channel marketing*. Where a company sells virtually the same product or service to both consumers and businesses (Biemans, 1998).

The influence of the internet on B2B marketing has been dramatic. Advert-like messages on a company's home page are also an option, as well as other internet advertising at appropriate sites. There was a significant movement by B2B marketers towards internet advertising in the 1990s, and away from more traditional print media. But now there is a notable return to traditional print media, as well as the use of television (especially on business-oriented programming). This follows a realization that while business decision-makers do go to the internet for specific, targeted information, there is a need to raise the salience of a company's products *before* they are looking for more targeted information. More traditional media provide this opportunity, although even here digital media, beyond the company's website, is making inroads.

Corporate image advertising

Corporate image advertising is traditionally defined as advertising that addresses a company rather than a specific product or service. The decision to include corporate image advertising as a part of an IMC programme in addition to other brand-oriented advertising is an important strategic decision. It is important because it helps in building and sustaining corporate image, identity, and reputation (as discussed in Chapter 3). Overall, it tends to be used more by larger companies than smaller companies.

Corporate image advertising is generally used to reinforce or increase corporate reputation, but it must first increase *corporate brand* awareness. Unfortunately, the more well-known a company the more likely its stakeholders will not only hold strong positive beliefs about the company, but also simultaneously hold strong negative beliefs. This means that a company's reputation will reflect the net differences between these beliefs (Brooks et al., 2003).

Back in Chapter 3 we talked about how Dowling (2001) looked at corporate image advertising as either 'image-' or 'issue-' oriented. In that same book on corporate reputation he also suggested where to use corporate image advertising: to advertise to stakeholders who are not often exposed to the brand's advertising; if the corporate brand name will contribute to value equity to its other branded products; if purchase cycles are longer than one year; when 'issue management' is a need; or simply to occasionally thank one's employees.

Many managers feel that corporate image advertising sends an important message to other businesses, reinforcing the company's reputation within its market. Studies have suggested that the more a company uses corporate image advertising, the more it is 'admired' among B2B marketers (Clow and Baack, 2004). In the USA in the early 1990s, 65 percent of service companies, 61 percent of business goods manufacturers, and 41 percent of consumer goods companies included corporate image advertising as part of their marketing communication programme (Schumann et al., 1991).

An important consideration with corporate image advertising follows from something McGuire (1969) talked about many years ago: inoculation theory. If corporate image advertising is effective in building a strong positive attitude toward the company, over time this will lead to a certain 'immunization' against possibly negative news about the company. In effect, it is working in much the same way as a small inoculation of a virus stimulates resistance to the flu. Of course, in the event of any sudden negative news, the message in the advertising will be specifically tailored to deal with it, but the foundation for a positive response to that message will have been laid. Later in this chapter, we look at the important consideration of involvement in how such messages should be constructed.

Because corporate image advertising does not promote any one product or service, some consider it an extension of public relations (PR). But PR relies on a company's message being delivered by various media without cost to the company, and with PR a company does not have control over the final message that is delivered. For those reasons, we feel corporate image advertising should be considered as a part of the advertising component of IMC, and not as an extension of PR.

In addition to direct corporate image messages, there are two *indirect* ways in which corporate image advertising may be used to help enhance the image and reputation of a company: advocacy advertising and cause-related advertising (Meyer, 1999). Corporate advertising that deals with important social, business, or environmental issues is known as *advocacy advertising*. To the extent that the issues addressed are salient and important to a company's target market, and the message succeeds in positively associating the company with that issue, it will help build positive attitudes towards the company. When a company is linked with a charity as part of cause-related marketing, and that link is advertised, it is referred to as *cause-related advertising* and part of social marketing. This too can help build positive attitudes towards the company. Research has shown that 80 percent of consumers report a more favourable attitude towards a company that is seen as supporting a worthy cause (Meyer, 1999).

Corporate image advertising and brand strategy

In Chapter 2, we discussed branding strategy and talked about stand-alone, source and endorser brands. Rossiter and Percy (1997) have identified four cases that follow from branding strategy, and which will inform the decision to use corporate image advertising. The four cases they discuss are: (1) when the corporate name is not apparent on the product or service offered; (2) when the corporate name is used with some brands but not others, such as Nestlé's Crunch and Taster's Choice (which is a Nestlé brand); (3) where the company always uses the corporate name along with its brand names; and (4) when the corporate name is the brand name.

In the first and last case, a company would be using a stand-alone branding strategy for all its products or services. When the company name is completely separate from its brands, it will be important to include corporate image advertising in an IMC programme because it will be the only way advertising can help build awareness and positive attitudes towards the company. When such a company has brands with strong brand equity, corporate image advertising that ties the company to the brands can be a useful tactic. When the company name and brand name are the same, in effect, brand advertising is serving as corporate image advertising as well. The stronger a brand's equity, the less necessary it may seem to run separate, specific corporate image advertising. But corporate image advertising goes beyond brand advertising. To help build a company's image and reputation beyond an association with well-regarded products, specific corporate image advertising will be necessary.

In the two mixed cases, where either a source or endorser branding strategy is used, corporate image advertising can be used in a number of ways. However, it is important *strategically* to separate the effects of corporate image on branding strategy from the need to establish a strong corporate image, identity, and reputation. Of course, a strong identity and reputation will carry over to a company's brands; this is a major reason for considering a source or endorser branding strategy. The positive equity in the corporate name, acting as a parent brand, helps to enhance brand awareness and brand attitude. But this positive brand association is *product*-based and does not necessarily work in the other direction, enhancing corporate identity and reputation in the broader sense which was discussed in Chapter 3.

This means that within an IMC programme, the role of corporate image advertising must be seen as separate from that of brand advertising, even when the corporate name is acting as a parent brand.

In the case of corporate image advertising, the choice of media will vary as a factor of both the size of the company and the size of the target market. With small companies, it is often the case that corporate image advertising, at least on a broader scale, is not affordable. If that is the case, the company's consumer-oriented advertising or B2B advertising should include some component that addresses corporate image. This could be as simple as a tagline in association with the company's logo that reinforces the desired corporate image and identity.

With medium or large companies, appropriate local and mass media should be used. The specific media, as with all market selections, must be consistent with awareness and attitude communication strategy.

Brand awareness and brand attitude strategy

Regardless of the type of advertising, in any marketing communication brand awareness and brand attitude will *always* be a communication objective. A brand will need to stimulate awareness, and positively contribute to its equity, with every piece of its marketing communication; and this includes corporate image advertising. As a result, brand awareness and brand attitude will always be an important part of IMC planning. We briefly introduce these effects now and will return to them in almost every chapter because of their significance in effective marketing communication.

Brand awareness strategy

If asked, marketing managers are certain to say that awareness of their brand is critical. But how often do you see an advertisement or promotion and not notice who the sponsor was? It is not unusual to talk about a funny or unique commercial in some detail, yet not be able to identify the advertiser! You are probably thinking of an example or two now. How can this happen?

One of the biggest dangers in creating advertising is the assumption that the target audience is going to 'get' the message. It is an easy and understandable trap to fall into. When it is your brand and you have spent a great deal of time and energy on an advertising execution, *you* certainly know what the brand is and what you are trying to communicate. Unfortunately, the target audience has not been involved in the creation of the advert, and they do not spend most of their waking hours thinking about the brand.

As a result, simply mentioning the brand name will not guarantee brand awareness. One must carefully think about where and how awareness of the brand will feature in the decision to purchase or use the brand by the target audience. What one is after is to provide the target audience with sufficient detail to identify the brand within the category at the time the decision to purchase or use is made. It may even be that sufficient detail does not require the identification of the brand name as such. Often it is no more than a visual image of the package that a consumer uses to identify a brand.

If an individual does not 'think aloud' about a specific brand, and simply waits until they see and recognize it at the point-of-purchase, then brand awareness does not require the recall of the brand prior to purchase. Of course, there are many cases when you do need to recall a brand prior to purchase. Understanding these differences in brand awareness is extremely important to IMC planning. Brand *recognition* and brand *recall* are two distinct types of brand awareness, and which one to use depends on which communication effect occurs first in the mind of the target audience (Figure 4.1). Does a category need occur and one looks for a product or service to meet it, which would be recall brand awareness, or does one see the product in the store and remember the need, which is recognition brand awareness?

Before we consider recognition and recall brand awareness in more detail, we need to address the idea of *brand salience*. Brand salience is more than just awareness of a brand, it results directly from having an effective brand awareness strategy. As we shall see when we talk about brand awareness creative tactics in Chapter 10, effective brand awareness follows from correctly

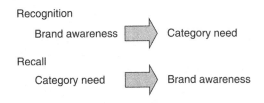

Figure 4.1 Brand awareness strategy.

linking in memory a 'need' for the product or service with the brand. The brand must be salient when the decision to purchase is being made. We want our brand to be immediately associated with the need or desire for a product or service when that need occurs.

Salience is often mistakenly called 'top-of-mind' awareness, but a top-of-mind brand may not be the most salient. It is all down to what brand is linked in memory first with a need. Top-of-mind refers to those brands that come to mind when thinking about a product category; salience reflects the brand most likely to be linked to a need when making a purchase decision (Ehrenberg et al., 2002). Salience is a consequence as well as a cause of many aspects of brand strategy. The more salient a brand, the more likely it will have strong distribution, and attract more media attention, especially on social media (Ehrenberg and Scriven, 1997).

Recognition brand awareness

In a number of purchase situations, it is seeing the brand itself in the store and recognizing it that reminds the consumer of the category need – Is this something I need or want? What goes on in the consumer's mind is:

Brand Awareness (in terms of recognition) reminds them of Category Need.

This brand recognition can be either visual or verbal. In the store, merely seeing the package may key awareness of the brand. On the other hand, especially with tele-marketing, *hearing* the brand name may key brand awareness. In either event, it is the recognition of the brand that constitutes the awareness, even though it may fail a recall test. As an example, think about how people shop in supermarkets. Market research consistently shows that few shoppers use lists, and those who do will usually only have category reminders rather than brand names (for example, bread, detergent, etc.). What happens is that as shoppers move up and down the aisles, when scanning the shelves they recognize a brand (usually the package) and mentally decide whether they need it or not.

What does this tell us about marketing communication? When brand awareness is likely to be based on recognition, one must be sure that the execution includes a strong re-presentation of the brand as it will be confronted at the point-of-purchase. This means large visuals of the package for most packaged goods products (in the advertising, on coupons, etc.), and repetition of the brand name for products likely to be sold or solicited over the telephone. The execution must establish a link in memory between the brand and the need, where seeing the brand (or hearing the name) triggers an association with the need.

Advert 4.3 provides an excellent example of this. There is a strong package presence ensuring easy recognition at the point of purchase, as well as a clear presentation of the benefit 'Ogx liquid pearl.' This too will be easily processed at a glance. In addition, there is support for the benefit on both the package and in the advert copy. This execution reflects everything we will be talking about later when discussing recognition brand awareness in more detail.

Recall awareness

In other purchase or usage decision-making situations, the brand is not available as a cue. The consumer first experiences a need, and then must think of potential solutions. In this case, the brand must already be stored in memory. But more than that, it must also be *linked* in the target audience's mind with the category need such that when the need occurs, the brand comes to mind. Just knowing the brand is not enough. It must come to mind when the need occurs, so that it is recalled from among the many brands someone may be aware of when they are ready to make a decision.

Advert 4.3 Ogx liquid pearl.

As an example, if you were to read a list of restaurants in your area, you would probably recognize most of them. However, when you decide to go out to eat, only two or three will come to mind and you will make your selection from one of them. The owner of an Italian restaurant wants people to think of his restaurant when they are in the mood for

Italian food. It doesn't help if the target audience is 'aware' of the restaurant when cued (recognition awareness); they must *recall* it when the appropriate need occurs (wanting to eat at an Italian restaurant). What must happen in the consumer's mind is:

Category Need (what is wanted) reminds them of Brand Awareness (recalled).

To achieve this sequence of effects, it is important that marketing communication strongly associates the category need with the brand name, and in that order: need–brand. Ideally, this link will be repeated often to seed the relationship in the target audience's mind.

Awareness and corporate image advertising

Consumer, retail, and B-to-B advertising all deal with brand awareness in a similar way, linking the brand to the need. But what is the 'need' with corporate image advertising? Generally, in most cases the need will be for stakeholders to recognize the company name. as a result, the awareness object will usually be recognition. Only rarely would recall awareness be an objective. This would be the case when the objective is for the company name to come to mind when government agencies or activist groups are looking for examples of good corporate citizens.

Brand attitude strategy

The issue of brand attitude is an involved one, and well beyond the scope of this book. Nevertheless, a general understanding is essential for effective IMC planning. We will be taking as our model the Rossiter–Percy Grid (Rossiter and Percy, 1997), which looks at brand attitude strategy for advertising and other marketing communication in terms of two critical dimensions: involvement and motivation.

Involvement

It is acknowledged that the level of consumer involvement in choosing a product or service will affect the choice and that this is probably a function of the complexity of the attitudes held towards a specific product or service. Without going into the research that underlies this, we will simply define involvement in terms of the psychological or financial risk perceived by the target audience in the purchase or use of a product. In low-involvement situations, trial experience will be sufficient because little or no risk is seen if the outcome is not positive. With high-involvement choices, there will definitely be perceived risk in purchasing or using the product or service.

This idea of involvement is reflected in how the consumer behaviour literature looks at it. Low-involvement decisions follow an awareness-trial-attitude model, and the one we like is the Ehrenberg Awareness-Trial-Reinforcement model (Ehrenberg, 1974). You first become aware of a brand and tentatively form an attitude toward it. If this tentative attitude is favourable (e.g., 'that sounds good'), you try the brand because there is little risk involved. If you indeed do like it, you begin to build a positive brand attitude. If you do not like it, a negative brand attitude is formed; but you have not lost much in trying the brand because of the low risk involved.

High-involvement decisions follow the well-known Hierarchy-of-Effects model, where you become aware of a brand, but before trying it you must form a positive brand

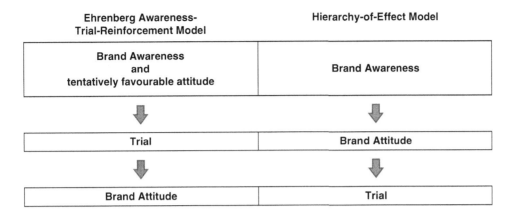

Figure 4.2 Low- and high-involvement models.

attitude because of the risk involved in making a bad decision. Once you are sure you will like the brand, you are ready to try it. These models are summarized in Figure 4.2.

An important point to remember here is that perceived risk is in the eye of the individual. It will always be important to 'check the obvious', and be certain whether there is a perceived risk in the mind of the target audience or not. It is also good to remember that this perceived risk could vary by situation, even for the same person. For example, the choice of what wine to serve at a routine family meal may entail little risk, but the perceived risk could certainly increase when important guests are dining.

Motivation

Psychologists all seem to agree that everything humans do is driven by a small set of motives. Of course, they all don't agree on exactly what constitutes that set of motives, but in general there is not a great deal of difference. To keep things simple, we will look at a basic distinction between positive and negative motives. There are three basic negative motives to consider: *problem removal* when the purchase is made to solve a problem, *problem avoidance* when the purchase is made to avoid a problem or *incomplete satisfaction* where one is looking for a better alternative (see Table 4.2). In terms of positive motives, we want to consider *sensory gratification*, where the purchase is made to enjoy the product, or *social approval*, where the purchase is made to achieve personal recognition for buying the brand.

Table 4.2 Motivations driving purchase behaviour

Basic motive	Description
Negative motives	
Problem removal	Looking for a product or service to **solve** a problem
Problem avoidance	Looking for a product or service to **avoid** a future problem
Incomplete satisfaction	Looking for a product or service that is **better** than what is currently available
Positive motives	
Sensory gratification	Looking to **enjoy** a product or service
Social approval	Looking for **personal recognition** for using a product or service

The important point to understand is that the reason why someone wants something, the motivation, causes attitudes to be formed in the first place. As a result, these motivations 'energize' the purchase or usage decision. In one sense, it is like a circle. The consumer is motivated to buy something and choose a particular brand because their attitude towards that brand suggests it is the best solution to satisfying that motivation. With purchase and usage, the attitude based on the motive is strengthened with a good experience (or weakened with a bad experience). This will involve addressing the motivation underlying the purchase decision, and the perceived risk in the purchase, as we shall see later in the chapter when we discuss the Rossiter-Percy grid.

To illustrate: if you have a bad headache, you will be motivated to do something about it (the negative motivation of problem–solution). You consider Neurofen which you feel is the strongest and fastest-working brand of pain reliever (the attitude associated with the motive) and take some. The headache goes away, and the attitude-motive link is strengthened. But motives are specific to attitudes. Continuing our example, if you have a sinus headache, while the general motive remains the same (problem–solution), the attitudes associated with *sinus* headaches may lead to the choice of another brand such as Sinutab.

This example shows not only how attitudes are dependent on motives, but also how brand choices are linked to motives through attitudes. It also serves as a good example of how the brand awareness link must be carefully established. If your target audience makes a distinction between types of pain (i.e., their attitudes towards pain and hence towards brands), managers must be sure that the link between category need and brand awareness forged in the brand's marketing communication reflects these attitudes.

Look at Advert 4.4 for Neutrogena. This is a very good example of how to execute a problem-solution negative motive. Problems with dark spots? A Neutrogena capsule a day will make them fade away. So, if you have a problem with dark spots and see the Neutrogena advert because trying it would be a low-involvement decision with little risk if it didn't work, you form a tentatively positive attitude and give it a try.

Attitude and corporate image advertising

The same reasoning that drives brand attitude strategy also applies to building a strong attitude toward companies with corporate image advertising. The motivation involved here will almost always be positive because the goal is usually for stakeholders to 'like' the company. Whether the level of involvement should be considered low or high will, just as with brands, be function of the perceived risk involved with 'liking' the company.

In many situations, corporate image advertising is only meant to foster a sense of goodwill toward the company, which will likely be low involvement. But in some situations, the risk will be higher, and the objective will be more than simply liking the company in a general way. This will certainly be the case for investors. They want to be certain before investing. It will also be high involvement, for example, when dealing with government regulatory agencies. You want to build the strongest possible positive attitude toward the company so that if it becomes involved in some regulatory issue they will be starting from an initial positive association in memory, not an indifferent or only moderately favourable association. This reflects something known as assimilation-contrast theory, and it is important to understand for all high-involvement marketing communication. We shall have more to say about this in Chapter 8.

Advert 4.4 Neutrogena.

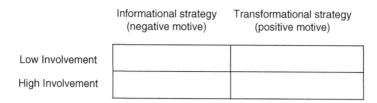

Figure 4.3 Brand attitude strategy: The Rossiter–Percy Grid.

The Rossiter–Percy grid

Given these dimensions of involvement and motivation, a 'grid' that easily reflects the interaction of the two follows. In effect, we are saying that if the fundamental criterion involved in choosing a product or service is the amount of perceived risk in the outcome of the decision and whether the need to be satisfied by the choice is negatively or positively motivated, then IMC planning must take into account the combination of involvement and motivation evidenced by the target audience. These strategic quadrants are represented by the 'grid' shown in Figure 4.3.

Before going further, we need to point out that the Rossiter–Percy Grid is *not* the same as the old, so-called FCB advertising planning grid that surprisingly still finds its way into some textbooks despite its many problems. It too uses involvement (although defined differently), but a second dimension called 'think–feel'. The two should not be confused. The full Rossiter–Percy Grid also includes an overlay of the brand recognition–brand recall distinction within each quadrant. But even just looking at the brand attitude component there is no comparison, and there are significant strategic planning advantages in using the Rossiter–Percy Grid (Rossiter et al., 1991).

What are the strategic implications for IMC planning suggested by the four quadrants of the brand attitude grid? Depending on where a brand's purchase or usage decision lies within the grid, creative tactics will differ significantly as we shall discuss in Chapter 10. For example, when a decision implies no risk, one does not need to convince the target audience. All one need do is titillate, or create what Maloney (1962) calls 'curious disbelief'. This opens up the choice of media for delivering the message. On the other hand, with high-involvement decisions one needs to convince. This means more permanent media should be considered (as opposed, say, to a 15-second commercial).

We have seen that motivation is important to attitude formation; it helps provide the link between a brand and its benefit. It is also linked to emotion, which plays a critical role in message processing. When dealing with positive motives we are concerned with the 'emotional authenticity' of the message. The target audience must sense that the emotional portrayal in the advert is 'real' and not contrived. When that happens, the emotion is embodied by the person seeing the advert or commercial, and that 'good feeling' quite literally becomes the benefit associated with the brand. You are creating a positive feeling, transforming your mood, which is why the brand attitude strategies associated with positive motivations are labelled 'transformational' in the grid.

This has significance for IMC planning. One of the reasons advertising is more effective than other IMC options in building brand attitude is its broader availability via television, and digital media advertising. Of all the means of delivering marketing communication, television, followed by digital media, offers the greatest opportunity for eliciting emotional responses, as well as an advantage in portraying a sequence of emotions consistent with how emotion is experienced. All of this means television and digital media have built-in advantages when dealing with purchase decisions that are driven by positive motives.

When dealing with negative motives, one has a lot more creative latitude. Here the basic task is to communicate information that supplies the 'answer' to the need driven by one of the three negative motives. For that reason, brand attitude strategies dealing with negative motives are labelled 'informational' in the grid. It is important to understand that emotion will also be involved here as well. But unlike when dealing with positive motivations where the emotional response that is aroused becomes the benefit, here emotion is only associated with the processing of the message. The benefit is in the information provided about the brand.

Returning to our 'pain' example, when you are experiencing pain there is a certain anxiety associated with it and when you take something to eliminate it you feel relief. This anxiety-to-relief sequence of emotion should be reflected in the execution. An emotional sequence is important for all advertising, whether dealing with negative or positive motives. We experience things over time, and there are likely to be different emotional associations with the experience. Advertising should reflect this, and we consider this in more detail in Chapter 8.

Advert 4.5 for Creative Roots provides a really good example of what we are talking about here. The emotional response to the headline that '1 in 2 kids is underhydrated' is likely to cause a strong feeling of concern, especially if you are a parent of young children. This will lead you into the copy, and the benefit: 'Access to Creative Roots has been clinically shown to increase hydration levels in children.' Here is the solution to the problem, and the initial anxiety is resolved by the brand.

To summarize, the Rossiter–Percy Grid helps with IMC planning in the following ways:

1   It helps focus the manager's thinking about a brand in terms of the target audience's involvement with the decision and the motivation that drives their behaviour.
2   When involvement is low and the motivation is negative, a wide variety of options are open because the target audience does not need to be convinced (only interested), and the key is in the information provided.
3   When involvement is high and the motivation is negative, the target audience must be convinced by the message, so the communication options considered must be able to accomplish this.
4   When motives are positive, 'emotional authenticity' is the key to successful communication, whether involvement is high or low, and the communication options considered must be able to deal with this. Also, when involvement is high, the target audience must personally identify with the emotion.

Beyond these general strategic implications, there are quite specific tactical considerations associated with each of the quadrants. These will be dealt with in Chapter 10. For now, it is important to know that the brand attitude quadrants will inform executions for both advertising and promotion.

Summary

In this chapter, we have looked at traditional advertising and its role in IMC. The key to understanding this role is the important distinction between advertising and promotion. All marketing communication where the primary objective is building brand awareness

1 in 2 kids is underhydrated.[1]

American Journal of Public Health

CREATIVE ROOTS

Access to Creative Roots has been clinically shown to increase hydration levels in children.[2]

- ☑ 1g of sugar
- ☑ Taste kids love
- ☑ Plant-powered hydration

[1]Harvard School of Public Health article
https://www.hsph.harvard.edu/news/press-releases/study-finds-inadequate-hydration-among-u-s-children/ ,
Kenney E, et al. Prevalence of Inadequate Hydration Among US Children and Disparities
by Gender and Race/Ethnicity: National Health and Nutrition Examination Survey, 2009–2012.
Am J Public Health. 2015;105:e113–e118

[2]Dr. Douglas Casa, "Nutrition, Urinary Markers and Sleep Habits in Children"

Advert 4.5 Creative Roots.

and positive brand attitude may be thought of as advertising, regardless of how the message is delivered. It differs from promotion in that promotion messages, while addressing both awareness and attitudes, have as their primary objective initiating immediate brand purchase intention.

There are four basic types of advertising: consumer advertising, retail advertising, B2B advertising, and corporate advertising. Consumer advertising is brand-focused and directed towards individual consumers, delivered through any of a broad range of media. Retail advertising involves both the store and the products or services it offers, and is generally local in nature. B2B advertising differs from the other types in addressing not only a customer base but also the trade and other aspects of the distribution system. Corporate advertising promotes the company, rather than its products or services, and addresses a wide range of target audiences.

Important to retail advertising is something called channels marketing. Channels marketing grew out of a recognition by marketers of the need for more control over traditional co-op advertising. With co-op, there is an arrangement between a marketer and retailer to cooperate in joint advertising and promotion for the brand. While the advertiser may bear most or even all of the cost of the programme, they have little control over implementation. Channels marketing differs in offering trade-specific programmes paid for by the advertiser or on an earned basis. This is important for IMC because it means the message will be consistent with other marketing communication for a brand as it is developed and controlled by the marketer.

Brand awareness and brand attitude strategy are intimately involved in IMC planning. Brand awareness strategy addresses the important distinction between recognition and recall brand awareness. When the brand choice decision is made at the point-of-purchase, where seeing the brand stimulates a need for the product, a recognition brand awareness strategy is required. When this is the case, to be effective advertising must show the brand as it will be seen at the point-of-purchase. When brand choice follows in response to need arousal, a recall brand awareness strategy is required. In such cases, advertising executions must link the need to the brand, and in that order, so that when the need occurs the brand will come to mind.

Brand attitude strategy follows from whether the purchase decision is low or high involvement, and driven by negative or positive motivations. These dimensions of choice are important to strategy because the creative tactics needed will differ significantly depending on involvement and motivation. When involvement is low, it is not necessary to convince the target audience with the message, only to excite curiosity. But when involvement is high, the message must be convincing owing to the perceived risk associated with brand choice. When dealing with negative motivations, the advertising must provide information that will help address the problem posed by the category need involved. If the underlying motivation is positive, the execution must deliver an emotional authenticity that associates an appropriate positive feeling with the brand. The relationship between brand attitude strategy and involvement and motivation is summarized by the Rossiter–Percy Grid.

Review questions

1 What is the fundamental difference between advertising and promotion?
2 What is the primary role of advertising in IMC?
3 Why is it important to distinguish between different types of advertising?
4 Why are television and digital media the strongest medium for consumer advertising?
5 In what ways might digital media offer advantages in creating brand awareness and attitudes for consumer advertising?

6　Find examples of retail advertisements that address the store's image and examples that deal with the products they sell.

7　Why are co-op advertising programmes not always good for a brand?

8　How does co-op advertising differ from tactical marketing?

9　Discuss B2B advertising and how it differs from other types of advertising.

10　When should you use corporate image advertising?

11　How does branding strategy inform corporate image advertising?

12　What is the difference between brand awareness and brand salience?

13　Why is it important to understand if a purchase decision involves recall versus recognition brand awareness?

14　Why is it important to know if a purchase decision is high or low involvement and negatively or positively motivated?

15　How does corporate image advertising help build strong attitudes toward the corporation?

16　Find examples of advertisements for each of the four quadrants of the Rossiter–Percy Grid, and discuss why you selected them.

References

Biemans, W.G. (1998) Marketing in the twilight zone. *Business Horizons, 41*(6) (November/December), 69–76.

Brooks, M.E., Highhouse, S., Russell, S.S. and Muhr, D.C. (2003) 'Familiarity, ambivalence, and firm reputation: is corporate fame a double-edged sword? *Journal of Applied Psychology, 88*(5), 904–914.

Clow, K.E. and Baack, D. (2004) *Integrated Advertising, Promotion, and Marketing Communication*. Upper Saddle River, NJ: Pearson Prentice Hall, p. 35.

Dowling, G. (2001) *Creating Corporate Reputation*, Oxford: Oxford University Press.

Ehrenberg, A.S.C. (1974) Repetitive advertising and the consumer. *Journal of Advertising Research, 14*(2), 25–34.

Ehrenberg, A.S.C., Barnard, N., Kennedy, R. and Bloom, H. (2002) Brand advertising as creative publicity. *Journal of Advertising Research*, July/August 42, 4, 7–18.

Ehrenberg, A.S.C. and Scriven, J. (1997) Differentiation as salience. Journal *of Advertising Research*, November, *37*(6), 9–14.

Jones, J.P. (1999) *How to Use Advertising to Build Strong Brands*. Thousand Oaks, CA: Sage, p. 2.

Maloney, J.C. (1962) Curiosity versus disbelief in advertising. *Journal of Advertising Research, 2*(2), 2–8.

McGuire, W.J. (1969) The Nature of Attitudes and Attitude Change. In G. Lindsey and E. Aronson (eds.), *The Handbook of Social Psychology*, iii. Reading, MA: Addison-Wesley Publishing, pp. 136–314.

Meyer, H. (1999) When the cause is just. *Journal of Business Strategy, 20*(6) November/December, 27–31.

Pickton, D. and Broderick, A. (2005) *Integrated Marketing Communication*, 2nd edition. Harlow, UK: Prentice Hall.

Rossiter, J.R., Percy, L. and Berkvist, L. (2018) *Marketing Communications: Objectives, Strategy, Tactics*. London: Sage.

Rossiter, J.R., Percy, L. and Donovan, R.J. (1991) A better planning grid. *Journal of Advertising Research, 31*(5), 11–21.

Rossiter, J.R. and Percy, L. (1997) *Advertising Communication and Promotion Management*. New York, NY: McGraw-Hill.

Schumann, D.W., Hathcote, J.M. and West, W. (1991) Corporate advertising in America: A review of published studies on use, measurement, and effectiveness. *Journal of Advertising, 20*(3) (September), 38.

Starch, D. (1926) *Principles of Advertising*. Chicago, IL: A.W. Shaw.

White, R. (1999) Brands and Advertising. In J.P. Jones (ed.), *How to Use Advertising to Build Strong Brands*. Thousand Oaks, CA: Sage, p. 57.

5 Promotion

In the last chapter, we introduced the fundamental distinction between advertising and promotion, emphasizing their *strategic* character. Advertising is strategically aimed at building brand awareness and positive brand attitudes, leading to a strong brand equity. This is reflected in the etymology of the word, 'to turn towards'.

Promotion is strategically aimed at driving short-term sales or brand usage. This, too, is reflected in the etymology of the word, to 'move ahead'. Even though brand purchase intention is the primary objective of promotion, as with *all* marketing communication, it too must contribute to building brand awareness and brand attitude, something Prentice (1977) long ago referred to as 'Consumer Franchise Building' promotion. This is a point to keep in mind as we discuss specific types of promotion.

Promotion strategy

As part of integrated marketing communication (IMC) planning, the manager must decide how promotion should be used as part of the communication strategy for the brand. It is a *strategic* issue. It will of course almost always be needed when brand purchase intention is an objective; and must be used when this is the primary communication objective. As we have seen, while advertising is certainly meant to *lead* to sales by building positive brand attitude, when immediate action is required promotion must be a part of the overall strategy for the brand.

But even if brand purchase intention is not an objective, a need for promotion may arise during the campaign for tactical reasons. A competitor may be about to introduce a new version of its product, so it would make sense to encourage an accelerated purchase of your brand using an incentive in order to 'pull' potential triers of your competitor's new product out of the market. Or, for whatever reason sales may be soft and a promotion could be used to help energize sales.

All promotions must be consistent with the brand's positioning in its advertising. It must also be coordinated with the brand's advertising. In Chapter 11, we will see how a successful promotion strategy, when coordinated with advertising, will increase the overall effectiveness of an IMC programme.

When most people think about promotion, they are usually thinking about what has traditionally been called 'sales promotion' and specifically some incentive for immediate action. Sales promotion is defined along the lines of any direct purchasing incentive, reward, or promise that is offered to the target audience for the purpose of making a specific purchase or taking a specific action that will benefit those responding to the promotion. But we must remember that not all promotions are sales promotions. An

DOI: 10.4324/9781003169635-7

incentive is not required, even if that is almost always the case. All that is needed for a promotion is for the primary communication objective to be immediate action.

Rossiter and Percy (1997) introduced an interesting and important consideration in how one should think about promotion: the notion of *time*. Consistent with the importance of understanding how consumers make purchase or usage decisions (which we have already talked briefly about and will cover in more detail later in Chapter 12), they remind us that promotion should be integrated over time in relation to the target audience's decision process. This suggests that promotion may be helpful prior to the actual purchase or use of a product or service, if a consumer is looking for information about a brand prior to making a decision during the actual purchase, or even after the purchase.

Promotion and specific incentive promotional techniques should be considered for each stage in a consumer decision process, but it is not necessary to always include one. Promotion may be inappropriate at any one step, or, while appropriate, may not be the best place to spend the brand's budget. If a promotion of some kind makes sense in order to accelerate the decision process, one must then choose a promotion that is appropriate for that stage.

Thinking about promotion in this general way, not as sales promotion but as part of marketing communication to help speed up the decision process – whether an incentive is involved or not – it is impossible to consider promotion in isolation. In developing an IMC programme, the manager should be thinking about whether a promotion or a particular type of incentive promotion will be an effective *part of the whole* marketing communication effort. As we have been underscoring all along, this is what we mean by IMC – looking at all available communication options and using those which best help effectively and efficiently to meet a brand's marketing communication objectives. In Chapter 11, we deal specifically with how advertising and promotion should be used together to maximize effective IMC. Now we turn our attention to specific incentive promotions. In the following discussion, as we talk about 'promotions', we will be referring to *incentive promotions* unless otherwise noted.

Basic types of promotion

When most people think of promotions, they usually are thinking of consumer promotions, but promotions can be directed at the sales force and trade as well. In reality, there are at least three major types of promotion to consider: consumer, retail, and trade. While this is how promotions are generally classified, Rossiter et al. (2018) take a somewhat different view. They talk about promotion within channels of distribution for products and services. In this view, they see three forms of manufacturer promotion: trial promotion to retailers, trial promotion to consumers, and repeat-purchase promotion to consumers. With retail promotions, they see only one channel, direct to consumers. While we will be talking about retail advert promotions, price-off promotions, and point-of-purchase display retail promotions, they go on to identify five more types of retail promotion, store layout and retail atmosphere, which we will deal with separately in Chapter 7, as well as store brands, card-based loyalty schemes, and home shopping.

Incentive promotions are divided into two broad categories: immediate reward promotions and delayed reward promotions. Immediate reward promotions are offers that provide something immediate, such as price reductions, bonus packs, free gifts with a purchase, etc. Delayed reward promotions defer the benefit of the promotion and usually require the target audience to do something before they receive the benefit of the promotion. These would include such things as sweepstakes, refund offers that require a proof-of-purchase, frequent flyer programmes, etc. Immediate reward promotions are usually more effective because of their immediacy. This, of course, is consistent with the primary use of promotion-like messages to influence action now.

Different incentive promotions will have specific strengths for either attracting new users to a brand (trial objectives) or for gaining additional business from existing users (repeat-purchase objectives).

While any type of promotion might be used to generate either a new trial for a brand or to encourage more purchases from existing customers, certain promotions tend to be more suitable for one objective than another. For example, as we shall see below, for consumer promotion the types most appropriate for a trial objective are coupons, sampling, and refunds or rebates; those most appropriate for a repeat purchase objective are loyalty and loading devices, sweepstakes, and games and contests. Depending how they are used, premiums have strength for both trial and repeat purchase objectives. Offering an appropriate premium can have a strong attraction for consumers who regularly switch among brands within a category, providing an incentive to add an additional brand to the set they already purchase. On the other hand, with current brand users, especially when dealing with products that have a long purchase cycle (for example, home appliances or computers), an attractive promotion could help initiate an earlier consideration of replacing an older product.

Before we review some of the situations where different incentive promotions might be effective, it would be well to point out that since promotions are used in a tactical sense to accelerate brand purchase intention, there are many, many unique ways such promotions might be applied. All we are attempting to do here is outline some of the conditions where a particular type of consumer promotion might be applicable. This should help further distinguish the specific strengths of the various types of basic consumer promotion.

Trade promotion

Overall, as much as half of all marketing communications spending goes to trade promotion. A trade promotion is a programme of discounts aimed at increasing distribution or some sort of merchandising activity at the retail level. This may include everything from slotting allowances to sales incentives designed to reward individual retail salespeople for meeting specific sales goals. We will look specifically at three basic trade promotion techniques.

We noted earlier that spending in trade promotion accounts for about half of all marketing communication expenditure; about twice that spent on consumer promotion. This trend is a function of many things, including a growing understanding by the trade of their power in the marketing mix. But perhaps the key reason has been the short-run emphasis of too many marketers attempting to use promotion to 'buy share' to satisfy immediate sales goals.

It cannot be emphasized enough that this is *not* the way to deal with trade promotion. It is certainly true that without good distribution consumers do not have an opportunity to purchase. But it must be remembered that the brand's goals and the goals of the trade are not always the same. The trade makes its money from *category* sales. They are indifferent to what brands sell, as long as their margins for the category are sustained. The brand, of course, is only interested in its own sales. So, while trade

Table 5.1 Basic trade incentive promotions

Promotion	Examples
Allowance	• Performance allowance • Trade coupon • Free product • Slotting fees
Display material	• Point-of-purchase • Special display
Trade premiums and incentives	• Dealer loaders • Sales goal incentives

promotion must be seen as a cost of doing business, *strategically* it must be considered within overall IMC planning. This means integrating trade promotion with consumer promotion and advertising.

Table 5.1 details a number of trade promotions. As already mentioned, trade promotions are usually a short-term incentive or deal that is offered to retailers or other key participants in the distribution channel to stimulate stocking an item or to feature and/or promote a brand. These promotions depend entirely on trade cooperation for any sales increase.

Success for any brand depends on trade or dealer support. The purpose of trade promotions is to improve relations with the trade in order to gain and hold new distribution, build trade inventories or obtain trade merchandising support. There are three principal classifications of trade-oriented promotions:

1 Allowance promotions.
2 Display material promotions.
3 Trade premiums and incentives.

Allowance promotions offer the trade something in return for purchasing or promoting a specific quantity of a brand, or for meeting specific buying or performance requirements. *Display material promotions* provide the trade or dealer with special in-store display material to use in featuring the promoted brand, often in conjunction with a trade allowance promotion. *Trade premiums and incentives* are promotions which offer the trade a free gift or a chance for an even higher-value prize in return for purchasing specific quantities of goods or meeting certain specified requirements.

There are both trial and repeat purchase trade promotions, just as with consumer promotion. Trial trade promotions are largely designed to gain an acceptance of a new product, or to encourage carrying an existing one. Repeat-purchase trade promotions are used to ensure a product is stocked and to get favourable shelf space. Various allowances are obvious usage promotions. All three types of trade promotion have applications as repeat purchase-promotions.

Before discussing the three basic types of trade promotion, we need to address slotting fees because they are likely to come out of the trade promotion budget. Slotting fees act like a trial promotion in that they are needed to secure distribution for a brand, but they are really simply a cost of doing business. While one can understand that with an ever-increasing demand to handle new products and line extensions – and their high failure rate – the trade is demanding some help in dealing with the overhead, the high fees charged are nonetheless worrisome. It has been estimated that as much as 70 per cent of slotting allowances go directly to the retailer bottom line rather than to defraying costs.

Allowances

Allowances to the trade can take many forms – everything from direct price reductions on invoices to free goods. We have just mentioned slotting fees, and their virtual necessity for achieving distribution, especially for consumer-packaged goods. As such fees increase, it becomes more and more difficult for those with small marketing budgets to compete.

A general weakness of most trade promotional allowances is that there is no guarantee that any significant portion of the money will find its way to the consumer, either through increased merchandising activity or lower prices. This is true of buying allowances, performance allowances and even free goods. As a result, while it is important that trade and consumer support are integrated, a manager must consider any consumer benefit a plus point. Trade allowances should be used for tactical purposes with the trade. For example, buying allowances and free goods helps build inventories in support of consumer marketing programmes (both promotion and advertising). Performance allowances, at least in part, will go to merchandising or retail advertising in support of the brand.

Trade coupons are actually coupons for the consumer, but distributed by the retailer rather than the marketer. They differ from retail promotions in that trade coupons are *controlled* by the marketer, not the retailer. Usually, the retailer pays for distributing the coupon in their advertising or other marketing communication and is then reimbursed by the marketer after the promotion. Because consumer promotions with coupons are keyed to trial, the same is true for trade coupons. Only in this case, it is not *trial* by the trade but by the consumer. It is a *repeat-purchase* promotion for the trade, in the same sense as the other allowances we have discussed.

This is an important point for IMC planning. Retailers as a rule like trade coupons because they help extend their own marketing communication budget. In this sense, trade coupons can help secure trade cooperation within an IMC programme – that is step one. Step two is the consumer response to the coupons. This must be considered in light of everything discussed about coupons as a consumer trial promotion.

Display material

Display allowances or materials are usually used to generate special in-store merchandising activity for a new product or brand extension, but they are also used to stimulate trade support for consumer promotions. The importance of in-store merchandising is underscored by the fact that more than 70 per cent of brand choices are made in-store (Advertising Age, 1995).

Point-of-purchase refers to all those things that are used at the point of sale in order to attract the attention of the customer to the brand. The objective of point-of-purchase material is to draw attention to a particular brand or product on the shelf, or wherever it may be displayed, or to provide information. It should encourage consumers to make an impulse purchase or trial decision, or to learn more about the item being featured. Sometimes, it can even guide consumers to other areas of the store for cross-merchandising opportunities. Well-designed point-of-purchase frequently acts as a trigger mechanism to remind the consumer of a brand's advertising.

One of the more interesting applications of point-of-purchase is interactive computer-driven displays. The consumer interacts with a computer displayed within the point-of-purchase unit in order to gain information about a product or service. Through the computer, the consumer can request a catalogue, ask questions, receive data in print-out form and much more. Interactive point-of-purchase is used at car dealerships to provide consumers with information about specific models, in retail stores to access store catalogues and it is even being introduced in fast food chains to place orders. The most common application, however, is where a high-ticket, high-margin purchase is involved, or where a purchasing decision process is more complex.

One of the advantages of using display materials as a trade promotion is that it encourages the trade to actually promote a brand in the store, because the incentive to the retailer is only available upon proof of compliance. It can also usually be quickly implemented, making it a useful tactical tool. The disadvantage is that it does require widespread trade acceptance to be effective, and often must conform to various store guidelines for in-store merchandising.

Trade premiums and incentives

These last trade promotions centre more on individual stores or personnel, and as a result are popular with the trade. Premiums offered to the trade are usually in the form of *dealer loaders*. Their goal is much the same as for consumer loading devices: to 'load up' the store or distributor with product. This is done with a product display where a premium is offered to the consumer, usually as part of the display. For example, a cooler might be offered at a very low price with the purchase of a 12-pack soft drink brand.

Incentives are offered to various levels of the trade, and for any number of reasons. Awards or gifts might be offered to individual counter or sales staff at retail for reaching a set level of sales for a brand, to a manager for store sales of a brand or to staff for devising new or innovative ways of promoting a brand. Incentive programmes are an especially good idea for new product introduction or for slow-moving products, and they have the advantage of being quick and easy to implement, as well as relatively inexpensive.

The problem with all trade premium and incentive promotions, however, is that many mass merchandisers do not allow them, or have rules that tightly restrict the type of programmes that are acceptable.

Retail promotions

As we look at retail promotion, keep in mind that the trade promotions we have just reviewed are also used by retailers. And, to the consumer, there is not much of a difference between a retail promotion and a consumer promotion. All they see is a price incentive or special display. In both cases, an inducement is offered to accelerate the decision process. But from a planning standpoint, there is a *crucial* difference. Retail promotions are independent of the brand, initiated either by a distributor or the retailer. This often puts retail promotion *outside* the scope of IMC planning. To help bring retail promotion within at least the planning control of the marketer, more companies are turning to *tactical marketing*, which we discussed in the last chapter.

There are three major goals for retail promotion: drive traffic to the store, increase profit for a category, and clear stock. But it is also important to understand that retailers are usually interested in *category* sales, not the sales of a particular brand. Suppose Adidas is running a consumer promotion, and your store sells Adidas along with other brands such as New Balance. The manager may decide to run a retail promotion for New Balance at the same in order to drive more traffic to the store.

The importance of coordinating retail and consumer promotion is underscored by research on consumer perceptions of promotional activity (Krishna et al., 1991). It has been found that consumers are reasonably accurate about sale price and deal frequency. This is significant in light of the general notion in the consumer behaviour literature that consumers tend to plan their brand choices and how much they buy based on when they expect a promotion. If consumers 'sense' when a product or service is likely to be on promotion, they are not making a distinction between a retail and consumer promotion. The retail promotion will certainly be a factor in the consumer's purchase or usage plans. If the marketer does not control or at least track these promotions, there is potential for conflict between the promotion objective of the retail store and the marketer. Even if a retailer insists on control of their promotions, it is essential that managers stay informed about them and do their best to influence the message content and execution.

Retail promotions are almost always price-related, so before we look at specific types of retail promotion, we should consider how best to present a price in the promotion. In the wording of a price-off promotion, you can use an *explicit comparative* format such as 'total value/sale price' or 'regular price/sale price', or *implicit comparative* wording such as 'now only'. Generally, explicit language is perceived to provide a better value (Friedmann and Hains, 1991). Price savings may be stated in terms of a *monetary* savings in euros or as a *percentage* saved. Most retailers tend to favour monetary savings. Alternatively, a *tensile price* claim may be used, where vague reference is made to how much you will save: e.g., 'Save up to 40 per cent' or Save 10 per cent to 40 per cent?'

Price endings are something else to be considered. Schindler (1991), perhaps the leading researcher on price-ending effects, has pointed out that an ending of .95 or .99, such as €34.99, will suggest a discount. An unusual ending such as .63 in €5.63 will suggest a carefully determined price, one where the retailer has offered the largest savings possible. A rounded ending such as €25.00 will suggest a high-quality product or store.

Next, we shall look at the three most common types of retail promotion: retail adverts, specific price-off promotions, and point-of-purchase display promotions.

Retail adverts

For years retail advertising has been associated with newspaper, especially for supermarkets, big box retailers, and automotive dealers. Today, of course, you will find retail adverts of all sorts on digital media. Typically, retail adverts as promotion will feature a number of products, and usually at a 'special' price. There can be a number of strategic reasons for choosing the particular items to feature, but often they are items that are on promotion to the retailer from the trade. It should be noted that a retail advert is a promotion when they feature products, whether or not they are discounted. Just as with brand adverts, they are a promotion when the objective is immediate action. Also, retailers use trade adverts as well, and the two should not be confused.

Price-off promotions

We have already addressed the three main variables in price-off promotions: how they are worded, whether the savings is expressed in terms of money or a percentage, and the price-ending. To this list, we may also add specific savings based upon the number of items purchased or amount spent. Retailers employ a number of pricing strategies for price-off promotions. They must consider any current recent price promotions, their inventory balance, as well as competitive activity. Price-off promotions are almost always a part of retail adverts as we have just seen, but may also be a part of point-of-purchase displays (discussed next). But, price-off promotions are used in many other ways as well, everything from in-store flyers to 'shelf-talkers', those small posters on shelves.

Point-of-purchase displays

In-store displays are a major part of retailers' promotional efforts. They include such things as end-aisle displays, stand-alone displays anywhere in the store, as well as store banners. By their very nature point-of-purchase displays stand out from the usual store environment, and for this reason will elicit reflexive attention to what is being promoted. In addition, selective attention may result because people will perceive that what is in the display is 'on special', even if it is not.

While not a point-of-purchase display as such, a retail store's physical layout and atmosphere can have a significant effect upon what is purchased. In a supermarket, for example, most shoppers will not visit all of the 30 to 50 product areas in the store. In fact, on average shoppers will only pass around 25 per cent of them on a typical trip to the store (Sorenson, 2003). As a result, attention must be paid to the layout of the store and how products are displayed on the shelf to increase the likelihood of visiting more aisles and purchasing more. Interestingly, how brands are displayed on the shelf within a product category can increase category sales for the store (Gibson, 1992). For example, stocking cereals by brand rather than type results in general overall cereal sales; placing toothbrushes in the middle of the toothpaste section rather than next to it will result in more sales.

The atmosphere of a retail store will also have a significant effect upon how long someone will shop and how much they will purchase (Donovan et al., 1994). The initial impression will immediately be encoded emotionally in terms of both arousal and pleasantness. This will be informed primarily by music and colour. To keep the arousal level high, such things as bright colours or fast music should be used. On the other hand, if the retail environment is intrinsically unpleasant, such as a dentist's consulting room or even some supermarkets, arousal should be lowered by using softer colours or slow music (Milliman, 1982).

Consumer promotion

Consumer promotions are developed by the marketer or its agency and directed towards the target audience to accelerate the decision process. Often these promotions are experienced at the retail level. Shelf-talkers (messages found attached to a shelf in the store), in-store coupons or bonus packs, special displays, price-off offers, all are promotions received at the point-of-purchase. What makes them different from an identical-looking retail promotion is that they were initiated and delivered by the marketer, not the retailer.

As seen in Table 5.2, there are seven basic types of promotion aimed at consumers (whether initiated by the marketer or retailer). Of these, three have a trial objective and four repeat purchase objectives. Those with trial as an objective are coupons, sampling, refunds, and rebates; those with repeat purchase as an objective are loyalty and reward

Table 5.2 Seven basic consumer incentive promotions

Promotion	Examples
Coupons	Coupon for reduced price delivered via FSI or other print media, also internet
Sampling	Free distribution of product to home, in-store samples, free trial of product
Refunds and rebates	Automatic rebate on initial purchase price of expensive goods, or mail-in proof of purchase for refund
Loyalty and reward programmes	Continuity programmes such as frequent flyer or frequent stayer
Loading devices	Multiple or bonus packs, price-off marked on package
Premiums	Product-associated items such as Pepsi-wear, use of other products as premium with purchase
Sweepstakes, games and contests	Free products or trips as prizes for mail-in participation, entry for chance or prize for accepting product demonstration, 'scratch' cards or bottle caps identifying winners

programmes, loading devices, premiums, sweepstakes, and games and contests. There are, of course, many others, but for our purposes we only consider these six basic techniques. It should be noted that not all types of promotion are permitted in all countries.

Trial promotions

In this section, we shall be reviewing the three major promotions used when trial is the objective.

COUPONS

There are two types of coupons: brand sponsored (consumer promotion), and distributor or store sponsored and distributed (retail promotion). As mentioned earlier, however, this is *not* a distinction a consumer is likely to make, but one that must be considered in IMC planning. Couponing is an effective promotion technique which uses a variety of means for discounting the purchase price. Coupons are an excellent way of inducing trial for a new product. There is a danger in using coupons too frequently, however. Over 80 per cent of coupon users stockpile coupons for the same brand, effectively lowering the price for all of their purchases of the brand. Today, especially with coupons delivered via digital media, there is more targeted couponing.

While there are some indications that marketers may be taking a harder look at the cost of using coupons, and that overall coupon distribution levels may have peaked, or even begun to drop slightly (Triplett, 1994), they remain very popular with consumers. In fact, consumers hold more favourable attitudes towards grocery product brands that offer coupons or other price incentives, and that feeling has been increasing. Even though only 2 or 3 per cent of the more than 300 billion coupons that are distributed each year are ever redeemed, coupons remain an important promotion option. One of the suggested reasons for a possible decline in coupon redemption is a significant shortening of expiration periods in an effort by marketers to control coupon liability.

Traditionally, coupons have been distributed via print media or direct mail. In the United States, in the early 2000s, the vast majority of coupons were in FSIs (free-standing inserts) – those annoying cards and papers that fall out of magazines and newspapers. Occasionally, coupons are included in and on a package, good for a future purchase of the brand (known as a bounce-back coupon) or of another of the company's brands (known as 'cross-couponing' or 'cross-ruff couponing'). In a very creative use of couponing, the Rijksmuseum of Amsterdam offered €5 coupons for admission to the museum on milk cartons. The cartons featured various masterpieces such as Vermeer's *Milk Maid* and Rembrandt's *Night Watch* (Fabrikant, 2015).

But as technology has increased in both stores and homes, the use of electronic couponing has become more prevalent, especially with smartphones. Today there are online electronic coupon programme services, where all one need to do is select the coupons wanted and print them out (Stecklow, 2005). Unlike more traditional ways of delivering coupons, these new electronic means offer much tighter control over who receives the promotion. Groupon, a leader in online coupons and promotions, was in over 300 marketers worldwide in 2010 (Weiss, 2010). Unfortunately, this has also led to coupon fraud, as hackers have ways to capture online images of coupons.

It is also possible to offer consumer coupons at the till, based upon a person's packaging behaviour. These 'check-out' coupons have redemption rates up to 6–8 per cent higher than the typical coupon redemption rate of 3–5 per cent (Fill, 1995).

Small business and social media

American Express initially got into social media with Foursquare in 2011, enabling small businesses to attract new customers with location-based offers by letting cardholders match accounts to the mobile app. They went on to use Twitter and Facebook. They introduced a service called 'Sync', that translated social media activity into savings for cardholders. For example, one programme offered Sync paperless coupons that are loaded onto an American Express card when the user tweets certain hashtags.

Source: *Advertising Age*, 14 May 2012

SAMPLING

Sampling is when the target audience is given an opportunity to try or use the product directly, with little or no cost. It can range from an actual product sample, either in a regular size or a special sample size that has been developed for the promotion, or the use of a product or service for a limited time (for example, a 30-day trial offer). The objective of sampling is to encourage trial of a product or service among a broader consumer base for an established product or service, or to introduce a new product or service. Because of market and media fragmentation, and the high cost of buying shelf space in stores, sampling has grown in popularity. Products with low trial or a demonstrable product difference are ideal candidates for sampling.

Samples can be delivered in a variety of ways, each with its own specific advantage and disadvantage. For example, sampling in-store or at a central location has the advantage of low distribution cost, but it is difficult to control who receives the sample. Direct mail offers an effective way of sampling either a broadly based target market or a highly targeted market, but there are obvious limits to what one can efficiently sample through the mail. Often, cosmetics or skin care products are offered in magazines by attaching a sample packet to the brand's advertisement. Even luxury brands use this technique. In one issue of *Vogue*, Chloé, Armani and Hermes advertisements all included a sample of the advertised fragrance. Door-to-door offers the only means of sampling products containing hazardous ingredients, but it tends to be inefficient and expensive. Overall, the most effective way of reaching a broadly based target market with sampling is through direct mail or samples in magazines where appropriate. In-store sampling is less expensive, but offers a more limited reach. Using more traditional advertising media, or even digital, to ask people to call or write for a sample is ideal for low budgets, but again has a very limited reach.

This would be a good place to point out that when a high-involvement product is offered on a trial basis, this is essentially 'sampling'. So, if a company or business is given an opportunity to try a product before finalizing an order, this is a sample promotion even if it is not accompanied by a price incentive.

REFUNDS AND REBATES

A refund or rebate promotion is an offer that is made by a marketer to refund a certain amount of money after purchasing a product and on the basis of proof-of-purchase. While most refunds and rebates are made directly to the consumer, they can be passed along by the retailer (for example, car rebates used to lower the initial purchase price). These refunds and rebates can be either a specific amount or a portion of the actual retail value of the purchase, ranging from a certain percentage all the way up to a full refund of the purchase price.

Refunds and rebates are used to encourage purchase or trial of a product, and there are a number of ways of delivering the promotion message: everything from direct mail, FSIs (in newspapers or magazines) and in or on the package, to digital media and e-marketing. The most common use for refunds or rebates is as a temporary sales stimulus or as a defensive measure to help counteract some competitive activity. Some of the strengths of using refunds or rebates include such things as:

- It effectively reduces the price *without* using the retailer.
- It can be especially useful in stimulating interest in high-priced products or services.
- There is a high level of non-redemption among those intending to apply for the rebate, reducing overall cost.

On the other hand, the value of refunds or rebates to the consumer is delayed, limiting their appeal. Many people perceive the effort involved as not worth it.

FAVOURABLE SITUATIONS FOR TRIAL PROMOTIONS

While coupons, sampling, and refunds and rebates are especially effective in generating trial, this is not to say they are ineffective as repeat-purchase promotions. Strategically, however, when trial is the objective, these three promotions should be considered. Of the three, sampling is probably the *most effective* promotion for generating trial, followed closely by coupons. Refunds and rebates, because they are less immediate, are somewhat

Table 5.3 Favourable situations for trial promotions

Promotion	Favourable situations
Coupons	• When a brand has a small budget • New product introductions
Sampling	• When a brand has low trial but a demonstrable positive difference • When advertising cannot adequately demonstrate a brand's benefit
Refunds and rebates	• Incentive for trying expensive products or services • Defensive tactic against strong competition

less effective, but they are perhaps the best means of accelerating trial of expensive products or services. They are also useful in defending against strong competitors when the purchase cycle for the category is long.

Sampling is particularly effective where category or brand trial is low, especially if a brand has a demonstrable difference that will be readily apparent with use. It is also a good way of beating the competition to the punch when a new category is being introduced. As potential users consider a new category, sampling helps 'push' them into action, and with the sample brand. Sampling is also an effective technique when advertising may not be able to adequately demonstrate a brand's advantage. Is a hand lotion really less messy? Is the crust really crispier? Does someone really feel pain relief faster? If using a brand will easily and quickly demonstrate a positive benefit, sampling can be an effective way of making the brand's benefit claims believable.

While couponing is less effective than sampling in generating trial, it has the advantage of being much less expensive. The introduction of a new product or service is an ideal time to use coupons in stimulating trial, or when wanting to attract new users to the brand. The problem here, of course, is that current users will use the coupon as well. Table 5.3 reviews favourable situations for trial promotions.

Repeat-purchase promotions

In this section, we shall be reviewing the four major promotions used when repeat-purchase is the objective.

LOYALTY AND REWARD PROGRAMMES

Loyalty and reward programmes are promotions that are designed to reward a brand's customers for being loyal. They are designed to build repeat purchase for the brand and have the advantage of enabling the manager to develop a strong database of their loyal customers, which in turn can be used to monitor satisfaction over a period of time. However, loyalty programmes generally only keep market shares constant in the category, likely because they mainly cause already loyal consumers to join (Leenheer et al., 2007).

The most common loyalty promotions are *continuity programmes*, which require the consumer to do something like save stamps, coupons, or proofs-of-purchase over a period of time in order to accumulate enough to qualify for a gift, trip, or reward of some kind. These seem to work best for low involvement products or services, especially when the incentive overlaps with brand meaning (Roehm et al., 2002). But perhaps the best-known continuity promotions are frequent flyer programmes of major airlines and frequent stayer programmes offered by major hotel chains. One variation on the continuity programme is points offered by credit card issuers for the amount charged, redeemable for products or services.

The objective of continuity programmes is to hold on to current users and to encourage occasional users to become more frequent users. There is some evidence that targeting light or occasional users can lead to cost-effective incremental sales (Wansink, 2003). Continuity programmes do a good job of retaining customers and they help build brand loyalty, but they do require long-term commitment, both on the part of the target market as well as the marketer, who may find the cost in the long run much greater than expected.

LOADING DEVICES

Loyalty and loading devices are often considered together because the aim of both is to help retain existing customers. Loading promotions differ in that they are designed to take consumers out of their normal purchasing pattern by encouraging the purchase of such things as a larger size, a special bonus offer or multiple packs. The reasons for wanting to do this can range from trying to upgrade the value or revenue of a purchase to a defensive measure against competitive strategy. For example, if a brand knows its major competitor is about to introduce an improved version of their product, a loading promotion will effectively take the brand's customers out of the market, making them less likely to try the competitor's improved product.

Some of the more common ways of implementing loading promotions are with such things as bonus packs, and money-off and price packs. *Bonus packs* are a particularly effective technique for moving additional product to the consumer, offering more of the product for the regular price. *Money-off and price packs* are extremely effective and efficient promotion techniques, especially where the opportunity exists to stimulate brand switching, and as a strong defensive move when one is needed quickly.

The manager must consider the strengths and weaknesses of the various loading promotions available to them. Bonus packs, for example, while creating an immediate incentive to buy because the 'bonus' is immediate, are unpopular with the trade because they interfere with normal stocking and take up extra shelf space without adding additional profit for the retailer. Money-off and special price packs (where the discounted price is specifically marked on the package by the manufacturer) again offer an immediate value at the point-of-purchase, but tend to subsidize regular users rather than encourage new trial or switching.

PREMIUMS

There are numerous types of premiums and just as many ways of delivering them. The goal of premiums is to influence consumers to take a specific action, with the premium as a reward. There are a wide variety of premiums one might consider. But it is important to remember that the premium must appeal to the target audience, and they must perceive a value in the offer.

Additionally, the premium should have an obvious association with the product, and ideally reinforce the image of the brand and reflect its benefit. Premiums may be offered for a one-time purchase or as part of a continuity programme. The premium may require a mailed or digital response, or be available at the point-of-purchase. When a premium is part of a package, it has the advantages of attracting attention to the product (usually with the enticement 'FREE!') and the reward is immediate, but it can occasion packaging problems and additional distribution costs. When a premium is available at the time of purchase (but not in or on the package), it too offers an immediate reward to the consumer and permits a marketer to offer larger premiums, but it does require significant retailer support.

Premiums may also be 'self-liquidating'. This is where a premium is made available at a reduced price, usually 30–50 per cent below regular retail prices – enough to cover the out-of-pocket cost of the merchandise for the marketer. While generally a low-cost promotion, and able to selectively target consumers through the type of premium offered, it does require advertising support to generate interest.

Sweepstakes, games and contests offer the consumer a chance to win a cash prize, merchandise or travel in return for using the promoted brand or taking a specific action, such as visiting a dealer for a demonstration. They are used to create interest in a brand or to provide a unifying theme for a group of promotions. It is important to ensure that they are *fully integrated* with all aspects of the brand's IMC programme, and that they are consistent with the brand's image. A successful sweepstakes for Hawaiian Tropic Sunscreen should not send the winner on a European holiday, but a trip to Hawaii, or at least to some tropical island.

A significant concern with sweepstakes, games and contests that is less of a problem with other types of consumer promotion is the legal aspect. As an attorney specializing in this area has put it, once you have decided on your objectives and what type of sweepstake, game or contest might satisfy those objectives, the next step is to involve a legal expert (Lans, 1994). While we do not want to get into details (something beyond the scope of this book), perhaps it would be useful to relate some of the advice this attorney offers marketers in order to provide a sense of the potential complications involved.

The most important thing from a legal standpoint is official rules of the promotion, which are regulated by the government and differ from country to country. It is impossible to include a full set of rules on a package or in advertising, but an abbreviated set of the official rules must appear. In fact, marketing communication that includes a consumer sweepstake should, at a minimum, include the following information: (1) no purchase necessary; (2) void where prohibited; (3) any age and geographic limitations for eligibility; (4) an end date for the sweepstake; (5) that the sweepstake is subject to complete official rules; (6) how consumers may obtain a copy of those rules; and (7) the name and address of the sponsor. Clearly, this is an area where expert help is required, and it varies between countries. Even if you have been running the same promotion for some time, it is important to check because even a seemingly insignificant change in the wording could mean that a new law applies.

There are weaknesses when using sweepstakes, games and contests as a part of an IMC programme. They do not require a purchase; the reward is not only usually delayed, but limited to only a small number of participants. Where they do work, they can help reinforce the image of a product or service at a relatively low cost. When well designed, they can also create excitement and interest.

FAVOURABLE SITUATIONS FOR REPEAT-PURCHASE PROMOTIONS

Strategic application of repeat-purchase promotions tends to address more short-term issues than trial promotions do. Trial promotions are meant to bring in new customers for the long-term health of the brand. Repeat-purchase promotions are used to alter the timing of a purchase, capturing users in the short term to take them out of the market, or to accelerate purchase for some other tactical reason.

Of the repeat-purchase promotions discussed, loyalty or continuity programmes are the ones most directly aimed at creating and maintaining brand loyalty. The others are aimed at people who tend to switch among various brands, with the intention of attracting them to the promoted brand on their next category purchase. Again, if the promotion is well executed with building a more positive attitude in mind, the result will bring more frequent switching to the brand, resulting in more frequent usage.

All usage promotions, but especially premiums, can be conceived in a manner that targets particular segments of a market. The appeal of the premium can easily be matched to specific audiences, as can the prizes in sweepstakes, games and contests. Both premiums and sweepstakes, games and contests also have the potential of generating in-store merchandising activity such as point-of-purchase display, banners, special displays, etc. This has the advantage of drawing switchers' attention to the brand as well as the opportunity of reinforcing key benefit claims. Sweepstakes, games and contests also present a good way of providing a unifying theme for an IMC campaign.

Loyalty programmes, and especially loading devices, are a good way of defending against competitor activity by removing people from the market. They help hold current brand-loyal customers and retain switchers by building repeat purchase or use. Loading devices, such as price packs and bonus packs help attract switchers to a brand, and deter switching to other brands. However, this can only be seen as a short-term, tactical application. For example, if a competitor is about to launch a new brand or otherwise challenge a brand, a bonus pack will temporarily disrupt the introduction by reducing category demand.

Repeat-purchase promotions can be very effective, but one must guard against using them in a predictable or ongoing way (with the exception of loyalty programmes, of course). They are meant to stimulate short-term usage, but the actual reward can only be a transition or aid to a more positive brand attitude. As with all promotions, they should contribute to long-term growth. Table 5.4 reviews favourable situations for repeat-purchase promotions.

Table 5.4 Favourable situations for repeat-purchase promotions

Promotion	*Favourable situations*
Loyalty and reward programmes Loading devices	• To defend against switching • When a new competitor is about to enter the market
Premiums	• Capitalize on selective appeal • Encourages point-of-purchase display
Sweepstakes, games and contests	• Provides a unifying theme for a group of promotions • Reinforces a brand's positioning and advertising • To gain in-store merchandising activity

Building brand attitude with consumer promotion

As pointed out at the beginning of this chapter, even though brand purchase intention is the primary communication objective for promotion, like all marketing communication, incentive promotions as well as promotion-like messages must also address brand awareness and brand attitude. A well-conceived promotion will help enhance brand equity by communicating a positive brand attitude consistent with the brand's positioning. To quote Mittelstadt (1993), a long-time consultant to the Interpublic Group of Companies, 'Promotions must be as creative as image advertising, and fully as effective in building brand equity'.

Each of the seven basic consumer promotion techniques reviewed offer opportunities for building positive brand attitude.

Coupons

Coupons are frequently used to introduce a new or improved product, and as such help initiate a positive brand attitude. But to be effective, they should be *tied to the introductory advertising*. This helps channel the good feeling occasioned by being offered a chance to try the new product at a discount with a positive message about the product itself. Even when used as a short-term tactic with established brands, this good feeling will occur *as long as the coupon is not expected*. When a brand regularly uses coupons, they are no longer seen as a 'gift' from the company, but merely as the means of sustaining a lower price.

Regardless of whether a coupon is used for a new or established product, it is important to carry over the key benefit claim from the advertising to the coupon itself. If a brand is not currently advertising, the key benefit inherent in the brand's positioning should be conveyed *on the coupons*. This connects the positive reward of the discount with the brand's key benefit claim, reinforcing positive brand attitude. Additionally, this message will be reinforced each time the coupon is reviewed by the consumer, right up until it is surrendered at the store. If there is a clear image or representation of the package on the coupon, it will help facilitate recognition brand awareness where appropriate (which is generally the case for all fmcg products).

Sampling

Sampling is a promotion technique that should stimulate a positive brand attitude. The consumer is being offered something for nothing (or a significantly reduced price), and, especially for new products, this provides an opportunity to quickly establish a positive brand attitude. In one sense, a person is already at least somewhat favourably inclined towards the brand or they would not accept and use the sample. But the sample itself will help nurture that initial positive attitude. The packaging and representation of the sample also offers an opportunity for building positive brand attitude.

Refunds and rebates

Refund and rebate offers made through traditional advertising media have a built-in opportunity of integrating the promotion and advertising message, and any offer that requires clipping something for mail-in provides a means of delivering the key benefit claim on the refund certificate itself. The offer should be worded in a positive way, linked to the brand, and, importantly, *unique*. Too often there is little imagination used in a refund or rebate offer. Most car rebate offers, for example, usually say nothing more than something like: 'Get 1,000 euros back!' It is important to avoid the impression that the offer is just another price-off deal.

Loyalty and reward programmes

Loyalty and reward programmes build positive brand attitude, and hence brand equity. By their nature, such programmes require product use over time before rewards are forthcoming. This provides a good opportunity for reminding the consumer of the coming reward within a positive brand attitude message, either on the package, through advertising or by direct mail. On the other hand, if the requirements for earning a reward are seen as too difficult, or if the rules change over time, this can have serious negative consequences for brand equity. Since the mid-1990s, airline frequent flyer programmes have found themselves in just such a bind. Not only are reward levels increasingly more difficult to reach, but it has also become more and more difficult to actually use frequent flyer miles for free flights because of high demand for seats. As a result, participants feel trapped in a programme and cheated by the airlines, seriously affecting the brand equity of the airlines among their most loyal customers.

Today, most people associate loyalty programmes with their frequent traveller programmes for hotels and airlines and increasingly with credit cards. But many retailers and consumer products have included reward programmes as part of their brand strategy for decades. The goal is the same, to retain customers and build brand loyalty. In the 2000s, improved digital technology provided the ability to deliver much more effective programmes by linking a reward account to a specific customer via a user ID number. This enabled brands to collect data and build profiles in real time.

As the cost of establishing and implementing reward programmes fell, more and more businesses adopted them. This, of course, presented a new problem: how to differentiate your brand's programme from your competitors. With the identification numbers a brand can track and measure specific consumer responses to a particular reward programme. Looking at who responds and what they purchase, as well as what is being talked about on social media, a brand can gain a good understanding of its users. This then provides better opportunities to forge deeper connections with customers. This works much the same way as direct marketing, which we will be talking about in Chapters 7 and 11.

Well-designed and targeted reward programmes can help build brand loyalty, but when a programme doesn't work there is always the potential for a negative impact upon brand attitude. In 2016, Starbucks announced changes in its long-time rewards programme, but it caused such a severe backlash that measures of brand perception fell by 50 per cent in just eight days following the introduction of the new programme. This led to a major European bank downgrading its outlook on Starbuck's stock (Brooke, 2016).

Loading devices

Like sampling, most loading devices automatically effect brand attitude – or should. But, loading devices such as bonus packs and money-off or price packs must *not* automatically contribute to an increase in positive brand attitudes, and when misused (for example, when offered too frequently) can have a *negative* effect on brand equity. How? If a brand has a premium image yet is often seen in price packs, it will assume a lower-price image. Even a regular-priced brand can suffer from too frequent use of reduced-price packs. This is, of course, true of *any* price promotion if it is used too often, but especially with loading devices because the lower price is visually reinforced on the package.

Bonus packs offer a better opportunity, especially when the 'bonus' is offered by way of a larger package. This offers an opportunity on the package label to reinforce brand attitude, which, coupled with the positive reward of the 'bonus', should nurture or increase positive brand attitude. If multiple unit packaging is used, while the wrapper does offer some opportunity for a reinforcing brand attitude message, it will be discarded with use. Consideration should be given to a special package as well, so that the initial favourable attitude stimulated by the multiple bonus pack at the point-of-purchase will be reinforced each time the consumer uses the product.

Premiums

Ideally, a premium is chosen to reinforce the choice of the original product or service, appealing to the same motivation as the product or service. For positively motivated brand choices, this means reinforcing the emotional response to the brand. When a brand decision is motivated by social approval, almost anything that will be seen by others and carries the brand's logo will help reinforce user brand attitude because it announces to the world the user's brand choice. Everything from jackets or other apparel with the brand's logo to things like insulated holders for beer cans might be used, but it is important that the premium, too, is consistent with the image projected by the brand.

Negatively motivated brand decisions call for premiums that are more directly related to the product or service offering the premium. For example, special folders for storing insurance policies or sun visors with a sunscreen provide positive, long-running association with the brand. As with positively motivated products, these premiums should also include the company logo or brand name. In this case, it is to remind the user of the brand and not necessarily to be noticed by others.

Selecting premiums congruent with motivation ensures positive brand attitude and the nurturing of brand equity. The most common mistake marketers make in selecting premiums is not relating them to the brand itself in a meaningful way, and not making certain they appeal to the same motivation that drives choice of the brand. But the *biggest mistake* a marketer can make is to offer a premium that is either inappropriate or unappealing to the target market. This may lead to negative attitudes towards the brand and a weakening of the brand's equity.

Fairy has not made this mistake when they offered free Timmy Time bedtime books with the purchase of their Non-Bio detergent or fabric softener (as we see in Advert 5.1). While this may not seem obvious at first, it is important to understand that the concurrent advertising campaign targeted mothers of toddlers and young children with the theme 'soften their world'. *Timmy Time* was a popular UK television show for young children for several years, making this a perfect tie-in. Additionally, by offering up to three books, one book for each proof of purchase, the promotion also acts as a loading device, encouraging multiple purchases before the offer closes.

Advert 5.1 Fairy/Timmy Time.

Source: © 2013 Aardman Animations Ltd and © 2013 Procter & Gamble.

Sweepstakes, games and contests

One of the more subtle benefits of a sweepstake or contest promotion is that by its nature it attracts people to the advertising or other sources used to announce the promotion. This is itself a good opportunity of associating the promotion with a strong brand attitude message. Beyond this, the sweepstakes, games or contests themselves should be created around the brand's perceived benefit. The stronger the link between the motivation associated with the brand decision and the promotion, the more likely it will be reinforcing a positive brand attitude and corresponding brand equity.

For example, consider Mars' Bounty bar. Bounty's positioning for many years has been based on the general theme of a tropical setting and 'a taste of paradise'. If they were to consider a sweepstake or contest where the prize was to be a holiday, what destination should the manager consider? The prize should be consistent with, and reinforce, the brand's positioning and benefit claim as we saw earlier with our Hawaiian Tropic Sunscreen example. In the same way, this would mean offering a trip to somewhere like Tahiti or some other tropical 'paradise', *not* a skiing trip in the Alps.

Incentive promotion cost

Unlike advertising, where the cost is fixed, at least in the sense of knowing what it will cost to produce and place the advertising, the cost of incentive promotions is *variable*. The eventual cost of a promotion will be directly related to the number of people responding to it. This will be true with trade and retail promotion as well as consumer promotion. For example, if a manager is expecting a normal 2 per cent redemption on a coupon drop but experiences a 10 per cent redemption, the cost of the promotion will have increased four to five times!

This will obviously have severe consequences for the brand's marketing budget. In such circumstances, it is rare that the additional business generated will be enough to cover lost revenue from otherwise-full-price purchases. The working margins for the brand will have been significantly lowered. With the surprise increase in cost from a too-successful promotion, money will need to be found from other parts of the brand's budget, disrupting the IMC plan.

Managers must carefully consider the likely cost of a promotion, thinking through all the possible consequences of a too-successful promotion. Another 'cost' of a too-successful promotion, for example, could be bad publicity following from an inability to meet demand for premium merchandise. Unless there is a prior history of a specific promotion's performance, research should be conducted to test its likely performance.

Summary

In this chapter, we have looked at promotion and its role in IMC, with special attention to incentive promotions. We began by looking at promotion strategy, noting that the primary communication objective for promotions is to stimulate immediate brand purchase intention, either for trial or repeat-purchase. In terms of IMC strategy, promotion is used as a short-term tactic, and should not be used as an ongoing programme that effectively lowers the price of the brand. The use of promotion should be carefully integrated over time in relation to the target audiences' decision process. Like all marketing communication, promotion too must address brand awareness and brand attitude.

There are three basic types of promotion: trade, retail, and consumer. Trade promotions provide incentives or merchandising activity for the trade, and make it the largest proportion of most brands' marketing budget. These promotions fall into three categories. First, allowance promotions, which include trade coupons, free product, and allowances for meeting performance goals. While not exactly a promotion, one must also consider slotting fees here. Second, promotional display material, and third, trade premiums and incentives. Retail promotions are independent of the brand, and are initiated either by the retailer or a distributor. They too fall into three categories: retail adverts, price-off promotions, and point-of-purchase displays.

Consumer promotion and retail promotion are aimed directly at consumers. While it is important from an IMC planning standpoint to discriminate between consumer promotion initiated by the manufacturer and the retailer, from the consumer standpoint there is no difference. Incentive promotions to the consumer, whether initiated by the manufacturer or retailer, fall into seven basic types: coupons, samples, refunds or rebates, loyalty and reward programmes, loading devices, premiums, and sweepstakes, games and contests. Coupons, samples and refunds or rebates are used primarily to generate trial, while loyalty and reward programmes, loading devices and sweepstakes, games and contests are used for stimulating repeat purchase. Premiums may be used for either trial or repeat-purchase objectives, but usually repeat purchase.

Coupons make sense when the brand has a small budget, and for new product introductions. Sampling is a good promotion technique when a brand has a demonstrable difference, or when advertising cannot adequately demonstrate the brand's benefit. Refunds and rebates are effective for expensive products or services, and can be a good defensive tactic against a strong competitor. Loyalty and reward programmes are used to defend against switching and loading devices when a new competitor is about to enter the market. Premiums provide an opportunity for selected appeal, and can also encourage retailers to use point-of-purchase displays. Sweepstakes, games and contests can provide a unifying theme for all promotional activity, and a chance to reinforce a brand's positioning in advertising. They also provide an opportunity for in-store merchandising activity.

Finally, it must be remembered that there are costs associated with promotion, and when a promotion is too successful, the unexpected increased costs can have a significantly negative effect on the marketing budget.

Review questions

1 How would you describe promotion?
2 What is the role of promotion in IMC?
3 Discuss how trade promotion is used in IMC.
4 What are the primary goals for retail promotions?
5 Discuss how best to present prices in a retail promotion.
6 In what ways can a retail store environment effect sales?
7 What are the key differences among consumer promotions?
8 How do retail promotions differ from consumer promotions?
9 What are the similarities between trade promotion and consumer promotion?
10 Why are some incentive promotions more appropriate for gaining trial and others for repeat purchase?
11 Discuss the advantages and disadvantages of both printed and electronic coupons.

12 When would you be likely to use a coupon rather than a rebate, and when a rebate rather than a coupon?

13 Discuss situations where it would be effective to use loading devices.

14 How can promotion be used to help build positive brand attitude?

15 Find examples of sweepstakes where the prize is not consistent with the brand's image, and discuss the implications.

16 What might be a good premium for a beer brand? What about for a major appliance, a tanning salon, a restaurant?

17 Why can a too-successful promotion be harmful for a brand?

References

Advertising Age (1995) Report on a study of consumer buying habits, 20 October.

Brooke, Z. (2016) Rewards, Refunds, and Ringside Seats. *Marketing News*, 31 May.

Donovan, A.J., Rossiter, J.R., Morcoolyn, G. and Nesdale, A. (1994) Store atmosphere and purchasing behaviour. *Journal of Retailing*, *70* (3), 283–294.

Fabrikant, G. (2015) Rembrandt and the buttocks-bearing dress: The Rijksmuseum's risk-taking director. *ARTNews*, September, 66–73.

Fill, C. (1995) *Marketing Communications: Frameworks, Theories, and Applications.* London: Prentice Hall, p. 376.

Friedmann, R. and Hains, P. (1991) An investigation of comparative price advertising and newspapers. *Journal of Current Issues and Research Advertising*, *13*(1), 155–173.

Gibson, R. (1992) The fine art of stocking supermarket shelves. *The Wall Street Journal*, 15 October, B1 and B10.

Krishna, A., Currin, I.S. and Shoemaker, R.W. (1991) Consumer perceptions of promotional activity. *Journal of Marketing*, *55*(2), 4–16.

Lans, M.S. (1994) Legal Hurdles Being Part of Promotion Game. *Marketing News*, 24 October, *15*.

Leenheer, J., van Heerden, H.J., Bijmolt, T.H.A. and Sundh, A. (2007) Do loyalty programs really enhance behavioural loyalty: An empirical analysis accounting for self-selecting members. *International Journal of Research and Marketing*, *24*(1), 31–47.

Milliman, R.E. (1982) Using background music to effect the behaviour of supermarket shoppers. *Journal of Marketing*, *46*(3), 86–91.

Mittelstadt, C.A. (1993) The coming era of image-building promotions, lecture given at Yale University, 3 March.

Prentice, R.M. (1977) How to Split Your Marketing Funds between Advertising and Promotion. *Advertising Age*, 10 January, *41*.

Roehm, M., Pullins, E. and Roehm, H. (2002) Designing loyalty-building programs for packaged good brands. *Journal of Marketing Research*, *XXXIX*, 202–213.

Rossiter, J.R. and Percy, L. (1997) *Advertising Communication and Promotion Management.* New York: McGraw-Hill.

Rossiter, J.R., Percy, L. and Berkvist, L. (2018) *Marketing Communications: Objectives, Strategy, Tactics.* London: SAGE Publications.

Schindler, R.M. (1991) Symbolic meanings of price-endings. in R.H. Holman and M.A. Soloman (eds) *Association for Consumer Research: 18.* Provo UT: Association for Consumer Research, 794–789.

Sorenson, H. (2003) The science of shopping. *Marketing Research*, *15*(3), 30–35.

Stecklow, S. (2005) Obsessive coupon disorder. *The Wall Street Journal*, 19–20 November, *5*.

Triplett, T. (1994) Report of couponing's death has been greatly exaggerated. *Marketing News*, 10 October, *1*.

Wansink, B. (2003) Developing a cost-effective brand loyalty program. *Journal of Advertising Research*, *43*, 301–309.

Weiss, B. (2010) Groupon's $6 billion gamble. *The Wall Street Journal*, 15 December, *A15*.

6　Media

The world of media continues to change, providing an ever-expanding variety of options for delivering integrated marketing communication (IMC) messages. But as these options grow, it is important to remember that regardless of how a message is delivered, the principles of message processing remain the same because the brain is still only dealing with audible or written words and visual images. One must still pay attention and learn something. It is also important to understand that any medium, traditional or digital, may be used to deliver an IMC message. The specific media chosen, however, as we shall see in Chapter 12, will depend on the processing requirements of the message.

The media environment has indeed been changing rapidly over the last several years, fuelled by the growth in digital media. In 2020, worldwide advertising spend on digital media was US$ 341 billion versus all other traditional media spend at US$ 379 billion (print, video, and television). But in the United States digital media had surpassed all other traditional media, with digital advertising at US$ 151 billion versus US$ 107 billion.

Things are much changed since the first text message was sent to a mobile phone in the United States in 1992, and since banner adverts made their debut in 1994. Along with these changes has also come significant audience fragmentation within media and new ways of delivering IMC messages that now include something called 'street media'. Often intrusive and far-out, it could be adverts on the walls of toilets, graffiti-style adverts on sidewalks (used to introduce Xbox in Sydney), or semi-permanently tattooed adverts on the foreheads of university students, who in London were paid around £10 to wear the tattooed advert for three hours.

With digital media, while one might expect very little audience concentration, in fact there is. This is because a very few players account for huge audiences (in terms of monthly reach), with significant fall-off after the market leaders: Google at 59 per cent and Yahoo at 52 per cent, along with a few others in the 30–36 per cent range – YouTube, MSN, ACL, and Facebook (Webster, 2014). As a result, the internet audience tends to be much more concentrated than television audiences.

Finally, as a result of all the changes in media, companies are looking outside of traditional marketing communication agencies, working with more groups, and giving assignments to smaller firms. This, of course, makes IMC even more important for effective communication of a brand's message, and, unfortunately, more difficult. More than half of the top 50 global advertisers now work with groups of staff from Google and Facebook, sometimes even embedded in their own marketing department. They help them learn the intricacies of the constant changes in their digital platform and help the brand with new technologies, and what is likely to work for them. For example, Omnicom Group's (one of the largest advertising agency holding companies) new

DOI: 10.4324/9781003169635-8

'agency of the future' for McDonalds included people from Google and Facebook on the brand's team (Neff, 2016). In this chapter, we will be discussing some important media concepts, followed by a more in-depth look at digital media. We shall also look at a few interesting consequences, or what one might think of as unintended 'side effects', of the application of new technology to viewing and purchasing media.

Media concepts

While the media world has certainly changed over the last 25 years, and continues to change, providing many more potential mediums to deliver an IMC programme, the basics of media planning have not changed. There are indeed more choices and different ways of buying media driven by technology. But in the end, one must still match the media to the processing requirements of the communication strategy. We shall be dealing with media strategy in Chapter 12, 'The IMC Planning Process'. Here, we shall be looking at some general media concepts important to IMC.

Target audience factor

Obviously, the first step required for successful IMC is for the target audience to have an opportunity to be exposed to the message. We shall be talking about how to select a target audience in Chapter 12, but here we want to look at the relationship between the target audience and media generally. Of course, the target audience must *choose* to be exposed to media.

There have been important changes in how people consume media with the growth of technology and digital media. In the past, radio and television were listened to and watched in a 'linear' way, with a stream of programming designed to keep viewers and listeners engaged with the same channel or station from one programme to the next. Today, even with the traditional broadcast media there are DVR's (digital video recorder) and VOD's (video on demand), as well as online access to it, where users can decide what and when to tune in, and, of course, this is the case with digital media and web-based platforms such as YouTube and Netflix. Most media today is now consumed in a non-linear fashion.

People have relationships not only with brands, but also with media; and this has become even more important with the growth of social media. Out of the wide range of available media, individuals can assemble their own 'network' and actively edit what they are using (Tillery, 2011). This relationship of the target audience to their personal media can be as important as their relationships to brands because (especially with social media) this relationship helps define their worldview. It is the source of their information and entertainment, and more.

Just as with brands, the target audience's attitudes and emotions associated with various media will drive the choice of the media they use. What programmes are 'must see'? What print media (newspapers and magazines) are 'must reads'? It would clearly be better to advertise in 'must' media, not just media that is watched or read. The emotional and attitudinal involvement will mean greater attention is paid to the message, and it will be processed within a more favourable context. Again, this is especially true with social media. Any particular medium may be seen as trustworthy or not, elicit positive emotional associations or none at all (or worse, a negative association). Understanding such personal relationships with a particular medium helps maximize the potential effectiveness of IMC media choice.

Reach and frequency

While there are many media concepts that are important to effective IMC media planning, most are beyond the scope of this book. However, it is essential to understand reach and frequency, and their relationships to continuity (the number of advertising cycles over the planning period, usually one year) in an IMC campaign. In developing a media plan, managers must take into account the trade-offs among these concepts that underlay all media plans. Given a fixed budget, any change in reach, frequency, or continuity will require a change in one or both of the other factors. If you want to reach more people with the same budget you will need to either lower the frequency of reaching them, or advertise less often. The same goes for any changes in frequency or continuity. To increase the frequency with which you reach your target audience, you must lower the overall reach, or settle for less continuity. And if you want to advertise more frequently, say every week rather than every other week, this will take up more of the budget, necessitating less reach and/or frequency when you are advertising. The only way around this, of course, is an increase in the media budget.

Broad reach vs. frequency

In 2014, Proctor and Gamble ran a coupon for their air freshener Febreze, targeting pet owners and large families because of their heavier usage of air fresheners. Sales did not increase during the campaign, but did when the target audience was broadened to anyone over 18 years of age. As the chief executive of a company that tests the effectiveness of adverts put it: 'If you could run an ad and reach a million people or run a targeted ad to reach 5,000 you would have to have a pretty impressive return on that 5,000 to make it worth it'.

Source: Terlep and Seetharaman (2016)

By definition, *reach* is the percentage of the target audience that is exposed to an IMC message within a given time period (usually four weeks). *Frequency* is the average number of times any one member of the target audience has the opportunity to see or hear the message within a time period. Unfortunately, neither of these common definitions are of much use in advanced IMC media planning, because they simply are not related to the IMC media plan's effectiveness (Rossiter and Percy, 1997).

Consider the idea of reach as the percentage of the target audience exposed to an advert or promotion at least once in a given time period, or even the idea of *communicative reach*, the percentage reached at least once over a larger time period (say the length of a campaign). Truly effective reach would only occur in the very rare case where the minimum effective frequency (a concept discussed below) is equal to one and the advertising cycle corresponds to the standard period used in conventional media measurement; or in the case of cumulative reach, corresponds to that longer period. What is needed is *effective* reach, which is the number of individuals in the target audience that will be reached at the minimum effective frequency level.

The problem with using average frequency in media planning is the same problem you have with any average. You do not know what the distribution is. If the average frequency is four, that might mean everyone in the target audience is exposed four times, or half the target four times, a quarter two times, and the remaining quarter six times. We know nothing about the plan's effectiveness. Additionally, as Rossiter et al. (2018) have correctly pointed out, average frequency will almost always exaggerate the frequency with which the typical target audience member is reached.

What is needed is an estimate of the *effective* frequency. Media planning should focus upon the role of effective frequency in increasing the disposition to purchase or act. Effective frequency must reflect the number of exposures required in an advertising cycle for each member of the target audience to successfully process the message. The issue is, within an advertising cycle, how many exposures will be needed to effectively process the message at least once?

In estimating the effective frequency needed for a campaign, you must be primarily interested in the *minimum* frequency needed to increase the target audience intention to act. In most IMC situations, the minimum effective frequency (MEF) will be at least two or three exposures within an advertising cycle, which is generally one week. Factors that go into estimating MEF include the target audience, brand awareness and brand attitude communication objectives, and the extent that personal influence is involved. Essentially, these factors will inform the extent to which more than one exposure will be required to optimize the likelihood the message will be attended to and processed. A complete discussion of this and a formula for estimating MEF, along with adjustments for specific advert units such as commercial length, print advert size, etc., may be found in Rossiter et al. (2018).

Fixed versus mobile media

Wilson and Till (2012) have offered an interesting way of looking at what they call non-traditional media; media other than traditional broadcast, print, and digital. These non-traditional media often play an important part in IMC. While Wilson and Till do not deal with the actual processing of the message, they make some good points about *how* these non-traditional media are attended to. In their framework they are looking at non-traditional media in terms of whether the message and/or target audience is 'fixed' or 'mobile'.

Messages would be 'fixed' in such non-traditional media as in-store videos, grocery shopping cart boards or video games, and they would be 'mobile' in such media as taxi boards or bus wraparounds. Note, however, that they are not talking about mobile in the sense of mobile phones as discussed later in this chapter, but advertising that is itself moving. The second dimension in their framework deals with the target audience and whether they are 'fixed' (or in their terms, 'captive') or 'mobile'.

They use this framework, in a sense, to identify how much effort will be needed to attend to and effectively process a message delivered in non-traditional media. If the target audience and the media delivering the message are both fixed, it should be easy for the target audience to process the message. This would be the case, for example, if someone was queuing at a store check-out and a video was easily seen. If the target audience is fixed but the media is not, there will be much less time available to fully process the message. This would be the case, say, if you were sitting on a bench and a bus with a wrap-around message went by. Just the opposite would occur if the person was moving and the media delivering the message fixed, but the processing potential would be same – much less time to attend to the message. Finally, when both the target audience and the media are moving, it would require a special effort to attend to and process the communication.

Why might it be important to look at media in this way? If the target audience and the media delivering the message fall within this fixed versus mobile framework, there will be different levels of distraction competing for the target audience's attention, and this should inform how complex the message might be. Wilson and Till (2012) call this 'matching cognitive congruency', but simply put it means the more likely there is to be a distraction, the simpler the message should be.

It is critical for the manager to understand what will be required for the effective processing of a message, which differs depending on the brand awareness and attitude strategies involved. This is because the processing requirements will dictate media selection. What we have been discussing above relates to the *available time to process* the message. Some advertising, for example that for high-involvement products (which we talk about in Chapter 10), requires more time to process. Other media selection criteria linked to processing requirements include visual content and frequency. We will be dealing with this in more detail in Chapter 13 when we talk about media selection.

Digital media

Again, there is no question that technology is changing the way in which people live. Inevitably, this means new opportunities for marketing communication and how it might be used in an IMC campaign. As this section is being written, the world of digital media continues to expand, fuelled by social media. As you read this, things may have moved well beyond what we are about to discuss; just as much of what we are talking about here would not have been a part of a textbook written five years ago.

Nevertheless, the really important point to bear in mind is that while 'digital media' will continue to evolve and new means of delivering messages will be introduced, those messages will still be made from text, audio, and visuals. Media change, but how the mind processes the message remains the same. Bavelier and Green (2011) have under-scored this, pointing out that technological change does not alter the fundamental abilities of the brain, and the general principles of brain organization are not likely to have changed since the advent of language. The strategic planning process remains the same. Digital media is only that; new ways of delivering a message to a brand's target audience that may or may not make sense as part of the brand's IMC programme.

There is no denying that there has been a tremendous surge of ever-evolving options for delivering marketing communication. However, even as increasing shares of media budgets are directed to digital media, there is no evidence that this is actually an *effective* way to deliver advertising and other marketing communication. For example, adverts on Snapchat only average about three seconds in length, which raises very real questions about attention and processing (Sloane, 2016). Facebook, in the autumn of 2016, ad-mitted that for two years they gave marketers inflated estimates of the average time users spent watching their online clips (Meyer, 2017).

While there appears to be at least some anecdotal evidence, especially for promotions, the rush by marketers to digital media may be nothing more than a desire not to be left behind. As Don Schultz (2010), one of the early 'fathers' of IMC, put it a decade ago, 'The question, though, is are all these heady measures of new media a sign of a gold-rush of a new-and-improved advertising and marketing opportunities or simply fool's gold?' Rance Crain (2011), who was the long-time editor of the leading advertising trade publication, *Advertising Age*, has said, 'It seems to me that the more prevalent social media becomes, the less we know about the power of persuasion', and 'Advertisers don't even know what the primary purpose of social media is supposed to be'. This would still seem to be true even as more and more money is being spent on advertising in digital media.

A disturbing misconception linked to the rapid growth of digital media, especially social media, is that owing to this incredible growth the nature of advertising must be changing. It is not, period. As we just saw, the way people process messages in digital media is no different to how they process messages delivered in any other media. And as we pointed out at the beginning of this book, the role of advertising and other marketing communication has not changed (Rossiter and Percy, 2013). Its role is, and always has been, to lead to more sales of a brand or service, or to obtain a higher price than consumers would be willing to pay in the absence of marketing communication.

With all this in mind, we now turn to a discussion of some specific digital media.

Internet

The first banner advert appeared on the internet in October of 1994 with an ATT 'teaser' advert in the online edition of *Wired* magazine. In the years that followed, relatively little was spent on internet advertising, but in 2005 global spending was around US$ 18 billion, and by 2010 was US$ 63 billion (Advertising Age, 2015). By 2014, worldwide spending on internet advertising was 24 per cent of total advertising worldwide, estimated to reach 42 per cent a total of online spend worldwide of US$ 333 billion (AdAge, 2018). In 2020, digital advertising passed traditional television advertising in the United States for the first time, although not worldwide. Projections have spending on digital advertising exceeding two-thirds of all advertising spending by 2023 (Shabam, 2019). The increases in digital advertising spending in part comes from a sharp decline in print media, especially newspapers, and other traditional media. In effect, brands were almost forced into digital media in order to achieve their reached frequency objectives.

Google enjoys by far the greatest share of digital advertising, reaching an estimated 1,200 million users monthly worldwide. Their share of digital advertising revenue is 29.8 per cent, well ahead of Facebook at 23 per cent, Amazon at 10 per cent, and all others accounting for only 32.9 per cent. There are many reasons for Google's dominance in the market. They can place adverts almost anywhere, from new sites to apps to online games; and they can be placed next to articles or within videos. However, in 2022, the European Union and the United Kingdom opened formal antitrust investigations into whether Google and Facebook sought to illegally cooperate in digital advertising, and in the United States a group of states were also suing, claiming that Google gave Meta (Facebook's parent company) preferred terms in order to exclude or hinder competition (Schenchner, 2022).

But in 2018, a shift of advert-spending to Amazon began. Up until then, most retailers and brands, with the exception of small local ones, almost by necessity needed to advertise on Google search engines. But owing to changes in shopping behaviour, much of the money spent on Google for advertising began shifting to Amazon. In 2018, the world's largest advert buyer, WPP PLC, spent US$ 300 million for search adverts with Amazon, and 75 per cent of that came from previous Google search budgets (Vranica 2020).

While there is no questioning the growth of digital media and internet advertising, there are some signs that all is not necessarily well. By 2013, many websites began to significantly cut back on their use of banner adverts, for example. And according to Google, by 2014, banner adverts were only being clicked 0.09 per cent of the time, and over half the adverts were never seen by anyone (Kantrowitz, 2014). Add to this that users of digital media are irritated by *all* digital advertising. A 2016 study covering 28 countries worldwide underscores the problem, finding large numbers of users unhappy with digital adverts, and thinking about purchasing adblocking systems. We shall have more to say about this later in the chapter when we deal with a number of concerns over digital media.

An increasing concern with using the internet (and other new media) for marketing communication is the extent to which the marketer can maintain control over the brand's message. Traditional media allow for tight control over the brand's message. But with new media a brand's message is increasingly beyond its control, especially with what has become known as 'word of mouse', messages within a brand or anti-brand community that are user generated (about which more in the section on social media). This potential for unauthorized and uncontrolled brand messages raises serious concerns about how and where to include new media as part of an IMC media strategy.

Widgets, which are small computer programmes that allow people to incorporate professional-looking content into their personal web pages on desk-top computers, are seen by many major marketers as the next generation of advertising on the internet. They see sponsoring widgets as a promising way to reach consumers because they integrate advertising onto their web pages. Widgets are considered a better approach than banner advertisements and less annoying than a video that takes over the screen. Reebok, for example, created a widget that allows users to display customized RBK shoes for others to critique (Steel, 2006).

Some other ways in which the internet is being used to deliver online advertising include delivering advertising-like messages using video games (more about this later in the chapter); online radio, where listeners can respond to an advertisement by clicking on a box at the station site to be directed to the advertised brand's website; entertainment programming created for the web that weaves product endorsements into the storyline; the ability to stop video and click to purchase clothing worn by the actors, and in-text advertising, appearing on some mainstream journalistic websites, where a pop-up advertisement appears when the cursor is moved over a keyword. And in New York and London campaigns that let people interact with posters at bus stops, train stations, airports, and ferries have been tested (Ante, 2011).

Streaming video is also used to offer mini movies where a brand features prominently. These videos are often cutting edge, and can quickly create an incredibly strong 'buzz'. BMW, on their BMWfilms.com site (separate from their home page), offer short, streamed films produced by well-known producers and directors, and with well-known actors (Iezzi, 2010).

In addition to advertising on the internet, promotion-like messages and specific incentive promotions are delivered on websites such as Fatwallet.com and send out daily early-morning email alerts for online bargains; sites like GottaDeal.com provide information about mail-in rebate, and sites such as CouponMountain.com and CouponCraze.com make it possible to print out coupons for both store and online retailers.

Unlike other digital media, there are good measures of exposure for the internet. For any time period, it is possible to measure the number of times someone clicks on an advertisement, opens it or downloads it. This provides an opportunity to test and make modifications at short notice. However, as we shall see later, there are potentially serious issues with fraud that could significantly distort these measures.

Internet and online marketing communication companies are acquiring better tools for targeting display advertisements to specific groups of users. Yahoo and Microsoft monitor the search habits of users in order to better direct messages to people visiting their own or partner websites. This is done through something called 'behaviour targeting' that analyses online activity (Delaney and Steel, 2007). The ability to target specific consumers has often been considered one of the real strengths of digital media and internet advertising. Facebook has spent years developing an ability to tightly target users in terms of demographics, shopping behaviour and life milestones. But such targeting is now thought to have limited effectiveness. Case studies have shown that advertisers gain more sales by reaching a larger proportion of a platform's overall audience, as we noted in an earlier 'box'. The thinking now, especially among major brands, is to return to the more traditional idea of the need for broad reach and less targeted media (Terlep and Seetharaman, 2016).

Network TV targeted adverts

Despite the fact that some large advertisers are questioning the use of highly targeted media to optimize reach, targeted adverts are now possible on network television. Sometimes described as the television industry's Holy Grail, targeted adverts where next-door neighbours watching the same program could see different commercials are finally possible. With the ability of digital media to tightly target, the model for network television advert sales that relied upon broad, general target audience descriptions based on demographics was long outdated. It was the lack of a natural measurement for such targeted television adverts that had proved to be the impediment. There was not the types of data needed to make it work. But now, Nielson, a leading TV-rating company, is measuring targeted television adverts. This was a fundamental shift in how they had previously measured commercial viewership. Now, instead of calculating an average audience for all adverts in a program, they measure each advert individually, something necessary for targeted adverts on television to work.

The Wall Street Journal, 11 November 2020

Social media

Facebook is by far the largest social networking site, reaching some 1,900 million monthly users, with an estimated annual revenue from advertising of US $18.76 per user (Rossiter et al., 2018). Twitter, the next largest social networking site has only 313 million monthly users, while other social networking sites such as Snapchat and BuzzFeed are only a fraction of that. LinkedIn, a business networking site, has an estimated per user revenue of US$ 10.74, comparable to Twitter.

What exactly is social media? While there are many definitions, perhaps the most widely used is that offered by Kaplan and Haenlein (2010). They talk about social media as 'a group of internet-based applications that build on the ideological and technological foundation of Web 2.0, and that allow the creation and execution of User Generated Content'. Some distinguishing features of social marketing identified by Mayfield (2008) are that it uses techniques that enable a high level of user participation, encourages 'openness' and conversation with few barriers to access, and has a high degree of 'connectiveness' that enables users to find and interact with others.

According to Gangadharbatla (2012), a common thread found running through all the services and websites comprising social media is that most content is created by users, and there are no gatekeepers to content. This, of course, can lead to the problem of un-authorized brand messages, as pointed out earlier. Another very real potential for trouble is the incredible speed with which damage to a brand can be done, even by a single individual who in seconds can tell a hundred of their closest friends about their 'problem' with a brand. This then grows exponentially, reaching millions by way of their social grid, on YouTube, or any number of other ways (Iezzi, 2010).

Like traditional media, social media rely heavily on advertising revenue for survival. But, unlike traditional media where advertising has become more-or-less accepted as the price to be paid for access to the content, users of social media are not at all happy with the intrusion of advertising. Yet at the same time, they are not willing to pay for social media content (Nielson, 2010). This no doubt follows from the fact that social media were not created as marketing communication venues, but as personal media.

Marketers have found some unique ways of capitalizing on social media. Pinterest, a social network with some 70 million unique visitors a month permits users to 'pin' unique images of their favourite places. Some marketers have directly commissioned 'influencers', users who have cultivated large followings on Pinterest (often bloggers), to pin up their brands. But, Pinterest earns nothing from this. As a result, in 2014, they introduced a service for marketers that would enable them to purchase what they called 'provided pins'. While many brands continue to only use influencers, others are now using both. Those using both have found it provides a significant lift, doubling traffic to their websites (Shields and Marshall, 2015). Some popular Instagram users now provide product placements in their pictures, charging a nominal fee like €1 per 'like' of a picture that includes the brand.

As with the internet generally, there are a number of concerns with using social media for IMC. Issues of privacy have become even more of a concern given the more persistent nature of social media. Often users are unaware that personal data are being collected and sold. Digital marketing companies such as Ditto Labs and Pijora analyse pictures that are culled from 'selfies' on some social media for indications of brand and product usage to use for better targeting. They look for images with, say, logos or a particular food product, and see if the faces look happy or are smiling. Taking this even further, they can check for certain behaviour patterns, for example seeing if certain brands of a beverage are being drunk with particular foods or snacks, and whether people are smiling in the picture. Child advocacy groups have warned that such practices could lead to predatory marketing.

Another concern for marketers is that social media users often cannot be sure if an advert they see is actually from the brand. Yet another is how quickly a brand's image can be affected through social media. Just one person's displeasure, real or imagined, or for revenge or spite, can be sent in a second to their 100 closest friends, then by way of their social grid on YouTube or countless other ways, on to millions. We shall be addressing a number of digital media concerns later in the chapter.

Additionally, there is no evidence as to the effectiveness of social media as advertising vehicles. At the beginning of this chapter, we pointed out the doubts of Rance Crain, editor of *Advertising Age*, and Don Schultz. Schultz has also suggested that marketers seem to feel a certain 'need' for social media strategies, regardless of any evidence of measurable results, because of the 'boxcar numbers of participants or the fear of being left behind' (Schultz, 2010). The editor-at-large of *Advertising Age* has wondered what a 'tweet' in-fluences a person to do, think, or behave. Burger King's extremely popular Subservient

Chicken promotion, while marking a 'watershed in the new era of interactive creativity', according to Iezzi (2010), seems to have had little, if any, effect on sales (Ries, 2011).

Social-traditional media interactions

Integrating traditional media and social media can often make good sense. A well-known example involves Mentos. In 2006 a group called Eepybird began dropping Mentos mints into 2-litre bottles of Diet Coke, resulting in a fountain of soda exploding from the bottle. The images were posted on YouTube, and in four years over 500 million people had seen them. While Diet Coke was slow to pick up on the marketing potential, Mentos was not. They created a tie-in with Eepybird and the fountain images, leading Mentos heavily into social media. On the other hand, Mentos chewing gum spends millions on traditional media. This interaction between traditional media for one product and social media for another builds Mentos *brand* awareness and positive attitude for both the mints and chewing gum.

Source: *Advertising Age*, 3 January 2011

We do not want to forget that the applications of digital media are being incorporated into more traditional media as we see in the English Heritage Buildings advertisement shown in Advert 6.1. It provides an excellent example of how a brand can use traditional media, print in this case, to drive people to their website. Other examples include new single-advertiser issues of magazines, delivered electronically, and advertisements with microchips embedded in them allowing for sound.

Elaborate online campaigns now marry brand pitches with high-tech entertainment. For example, someone opens an email that presents a fictional newspaper with a headline reading: 'Another slaying at Datadyne HQ'. There is a link that sends you to a video of an autopsy, and the camera pans down to a tag on the toe of the body with the person's name. A video game from Microsoft's Xbox is then advertised, with an invitation to send the link to a friend. If the link is forwarded, the person's phone rings and a recorded message from the video game's heroine announces, 'The job is done'. An email then arrives from the heroine with a picture of another dead body, but with their friend's name on the toe tag.

Mobile

In 1992, the first text message was sent in the United Kingdom from a computer to a mobile phone. But it was the new millennium that saw an expanding use of web-enabled mobile handsets. This was especially true in Scandinavian and Asian countries. Today, 2.1 billion people worldwide own a smartphone. While banner advertisements appeared on mobile phones as early as the year 2000 on the Pacific Rim, they did not immediately catch on in other areas because major carriers in the United States and Europe feared they would not be acceptable to their customers. A study (Katsukura et al., 2005) reported that in the early 2000s, for example, roughly 55 per cent of people in Japan had signed up for internet access on their mobile phones compared with only 12 per cent in the United States. But by the mid-2000s, major mobile phone networks in the United States (Sprint Nextel and Verizon) and the United Kingdom (Vodafone Group) had introduced advertising on their wireless information and entertainment services (Yuan and Bryan-Low, 2006). This was

Where
your
building
starts.

Where your imagination begins.

Announcing the launch of our brand new website, where you will find
endless inspirational ideas for your new oak framed building.

What's more, we've included information covering all aspects of
the building process, from Building Regulations to finishing touches.
You'll even be able to watch actual time lapse films of existing builds,
erected from start to finish.

Visit **www.ehbp.com** and take a look for yourself.

NEW WEBSITE ONLINE NOW

Advert 6.1 English heritage buildings.

Source: © English Heritage Buildings.

encouraged by advances in phone technology. Early mobile phones were designed solely
for calling, not downloading. But mobile phones now offer large colour screens and data
connections, making them much like small computers. In the United States, people spend
more time with mobile devices than with print media (Advertising Age, 2012).

As we have already noted, mobile is driving the growth of digital media advertising revenue, accounting in 2016 for US$ 100 billion or 50 per cent of all digital advertising spending worldwide. It is expected to be US$ 215 billion by 2020, or some three-quarters of all digital media advertising revenue worldwide. However, this revenue is concentrated, with only a few players. Google accounts for about one-third of all mobile internet advertising revenue worldwide, some US$ 34 billion, with Facebook a distant second at about US$ 18 billion. Only two others have revenue over US$ 5 billion, Alibaba (US$ 9.2 billion) and Baida (US$ 7.1 billion), with all the remaining one-third (US$ 31.8 billion) spread among all the other mobile media (*The Wall Street Journal*, 2016).

The Mobile Marketing Association (2005) in the United Kingdom has defined mobile marketing as: 'The use of the mobile medium as the communications and entertainment channel between a brand and an end user. Mobile marketing is the only personal channel enabling spontaneous, direct, interactive and/or target communications, any time, any place'. But as pointed out by Vittet-Philippe and Navarro (2000), mobile marketing involves much more than simply mobile telephoning. The key is the target audiences' willingness to receive advertisements on their mobile devices.

Research indicates that users find mobile advertising far more annoying than television advertising (Advertising Age, 2012). In fact, as discussed in the box below, there are questions about the actual potential for mobile advertising. But advertising on mobile devices appeals to marketers because they can tightly target their messages, as well as control message environment and time of exposure.

Mobile–advert tactics

While mobile advertising has been heralded as the 'next big thing' in delivering marketing communication since the introduction of the iPhone in 2007, it has not lived up to expectation. In 2010, Apple's Steve Jobs is quoted as saying, 'Mobile advertising really sucks'. Even though smartphones continue to proliferate, the research company eMarketer estimated that in 2012 less than 2 percent of all US marketing dollars were spent on mobile advertising. A number of issues militate against mobile advertising, including not being able to buy extensive exposure and a lack of good measures of effectiveness.

Even without a good measure of effectiveness, marketing experience with mobile advertising is beginning to identify some of the things that seem to work, and some things to avoid. What seems to work are advertisements that play on mobile's unique properties for games and providing fast information. The largest expenditure in mobile goes for search advertisements. They not only offer something the user wants, information, but also a good measure of user responses. About half of all US mobile spending on advertising is for search advertisements, according to eMarketer. Large consumer marketers like Kraft Foods and giant retailer Macy's are trying to create advertising for mobiles that will be seen as fun, as well as providing desired information.

What doesn't seem to work is when companies simply take their web advertising and use it on mobiles. Banner advertisements, the boxes or rectangle advertising appearing on mobile websites or apps, have come to be known by marketers as 'Spray and Pray'. Even though there is a consensus among both users and companies that banner advertising on mobiles looks cheap and is annoying, eMarketer found that it represents about 20 percent of all US mobile advertising.

Source: *The Wall Street Journal*, 28 September 2012

Coupons are available on mobile phones, sent via display advertisements in text messages. However, redemption can pose problems if retailers cannot read the mobile barcodes. But, technology is in place to overcome these difficulties. Another interesting application of mobile advertising involves one of the oldest forms of advertising, outdoor. Outdoor advertising has become the second fastest-growing form of advertising, behind the internet. Billboards now have the ability to electronically beam information to mobile phones. There are also mobile servers that permit targeting based on where the phone is so the user can receive localized content or offers. But, marketers should have the user's permission to communicate with them through location-based services, or risk irritating their consumers and affecting brand attitude.

This perhaps represents the optimum in tracking message exposure, although the potential is there for all mobile marketing communication. Additionally, this information enables the brand to build a strong database, and, much like direct marketing (discussed in Chapter 10), effective mobile marketing must be driven by consumer data (Peltier et al., 2003).

Yet with all of these applications, the phone itself constrains its potential for advertising and IMC. Not only do mobile users resent the intrusion of adverts, but if the medium itself is to continue growing and become a major platform for the future, it will need to deal with the challenge of generating impact with adverts on a small screen.

Online and in-game video

Marketers are increasingly tapping the growing video game market, creating another opportunity for IMC via in-game advertising. In 2007, online video became the fastest-growing category of internet advertising, spurred on by the internet user's dislike of pop-up adverts (Oser, 2004) and pre-roles, where you are forced to watch an advert before seeing the video clip (Delaney and Steel, 2007), which they confront with the traditional use of the internet. By 2015, in the United States alone 33 million adults were using their smartphones to play games online (AdAge, 2018). But as online-video continues to grow, there is no real consensus on what does and does not work.

There are two basic ways to include advertising in online games: product placement within the game and the creation of a free online game promoting the brand, known as an 'advergame'. One very innovative game created for Charles Chocolate, a small San Francisco brand, enabled players to actually purchase a version of the virtual chocolate they created in the game (Stutsky, 2011).

With advergames, there should be a strong congruence between the product category and the game created. Studies have shown that this generally results in a better memory (Gross, 2010). This likely follows from the notion of spreading activation theory (Anderson, 1983) because of the strong relationship between the brand and the game content. This same idea also applies to promotion sweepstakes, games and contests, as we shall see in the last chapter.

If product placement is used in online video games, there should be a carefully considered placement strategy developed to determine where to best place the brand in the game, something referred to as brand prominence (Caubergne and DePelsmaker, 2010) or product placement proximity (Lee and Faber, 2007). And as with any product placement, the product must make 'sense' within the context of the game, and be fully integrated within a central part of the game. Yet even then, there is little evidence of the effectiveness of product placement, something we shall discuss in the next chapter. With product placement, there are the same ethical considerations attending to any use of product placement, again something we will be addressing when we deal with product placement more generally in the next chapter.

Usage issues

The more people report using social media such as Facebook, the worse they feel after using it. In one study, over the course of two weeks, the more people used Facebook, the more their overall well-being declined (Kross, 2013). Also, Facebook use was found to cause a rise in feelings of jealousy and envy when compared with the perceived happy lives of friends. Studies of children and teenagers have shown that the more they use Facebook, the less satisfaction they report having with life, and the more time they spend seeking feedback on social media, the more they report depressive symptoms. Another study found that mobile phone use could exacerbate depression in young adults (Viskontas, 2020).

There also seems to be a correlation between video games and violence. A meta-analysis of 98 studies in 2014 involving 37,000 participants concluded that there were significant associations between video games and social outcomes. Violent video games were found to increase aggression-related variables; but it was also found that pro-social video games had the opposite effect (Greitmeyer and Mugge, 2014). There is also ample evidence that playing video games manipulates children's emotions.

Evidence is also increasing that smartphone use, or simply just having one with you even if you are not using it, can diminish cognitive efficiency, creating a diversion of attention that impedes reasoning and performance. As Adrian Ward, a cognitive psychologist working in the area, has put it, a smartphone is a supernatural stimulus that can 'highjack' attention when it is part of our surroundings, which it generally is for most people (Carr, 2017). The availability of attentional resources can be adversely affected by the mere presence of a person's smartphone, even when it is not being used (Ward et al., 2017). Additionally, there are studies that show that the mere presence of a smartphone will have a significant negative effect upon student performance (Clayton et al., 2015); and that relying upon the availability of digital services of information can have a negative effect upon memory, the so-called 'Google effect' (Sparrow et al., 2011).

Product placement in casual games

The popularity of casual games played on mobile devices has been unprecedented as more and more people play, spending more and more time playing. Zynga's CityVille attracts about 100 million players a month, and Angry Birds players spend some 200 million minutes a day with the game. Angry Birds only cost Rovio US$ 100,000 to create, but it earns about US$ 2 million a month. The Casual Games Association reports that in 2009 the industry earned US$ 3 billion in mobile revenue.

So how can advertisers become a part of this? The creator of Angry Birds, Peter Vesterbacka, has said that brands must first let go of the idea that they need their own games. He suggests that 'the smart brands are the ones who will work with the apps that have the audience already and create experiences that will be integrated into the app'. One way brands can integrate with casual game content is by placing products inside the game. As the CEO of one game marketer points out in talking about a shift in emphasis for the industry, while it used to be a software business it is now a content-access business, where users are paying for placement inside free content. Major advertisers such as Clorox, Axe and Dove are doing just this. But the key is to ensure the advertising does not interrupt the game play.

Source: Ries (2011)

Adblocking

Using many of the same ways the target audience is now watching programmes on media, they are also avoiding adverts. DVRs facilitate skipping over commercials, you click past adverts that pop up on the internet, and adblocking software is readily available for digital media. In 2016, around 10 per cent of desktop computers worldwide had online advert-blocking software (including over a quarter of all US internet users) on their desktop computers, and one in five smartphone users worldwide use some form of adblocking. Mobile adblocking is particularly widespread in emerging markets, and 36 per cent of smartphone users in the Asia Pacific area have adblockers on their mobile devices. In India and Indonesia, two of the world's fastest growing internet markets, the figure is almost two-thirds (Scott, 2016).

There have been signs of pushback. Eyeo Gmbit's Adblock Plus, at least in 2016, had an agreement with Google and 70 other companies where they charged them to participate in what they called the 'Acceptable Ads Platform'. This enabled certain adverts to get past their Adblock Plus filter. They would then take a 30 per cent cut of the advertising revenue for letting those adverts through. Facebook has been less cooperative, making it hard for Adblock Plus to distinguish adverts from the rest of its content. Rather than paying them to 'unlock' their advertising, they are enabling the user to limit advertising with updated advert preference controls (Stefo, 2016). And while Facebook gets most of its advertising revenues from mobile, they nonetheless in 2016 began forcing adverts to appear for all users of their desktop website, even if they have adblocking software. They did it by changing how advertising is uploaded onto the website (Marshall, 2016).

An irony here is that some makers of adblocking software, like Adblock Plus, also want to sell advertising. Many website publishers are not pleased with the Eyeo Gmbit Acceptance Ads Platform, pointing out that its business model erects barriers to adverts on their websites, and then asks for payment to take it down.

DVRs have enabled television viewers to skip past commercials for some time. Now Apple, which accounts for most of the audience for podcasts, is providing this same ability for them. Listeners will be able to skip ahead in 15-second increments. Spotify AB and Stitcha, along with others, also have a skip button. While podcast advertising formats differ by programme, the two most common types are those where the host of the programme reads the advert, or a commercial in the manner of a traditional radio spot. Marketers obviously prefer the former because the message tends to blend into the programme's content and is less likely to be skipped (Perlberg, 2016).

Not only do users not want adverts in digital media, they pose a very real problem, especially for mobile devices, because of the toll they take on data plans and battery life. Apple's OS 9 operating system tried to deal with this by including a content blocking feature that helped block cookies, pop-up adverts, and other undesirable content. If a web page carried an advert, the system blocked it from loading, and could also usually block the sending of tracking data to other sources like Google and Facebook (Wu, 2016). As a result, the iPhone worked faster and more effectively, using less power and band width.

Digital media concerns

While digital media growth remains strong, there are a number of concerns that could prove worrying. One such concern is the effect of a 2003 EU law that requires non-EU companies to collect a value-added tax on fees for internet services, as well as for products downloaded by users over the internet such as music, videos, and software. This would mean, for example, that Europeans using eBay must pay a VAT, and EU sellers must add VAT onto the fee they pay eBay to list their products (since eBay is not an EU company).

Then there are a number of real concerns over privacy, fraud, and programmatic buying, all of which we will be dealing with here. But beyond this, there are other signs that all is not well. In 2020, Google was accused of running an illegal digital-advertising monopoly, and of enlisting Facebook in an advertising auction-rigging deal, amid other federal antitrust lawsuits filed in the United States (McKinnon and Tracy, 2020). The US Congress has concluded that Amazon holds monopoly power over third-party sellers on its site, and that Apple exhorts monopoly power through the AppStore.

A glitch in Facebook's tool that tells advertisers how effective their adverts may be in driving results, such as getting consumers to download an app or make a purchase, skewed the data brands use to decide how much to spend on advertising with Facebook, significantly over stating results. While not the first problem with their metrics, this problem hurt confidence in their metrics among advertising buyers (Bruette and Patel 2020).

While there is no question as to the impact of digital media on IMC, there is also no denying that there are a number of potential problems that could affect its future growth and effectiveness as an advertising medium.

Privacy issues

The practice of installing tracking tools such as 'cookies' on computers without user knowledge, and often without the website's knowledge, is drawing more attention from government regulators as well as internet users. Prior to 2009, European law required websites to permit users to 'opt out' or decline cookie installation. In drafting new legislation in 2009, the EU Parliament proposed that users must 'opt in' before cookies were installed. This failed after pressure from marketers. In the end, a rather vague law was passed (Sonne and Miller, 2010), but at the time there was no agreement on its meaning. Most of the countries in the EU interpreted the law as meaning that a browser setting would be enough to indicate user consent.

But, in 2018, a General Data Protection Regultion (GDPR) went into effect that required companies doing business in the EU to specifically ask for consent before collecting any personal data. Even if this consent is given, only information for a specific job may be collected, and there are a number of restrictions on how it may be used. For example, having given consent, you may nevertheless ask for the information to be deleted at any time. Violators of the GDPA face fines of €20 million, or 4 per cent of their global revenue (O'Reilly, 2018).

At the end of 2018, consumer advocates from four EU countries sued Google, alleging they violated the GDRP in the way they tracked user locations (Michaels and Woo, 2018). They were fined a then record US$ 5 billion. Then in 2020, France's regulatory agency CUIL assessed a €100 million fine against Google, and a €35 million fine against Amazon, for improperly collecting information about website visitors (Schenchner, 2020a). Twitter was fined €450,000 in Ireland under the GDRP for failing to notify regulators of a data breech that exposed some user's private trends, the first in a long list of pending cases in Ireland involving Facebook, Apple, and Google (Schenchner, 2020b).

In the United States, the Federal Trade Commission (FTC) had long wanted a 'do-not-track' protocol in order to guard digital media users' privacy, a one-click option that users could use to prevent companies and websites from installing 'cookies' and then selling the data collected to advertisers. But after trying to find a solution through industry self-regulation, the effort failed. But this is changing. By 2021, a wave of new privacy regulations were introduced in a number of states, and the FTC was expected to update its own rules for various areas of disclosure (Bruell, 2020). This action by individual states lead to major brand's seeking a federal law governing how personal data is collected and used, obviating the need to deal with each state separately (Vranica, 2019).

Action by Apple in 2021, implementing new privacy requirements that made it harder to gather user data, as well as proof that adverts work on its platform, lead to significant challenges to the core business of Facebook and others (Haggin et al., 2021). The new software required apps to ask users whether or not they want their behaviour to be tracked for purposes of showing them personalized adverts. The change was particularly hard on small businesses by making it more difficult for them without sufficient tracking data. It meant they needed to spend significantly more for larger audience reach because targeting would be less precise (Mims, 2021).

Apple privacy feature for mobile devices leads to advertising loses for Facebook and Instagram

When Apple introduced a privacy feature for their mobile devices in 2021 that restricted user tracking, costs for small businesses to acquire prospects rose as much as ten times. This led to cutting advertising spending on Facebook and Instagram, and moving it to Google and others. One small business shifted their entire advertising budget from Facebook and Instagram to search adverts on Google. Another cut its spending on Facebook adverts and shifted 60 percent to Google search adverts after their cost to acquire new customers doubled. An e-commerce company that was spending US $7,000 a day on Facebook adverts cut its Facebook spending by about 80 percent and shifted money elsewhere, including Amazon search adverts.

Meta Platforms, Inc., the parent company of Facebook and Instagram said the privacy push appears to be the biggest threat to their once dominant share of advertising spending by small online businesses and e-commerce companies. But, just as Apple's change led to cuts in spending on Facebook and Instagram, proposed changes at Google could do the same for adverts delivered to Android users.

Source: *The Wall Street Journal*, 19–20 February, 2022

Digital advertising fraud

There is widespread fraud associated with advertising and digital media, including inflated measures of traffic, fake traffic, falsified 'clicks', and more. In 2018, it was estimated that the cost of online advertising fraud was US$ 19 billion, with some 16 per cent of global adverts 'click-throughs' fraudulent (Williams, 2018). A good example of the problem may be found with influencers on Instagram where it is estimated that in 2018 an average of 14 per cent of influencers were fakes, with even higher levels of fraud associated with some brands like Dove at 25 per cent and Amazon's Zappo at 38 per cent (Neff, 2019).

The trade group Interactive Advertising Bureau has estimated that as much as 36 per cent of all web traffic is fake. Much of this follows from fake websites known as 'bots' where programmes are used to infect computers and mimic human activity. This 'bot' traffic costs advertisers because brands typically pay for their adverts once they are loaded in response to web visitors, regardless of whether they are 'real' people or not. Sites are set up with false traffic and advertisers are billed and pay through middlemen who aggregate across many sites and resell the space for most publishers (Vranica, 2013). A study by the Association of National Advertisers in the United States found in 2014 that 11 per cent of display adverts were prompted 'bots', and 23 per cent of video adverts (Marshall, 2014).

Digital advertising fraud is most commonly associated with web video and display adverts, but as brands shift money into streaming TV, fraud on internet connected televisions is growing. Advert-spend on streaming TV in the United States in 2020 was estimated at US$ 8 billion, yet at the end of 2019 it was estimated that some 20 per cent of the adverts were likely to be fraudulent (Patel, 2020a). In just four months at the end of 2020 scammers were able to fool advertisers into paying US$ 14.5 million for adverts that were never seen (Patel, 2020c).

A number of tech companies and advertising measurement firms have been working on ways to develop applications to ensure safer insertions in streaming TV, but there are problems. Increasingly, adverts for streaming TV are purchased through automated marketplaces, with all their attendant problems (which we deal with in the next section). Also, there has been a reluctance to release what apps are involved with the advertising buying (Patel, 2020b).

Another aspect of digital fraud involves the use of the names and messages of well-known public figures in adverts without their permission. Facebook has been under scrutiny for this for some time. In 2019, they agreed to give US$ 3.3 million to a project to fight these scam adverts as part of the settlement from a lawsuit in the United Kingdom. But in 2022, they were again sued for the same thing in both the United States and Australia (Cherney, 2022).

Programmatic advert buying

As just mentioned, online advertising fraud has in part been facilitated by an increased use in recent years of computerized buying markets where advertising insertions are purchased or bid for, much like a stock market, rather than bought directly. This use of automated systems to buy and plan media rather than with actual media 'reps' (i.e., media salespeople) is known as programmatic buying. In 2017 it was estimated that as much as 80 per cent of all digital advertising space involved the use of such programmatic buying.

Programmatic buying in the United States alone was expected to grow at double-digit rates from the US$ 25.23 billion in 2016 according to eMarketer (Stefo, 2016). Yet, interestingly, a 2014 survey of 150 marketers in the United States by the Association of National Advertisers (ANA) found that only 28 per cent of those surveyed felt they understood programmatic buying well enough to use it.

A lack of transparency is seen as a real problem, along with questions of just what is being bought. This is aggravated for digital media by the rise of phony websites, whose programmes are used to infect computers and mimic human behaviour. These 'bots' disguise themselves as real users and create the illusion of authentic web traffic, fooling advertisers into thinking they are real people. A 2014 study by the ANA found that 11 per cent of display adverts, and 23 per cent of video adverts, were prompted to appear by bots (Marshall, 2014). The Interactive Advertising Bureau (a trade group) estimates that 36 per cent of all web traffic is false. Since marketers typically pay for advertising when it is loaded in response to someone visiting a web page, not only is a lot of money being wasted, but a much smaller audience is being reached and planned. Another concern is that with automatic buying systems insertions (i.e., the adverts) are going to sites with stolen copyrighted content. A study of 596 sites in 2014, estimated that these sites generated a total of some US$ 227 million in advertising revenue (Marshall, 2014). But perhaps the most disturbing development in programmatic buying involves so-called 'injection' schemes that force adverts that have been sold by a third party onto websites without that site owner's knowledge. A network browser extension offers users a benefit such as being able to download streaming video, but then injects advertising into other sites throughout the web. The consequences can be a major problem, as when a Target advert popped up in the middle of Walmart's website. Walmart and Target are major competitors.

Summary

The world of media continues to change, and marketers are looking beyond traditional agencies and media companies for their media planning and buying. There are new ways of looking at media, such as whether they are fixed or moving when delivering a message. Still, there are certain basic media concepts that remain essential to understand for IMC planning. In this chapter, we addressed issues related to how media are consumed by the target audience, and their personal relationship with them. We looked at the foundational concepts of reach and frequency, and the importance of understanding that it is *effective* frequency that is needed, not the traditional idea of average frequency; or average reach. An increasing portion of the money spent on marketing communication is now spent on digital media. This growth, however, has been largely limited to the largest providers like Google, and Facebook. But along with the growth has come increasing concern over privacy and other issues, along with a growing pressure to tax internet service.

Advertising delivered through digital media goes well beyond simple banner or pop-up adverts. Keywords used in searches and emails can now trigger related advertisements. Promotions, too, are delivered over the internet, with some websites devoted only to online promotions. Mobile marketing enables advertisers to send messages directly to mobile phones and other wireless mobile devices. With prior permission from mobile phone users, messages can be highly targeted and exposure tracked. It is even possible to direct messages to mobile phones from outdoor billboards. Online video and game now include product placements and even adverts, and marketers are creating their own advergames.

A potentially major problem with all media today is adblockers. A growing number of laptops and mobile devices now have software for blocking adverts, and DVRs enable viewers to skip past commercials. And, there is increasing concern over potential adverse effect from using, or simply having, a smartphone. With the growth of programmatic buying, there are real issues with whether adverts are ever even seen or not. Additionally, there are concerns over privacy, fraud, and more.

Review questions

1 Find examples of street media and discuss how they can be effective.
2 Discuss how the ways people consume media has changed over the last several years.
3 Discuss the problems inherent in using average reach and frequency for media planning.
4 What is effective frequency, and how does it differ from average frequency?
5 How might Wilson and Till's idea of fixed versus mobile be important for IMC media selection?
6 In what ways do you feel digital media have made a positive versus negative impact on delivering advertising?
7 Google has the greatest share of digital advertising. Discuss to what extent this may or may not be a problem.
8 Discuss the ethics of installing tracking devices through the internet without the user's knowledge.
9 Why is social media creating problems for advertisers, and can they be overcome?
10 How would you use mobile marketing as part of an IMC programme?
11 How might a phone in-and-of itself constrain the potential for mobile digital advertising?
12 Discuss the potential long-term effects of adblocking on brand advertising.
13 What are some of the major concerns with digital media?
14 How effective are government efforts in addressing privacy concerns with digital media?
15 How serious a concern is digital advertising fraud, and what can be done about it?
16 What is programmatic buying, and what problems are associated with it?
17 What are some of the concerns associated with social media use, and how serious are they?

References

AdAge (2018) *AdAge Marketing Fact Pack 2019* 17 December, *15*.

Advertising Age (2012) Mobile Fact Pack, p. 6.

Advertising Age (2015) Marketing Fact Book, 29 December.

Anderson, J.R. (1983) A spreading activation theory of memory. *Journal of Verbal Learning and Verbal Behaviour*, *22(3)*, 1–12.

Ante, S.E. (2011) Billboards join wired age. *The Wall Street Journal*, 4 February, B10.

Bavelier, D. and Green, C.S. (2011) Browsing the nature of the brain. *Nature*, *470(7332)*, 37–38.

Bruette, A. and Patel, S. (2020) Error hits Facebook and text. *The Wall Street Journal* 27 November, *B5*.

Carr, N. (2017) How smartphones highjack our minds. *The Wall Street Journal*, 7–8 October.

Caubergne, V. and De Pelsmaker, J. (2010) Advergames: The impact of brand prominence and game repetition on brand response. *Journal of Advertising*, *39(1)*, 5–18.

Cherney, M. (2022) Meta sued over scam ads shown on Facebook. *The Wall Street Journal*, 19–20 March, *B.1*.

Clayton, R.B., Leshner, G. and Almond A. (2015) The extended iSelf: the impact of iPhone separation on cognitive emotion and physiology. *Journal of Computer Mediated Communication*, *20/2*, 119–135.

Crain, R. (2011) Just how influential is your social-media program if it isn't helping sell product? *Advertising Age*, 17 January, *14*.

Delaney, K.J. and Steel, E. (2007) Are skins, bugs, or tickets the holy grail of web advertising? *The Wall Street Journal*, 13 August, B1.

Gangadharbatla, H. (2012) Social Media and Advertising. In S. Rodgers and E. Thorson (eds.), *Advertising Theory*. New York: Routledge, pp. 402–416.

Greitmeyer, T. and Mugge A.O. (2014) Video games do affect social outcomes: a meta-analytic review of the effects of violent and prosocial video game play. *Personality and Social Psychology Bulletin, 40(5)*, 578–589.

Gross, M.L. (2010) Advergames and the effects of game-product congruity. *Computers in Human Behaviour, 26(6)*, 1259–1265.

Haggin, P., Hagey, K. and Schenchner, S. (2021) Facebook ad business faces threat. *The Wall Street Journal*, 30-31 January, *B1*.

Iezzi, T. (2010) *The Idea Writers*. New York: Palgrave MacMillan.

Kantrowitz, A. (2014) The banner ad turns 20. *Advertising Age*, 27 October, *35*.

Kaplan, A. and Haenlein, M. (2010) Users of the world unite: The challenges and opportunities of social media. *Business Horizons, 53 (1)*, 59–68.

Katsukura, A., Nishiyama, M. and Okazaki, S. (2005) Evidence from Japan: A preliminary scale development of consumer perception of mobile portal sites. Advertising and Communication. Proceedings of 4th International Conference on Research in Advertising. Saarbruecken, Germany: Saarland University, pp. 254–259.

Kross, E., Verduyn, P., Demiraip, E., Park, J., Seungjae, Lee, D., Lin, N., et al. (2013) Facebook use predicts decline in subjective well-being in young adults. *Plus One no. 8*.

Lee, M. and Faber, J. (2007) Effects of product placement in on-line games on brand memory: A perspective of the limited-capacity model of attention. *Journal of Advertising, 36(4)*, 75–90.

Marshall, J. (2014) Bot fraud affects 11 percent of display ads on web. *The Wall Street Journal*, 9 December, *B3*.

Marshall, J. (2016) Ad blockers now filter to allow some ads. *The Wall Street Journal*, 14 September, *B7*.

Mayfield, A. (2008) What is social media. *Networks. V1.4 UPDAT*, 36.

McKinnon, J.D. and Tracy, R. (2020) Google is accused of enlisting Facebook to aid in ad-rigging. *The Wall Street Journal*, 17 December, *A1*.

Meyer, D. (2017) Facebook's ad metrics come under scrutiny yet again. *Fortune*, 6 September (n.p.).

Michaels, D. and Woo, S. (2018) Europe fines hit Google, Facebook. *The Wall Street Journal*, 28 November, *B4*.

Mims, C. (2021) Apple's collateral damage. *The Wall Street Journal*, 10-11 April, *B2*.

Mobile Marketing Association (2005) What is mobile marketing, www.mmaglobal.co.uk. Accessed 10 January 2017.

Neff, J. (2016) Marketers Embrace Facebook, Google Missionaries. *Advertising Age*, 17 October, 10–11.

Neff, J. (2019) Report finds fake followers are hard to shake. *AdAge*, 4 February, *14*.

Nielson (2010) What Americans do online: Social media and game dominate activity. Reported in Gangadharbatla (ibid.).

O'Reilly, L. (2018) The future of digital marketing in a data-privacy world. *The Wall Street Journal*, 19 June, *B1*.

Oser, K. (2004) Money, Mayhem to be first with pop-ups. *Advertising Age*, 25 June, *57*.

Patel, S. (a) (2020) Advertisers find fraud on streaming TV. *The Wall Street Journal*, 28 September, *B7*.

Patel, S. (b) (2020) Ad-tech companies look to make streaming TV safe for marketers. *The Wall Street Journal*, 12 October, *B4*.

Patel, S. (c) (2020) Scammers hit streaming TV advertisers. *The Wall Street Journal*, 18 December, *B6*.

Perlberg, S. (2016) Ad-Skipping's New Victim. *The Wall Street Journal*, 18 July, *B3*.

Peltier, J.W., Schibrowsky, J.A. and Schultz, D. (2003) Interactive integrated marketing communication combining the power of IMC, new media, and database marketing. *International Journal of Advertising, 22(1)*, 93–115.

Ries, A. (2011) *Advertising Age*, 10 January.

Rossiter, J.R. and Percy, L. (1997) *Advertising Communications and Promotion Management*. New York: McGraw Hill.

Rossiter, J.R. and Percy, L. (2013) How the roles of advertising merely appear to have changed. *International Journal of Advertising, 32 (3)*, 391–398.

Rossiter, J.R. and Percy, L. and Bergkvist, L. (2018) *Marketing Communication: Objectives, Strategy, Tactics*, London: Sage.

Schenchner, S. (a) (2020) French privacy fines hit Google, Facebook. *The Wall Street Journal*, 11 December, *B6*.

Schenchner, S. (a) (2020) Twitter fined in Europe over data breach. *The Wall Street Journal*, 16 December, *B4*.

Schenchner, S. (2022) EU, U.K. probe Google, Facebook. *The Wall Street Journal*, 12-13 February, *B2*.

Schultz, D. (2010) The Pyrite Rush. *Marketing News*, 30 September, *12*.

Scott, M. (2016) Rise of ad blocking software threatens online revenue. *NYTimes.com*, 30 May.

Shabam, H. (2019) Digital advertising to surpass print, TV for first time report says. *Washington Post*, 20 February.

Shields, M. and Marshall, J. (2015) Paid influences undercut ads on Pinterest. *The Wall Street Journal*, 16 January, *B5*.

Sloane, G. (2016) Are Snapchat ads worth the effort? *Advertising Age*, 5 December, *3*.

Sonne, P. and Miller, J.W. (2010) EU Chews on web cookies. *The Wall Street Journal*, 22 November, B.1–B2.

Sparrow, B., Liu, J., & Wegner, D. (2011). Google effects on memory: cognitive consequences of heavy information at our fingertips. *Science*, August, vol 333, 776–778.

Steel, E. (2006) Web-page clocks and other 'widgets' anchor new internet strategy. *The Wall Street Journal*, 21 November, *B4*.

Stefo, G. (2016) Whose side is Google on? *Advertising Age*, 26 September, 34–36.

Stutsky, I. (2011) Nothing casual about this game obsession. *Advertising Age*, 10 January, *2*.

Terlep, S. and Seetharaman, D. (2016) Biggest ad buyer rethinks Facebook. *The Wall Street Journal*, 10 August, *A1*.

Tillery, A. (2011) The Strategic Importance of Media. In L. Butterfield (ed.), *Excellence in Advertising*. Oxford: Routledge, pp. 193–215.

Viskontas, I. (2020) *How digital technology shapes us*. Chantilly Virginia: The Teaching Company.

Vittet-Philippe, P., and Navarro, J.M. (2000) Mobile e-business (M-commerce): State of play and implications for European play. *European Commission Enterprise Directorate – General E-Business Report*, *No. 3*, 6 December.

Vranica, S. (2013) The case of the invisible Web ads. *The Wall Street Journal*, 12 June, *B10*.

Vranica, S. (2019) How privacy rules will affect the ad business *The Wall Street Journal*, 12 June, *B6*.

Vranica, S. (2020) Digital takes lion's share of ads. *The Wall Street Journal*, 2 December, *B1*.

The Wall Street Journal (2016) Advertising's shifting winds. 22 June, *R2*.

Ward, A.F., Duke, A., Gneezy, A. and Bos, M.W. (2017) Brain drain: The mere presence of one's smartphone reduces available cognitive capacity. *Journal of the Association for Consumer Research, 2/2 April*.

Webster, J.G. (2014) *The Marketplace of Attention: How Audiences Take Shape in a Digital Age*. Cambridge, MA: The MIT Press.

Williams, H. (2018) What's an online ad worth? Blackchain may help with that. *The Wall Street Journal*, 19 June, *B8*.

Wilson, R.T. and Till, B.D. (2012) Managing Non-Traditional Advertising: A Message Processing Framework. In S. Rogers and E. Thorson (eds.), *Advertising Theory*. New York: Routledge, pp. 337–354.

Wu, T (2016). *The Attention Merchants* (New York: Alfred A. Knoff) 333–336.

Yuan, L. and Bryan-Low, C. (2006) Coming soon to cell phone screens – more ads than ever. *The Wall Street Journal*, 16 August, *B1*.

7 Additional delivery options

In the last chapter, we discussed some basic media concepts and looked at digital media. And while we will be considering digital media again, along with more traditional media, in the last part of the book when we are dealing with the integrated marketing communication (IMC) plan, we need to understand that there are many other ways of delivering an IMC message that should be part of our initial thinking. This includes everything from business cards and newsletters to the panels on the sides of delivery trucks. *Anything* that a potential customer sees is an opportunity to communicate the brand's benefit. In this chapter, we will be looking at a number of different options for delivering a message.

Regardless of how a message is delivered, the message must be the *same* everywhere, executed with the same 'look and feel' as the company's or brand's advertising. Trade show banners and brochures should focus on the same primary benefit; product placements should be consistent with the brand's positioning. A designer of traditional high fashion like Ralph Lauren should not sponsor a fringe group rock concert.

Any, and all, options for delivering IMC should be looked at, at least initially, as part of the strategic considerations for optimizing the development of the most effective IMC programme.

Sponsorships and event marketing

Sponsorships play an important role in IMC, and involve a company or brand providing support for an event, organization, cause, or even an individual. In return, the company has the right to display its brand name or logo, linked to the sponsored activity or individual, and to use the sponsorship in their other marketing activities. This makes sense for the company's brand because it enables them to be presented in a favourable environment where it has the potential of benefiting from an already favourable attitude towards the sponsored activity.

Of course, the sponsored activity or individual must be viewed positively by the brand's target audience. Otherwise, it makes no sense. There are three questions a manager should ask when considering sponsorships or events: will it communicate the brand's position; in terms of target audience reach, does it offer good media value, with what reach pattern, and at what cost; and will you be able to measure if it has worked (Rossiter et al., 2018).

Event marketing is similar to sponsorship, differing only in that with event marketing a company supports a specific event rather than an ongoing relationship. In effect, event marketing is a one-off sponsorship. For example, supporting a tsunami relief concert

DOI: 10.4324/9781003169635-9

would be event marketing, compared with sustained support of an organization dedicated to helping victims of natural disasters, which would be sponsorship. Sponsoring the World Cup would be event marketing; supporting a particular team throughout the season, sponsorship. In Europe, especially, brands are major sponsors of football teams. In fact, worldwide most sponsorships involve sports (Meenaghan, 1998). Visa has been a long-time sponsor of the Olympics, and while there is no obvious link to a brand benefit, as seen in the box nearby it is still possible to build positive *corporate* brand equity. Unfortunately, while there are obvious potential benefits to sponsorships and event marketing, there is little evidence that they have a measurable effect on sales or a company's stock price.

With sponsorships, there is always the risk of negatively perceived over-commercialization, or a negative association resulting from problems tied to the sponsored activity or individual. We pointed this out back in Chapter 3 when we indicated that sponsorships could be used as a potential symbolic strategy for corporate stories. Nevertheless, if well conceptualized, sponsorships and event marketing can make a positive contribution to IMC. The key here is the same as with all other marketing communication: establish brand awareness and effectively build positive brand attitude. With brand awareness, the event or individual should have a clear association with the product (ideally), or the category need should be immediately linked to the brand name or logo.

Olympic sponsorship risks

In addition to the questionable benefits of an Olympic sponsorship there are also potential issues with the host country. This was clearly a dilemma for many Olympic sponsors of the 2022 Winter Olympics in China. As China is seen as being more repressive, and with accusations of systematic human–rights violations against the Muslim Uyghur minority in the Xinjian region of China, companies that have positioned themselves as valuing social responsibility face potential risk to their credibility as sponsors of the Beijing Olympics. Even though the Chinese government has denied these allegations, the perception remains. A very real question is whether companies like Coke and Proctor & Gamble will still be seen as credible advocates for social change while also a Beijing Olympics sponsor.

Source: *The Wall Street Journal*, 5–6 February 2022

To facilitate building positive brand attitude, there must be a clear association between the sponsored activity, or individual, and the primary brand benefit (Poon and Pendergast, 2006). Beer and sporting events make sense together because beer is associated with sports, and those attending sporting events are likely to be beer drinkers. The positive emotional benefits associated with sporting events by their fans will transfer to the brand. Tea and sporting events would not make sense. Nor would high-fashion brands like Chanel or Gucci make sense sponsoring sporting events, but a sportswear brand like Lacoste – perhaps. Lacoste would certainly fit with golf or tennis, but not Formula 1 racing or NASCAR. The brand manager must ask if there is a good 'fit' between the brand and the event; just as the event manager should ask if there is a good 'fit' between the event and the brand (Gwinner and Eaton, 1999).

Experiential marketing

Experiential marketing, sometimes also referred to as engagement marketing, utilizes limited-run, pop-up, Instagramable events. It reflects a strategy that immerses you with a product, creating a meaningful connection between a brand and the consumer in order to build a positive brand attitude and drive sales. It goes beyond simply promoting the brand, it actively engages people with the identity and core values of the brand. It provides an opportunity to not only promote the brand, but to *experience* the brand by creating memorable and unique experiences linked to it.

With experiential marketing you are looking for opportunities to create an event that lends itself seamlessly to social content and social-media-based outreach (Nelson, 2019). A key benefit of experiential marketing is that it provides a personal engagement, a strategic emotional connection with the brand, and an opportunity to share the experience on social networks.

To promote its new Doc McStuffin's bear line, Build-a-Bear launched pop-up 'clinics' across the United Kingdom. At these Doc McStuffin's Bear Hospitals children could bring their torn bears to staff dressed like doctors who would then repair the bear. Even if the bear wasn't damaged, children could bring in their bear for a 'check-up' where the staff would give the bear a physical. And of course, you could buy a new Build-a-Bear at the po-up. Some 8,000 children attended the event.

In another example, at the FIFA world cup Coca-Cola placed a virtual reality experience in front of a train station where you could stand in front of a screen and see a famous footballer next to you. You could then practice football moves with the player, or compete in your own mini tournament.

The growth of experiential marketing in recent years has been credited to millennials. In a 2016 study, 72 per cent of millennials said they would prefer paying for an experience rather than an actual product. However, there is some concern that it may be reaching a saturation point. With this same group of young people, especially GenZ, there is a growing reluctance to sharing information on the internet owing to privacy concerns. Additionally, experiential events can be quite expensive, in excess of US$ 1 million, which raises questions about their return-on-investment (Pasquarelli, 2019).

Baskin-Robbins experiential event

During London Fashion Week in 2019, Baskin-Robbins teamed up with Netflix and their popular show *Stranger Things* to bring to life its Scoops Ahoy ice-cream parlour. They transformed their highest traffic shop into a real-life version of the shop from Scoops Ahoy. It featured the same interiors, signage, uniforms, products, and personalities as those in the show. They offered a number of different Instagram opportunities, including a Scoops Ahoy 'Employee of the Month' cardboard cut-out for visitors to stick their head in for a picture. People were lined up around the block. The experience ran for two weeks, and crowds were lined up around the block for a chance to get in.

Source: *AdAge*, 29 July 2019

Product placement and branded content

Product placement and branded content are similar in that both involve an *unannounced* inclusion of a brand in an article, programme, or movie. They are considered by many (ourself included) to be unethical because they attempt to persuade without the recipient's awareness. Additionally, it doesn't really matter if people recognize a product placement in a movie, television programme, or online video, or concocted stories in various media, for what they are – adverts for a brand. According to regulatory agencies in most countries it is a deceptive practice if it is the *intention* of the brand to deceive, regardless of whether actual deception occurs (Rossiter et al., 2018).

Product placement

Product placement may be defined as the reference to or actual inclusion of a product or service within some context in return for payment or other consideration. That context may be anything from movies and television programmes to video games (as discussed in the last chapter) or even books. While generally referred to as product placements, in actuality, of course, one is talking about *brand* placement. Nonetheless, we use the more common term, product placement.

It was not until the mid-2000s that the European Parliament's culture committee gave approval for product placements. Yet despite this, not all the EU countries are keen to adopt it. In the United Kingdom, product placement has long been a controversial issue, and even with EU approval adoption is not expected in the near term. Even though many US television shows are seen in the United Kingdom, product placement in that programming is pixilated (digitally blurred out) (Hall, 2007).

Beyond the ethical concerns, there is an issue of whether product placement works or not. There are certainly many anecdotal stories about the effectiveness of product placements. An oft-told story concerns the 1986 movie *Top Gun*, where Tom Cruise is wearing Ray Ban Aviator sunglasses. It is said that this led to a turn-around in the fortunes of the company, which before the release of the movie, was in financial difficulties (Fischer, 1996). Nevertheless, there are few empirical studies of product placement, and those that have been conducted are not encouraging (Johnstone and Dodd, 2000).

Assuming product placement can be effective, *how* the brand is placed will have an obvious impact. If a brand is clearly seen being used by a celebrity or specifically talked about, the potential effect will be greater than if it is simply part of the background (Semenik, 2002). If well placed, the most likely effect will be raising brand awareness and salience. But even this will require *conscious* attention to the brand.

The likelihood of product placement positively effecting brand attitude for significant segments of a brand's target audience is much more problematic. Even though the actual cost of a product placement in absolute terms is likely to be less than that for other forms of marketing communication, it is difficult to predict whether any positive effect will offset the cost of the placement. The key to effectiveness is the number of people *consciously* aware of the brand and positively associating it with the environment within which it is placed. While there may be implicit processing of the brand's placement, this will have *no* effect on brand attitude or behaviour (Percy, 2006).

To be effective, product placements must stimulate explicit positive associations in memory with the celebrity or environment linked to the brand, and within the correct emotional context. If this occurs, the placement should contribute to brand attitude, because the audience may feel as if it has had a personal experience with what is going on. But this is a lot to ask of all but the most rabid fan of the principal actor or setting involved.

In any event if you are willing to set aside the question of ethics, product placement may have the potential to build brand awareness and contribute to brand attitude. But it must be seen within a context consistent with the brand's positioning, attended to consciously, and positively linked to the appropriate emotional and explicit memories, as with any other effective marketing communication.

Branded content

Branded content, also known as 'native advertising' or sponsored content, is what drives content marketing, and is another outgrowth of the rise of digital media. It is where a brand creates 'content' of some sort, for example entertaining short videos or articles. It is then 'shared' on digital media with the aim of attracting and energizing consumers. A problem is that it can often be hard to distinguish it from advertising. A good example of where this problem was avoided is when Red Bull filmed someone skydiving from the edge of space. It created an incredible amount of positive word-of-mouth, and while not an obvious advert for the brand, it nevertheless had a positive effect upon brand awareness and attitude.

Content marketing differs from advertising in two fundamental ways. First, it is not paid for in the traditional sense of a media buy. If it was, it would be advertising. Second, content marketing relies upon a pull, not a push strategy. This is often referred to as 'earned' digital media as opposed to 'paid' digital media. Content marketing should not be confused with public relations, as it often is. We shall be dealing with public relations at the end of this chapter.

A perceived advantage to using branded content is that because the advertising cost of production are front-loaded it will enable the brand to be more strategic with their paid media budget. Ideally, if it does well, the content can be edited into multiple clips that can then be customized for distribution to any number of social networks, or it can be hosted on websites. But, studies have shown that brands spend almost as much to create and manage the branded content as they would with paid online adverts (Neff, 2013).

The best branded content is not obviously touting a brand, but offering something of interest to the target audience. The key here is that the content should be a story or some form of entertainment that is not about the brand. This is why content marketing is often developed by someone with a journalism background rather than an advertising copywriter. Still, there must be a link to the brand, and this raises some of the same ethical issues as with product placement in general.

A major component of branded content in content marketing is digital influencers. In North America alone, it was estimated that over US\$ 1 billion was spent on influencers in 2018. Influencers initially were paid for the number of followers, but as the problems with fake followers grew, brands switched to paying based upon such things as clicks, likes, and sharing. However, this can also be faked, which then led brands to simply paying for content, and then placing it online themselves (Neff, 2019). Of course, as we saw in the last chapter, there can be fraud here as well.

Most people do understand that influencers are being paid to endorse a brand, and regulators do require disclosure. Interestingly, however, studies have found that people respond more positively to influencer-created content than to adverts. This follows from something McGuire pointed out many years ago, that when there is a forewarning of an intent to persuade it is actually more effective than not doing it (McGuire, 1985).

Packaging

Packaging is a critical element in IMC. Even though there is evidence that marketers are coming to realize that packaging is an important part of a brand's identity (Walczyk, 2001), the powerful role packaging can play in building and reinforcing positive brand attitude and equity is often underestimated by managers (Southgate, 1994).

In a study among brand managers, Chareonlarp (1997) identified a number of key emotional and psychological benefits associated with packaging. The findings may be summarized as the ability to attract attention and provide an expression of a brand's image: in other words, brand awareness and brand attitude, the key communication objectives for all marketing communication. As with all other forms of marketing communication, the visual elements of a package, its 'message', should differentiate it from competitors.

Well-designed packages can attract attention at the point-of-purchase, a critical attribute for any product where the brand purchase decision follows from recognition brand awareness. Studies by the Point-of-Purchase Advertising Institute (2000) have shown that over 70 per cent of brand awareness decisions in supermarkets are made in the store. A package, if effectively linked to the brand in the consumer's mind as a result of other marketing communication for the brand (especially advertising), and if visually impactful and unique relative to competitors, will be easily recognized at the point-of-purchase. Given the large number of package facings in a store vying for attention, packaging must be able to 'cut through' the competitive clutter.

A good example of this is how a number of small wineries around the world are using very creative and fun labels. They certainly help the wine stand out from other bottles on the shelf, but they also seem to make the wine more 'approachable' for younger drinkers (Dawson, 2015). Some wineries are even commissioning well-known artists to design their labels, and others are obtaining permission to reproduce well-known art for their labels. Additionally, some wine labels are now using augmented reality apps to interact with potential buyers at the point-of-purchase.

Another really good example of this is the Black Rooster mark used on bottles of Chianti Classico. As Advert 7.1 for Chianti Classico makes clear, the Black Rooster on the bottle identifies the wine as coming from the Chianti Classico region, the first-ever wine territory, differentiating it from imitations. The Black Rooster on the neck of the bottle will easily and quickly identify authentic Chianti Classico on the shelf.

In 2016, McDonalds changed its bags and cups, making the lettering brighter and updating its iconic golden arch in a global packaging update. In addition to their signature red and yellow, a range of new colours were introduced, with names like Passionate Purple, Optimistic Orange, Ocean Fresh Blue, Zesty Lime, and Magical Magenta. Other ideas were tested but not adopted because consumer feedback suggested they were too much of a departure. As McDonald's global brand development director put it: 'They really liked the designs that leaned into our core assets and icons'. While there were new colours, the overall design update made prominent use of the golden arches (Wohl, 2016).

While McDonalds made packaging changes within its core iconic structure, in 2016 Coca-Cola's Mellow Yellow brand of white soft drink introduced what they referred to

Advert 7.1 Chianti Classico.

as an 'extreme' package makeover (in this case their bottles and cans). Long a distant second to Pepsico's market leader Mountain Dew, they felt a radical change was needed. The change featured a vertically scripted 'MY' and used black and yellow with touch of green, a significant change from their traditional green and orangish-red against a yellow background (Schultz, 2016).

But there is much more packaging must do. It should help reinforce the brand's image and key benefit. For many products, the package is always there when the product is being used, providing an ongoing reminder of the brand and an opportunity to reinforce its primary benefit. Products ranging from cold remedies, to breakfast cereal, to toothpaste to washing-up powder are used *from the package*. In a sense, packaging operates as post-purchase advertising. Rossiter et al., 2018 capture this idea in their definition of packaging, suggesting it may be thought of as 'takeaway or leave-behind' communication vehicles.

But interestingly, *where* the image of a package's content appears on the package could be important to what it says about the product. While the colours used can convey mood, and the shape of the package can affect the perception of how much is in it, where the product's image is placed will influence how 'heavily' it is perceived. Research has shown that products are seen as being heavier when the image is placed in the bottom or right area of the package's front, and lighter when placed at the top or left side. This can be important when the 'weight' of the item is viewed as a positive (or negative) attribute of the product. An example cited by Deng and Kahn (2009) from their research finds that for snack products, if a consumer is looking for a 'healthy' snack they are more likely to choose a package where the image of the snack is placed at the top or left of the package because that conveys 'lightness'.

Updating labels for easier shopping

In the US, Campbell Soup owns the condensed soup market. Any visit to even a reasonably sized food store would find a large shelf display of their familiar red and white labelled soup cans. Even after major merchandising improvements consumers continued to find this 'wall of red' confusing and difficult to navigate, overwhelming and frustrating. After extensive biometric and eye-tracking research, along with ethnographic interviews with shoppers, new labels and merchandising strategies were introduced. On the label the spoon in the bowl was moved, and the bowl itself redesigned. 'Steam' was added and the logo was made smaller. Colour coded banners on the labels and shelf-talkers were used to identify different varieties, such as 'Classic Favourites' or 'Great for Cooking'.

Source: *Advertising Age*, 25 July 2011

Trade shows and fairs

Trade shows and fairs fall somewhere between promotion and personal selling. Promotional incentives of some kind are often used to encourage attendance at trade shows and fairs; they are advertised through various media, and direct contact is made with customers and potential customers at the company's booth. Every industry has a trade show of some kind. They can be especially important for small marketers unable to advertise, and they play a significant role in the marketing communication for industrial companies. It has been estimated that between 20 and 25 per cent of an industrial marketer's communication budget is spent on trade shows (Gopalakrishna and Williams, 1992).

Because of the personal interaction afforded by trade shows and fairs, they offer marketers a number of opportunities (Shipley et al., 1993). They provide a chance to identify and meet new customers, as well as entertain old ones. New products can be introduced, and existing products demonstrated. They also help raise the salience of a company and to enhance its image: brand awareness and brand attitude. The key advantage is that this may be all done in a short period of time, and among nearly all of one's existing and potential customers. But as with all other forms of marketing communication, the trade show or fair, as well as all the advertising and promotion associated with it, should be consistent with other ongoing IMC efforts.

There is some debate about the effectiveness of trade shows and fairs, even though there is no question that they provide a good opportunity for marketers and customers to meet in an environment where the one is imparting information and the other seeking it. Some have shown that they generate awareness and interest, leading to sales (Gopalakrishna and Williams, 1992), while others have questioned their value altogether (Sashi and Perretty, 1992).

Many define effectiveness in terms of leads generated that result in sales (Sharland and Balogh, 1996). This is certainly in line with one way managers who are heavily involved in trade shows and fairs look at it (Blythe and Rayner, 1996). Yet Shipley et al. (1993), as well as others, have found that the non-selling aspects of trade shows and fairs are highly valued by the managers involved with them. The problem would seem to be that there are frequently no set criteria for success, and this is complicated by no good measure of cost-effectiveness. Additionally, when assessing trade shows and fairs, managers are apt to look at them in isolation rather than as part of an overall IMC programme.

Personal selling

In this section, we are not so much interested in personal selling as such, but rather with the role of the salesperson in delivering and reinforcing a brand's positioning and marketing communication. How to be an effective salesperson is a subject for another book (for example, Cialdini, 2001).

Personal selling may be looked at in terms of direct contact with consumers or a link to resellers or dealers in business-to-business marketing. In fact, personal selling is often the primary (if not only) form of marketing communication for industrial marketers. In either case, the message delivered must be consistent with that of the overall marketing communication programme. It will differ from most other forms of marketing communication in an IMC programme because the message moves *directly* from the marketer to an individual member of the target audience, providing an opportunity for interaction and modification of the basic message to address specific target audience concerns.

The principal advantage of personal selling, from a marketing communication standpoint, is that it involves a two-way interaction between the salesperson and the customer, unlike the one-way communication of other marketing communications (with the exception of those involving interactive media). Personal selling provides an opportunity for customizing the message for an individual customer, and, as mentioned above, the opportunity to adapt the message during the customer-salesperson interaction. Because of this, attention to, and involvement with, the message is likely to be high. Personal selling

Table 7.1 Advantages and disadvantages of personal selling

Advantages	• Two-way interactions and the opportunity to adjust message during presentations • Opportunity to customize message • Ability to demonstrate product
Disadvantages	• Difficult to maintain message consistency • Expensive relative to other forces of marketing communications • Low reach

also offers a chance to demonstrate product benefits that might be difficult or even impossible to effectively convey with other forms of marketing communication.

The key advantage of personal selling in marketing communication unfortunately leads to its primary disadvantage, especially for IMC. Because of the flexibility and multiple delivery sources (the different salespeople), it is difficult to maintain message consistency. Given the nature of personal selling, relative to other ways of delivering a message, it is expensive and has a low reach. These advantages and disadvantages associated with personal selling in IMC are summarized in Table 7.1.

Integrating personal selling into the development of IMC strategy can be difficult, for in many companies the sales force is not part of the marketing department, especially for consumer packaged goods. As Dewshap and Jobber (2000) point out, in packaged goods companies retailers are the brands for the salesforce, unlike for marketing managers, where the product is the brand. The focus is different, and they have separate budgets. Nevertheless, personal selling must be considered as part of IMC planning, using a message that is consistent with a brand's other marketing communication.

When marketing and sales are separate, it makes it difficult to include personal selling as such in the IMC strategic planning process. Regardless, the message from the sales force must reflect the brand's overall marketing communication. This should go beyond sales support material such as sales kits. The sales force should be thoroughly familiar with the brand's positioning and message when talking with the trade.

In their book, Rossiter, Percy and Bergkvist (2018) pointed out that the management of personal selling will depend upon the type of selling involved, and they identified six different types: regular retail selling, small-business selling, trade selling, telemarketing, high-end retail selling, and professional technical selling. They see regular retail selling and small-business selling as *passive*, where the customer tends to control the sales exchange. The other four types of selling are *active*, where both the customer and salesperson are involved in the exchange. It is only these four 'active' types of personal selling that are important to IMC.

In recent years, there has been a realization that retaining existing customers is a more profitable strategy for the salesforce than seeking new customers (not that a company should stop trying to gain new customers). This is what *relationship marketing* is all about. It also means that, with more long-term relationships in mind, there is a greater opportunity for personal selling to be used in reinforcing a brand's message.

While the ultimate objective of personal selling is to convince the target customers to stock or purchase the brand, like all marketing communication the message must address brand awareness and brand attitude objectives. With personal selling, the brand awareness objective will be recognition. For brand attitude, there is a key difference. As already discussed, one has the opportunity of adjusting the message to maximize interest in the brand's benefit for a specific target customer.

Much personal selling is directed to the trade or in straight business-to-business situations, where the purchase motive is likely to be negative and an informational brand attitude strategy required. Additionally, the purchase decision is likely to be high involvement. This means the salesperson must understand the target customer's *initial attitude* towards the brand because that understanding will be critical to framing the message for acceptance. The personal, interactive nature of personal selling allows for a certain amount of probing to ensure a good understanding of how the target audience sees the brand.

Interestingly, in these high-involvement cases, even if objectively a brand can deliver its key benefit better than the target customer believes it can, the salesperson should not try to convince them it will. They are not likely to believe the stronger claim, even if it is true. As long as the prospect is generally positive about the brand, talk about the benefit at the customer's level of belief. Research has shown that when used, if a product turns out to deliver a better benefit than anticipated, overall brand attitude will *increase* (Kopalle and Assuncão, 2000). This results from the difference between the anticipation and actual delivery of the benefit.

But one must be careful here in the case of the trade. While getting the trade to stock a brand will likely involve negative motives, and an informational message strategy to 'close the sale', this may not be the case for the brand. When talking about the *brand itself* and its key benefit, if the purchase decision by consumers for the brand reflects positive motives, the message about the brand must incorporate a transformational strategy consistent with its overall marketing communication brand attitude objective. In other cases, especially when personal selling is direct to the consumer (for example, with high-end luxury goods), when the motive driving the purchase decision is positive, the message strategy should be transformational. Here, one need not be as concerned with the target customer's initial attitudes toward the brand, and the salesperson should feel free to present the brand in the best possible light.

Direct marketing

What is direct marketing? According to the Direct Marketing Association, it is:

> An *accountable* system of marketing which uses one or more communications media to *effect a response*. It is an *interactive process* where responses from or about buyers are recorded in a *database* for building profiles of potential customers and providing valuable marketing information for *more efficient targeting*.

Obviously, the Direct Marketing Association has something rather definite in mind. It defines direct marketing as an accountable system using different media to effect a response, and is an interactive process that builds and uses a database for more effective targeting.

The basic characteristics of direct marketing, implied by this definition, are that it asks for a response and that it can be highly targeted. It can be aimed at both an individual or a very narrowly defined group of people. In addition, every aspect of direct marketing must be tied to a database so that statistical analysis can be used to access the effectiveness of any programme.

Jerome Pickholz (1994), when chairman and CEO of Ogilvy-Mather Direct, suggested that there are two significant hurdles for direct marketing to overcome. The first is building a good database. The problem is that it must be built over time, and, as Pickholz reminds us, this can be a real problem for marketers who are looking for immediate solutions. The second hurdle is the cost. Despite the fact that studies show direct marketing helps to build business, the cost per response can seem way out of line. As again Pickholz points out: 'It's hard for marketers accustomed to a $20.00 cost per thousand to acclimate themselves to a $500 CPM, no matter how much more effective the medium has proven to be'. But the nature of direct marketing does allow for close monitoring of costs, and provides the needed flexibility to evolve increasingly more cost-effective programmes.

We shall be looking at the role of direct marketing later in Chapter 11.

The database in direct marketing

When to use a database in one sense is the same as when one should consider using direct marketing. What we want to briefly cover here is how a manager can use a database to help make direct marketing decisions. Table 7.2 outlines five situations where information in a database can help guide strategic decisions as to whether to include direct marketing in a particular IMC programme or not. The first situation is where it is known that people on the list make *multiple or repeat purchases* of a product or service, especially where there are high gross margins. It also helps if the purchase cycle is neither too short nor too long. If the purchase cycle is too short, even if a person is a regular customer, the margins will not support specialized direct marketing. If the purchase cycle is too long, unless one knows it is time for the customer to repeat, too much of the direct marketing effort could be wasted on people not in the market at the time of the campaign.

A second situation is where specialized niche marketing or *segmentation* makes sense. Direct marketing is meant to be highly targeted, and a database can reveal important segments. Of course, this assumes that the brand has compiled the relevant dependent segmentation variables in its database. Because so much is known about the customers and prospects in the database, it offers unique opportunities for *increasing business* among them. An obvious example here would be to use the database for cross-selling. Beyond this, a third situation is that by knowing customers well, it is possible to tailor messages to reduce switching behaviour or increase their current usage or purchase of the brand. Finally, with a good database one can predict when customers are most likely to be in the market, and prevent defections by competitive attempts to lure them away. This is why service companies and brands that are used on a regular basis send out 'reminder' notes.

Analysing a database with these points in mind will help pinpoint potential direct marketing applications. If information that might help target particular segments is not in the database, thought should be given to what it might take to add it.

Table 7.2 Information in database that helps identify opportunities for direct marketing

- People who make multiple or repeat purchases
- Length of purchase cycle
- Potential for segmentation or niche marketing
- Knowledge of target audience to tailor message
- Understanding of behaviour to predict when consumers are in the market to prevent defection through competitive activity

Public relations

Where public relation (PR) fits within IMC is not an easy question to answer. Part of the reason is that neither academics nor practitioners seem to offer a consensus on the role PR plays with regard to an organization and its marketing activities. Many would argue, for example, that 'publicity' is only one part of PR. Is the advice a PR agency provides to corporate management 'publicity', or the speeches they write for a CFO to give to the financial community? What about help with employee relations, or lobbying activities?

From a marketing standpoint, the word 'publicity' is perhaps a good choice. But many PR practitioners would like to distance themselves from any association with 'marketing'. They like to see what they do as more concerned with enhancing the image and reputation of an organization. The Institute of Public Relations defines PR as 'the planned and sustained effort to establish and maintain goodwill and mutual understanding between an organization and its publics' (Pickton and Broderick, 2001). While this definition would seem to distance PR from consumers and marketing, with an emphasis more on the organization, obviously one of a company's most important 'publics' is the consumer. As we saw in Chapter 3, an organization's image and reputation cannot be separated from the marketing of its products or services.

Regardless of how one chooses to define PR, it plays an important part in the marketing communication mix, and the messages it delivers to various 'publics' must be consistent with the message delivered by more traditional marketing communications. While some PR activities are clearly outside of the normal strategic planning for IMC, whatever activities are undertaken on behalf of an organization should take cognizance of the overall marketing communication programme for that company's brands. While in this chapter we are only concerned with those areas of PR that have a direct effect on marketing issues, we must still keep this in mind. Regardless of the PR activity, to the extent that it reflects on the image and reputation of an organization or its products, it should be consistent with the overall IMC programme.

In terms of strategy, PR may be either proactive or reactive. With proactive PR, a company or brand is using it to attract attention and help build positive brand attitude. Reactive PR is what is involved when a company or brand responds to negative publicity. There are several different strategies that have been identified to deal with the need for 'damage control': attack it head-on with a denial; argue that it is a one-off occurrence and will not be allowed to happen again; try to deflect it with positive PR; neutralize it by downplaying the situation; or simply ignore it and hope it goes away (Rossiter et al., 2018). In social psychology, such damage control is known as impression management, where you are seeking to protect yourself by maximizing positive associations and minimizing negative ones.

Advantages and disadvantages

There are both advantages and disadvantages to using PR in marketing. Advantages include such things as low cost, the ability to reach very specific target audiences, avoiding 'clutter', and message credibility (see Table 7.3). Compared with other forms of communication, PR is much less expensive to use in an absolute as well as relative sense. Primarily, this is because there are no direct media costs involved. By its nature, PR activity can be directed to very specific target groups and can reach highly segmented publics effectively. Because PR messages are not delivered through traditional media,

Table 7.3 Advantages and disadvantages of PR

Advantages	• Low cost
	• Reach highly specific targets
	• Avoid clutter
	• Message credibility
Disadvantages	• Lack of control over message
	• Target audience may not link message to brand

they avoid the clutter associated with advertising-like messages. As they are not seen as 'advertising', PR messages are likely to be seen as more credible.

On the other hand, there can be disadvantages associated with using PR. Perhaps the greatest potential problem with PR is lack of control. There is rarely a guarantee that a message will be exposed, and, if it is, that it will necessarily be presented in the way the company desired. Owing to the fact that PR is not seen as 'advertising', the target audience may not make the desired link between the message and the brand or company.

Marketing public relations

In the mid-1990s it was estimated that 70 per cent of PR activities were related to marketing (Harris, 1993). It was at this time that Thomas Harris introduced the term marketing public relations (MPR) to describe PR activities in support of marketing objectives. There is every reason to believe that the proportion of PR activities that could be described as MPR is even greater today. Harris specifically defined MPR as 'the process of planning, executing, and evaluating programmes that encourage purchase and consumer satisfaction through credible communicators of information and impressions that identify companies and their products with the needs, wants, concerns, and interests of consumers'. In a sense, MPR helps define and communicate a brand's positioning, and Harris's definition outlines this point.

When we discuss positioning again in Chapter 9, we will see that effective positioning requires linking a brand with a need (defined as *category* need, a perceived need for a product in a particular category), and also linking the brand with a desired benefit. MPR, by identifying a company and its products with particular needs, is helping to provide the link between a category need and the brand, and by identifying a company and its products with a want, links the brand with a desired benefit that satisfies that want.

This understanding of PR as MPR becomes even more important for companies that use source or endorser branding strategies. With such branding strategies, the company name is part of the brand name and acts as an endorser or guarantor for the product, as we have seen. When Nestlé adds its name to its Crunch bar, in a very real sense it is contributing Nestlé's image and reputation to the brand. The potential importance of MPR here is obvious. Any PR that helps build and nurture Nestlé's image and reputation enhances the image of the Crunch brand. On the other hand, PR for Mars is unlikely to affect the image of Snickers unless one knows that it is made by Mars. Snickers is what is known as a 'stand-alone' brand, as discussed in Chapter 2.

In any event, MPR must be seen as consistent with a brand's overall marketing communication, and ideally should reflect the same visual and verbal 'feel'. This is why MPR must be considered within IMC strategic planning. When these objectives are achieved, the link between the MPR messages and the brand will be easily recognized, and help build positive brand attitude. The coordination between MPR and other elements of a brand's marketing communication is critical.

Some of the ways in which MPR can contribute to achieving a brand's overall communication objectives is through activities such as media relations, corporate communication, sponsorships, events and perhaps its most important activity, publicity. Maintaining good *media* relations helps to ensure a more likely acceptance for things like company press releases and feature stories, but it requires an ongoing nurturing of editors and journalists. *Corporate communication* involves much of what was discussed in Chapter 3, and includes not only corporate advertising and directed communication to specific stakeholder groups, but also things like internal communication and company news-letters. Both *sponsorships* and *events* may be initiated as part of MPR, just as discussed earlier where they were more directly involved in brand marketing communication.

Publicity is what most people think about as PR, and it is by far the most frequently engaged in PR activity. In fact, publicity in one form or another is likely to be involved along with most other forms of MPR. Often people think of publicity as 'free adver-tising', especially since it uses mass media to deliver its message. An argument can certainly be made that MPR is (or should be) an advertising-like message, but it is certainly not free. There may not be an actual media cost, but there is an ongoing cost for media relations in order to ensure the message will be broadcast and given favourable exposure. There are also costs for developing the message and overall management, and of course, unlike advertising, there is no control over the content or when and how the message will be delivered.

With the traditional MPR model, the marketing team creates a brief for the message, and MPR is used later as needed. However, given the role of social media in today's world, and the speed with which something can spread, if MPR is not involved early on you risk creating a programme that lacks what is called 'talk value', having a message that will be picked up by different media sources as well as being talked about on social media.

Publicity does have the advantage of being seen as more objective than advertising because it is generally viewed as 'news' or information rather than an attempt at per-suasion. While it is likely to reach far fewer people than other forms of marketing communication, it will likely be more persuasive among those who are reached. Yet in the world of digital media today, and especially with social media, the link between media advertising and earned media editorial coverage through MPR has all but been erased.

Buzz marketing

While not exactly PR as such, buzz marketing is the term given to a new trend in word-of-mouth brand communication that emerged in the mid-2000s in an effort to better reach younger consumers. Companies were created to actively enlist the help of 'ordinary people' in talking about specific brands. One such company in the United States (BZZ Agent) recruits people from the internet to talk about their client's brands to friends and family. They are given free samples of the product, along with an outline of things they might say. For example, 3,000 of these 'bzzagents' may be given a sample of a new perfume fragrance and asked to wear it, and to encourage people to talk about it. While they are encouraged to identify themselves as part of a marketing campaign, the 'buzz' created nevertheless has more credibility than traditional advertising because it is coming from someone who is known.

In other ways, companies are using their websites to encourage entertaining interactions to generate positive word-of-mouth about their brand. BMW and many other brands even create short films for use on the internet, featuring well-known actresses and directors, and they rely upon word-of-mouth to build buzz (Iezzi, 2010). There are even auditing services that track 'buzz' about a brand on blogs.

Summary

In this chapter, we have looked at alternative ways of delivering advertising and promotion. More and more, marketers are looking at non-traditional ways of delivering their message. Some alternative ways of delivering marketing communication include sponsorships and events, although there is little evidence that they offer a good return on investment. Nevertheless, when used within an IMC programme they can help in building brand awareness and positive brand attitude. More recently, experiential marketing has become an effective way of generating interest in a brand, creating events that lend themselves to social media.

Product placement and branded content are ways of presenting a brand unnamed in an article, programme, or movie. Product placement has also aroused ethical concerns, and there are also some questions as to its likely effectiveness. Branded content, sometimes referred to as native advertising or sponsored content, looks to provide something of interest without obviously promoting a brand. While a forewarning that branded content is sponsored by a brand is required by regulations, it is not always easy to find.

One non-traditional medium that does offer potential, yet is too often overlooked by managers, is packaging. For many products, especially fmcg, packaging offers an excellent opportunity for reinforcing not only the brand name but also the brand's primary benefit. Trade shows and fairs provide a personal way of delivering a brand's message, and are widely used, especially by industrial marketers.

Personal selling is an area that is often overlooked in terms of IMC, yet it offers a good opportunity for reinforcing brand positioning and message. The key is that the message must be consistent with the IMC message for the brand. It has the obvious advantage of personal interaction with consumers, which opens up the potential for customizing the message. But this obvious advantage can also lead to problems, because it is difficult to maintain consistency.

Direct marketing is an alternative to traditional promotion when an immediate response is desired. PR, too, should be considered as part of an IMC programme. But it must fit within the overall brand communication strategy, even when it is addressing specific corporate communication issues. This idea has been talked about as MPR. It has the advantage of not being seen as advertising, but also the potentially serious problems associated with a lack of control over message content and how it is delivered.

Review questions

1 Find examples of sponsorships or event marketing, and discuss whether you think they are likely to be effective for the brand. How might Wilson and Till's idea of fixed versus mobile be important for IMC media selection?
2 Under what circumstances might you want to include experiential marketing in an IMC campaign?

3 Discuss the ethics of product placement, and discuss their effectiveness.

4 Why is the package an important venue for advertising messages?

5 How would you define direct marketing?

6 In what ways is direct marketing similar to, and in what ways different from, other ways of delivering advertising and promotion?

7 What are some of the advantages of using branded content?

8 What ethical concerns might you have in using branded content?

9 What are the strengths and weaknesses of trade shows and fairs for consumer packaged goods brands? What about for business-to-business marketers?

10 What role does personal selling play in an IMC campaign?

11 How does the type of selling involved inform personal selling?

12 How can public relations be used successfully in IMC?

13 What is the biggest weakness of public relations in terms of IMC, and how can this be overcome?

14 What are the key differences between PR and MPR?

15 Find examples of buzz marketing, and discuss whether you think it works for the brand or not.

References

Blythe, J. and Rayner, T. (1996) The evaluation of non-selling activities at British trade exhibitions – An exploratory study. *Marketing Intelligence and Planning, 14(5),* 20–24.

Chareonlarp, S. (1997) *An Investigation of the Representation of Brand Image Through Packaging, MSC Marketing Management Dissertation.* Birmingham: Astor Business School, Astor University.

Cialdini, R.B. (2001) *Influence: Science and Practice,* 4th ed. Needham Heights, MA: Allyn & Bacor.

Dawson, M. (2015) 'Strong shelf life: more and more producers are using labels to attract a new generation of wine drinkers', Wine Enthusiast, April.

Deng, X. and Kahn, B.E. (2009) Is your product on the right side? The 'location effect' on perceived product heaviness and package evaluation. *Journal of Marketing Research, 46(6),* 725–738.

Dewshap, B. and Jobber, D. (2000) The sales-marketing interface in consumer packaged-goods companies: A conceptual framework. *Journal of Personal Selling & Sales Management, 20(2),* 109–119.

Fischer, B.R. (1996) Making your product the star attraction. *Promo,* July, *58.*

Gopalakrishna, S. and Williams, J.D. (1992) Planning and performance assessment of industrial trade shows: An exploratory study. *International Journal of Research in Marketing, 9(19),* 207–224.

Gwinner, K.P. and Eaton, J. (1999) Building brand image through event sponsorship: the role of image transfer. *Journal of Advertising, 28(4),* 47–57.

Hall, E. (2007) Product placement faces wary welcome in Britain. *Advertising Age,* 8 January, *27.*

Harris, T. (1993) *The Marketer's Guide to PR: How Today's Companies are Using the New Public Relations to Gain a Competitive Edge.* New York: John Wiley and Sons.

Iezzi, T. (2010) *The Idea Writers.* New York: Palgrave McMillan, pp. 37–45.

Johnstone, E. and Dodd, C.A. (2000) Placements as mediations of brand salience within U.K. cinema audiences. *Journal of Marketing Communications, 6(3),* 141–158.

Kopalle, P.K. and Assuncão, J.L. (2000) When (not) to indulge in 'puffery': The role of consumer expectations and brand goodwill in determining advertised and actual product quality. *Managerial Decision Economics, 21(6),* 222–241.

McGuire, W.J. (1985) Attitude and Altitude Change. In G. Lindsey and E. Armson (eds.), *The Handbook of Social Psychology,* Vol. 12, New York: Random House.

Meenaghan, T. (1998) Current developments and future directions in sports sponsorship. *International Journal of Advertising, 17(1),* 3–28.

Neff, J. (2013) Marketers adopt "content Darwinism", struggle with ROJ. *Ad Age,* 23 September, *31.*

Neff, J (2019). How to succeed with influencers, *Ad Age*, 23 January, *19*.

Nelson, T. (2019) Beyond the pop-up. *Ad Age*, 29 July, *24*.

Pasquarelli, A. (2019) Samsung overload. *Ad Age*, 29 July, 8–11.

Percy, L. (2006) Are product placements effective? *International Journal of Advertising*, *25(1)*, 112–114.

Pickholz, J.W. (1994) From the practitioners. *Journal of Direct Marketing*, *8(2)*, 2–6.

Pickton, D. and Broderick, A. (2001) *Integrated Marketing Communications*. Harlow: Pearson Education.

Point-of-Purchase Advertising Institute (2000) *An Integrated Look at Integrated Marketing: Uncovering P-O-P's Role as the Last Three Feet in the Marketing Mix*. Washington, DC: Point-of-Purchase Advertising Institute, p. 10.

Poon, D.T.Y. and Pendergast, G. (2006) A framework for evaluating sponsorship opportunities. *International Journal of Advertising*, *25/4*, 471–488.

Rossiter, J.R., Percy, L., and Bergkvist L. (2018) *Marketing Communications: Objectives, Strategies, Tactics*. London: Sage Publications, Ltd.

Sashi, C.M. and Perretty, J. (1992) Do trade shows provide value? *Industrial Marketing Management*, *21(3)*, 249–255.

Schultz, E.J. (2016) Hellow, yellow. *Advertising Age*, 11 January, *6*.

Semenik, R.J. (2002) *Promotion & Integrated Marketing Communication*. Cincinnati, OH: South-Western, p. 398

Sharland, A. and Balogh, P. (1996) The value of non-selling activities at international trade shows. *Industrial Marketing Management*, *25(1)*, 59–66.

Shipley, D., Egan, C. and Wong, K.S. (1993) Dimensions of trade show exhibiting management. *Journal of Marketing Management*, *9(1)*, 55–64.

Southgate, P. (1994) *Total Branding by Design*. London: Kogan Page.

Walczyk, D. (2001) Packaging should be a critical element in the branding scheme. *Marketing News*, *35(23)*, 14–17.

Wohl, J. (2016) McDonald's packaging gets bright makeover. *Advertising Age*, 11 January, *6*.

Part III

IMC Messages

In the first two parts of this book we have explored the general context of IMC, where it fits within corporate and brand strategy and its various component parts. In Part III, we turn our attention to the message itself, the importance of understanding how it is processed, how it is developed, and techniques needed to ensure that it is effective. IMC is made from advertising and promotion messages that may be delivered in a variety of ways, as we have seen. These messages are no more than a collection of words and pictures, without meaning for a brand, until successfully processed.

In Chapter 8, we discuss message processing and learn how difficult it is to get a target audience to successfully process marketing communication. To begin with, it is the job of the media carrying the message to make it available to the target audience. Once exposed, it is up to the execution itself to attract and hold attention, and encourage learning the brand name and key benefit (at minimum), and for high-involvement decisions, to accept the message as well. At each of these steps, emotion will be involved, informing how the message will be processed.

Chapter 9 looks at what is needed for developing an effective message. It begins with an overview of how a brand is to be positioned within its marketing communication (and, as always, we are using the word 'brand' in the widest possible way). This results in a positioning statement that clearly and simply outlines what the brand is, who it is for, and what it offers. What it offers is the benefit, and once chosen, an appropriate benefit focus is determined. With the positioning and benefit focus in place, communication objectives are established, and the correct communication strategy follows. All of this is then summarized in a creative brief. It is at this point, once the strategic decisions have been made, that it is time to come up with creative ideas to execute that strategy. The most promising creative ideas are then worked up into rough executions and *tested*. This pre-testing is essential to ensure that the message will be correctly processed and effectively communicate the positioning. The chapter concludes with a section on social marketing communication. While it utilizes the same basic strategic and planning objectives, the message development for social marketing communication is significantly different from other IMC.

Maximizing the likelihood of message processing and satisfying a brand's communication objective is, of course, the job of creative executions. While it is creative instinct and genius that brings marketing communication to life, especially advertising, effective executions require much more than a great creative idea to be successful. A great creative idea could be entertaining, but may not satisfy the brand's communication objective. An idea that is not consistent with the executional requirements associated with a brand's communication objective and strategy cannot be successful. This is why we pre-test.

DOI: 10.4324/9781003169635-10

In Chapter 10, we address some of these requirements, and looks at creative techniques that are known to help facilitate message processing, and specific creative tactics associated with brand awareness and brand attitude communication objectives.

There is a large and significant body of knowledge in psychology covering the ways in which words and pictures are used in the execution of a message that leads to successful processing. These fundamental creative techniques should be understood by everyone involved in the development, execution, and evaluation of IMC. They provide the foundation from which the creative mind must build its magic, ensuring not only a memorable and unique execution, but one that is likely to satisfy the brand communication objectives and positively influence brand choice. A number of these techniques are also discussed in Chapter 10.

8 Message processing

Processing is the general term that applies to the short-term attention paid to marketing communication and what follows. It occurs with *each* exposure to a message execution, however delivered: through advertising or promotion, the package, even the product itself, or just hearing the brand name. In fact, any reference to the brand. Processing reflects how the target audience deals with the message being delivered in an integrated marketing communication (IMC) campaign. Every part of an IMC campaign and each component of every execution will have the capacity to stimulate specific neural activity in the brain. This is why it is so important to understand what is involved in processing IMC messages.

Message processing is obviously dependent on exposure to the message, and if successfully processed will lead to the desired response. But it will also be dependent on the knowledge and assumptions associated in memory with all of the various elements in an execution, and these may differ among people. Even when processing the same advert or package, or however the message is being delivered, neural systems will react differently depending on our goals, moods, and memories. This underscores the critical importance of pretesting integrated marketing communication (IMC) executions.

Consciousness

Since the 1990s, the study of consciousness has been at the forefront of neuroscience research. There are at least three concepts of consciousness: vigilance, attention, and conscious access (Dehaene, 2014). Vigilance refers to the state of wakefulness, attention is the focusing of our mental resources onto something specific, and conscious access relates to the fact that we become aware of what we attend to and are able to tell others about it. Only the last two concepts are important for IMC.

To understand consciousness, we must first consider *preconscious* or what is accessible to us, but which we have not yet attended to. To all of the many things in our environment that are vying for our attention at any one time, we will only pay selective attention to a very few, and from this small group, only *one thing* can be brought to consciousness at any one time. Those things attended to, but before being brought to consciousness, make up our preconscious, which forms a sort of 'buffer' zone where things that we paid attention to wait to be called into consciousness. But, this wait is risky because at any moment new incoming stimuli or distracted thoughts can erase the buffered item, and this risk increases the longer they wait (Dehaene, 2014).

DOI: 10.4324/9781003169635-11

Unconscious processing

There is a great deal that people process, but are unaware of. It is impossible to consciously attend to everything in our environment, and much of our behaviour is unconscious. This is what enables a driver to stop at a red light, a person to type or to play the piano. One does not consciously think: 'That light just turned red, what should I do?' One simply applies the brake. In typing or playing the piano, one does not consciously recall where the letter g is located on the keyboard or where the note b-flat is on their instrument. They automatically type the letter or play the note. This is called procedural memory, a key part of nondeclarative or implicit memory, and behaviour associated with it is unconscious.

An interesting view of unconscious processing follows the work of Zajonc and his colleagues, and his notion of 'mere exposure', or priming effects (Zajonc, 1968; Murphy and Zajonc, 1993). For example, having seen or heard words or pictures briefly, even subconsciously, can increase the likelihood of using them later (Kalat, 2004). But priming effects are largely a response to familiarity among a set of otherwise unfamiliar alternatives. As we have pointed out elsewhere (Percy, 2006), even if there is unconscious processing of advertising, there is no reason to expect a priming effect because other brands, as well as attitudes toward the 'primed' brand, will be recalled from *conscious* memory during brand choice.

There are some people in advertising (including academics) who try to suggest that there is an 'unconscious processing' of advertising that can inform attitudes toward the advertised brand. This is simply impossible. Indeed, unconscious processing is occurring all the time; it is the source of what may eventually be brought to consciousness. Unconscious processing occurs largely within the narrow bounds of the left temporal lobe, where the language networks that process memory lie (Sergent, et al., 2005). Much larger neural networks in the frontal lobe are involved in consciousness. Only consciousness permits us to retain lasting thoughts.

Subliminal processing

This might be a good place to address the notion of 'subliminal' processing. The preconscious is *not* a subliminal state. While cognition might be influenced without our notice, the effects are too short and small to be of any practical use in IMC or any other field (Karremans, et al, 2006). Even when subliminal cues are purposely embedded in adverts, there is no significant effect on the advert's ability to communicate or persuade (Moore, 1982). In the early 1990s, a review of over 200 studies in this area failed to find any subliminal effects upon behaviour (Patkamis and Arousen, 1991).

Research into subliminal perception today continues to find little, if any, evidence that subliminal messages could influence attitudes or complex behaviour. Why? A subliminal stimulus will *never* become conscious, no matter how hard you try to perceive it. Subliminal thought only lasts for an instant, and while they do have the potential to create a certain 'feeling of familiarity' that a product has been seen before (Johan et al., 2006), basically a priming effect, it would have no effect upon choice. But what about that famous case where 'Drink Coca-Cola' and 'Eat popcorn' was subliminally flashed on the screen in a movie theatre and there was a rush to the concession stand? It never happened. In 1984 James Vicary, the cinema owner who was the man behind it, admitted he made it all up to promote his business (Sutherland and Sylvester, 2000).

Conscious processing

People respond 'consciously' to everything they are exposed to and to which they actively attend neurologically. Psychologists like to talk about this in terms of *cognitive response*, which is nothing more than a conscious activity that goes on when actively processing information. Even though someone may not consciously be aware of everything that is being processed, they are associating in working memory the new information (e.g., exposure to an advertisement or seeing a brand on the shelf) with all the relevant knowledge and assumptions already stored in memory. This is top-down processing, and involves declarative, explicit memory; our conscious memory.

People bring to brands and their marketing communication attitudes and beliefs associated with their expectations and experiences, and this will all inform how they think about that brand and process information about it. This follows from the two fundamental types of conscious memory: semantic memory and episodic memory (Tulving, 2002a, 2002b). Semantic memory may be thought of as 'fact-based', and will include a general knowledge and understanding of brands and products. Episodic memory is 'event-based', and will include a person's experience with brands and products. This would not only include using the brand, but memories of an event that was sponsored by the brand. Together, both semantic and episodic memory combine to form declarative, conscious memory and are integrated with new information as it is processed in working memory to form and build new memories linked to the brand.

In terms of cognitive response theory, it is assumed that people will try to make sense of what they are experiencing: looking at a product display in a store, reading an advertisement in a magazine, watching a commercial on television or attending an event sponsored by a company. How they make sense of what they are experiencing is by accessing the appropriate declarative memories from both semantic and episodic memory. It is the job of IMC to be sure that a consistent base of knowledge and experience is available for making judgements about a brand (brand attitude) and making choices (brand purchase intention).

Communication response sequence

William J. McGuire was one of the founding fathers of attitude change theory, and he described six processing steps that must occur for any message to be persuasive, which he called an *information processing paradigm*. He was referring to any type of persuasive communication, and this would include advertising. The six steps were as follows: the message must be presented to the target audience, they must pay attention to the message, comprehend what is presented, yield to the argument, retain that agreement, and then act on it.

Perhaps, the most important point to understand about McGuire's information processing paradigm is that it involves *compounding probabilities*. This is why persuasive communication is so difficult. What it means is that if one is 50 percent successful at each stage of the process, less than 2 percent of the target audience will actually act on their positive intention formed as a result of processing the message: this is the nature of compounding probabilities. If 50 percent are presented the message and 50 percent pay attention, that is 25 percent of the target audience; another 50 percent comprehend what the message is saying, meaning 12.5 percent of the total target audience; 50 percent yield, or 6.25 percent of the target; 50 percent form a positive intention, a bit more than 3 percent of the target; and 50 percent act on that intention, just 1.5 percent of the target audience. This should dramatically underscore the difficult job IMC has in effectively communicating with its target audience.

In an IMC sense, these six steps of the information processing paradigm may be thought of as a communication response sequence, where exposure leads to processing that brings about a communication effect leading to the desired target audience action:

Exposure → Processing → Communication Effect → Target Audience Action

It is the job of IMC to ensure that all the various executions in a campaign are contributing to this process.

Good planning will ensure exposure. The manager is responsible for scheduling media in such a way that the target audience will have ample opportunity to see and hear the messages. An important consideration at this first stage in IMC planning is how many opportunities, at minimum, will be necessary to ensure that enough processing of the message occurs to drive the desired communication effect. It may require several exposures before enough attention is paid to learn something about the brand's primary benefit, and even if a positive intention is formed, additional messages may need to be processed in order to keep that intention salient until an actual purchase is made. This can be true even with current users of a brand. If a brand is not routinely and frequently purchased, even users may need to be regularly reminded. This is why establishing what the minimum effective frequency should be in the media plan is so important.

Message processing responses

The communication response sequence is triggered by exposure to any part of an IMC campaign, as well as to the brand itself during usage. As Rossiter et al. (2018) have pointed out, even exposure to the marketing communication of competitive brands could influence processing for a brand. For example, if two competing brands are associated in memory, exposure to the competitor's marketing communication could trigger a sequence such as: 'Ah, this is the brand that claims to be better than my brand, but nothing can top my brand' for a brand loyal. Or for more casual users of the brand, perhaps: 'This is the brand that claims to be better than the one I'm using. I wonder if it is? Maybe I'll give it a try'.

The point is that the processing of information about a brand can be initiated by exposure to a wide variety of sources. Thus, exposure to anything related to a brand has the potential for initiating the processing of information about it. One cannot control the advertising or other marketing communication of competitors, but they must be taken into account when developing one's own message.

Processing itself is made up of four different responses that can follow from exposure: attention, learning, acceptance, and emotion (Figure 8.1). With the exception of emotion,

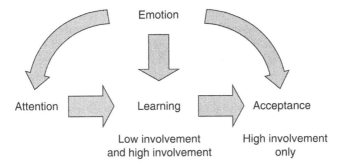

Figure 8.1 Processing responses.

which is involved with the other three, these responses reflect stages of McGuire's information processing paradigm (attention, comprehension, and yielding).

Attention is necessary before any of the other processing responses can occur. Without *conscious* attention being paid to the message (and again we mean message to include any reference to the brand), it will be impossible to *fully* process the message. While some have tried to argue that low attention or unconscious attention to marketing communication can be effective, with the exception of emotional responses it is very unlikely, and, with only unconscious attention, impossible (Percy, 2006) as we have just seen. Full processing begins in working memory, where the new information that has been attended to and accessible in preconscious is consciously integrated with existing knowledge and assumptions about the brand.

After attention comes *learning*, where some information is picked up from the execution and is stored in memory. With effective processing of the message, this will include at least the brand name and the key benefit. With low-involving products, for potential buyers learning is really all that might be necessary in order to stimulate a tentatively positive attitude toward the brand and an interest in trying it. They do not really need to accept the message as being true as such, only experience what Maloney (1962) called 'curious disbelief:' I wonder if that claim could really be true? Because it is a low-involvement decision with no real risk in trying it, you make the purchase to see if it is true. With existing users, relearning of the brand and benefit from an IMC execution serves to reinforce brand awareness and positive brand attitude. When we say 'relearning', we do not mean users have necessarily forgotten the brand, only that as they process the message it is consistent with existing memory for the brand and makes it salient.

With high-involvement products, the target audience must not only learn what the message is trying to communicate, they must also *accept* the message. In processing the message, they must take what they have learned and integrate it with all their knowledge and assumptions about the product category and competing brands, and believe that what the message says fits with this. This is because of the potential risk involved in making a bad choice decision. If it does, this will initiate the formation of a positive brand attitude for potential new users, and help reinforce or build brand attitude for users.

The fourth response in processing is *emotion*. At some level, there is an emotional response to everything one encounters in life so that necessarily includes marketing communication. It is important to understand that emotion will be involved in attention, learning and acceptance, and, in some cases, along with attention, may be all the processing that occurs. After attending to the message someone may have a negative emotional response and *never* learn anything, including the brand name. A person may simply hate the advertisement, package, etc. On the other hand, someone may only have a positive emotional response and connect it with the brand, which itself could be enough to drive preference if it is a low-involvement product (especially transformational). We look at emotion in some depth later in this chapter.

Processing of messages, once it moves beyond attention, has the potential to initiate, reinforce, or increase communication effects for a brand. For those unfamiliar with a brand, at the very least brand awareness will occur. Users of the brand will likely have their brand attitude and purchase intention reinforced; potential users familiar with the brand may have their attitudes toward the brand strengthened, and a purchase intention initiated. At the same time, if marketing communication for a competitor brand is being processed, there is the potential for those communication effects to interfere with the communication effects for the first brand. This would be the case in the example above for the casual brand user whose interest in another brand was initiated by advertising. Their existing positive brand attitude for the brand they use, built and sustained by processing the brand's IMC, was interfered with by processing the other brand's advertising.

Although a simple example, this is what is going on all the time in the market. The target audience is processing messages from a wide variety of sources for a number of brands in a category, with resulting communication effects: they are aware of many brands, they have at least some tentative positive brand attitudes, and, for some have, formed purchase intentions. The stronger a brand's marketing communication, the greater chance it has of 'inoculating' the target audience against competitor messages. This is something McGuire (1969) talked about as inoculation theory – how processing strong positive messages over time will build attitudes more resistant to the arguments of others.

In a sense, processing is where the target audience takes over from the marketing manager. It is the manager who provides the opportunity for exposure, but the target audience must then process the marketing communication before anything else will happen. True, the manager can help facilitate the likelihood of processing with effective creative executions, and we look at how this can be done in the next chapter. But in the rest of this chapter, we look specifically at how the target audience processes messages. When managers understand how a message is processed, they are in a much better position to develop more effective strategic IMC plans.

Attention

Our primary concern is with the *initial* attention paid to marketing communication. Once initial attention is achieved, it is up to the execution itself (the advertisement, package, brochure) to hold attention and ensure further processing. While the notion of attention may seem obvious, there is a great deal of debate in the fields of neuropsychology and neurology over what constitutes 'attention'. In the last 50 years, over a dozen different theories of attention have been proposed. Although no single theory has emerged, perhaps the work that has enjoyed the strongest influence on the meaning of attention is that of Broadbent (1958) and his filter theory. This theory posits that people have the ability to block or weaken the messages coming to the brain from their sense organs. It is not exactly clear how this is done, but there is ample evidence that it does occur. The result is that the content of consciousness in working memory after being filtered by attention is limited.

Today, attention is no longer seen as a simple process that enhances perception, but rather a complex process that helps us better understand what is going on around us, and provides strategies for, as well as control of, how information is processed (Gregory, 2004). In terms of marketing communications, we do not need to be concerned about the neural arguments, but we do need to understand that there is a difference between conscious and unconscious attention, and that most unconscious attention will not lead to a full processing of a message.

Unconscious processing is automatic and reflects something psychologists talk about as 'bottom-up' processing, which deals unconsciously with signals from our senses. This is in contrast to 'top-down' processing, which calls on the associations already in explicit or declarative memory (conscious memory) to help interpret the signals coming from our senses. However, just because someone is not aware of something does not necessarily mean they do not consciously process it. As someone flips through a magazine or glances at a television commercial, they are probably not aware that they are paying attention to the content. Do you consciously think to yourself 'that is an advertisement and I am not interested'? Unlikely, but your behaviour can indicate that you did pay some attention because you keep turning the pages, or leave the room to get something to eat. Visual input into working memory (bottom-up processing) was recognized as an advertisement or commercial (top-down processing) and the decision was made to not further process the message.

But people do pay unconscious attention to much of what is going on around them; they just tend to ignore it. When the conscious mind is occupied, all other possibilities for awareness that have been unconsciously attended to wait in our preconscious, as we have seen. For example, research suggests that our visual system is filtering out some information even if neurologically it is being held at an unconscious level. This is especially likely if one's attention is focused somewhere else. In a classic example of this, Simons and Chabris (1999) showed a group a film of people tossing a basketball back and forth and asked the participants to count the number of passes. About a minute into the exercise, someone dressed in a gorilla costume walked directly in front of the screen, yet incredibly 70 percent of those in the study did not notice the gorilla! When the exercise was repeated, and the participants were asked to look for the gorilla, they had no trouble seeing it. In a more recent audio version of the study (Dalton and Fraenkel, 2012), participants listened to a stereo recording of two men and two women independently talking about a party. Half were asked to pay attention to the men's conversation, half the women's. In the middle of the recording, a man began repeating 'I'm a gorilla, I'm a gorilla' for 19 seconds. When asked later if they heard anything odd, 90 percent of those asked to listen to the men's conversation mentioned the gorilla, but only 30 percent of those asked to listen to the women's conversation mentioned the gorilla.

Activity in the frontal–parietal network will filter out a lot of information when your attention is focused on something else. Things that would otherwise be obvious, like the person in a gorilla suit, are suppressed. This has clear implications for IMC. Both for elements within an execution, as well as for the environment in which it is exposed, if attention is drawn to something it could very well be to the exclusion of other parts of the execution, or to the message itself.

It is also important to understand that we can never actively consciously process two unrelated things at the same time. As one thing enters our conscious awareness, others must wait in our preconscious, something often referred to as the 'psychological refracting period' (Sigman and Dehaene, 2005). And, those other items in the preconscious can easily vanish with distracting thoughts or other incoming stimuli as already noted, and the likelihood of this occurring increases with time (Marti et al., 2012). As a result, it is not surprising that all too often when IMC messages are competing for attention, they will not make it into consciousness.

With marketing communication to be effective *conscious* attention is required, with one exception. Generally speaking, emotional responses are processed unconsciously. But as we see later in this chapter, they interact in working memory with conscious, declarative memory.

Learning

In processing marketing communication messages, after gaining attention, the target audience must 'learn' something. At the very least, the marketer must communicate the brand name and the primary benefit associated with that brand. With low-involving product decisions, that is really all that is necessary. But as we see later, for high-involvement decisions, the simple learning of the brand and the benefit will not be enough. The target audience must also accept the message as true.

Within a neurological or psychological context, learning means the stimulating of pre-existing synapses in the brain. It is rare that learning will involve something totally new, and the creation of a new synapse. Learning involves the integration of new information with existing knowledge and assumptions. In processing marketing communication, if a person pays attention and continues to process the message, they are 'learning' at least something. But what they are 'learning' may not be new information. They may be learning that they already know those things about the brand. For example, people familiar with a brand will recognize it and learn that the message is about that brand, and they will bring into working memory other associations they have with that brand, and integrate it with what they are processing from the message (top-down processing, as mentioned earlier). If the benefit has not already been associated with the brand in memory, what they do associate with that benefit will be brought into working memory and integrated with what they know about the brand. Then either a new memory will be formed coupling the benefit with the brand, an association with the brand will be rejected, or the message will simply be 'forgotten'.

In a psychological sense, all of this is 'learning'. The reason it is important to understand this is because when developing marketing communication executions (packages, advertisements, etc.) one must be aware that the images used and the benefits presented will be understood within the framework of already existing knowledge and assumptions about those images and textual content. In the following box, we see how important it is to get pictures and images correct.

The importance of good photos on websites

The website of many small businesses cannot afford to use professional photographers, and the pictures on the site reflect it. Poor images cannot only affect a company's image, but can also negatively affect sales. In 2005 the chocolate maker sweetrot received emails from customers asking what a blurry photo of their chocolate-covered cacao nibs was. The founder, Sarah Endling, was convinced the bad picture had a significant negative effect on sales, leading her to hire a professional photographer. She then reported that customers 'loved our photos' of their products and a picture of the company team. Now they include the pictures in their delivery boxes, and send them out as promotional postcards.

Other more subtle problems often occur when not enough attention is given to the picture a company uses on their website. As David Pries, co-founder of the presentation-design firm ProPoint Graphics, points out, all too often the photos of executives on a company's 'About Us' page end up as nothing but 'head shot soup' (as he put it). What is presented are pictures taken at different times with different backgrounds, which distracts from any sense of a cohesive unit of executives, and is more likely to communicate a sense of carelessness and inconsistency.

Increasingly, some companies use stock photos to represent company executives. Mr Pries recalls one company that was found out doing just that by a customer who saw the same images on another company's website; the same stock photos used to represent people at different companies. Not likely to instil trust in the firm.

Source: *The Wall Street Journal*, 21 May 2012

Learning and brand awareness

Learning, in the sense that we are using the term, refers to rote learning. Rote learning is a passive process, and occurs automatically whether we are aware of it or not (Langer et al., 1978). Because of the nature of rote learning, a certain amount of repetition is usually required before new memories for the learned response are retained. Part of that repetition comes from the consistency in message and execution that is part of IMC.

Those unfamiliar with a brand must obviously 'learn' the brand name, but this does little good if they do not associate the brand with the appropriate category need. The response that must be learned will depend on whether recognition or recall brand awareness is required, as discussed in earlier chapters. What must be learned with brand recognition strategies is that the brand will be associated with the need in such a way that when the brand is seen at the point-of-purchase, it is immediately linked with the need. With recognition brand awareness, seeing the package or hearing the brand name should always elicit in the target audience's mind the question: 'Do I need any of that now?' On the other hand, brand recall learning requires the brand to be the response to the need. When the need occurs, it should elicit from the target audience the brand as satisfying that need.

The key to learning the appropriate brand awareness association is something Tulving (1983) talked about as *encoding specificity*. As he defined it, 'successful retrieval depends on achieving a match between the information encoded at the time of learning and the information that is available at the time of retrieval'. With marketing communication, this means that the execution must present the brand in the same way as it is most likely to be presented when a brand choice is made. For brand recognition learning, the target audience must be able to recognize the brand at the point-of-purchase. As we have discussed, this means the execution must show the package as it will be encountered, and within the context of the product category. For brand recall learning, the need must be clearly shown with the brand as the solution and in that order, so that the connection is learned in such a way that the brand name is retrieved from memory when the need occurs. We deal with creative tactics in more detail in Chapter 10.

Learning and brand attitude

The key to learning for building a positive brand attitude is to learn the brand's primary benefit, and link it in memory with the brand. Remember, that benefit, at least in some form, will already be associated with other things in memory. The job of a brand's marketing communication is to highlight the degree of the connection between the brand and the benefit, and the job of individual executions (things like the package, advertisements, in-store collateral, etc.) is to tie in other positive associations with the benefit from memory in order to reinforce the positive nature of the benefit.

If the primary benefit for a brand of soluble (instant) coffee is 'great coffee taste', using images in executions that are likely to elicit this benefit will facilitate making that connection, and make it stronger as new memories are formed. For example, suppose the brand used a picture of an espresso machine in the background, with a steaming cup of coffee in the foreground alongside the package. The image of the steaming cup of coffee would be likely to elicit positive memories among the target audience of coffee's aroma, and this will be reinforced more positively by the association with coffee made by an espresso machine. Additionally, using a cup, not a mug, should activate a more high-quality association in memory. All of this is then linked to the brand, and a new memory formed. People know that soluble coffee really does not taste as good as fresh-brewed espresso. But because this is a low-involving decision, all that is necessary is to create a positive feeling that it might be good-tasting coffee. When seen in the store, that positive feeling will be retrieved as the audience thinks to themselves: 'I wonder if it really does taste that good. I think I'll try it and see'.

Advert 8.1 provides a really good example of what we are talking about here. The Greek Style Yogurt advert integrates the visual image with the benefit of 'natural', a benefit also clearly communicated on the package and in the copy. Additionally, the 'style' of the name is reinforced by 'stile' in the execution. This is an excellent example of linking multiple elements in an execution to reinforce one another, which helps to encode the brand name and benefit in memory.

For high-involvement decisions, however, this sort of simple rote learning will not be enough to drive positive brand attitude. To begin with, because of the risk involved, more than one benefit will usually need to be learned. Learning about the primary benefit is what will help hold the target audience's attention, and interest them in processing the rest of the message. Assuming the primary benefit is important to them, they will then be looking for more information before beginning to form a positive brand attitude and possible brand purchase intention.

To facilitate learning when dealing with high-involvement decisions, it is important to understand the target audience's existing knowledge and assumptions about the brand and product category. In order to process and learn the brand's benefit, they must be

Advert 8.1 Greek Style yoghurt.

Source: © Yeo Valley Farms.

pitched in the execution at a high level, but not so high that it is dismissed as un-
believable. Knowing where this line is drawn is critical because the message should not
undersell either. This idea reflects something that Sherif and Hovland (1961) talked
about long ago in their assimilation–contrast theory. People hold definite beliefs about

things, and if an advertisement for a high-involvement product makes a claim, that claim will either be accepted or not based on these existing beliefs. If a new hybrid car makes the claim that it is more powerful than a BMW, the target audience is likely to dismiss it out-of-hand. Such a claim would fall into what Sherif and Hovland called their 'latitude of rejection'. How could a hybrid be more powerful than a BMW?

But what if this new hybrid really was more powerful? If that were the case, marketing communication would need to gradually build toward that claimed benefit, perhaps with a refutational strategy. This can be accomplished by pitching the claim in what Sherif and Hovland call the 'latitude of indifference', an area between what is felt to be true and what is definitely not true. Perhaps the claim could be made that because of new technology this new hybrid has significantly more power. Unless the target audience believes a hybrid can never have much power, this claim could fall into their latitude of indifference: they don't necessarily agree, but they don't necessarily reject it either. They would be open to processing the message, especially if not having enough power was a significant concern among potential hybrid buyers. You can see from this example how important it is to know what the target audience's existing attitudes are when dealing with high-involving decisions. If they are to successfully process the message, learning the desired benefit, it is critical to understand where their latitude of rejection lies in order not to overclaim.

In summary, as with brand awareness, all that is required for low-involvement persuasion is rote learning of the brand benefit to initiate a positive brand attitude. The brand name has already been learned (brand awareness learning), and it is only necessary to associate that brand in memory with its benefit. The actual response learned will be that the brand has the benefit. Because it is a low-involvement decision, the benefit is only temporarily held in memory until the product is actually purchased. But with high-involvement decisions, persuasion requires acceptance, not just learning, of the brand's benefit as we discuss in the next section. The target audience must *personally agree* with the benefit claims being made for the brand.

This thinking follows directly from low-versus high-involvement models of decision-making. In psychology, low-involvement decisions follow a cognitive-conative-affect model and high-involvement decisions a cognitive-affect-conative model (where cognitive reflects learning, affect attitude formation, and conative behaviour). This has been translated in the marketing and communication literature to various low-involvement choice models and the traditional hierarchy-of-effect model.

In low-involvement models, such as Ehrenberg's Awareness-Trial-Reinforcement model (Ehrenberg, 1974), one first becomes aware of the brand, then, on the basis of a tentatively formed favourable attitude ('I think I might like that'), the brand is tried. *After* trial, more permanent attitudes are formed. Trial of the brand will either re-inforce the initial positive attitude or bring about a rejection of it. One does not necessarily need to accept that the message is really true because there is little, if any, risk involved. If the person does not like the product after trial, they do not buy it again. On the other hand, when dealing with high-involvement decisions, a hierarchy-of-effects model holds. One becomes aware of the brand, but because of the risk associated with making a bad choice, a *definite* positive attitude must be formed prior to trial. The buyer must be convinced they will like the brand before buying. These basic models are illustrated in Figure 8.2.

An experience of *Wine Enthusiast* magazine in the United States offers an excellent example of the need to consider every aspect of marketing communication in terms of

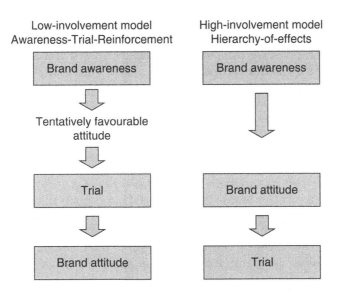

Figure 8.2 Basic consumer decision models.

how the message is likely to be processed (Strum, 2004). Wine retailers often use ratings and reviews at the point-of-purchase for wines on offer. The value of these ratings comes from the consumer's perception of the credibility of the reviewer or publication offering the rating. Thousands of wine retailers used the ratings from the *Wine Enthusiast* taste panel on 'shelf-talkers' (those small notices fixed to a store shelf with an announcement or promotion).

But there was a problem. Retailers brought to the magazine's attention that its logo was presenting a problem. The logo used the word 'Wine' in large letters, stacked over the smaller 'Enthusiast' (Figure 8.3a). When the logo was used with a rating on a shelf-talker, the word 'Wine' was clearly visible, but the key word 'Enthusiast' that identified the magazine, and the source of the rating, was so small as to be barely perceptible. Consumers seeing the shelf-talker would likely only process the word 'Wine' and the rating.

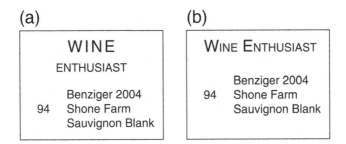

Figure 8.3 (a) Original *Wine Enthusiast* shelf-talker. (b) Revised *Wine Enthusiast* shelf-talker using new logo.

This was obviously not what the retailer wanted to convey, and the magazine was receiving no exposure. The retailers wanted consumers to understand that the *Wine Enthusiast* had rated the wine highly, and in effect was recommending it. All the consumer was processing, however, was that the wine was rated highly by 'someone'. This may have been sufficient if the purchase was low involvement, but most wine purchases are likely to be high involvement. The buyer wants to be sure the wine will be good; especially for special occasions. In response to this problem, the *Wine Enthusiast* redesigned their logo (Figure 8.3b). With the new logo, ratings can be quickly and easily processed and linked to *Wine Enthusiast*, and with the new logo, the magazine had a new face.

Acceptance

With high-involvement decisions one must *accept* the message; you must be convinced it is true prior to purchase because of the risk involved in making a bad decision. When processing the message, the target audience must believe what they learned about the brand is true, *and* that the main benefit corresponds to what they are most looking for in the product. In order for this to happen, the message must fall within their latitude of acceptance.

With low-involvement decisions, acceptance as such is not necessary because there is little risk in making a bad choice. If the target audience thinks that the advert's message might be true, that constitutes acceptance.

Emotion

We have seen that processing marketing communication requires attention, learning, and, for high-involvement decisions, acceptance as well. But processing also involves emotion, it is a critical component of all message processing, and it is essential for managers to understand the role it plays (Percy, 2012). Emotion operates in two fundamental ways as it influences how marketing communication is processed. First, there are emotional associations in memory linked to almost every object and experience in a person's life, and these emotional associations will be activated by the text and, especially, the images used in an execution. Second, when there are people shown in an execution, the emotion expressed by those people will stimulate a corresponding emotion in anyone paying attention to it (something known as embodiment).

The way these two emotional responses mediate the processing of marketing communication will be discussed next, but first, it would make sense to look at what is meant by an 'emotion'. To begin with, it is important to understand that emotions and feelings are *not* the same thing. In an emotion it is the unconscious underlying process that embodies all the components that go into making up an emotion, while a feeling is only the 'conscious' expression of that emotion. Damasio (1999) has described this difference well: 'The full human impact of emotions is only realized when they are sensed, when they become feelings, and when those feelings are felt. That is when they become known, with the assistance of consciousness'.

Most people who study emotion described it in terms of three different components referred to as the 'reaction triad': physiological arousal, motor expression and subjective feeling. To illustrate this, suppose you came across a coiled snake on a path as you were walking through the woods. Before you are even conscious of the snake, your limbic system is at work signalling the body to release adrenaline and the heart to beat faster (physiological arousal), you 'freeze' (motor expression), and only then do you become aware of the sense of danger and fear (subjective feeling). All of these responses are part of emotion. The first two have little practical value for marketing communication; subjective feeling certainly does. It is these 'feelings' with which we are concerned.

Our conscious response to an emotion, our feelings, become a part of the cognitive process that leads to logical thinking. It helps increase attention and learning when consistent with the relevant underlying motivation driving behaviour and choice in the brand's product category. Damasio (2003) has stated that reasoning is influenced not only by conscious signals, but also by unconscious signals from the neural networks associated with emotions. This means that, along with a person's knowledge and experience with a brand, the emotional associations with these memories will influence brand choice.

Recent studies in neuroscience using neuroimagery with positron emission tomography (PET) scans and functional magnetic resonance imagery (fMRI) that measure brain activity when information is being processed have confirmed the role that emotion plays in brand choice decisions. In one study (McClure et al., 2004), brain activity was measured with fMRI as people made a choice between two colas. When they did not know what they were drinking, the only areas of the brain that were active were those associated with taste perception. But for those whose favourite brand was Coke, when they were asked to choose between Coke and Pepsi, knowing what they were tasting, those areas of the brain associated with emotional memory were active when they stated their preference.

Clearly, if managers understand the emotional associations with their brands and their markets, and with their marketing communication executions, they will have a powerful tool for developing more effective messages; messages more likely to be positively and fully processed. Gaining this understanding is not as difficult as one might think. Measuring emotional associations is done by asking about the *feelings* associated with something. According to Bradley and Lang (2000), people become conscious of their emotions when asked, and are quite capable of describing their feelings when asked to think about them.

Emotional associations in memory

Few, if any, objects or experiences are emotionally neutral. Everything one experiences and forms long-term memory traces of will have an emotional component. Advertisements, packages, and other marketing communication for a brand will activate not only cognitive, conscious associations from memory (declarative, or explicit memory as we see later in the chapter when we talk about memory), but also unconscious emotional associations (non-declarative emotional memories) with the brand. These memories are stored in the amygdala, part of the limbic system, and located in the paleomammalian region of the brain.

As one begins to process marketing communication, the emotional memories associated with the imagery used in the execution, as well as the brand itself, will proceed into conscious working memory, and it will arrive *ahead* of whatever conscious memories are activated. These emotional memories help 'frame' the knowledge and assumptions activated in conscious memory (largely from the hippocampus), and inform how the message will be initially processed. One of the most important jobs in IMC, which we look at in the next chapter, is ensuring a consistent look and feel among all the various executions in different media. This helps ensure that the same emotional memories are activated in the processing of the messages.

This means that when an advertisement or other marketing communication for a brand cues either positive emotional associations with the brand or with the imagery in an execution, those unconscious emotional memories will mix with conscious memory and enable a person to become aware of the fact that they are emotionally aroused. For example, they may experience a good feeling, or even a happy feeling. Out of the processing that occurs, new associations in memory are possible and likely. Any emotional learning, if linked to the brand, as well as learning associated with the benefit in the message, will be in play and ready to be activated when exposed to new advertising for the brand, when the brand is seen at the point-of-purchase, even when just 'thinking' about the brand. Effective marketing communication, using consistent executional elements within an IMC campaign, will ensure this happens.

Advert 8.2 for Cardrona Distillery is a perfect example of this. The 'Angels' Share' imagery will elicit a strong positive emotional response from any whisky drinker, and that feeling will be linked to the brand. It is this feeling that is the benefit, and it will be re-experienced when thinking about Cardrona single malt whisky, or when the bottle is seen on the shelf.

Still, it must be remembered that while positive emotional associations in memory will provide an initial positive context within working memory for processing the message, this does not have the strength to override negative conscious elements in the processing (e.g., noticing that the price of the brand has increased significantly). But in all other cases these positive emotional associations will facilitate positive processing of the message and the formation of new positive memories: in other words, learning.

Interpersonal emotion

The second area of emotion important to understand in the processing of marketing communication is interpersonal emotion and the notion of *embodiment*. Other people's emotions influence our own by virtue of the information they convey. This is thought by some social and evolutionary psychologists to be part of our natural response to our environment in order to survive. Sensing fear or anger in someone conveys potential threat or danger; happiness, safety, or comfort. When people are shown in advertisements, on packages, storefronts, or in other marketing communication, and they convey particular emotions, those perceived emotions will tend to influence parallel emotional responses in the target audience.

This is known as embodiment. In other words, people will embody, that is, take on or initiate the emotional behaviours of others as perceived in their facial expression, body posture or prosody (tone of voice). As Niedenthal et al. (2005) have defined it, embodiment means 'the bodily states that arise (e.g., posture, facial expression and use of the voice) during the perception or an emotional stimulus, and the later use of that emotional information (in the absence of the emotional stimulus)'. In effect, the emotions exhibited by people in, for example, an advertisement, will be 'felt' by those attending to it, and that emotion will become part of the processing in working memory of that message. This will be available for later use when processing other messages about the brand.

The most important component in assessing someone else's emotional state is their facial expression, and this has been studied more than any other aspect of emotional expression (deGelder, 2005). It seems that people have a very efficient system for recognizing and processing the emotional content of facial expressions. As with emotional

Advert 8.2 Cardrona.

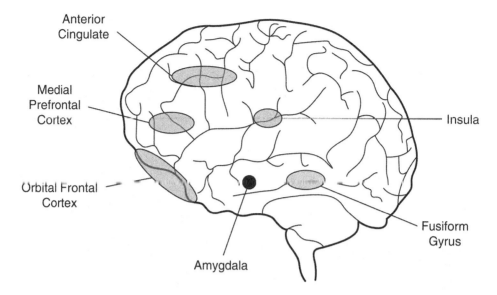

Figure 8.4 Brain areas believed to be involved in the perception of emotion from facial expression.

memories, the amygdala is at the heart of how emotional expressions are processed (Wright et al., 2002).

The amygdala plays the most important role in emotional responses. However, other areas of the brain are also involved, especially in the response to facial expressions. Some of these include the medial prefrontal and orbitofrontal cortex, which neurological studies have shown to be activated by facial expression, as well as the anterior cingulate, insula and regions of the occipital cortex such as the fusiform gyros (Del–Ben et al., 2005). Figure 8.4 illustrates where these areas are located in the brain.

When looking at someone's facial expression, it is the eyebrows, mouth and eyes that convey emotion. Based on a study of schematic faces representing happy or threatening expressions (as illustrated in Figure 8.5), Lundqvist and Öhman (2005) found that

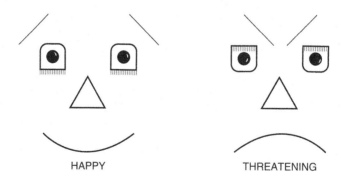

Figure 8.5 Happy versus threatening schematic faces.

Source: Adapted from Lundqvist and Öhman (2005).

V-shaped eyebrows conveyed a threatening emotion while ∩-shaped eyebrows were seen as friendly. They also found that a U-shaped mouth conveys a happy feeling while a ∧-shaped mouth was seen as unhappy. Using eye-tracking, they also determined that the most important facial cue communicating threat or anger was the eyebrows, and for communicating a happy feeling, the mouth. Subsequent work using image analysis of real faces supported these findings.

This of course has direct implications for executions in marketing communication. To communicate a positive, happy emotion requires attention to a true 'smile'. Rossiter and Percy (1997) pointed out the need for depicting an authentic emotion, critical for transformational strategies. But this is not easy to effect. Even experienced actors have difficulty realistically projecting an emotion that is not truly felt, and this is especially true of smiles. This is because of the evolutionary importance of smiles. The facial muscles that control smiles are affected by two distinct neural systems. First, the evolutionarily older one originates in the striatum and exerts an involuntary control over facial muscles, reflecting truly felt emotions (Fridland, 1994). The second, in terms of evolution, is newer and involves voluntarily controlled muscles (Gazzaniga and Smylie, 1990). As a result, the use of the intentionally controlled muscles for a smile that an actor may use in smiling might not reflect a true positive emotion.

These voluntary smiles need only involve the mouth, and are consciously seen and interpreted as a smile, as the work by Lundqvist and Öhman (2005) has shown. The truly felt positive emotions such as happiness will also involve the muscles around the eye, and this will initiate an embodiment of the emotion. Such smiles are known as 'Duchenne Smiles' after the 19th-century French anatomist Duchenne de Boulogue. A true Duchenne Smile is an unintentional emotional signal that occurs spontaneously on the experiencing of the positive emotion of joy or happiness, reflecting a true emotional state. This is what one is looking for when using people in marketing communication and one wishes to elicit a positive emotional response (essential for transformational brand attitude strategies). It will be this true smile that will be embodied and elicit a positive emotional response.

The role of memory

One must be concerned with memory in any consideration of IMC because of the nature of IMC. With multiple messages, delivered through different media, how these messages are processed and stored in memory will be critical to the overall effectiveness of the campaign. It is essential that as different messages are processed they become part of a unified memory for the brand. Even though various messages, and various aspects of individual messages, may be processed differently, they must be associated in memory with the brand, and available for subsequent processing when the brand is being considered.

In this chapter, we have referred a number of times to 'conscious' and 'unconscious' processing. In many ways, what we are really talking about here when talking about processing and its result is *memory*. Conscious processing involves the use of what psychologists call declarative or 'explicit' memory. Unconscious processing involves what is known as nondeclarative or 'implicit' memory, and reflects what we have talked about as 'bottom-up' processing. It is important to understand that even if there happens to be unconscious processing of marketing communication leading to implicit memory (unlikely in any case), those memories cannot inform brand attitudes or choice as we have seen. The only exception here is nondeclarative emotional memories (Percy, 2006).

Declarative and nondeclarative memories recruit different brain systems and use different strategies for storing memory (Heilman, 2002). One's declarative memory is for facts, assumptions and events, the sorts of things that one can bring consciously to mind as either a verbal proposition ('that is an expensive, luxury product') or a visual image (in our mind's eye we 'see' the product). Nondeclarative memories also come from experiences, but they are expressed in terms of unconscious changes in behaviour, not as conscious recollections. With the exception of emotion, non-declarative memories are generally inaccessible to the conscious mind. Such memories tend to involve knowledge that is *reflexive* rather than *reflective* in nature (Heilman, 2002). Importantly, in terms of IMC and brand learning, once something is stored in non-declarative memory, that unconscious memory *never* becomes conscious.

Processing messages in digital media

Earlier in the book, we pointed out that processing a message in digital media is just like processing any other message. They all use words, images, and sound, and the brain does not really care how it receives them. Everything we have been talking about in this chapter applies to the processing of messages in digital media.

But beyond the processing responses we have been discussing (attention, learning, acceptance, emotion), *how* some digital media messages are processed may be different from how messages in traditional media are processed. For some digital media, especially the Internet, there may be more than one stage of processing involved. This has been discussed by Rossiter and Bellman (1999) in terms of micros and macro-structure.

They suggest that all marketing communication shares a common micro-structure, which they define as the link between content variables. But if you click on an Internet advert, it may be necessary to "navigate through the web ad" as they put it. This is what they mean by a micro-structure, where there can be links between pages. In that case, a person is free to navigate the site in any way they wish. This reflects what they call a 'self-constructed web ad scheme', and this may not follow the path the marketer would prefer they follow. This has the potential for a loss of control for the marketer, something especially likely with the emotional responses associated with processing.

Summary

In this chapter, we have discussed what is involved in processing marketing communications. It is important for managers to understand this because every aspect of IMC must be conceived to maximize the likelihood that a message will be positively processed, leading to the appropriate target audience action. We began this chapter looking at consciousness and the unconscious, with specific attention to the preconscious. We also addressed the question of subliminal processing, noting that even with subliminal priming there could not be any significant effect on attitude or behaviour. Although some have tried to argue for unconscious processing of marketing communication, while some messages or parts of messages may be processed unconsciously and enter non-declarative, implicit memory, those memories cannot inform attitudes or brand behaviour. It is impossible because different brain systems are involved. Emotion is the only component of non-declarative memory that has any effect on IMC message processing.

Information is generally dealt with hierarchically, following the six steps of McGuire's information processing paradigm. The message must be presented to the target audience; they must attend to it, understand what is presented and yield to the argument; they must retain that agreement and then act on it. The important point here is that the process is hierarchical, involving *compounding probabilities*. This means each step is dependent on the successful completion of the previous step, and the percentage of the target audience positively responding at each step is multiplied over the six steps. So if 60 percent of the target audience is exposed to a message and 45 percent pay attention, that means only 27 percent of the target audience is even available to learn something, and so on through the last step, acting on the message.

For IMC planning, McGuire's information processing paradigm has been reconfigured into the Communication Response Sequence, where *exposure* is followed by *processing* in order to achieve the desired *communication effect*, which should lead to *target audience action*. Obviously, the target audience must have the opportunity to see or hear an execution (exposure), and this is the job of media planning – the final step in the strategic planning process for IMC. Once exposed, the message must be processed, and successful processing involves attention, learning, acceptance (for high-involvement decisions), and emotion.

Conscious attention is required to fully process the message. One may not necessarily be aware of the message at first, but neurologically it must activate conscious processing in working memory, which will then lead to active, conscious learning. At minimum for successful processing, the target audience must learn the brand name and primary benefit. With high-involvement decisions, because of the risk involved in making a bad choice, the target audience must accept the message as true. With low-involvement decisions, acceptance is not necessary because there is no real risk involved. The target audience need only think the message might be true in order to be motivated to try the brand.

Mediating attention, learning and acceptance is emotion. People have emotional responses to everything with which they come into contact, and this includes marketing communication. These emotional responses, along with already existing nondeclarative emotional memories linked to the brand and to elements within an execution, will all be at work to attract and hold attention, and facilitate learning and acceptance. New memories are then formed based on what has been processed, mediated by those emotions. These new memories are available, with the emotional associations, when thinking about a brand and when brand purchase decisions are made.

This last point is important. By its nature, IMC will most often involve multiple messages being delivered through various media. The need for a consistent look and feel over all IMC executions will be discussed in Chapter 10. But, additionally, it is critical that the processing of each message leads to a unified memory for the brand. Even though each message is processed individually, it must be associated with the brand consistently in memory. These memories become part of the knowledge and assumptions about the brand, stored in declarative, explicit memory. This is our conscious memory and is required for attitude formation and purchase behaviour.

Review questions

1 What must be considered before you can fully understand consciousness, and why?
2 Discuss the pre-conscious and why it is important in understanding message processing.
3 How is the pre-conscious different from the unconscious?
4 What is subliminal processing, and can it be a factor in processing IMC?
5 Why is the notion of 'multi-tasking' problematic?
6 What must happen for a message to be successfully processed?
7 Why is it so difficult for marketing communication to lead to a brand purchase?

8   How can processing advertising for a competitor help a brand?
9   Can unconscious processing of marketing communication be effective for a brand?
10 Discuss attention and its role in message processing.
11 What is the role of learning in building brand awareness?
12 How does learning differ for high- and low-involving product decisions?
13 What is the role of emotion in message processing?
14 Discuss the two ways in which emotion can affect the way in which marketing communication is processed.
15 Look at some advertisements and record your 'feelings' as you look at them. Where do they come from? What is it about the executions that elicit those emotions?
16 Why is it important for managers to understand the role of memory in processing marketing communication?
17 In what ways is processing digital media the same as, and in what ways different from, processing messages in traditional media?
18 What is the difference between semantic and episodic memory? Find examples of advertising that are likely to involve each.
19 Why is it unlikely that unconscious attention to advertisements will affect brand attitude?
20 Look at some advertisements and think about the various associations in memory that are aroused by the words and images.

References

Bradley, M.M. and Lang, P.J. (2000) Measuring Emotion: Behaviour, Feeling, and Physiology. In R.D. Lang and L. Nadel (eds.), *Cognitive Neuroscience of Emotion.* Oxford: Oxford University Press, pp. 242–276.

Broadbent, D. (1958) *Perception and Communication.* London: Pergaman.

Dalton, P. and Fraenkel, N. (2012) Gorillas we have missed. *Sustained inattentional deafness for dynamic extents. Cognition, 124(3)*, 367–372.

Damasio, A. (1999) *The Feeling of What Happens.* San Diego, CA: Harcourt.

Damasio, A. (2003) *Looking for Spinoza.* Orlando, FL: Harvest Books.

deGelder, B. (2005) Nonconscious Emotions: New Findings and Perspectives on Nonconscious Facial Expression and its Voice and Whole Body Context. In L.F. Barnett, R.M. Niedenthal and P. Winkielman (eds.), *Emotion and Consciousness.* New York: The Guilford Press, pp. 123–149.

Dehaene, S. (2014) *Consciousness and the Brain: Deciphering How the Brain Codes our Thoughts.* New York: Viking.

Del-Ben, C.M., Deakin, J.F.W., McKie, S., Delvai, N.A., Williams, S.R., et al. (2005) The effect of citalopram pretreatment on neural response to neuropsychological tasks in normal volunteers: An fMRI study. *Neuropsychopharmacology, 30(9)*, 1724–1734.

Ehrenberg, A.S.C. (1974) Repetitive advertising and the consumer. *Journal of Advertising Research, 14(2)*, 25–34.

Fridland, A.J. (1994) *Human Facial Expressions: An Evolutionary View.* New York: Academic Press.

Gazzaniga, M.S. and Smylie, C.S. (1990) Hemispheric mechanisms controlling voluntary and spontaneous facial expressions. *Journal of Cognitive Neuroscience, 2(3)*, 239–245.

Gregory, R.L. (2004) *The Oxford Companion to the Mind,* 2nd ed. Oxford: Oxford University Press.

Heilman, K.M. (2002) *Matter of Mind.* Oxford: Oxford University Press.

Johan, G.V., Maheswaran, D. and L. Pieracchio. (2006) MAPping the frontiers: Theoretical advances in consumer research on memory, affect, and persuasion. *Journal of Consumer Research, 33*, 139–149.

Kalat, J.W. (2004) *Biological Psychology,* 8th ed. Belmont, CA: Wadsworth.

Karremans, J.C., Stroebe, W. and Claus, J. (2006) Beyond vicarys fantasies: The impact of subliminal priming and brand choice. *Journal of Experimental Social Psychology*, *42/6* November, 792–798.

Langer, E., Blank, A. and Chanowitz, B. (1978) The mindlessness of ostensibly thoughtful action: The role of 'placebic' information in interpersonal interaction. *Journal of Personality and Social Psychology*, *36(6)*, 635–642.

Lundqvist, D. and Öhman, A. (2005) Caught by the Evil Eye: Nonconscious Information Processing, Emotion, and Attention to Facial Stimuli. In L.F. Barnett, P.M. Niedenthal and P. Winkielman (eds.), *Emotion and Consciousness*. New York: The Guilford Press, pp. 97–122.

Maloney, J.C. (1962) Curiosity versus disbelief in advertising. *Journal of Advertising Research*, *2(2)*, 2–8.

Marti, S.J., Sigman, M., and Dahaene, S. (2012) A shared cortical bottleneck underlying attentional blink and psychological refractory period. *Neuroimage*, *59/3*, 2883–2898.

McClure, S.M., Li, J., Tomlin, D., Cypert, K.S., Montague, L.M. and Montague, P.R. (2004) Neural correlates of behavioural preference for culturally familiar drinks. *Neuron*, *44(2)*, 379–387.

McGuire, W.J. (1969) The Nature of Attitudes and Attitude Change. In G. Lindsey and E. Aronson (eds.), *The Handbook of Social Psychology*. Vol. 3. Reading, MA: Addison-Wesley.

Moore, T.E. (1982) Subliminal advertising: What you see is what you get. *Journal of Marketing*, *46*, Spring, 38–47.

Murphy, S. and Zajonc, R.B. (1993) Affect, cognition, and awareness: Affective priming with optimal and suboptimal stimulus. *Journal of Personality and Social Psychology*, *64(5)*, 723–739.

Niedenthal, P.M., Barsalou, L.W., Riz, F. and Krauth-Gruber, S. (2005) Embodiment in the Acquisition and Use of Emotion Knowledge. In L.F. Barret, P.M. Niedenthal and P. Winkleman (eds.), *Emotion and Consciousness*. New York: The Guilford Press, pp. 21–50.

Percy, L. (2006) Unconscious Processing of Advertising and its Effects Upon Attitudes and Behaviour. In S. Diehl and R. Terlutter (eds.), *International Advertising and Communication*. Wiesbaden, Germany: Deutcher Universitäts-Verlag, pp. 110–121.

Percy, L. (2012) The Role of Emotion in Processing Advertising. In S. Rogers and E. Thorson (eds.), *In Advertising Theory*. New York: Routledge, pp. 69–84.

Patkamis, A. and Arousen, E. (1991) *Age of Propaganda*. New York: Freeman.

Rossiter, J.R. and Bellman, S. (1999) A proposed model for explaining and measuring web ad effectiveness. *Journal of Current Issues and Research in Advertising*, *21/1*, 13–31.

Rossiter, J.R. and Percy, L. (1997) *Advertising Communication and Promotion Management*. New York: McGraw-Hill.

Rossiter, J.R., Percy, L., Bergkvist L. (2018) *Marketing Communications: Objectives, Strategies, Tactics*, London: Sage Publications, Ltd.

Sergent, C. Baillet, S. and Dahaene, S. (2005) Timing of brain events underlying access to consciousness driving the attentional blink. *Nature Neuroscience*, *8/10*, 1391–1400.

Sigman, M. and Dehaene, S. (2005) Parsing a cognitive task: A characteristic of the minds bottleneck. *PLOS Biology*, *3/2*, 37.

Sherif, M. and Hovland, C.I. (1961) *Social Judgement*. New Haven: Yale University Press.

Simons, D.J. and Chabris, C.F. (1999) Gorillas in our midst: Sustained inattentional blindness for dynamic events. *Perception*, *28(9)*, 1059–1074.

Strum, A. (2004) The Changing Face of *Wine Enthusiast*. *Wine Enthusiast*, May, 10.

Sutherland, M. and Sylvester, A.K. (2000) *Advertising and the Mind of the Consumer*. St. Leonards, Australia: Allen and Unuru, p. 35.

Tulving, E. (1983) *Elements of Episodic Memory*. Oxford: Oxford University Press.

Tulving, E. (2002a) Episodic Memory: From Mind to Brain. *Annual Review of Psychology*, *53*, 1–25.

Tulving, E. (2002b) *Elements of Episodic Memory*. Oxford: Clarendon Press.

Wright, C.H., Martis, B., Shin, L.M., Fischer, H. and Rauch, S.L. (2002) Enhanced amygdala responses to emotional versus neutral schematic facial expressions. *Neuroreport*, *13(6)*, 785–790.

Zajonc, R.B. (1968) Attitudinal effects of more exposure. *Journal of Personality and Social Psychology Monographs*, *9(2, part 2)*, 1–27.

9 Message development

In the last section of the book, we deal with the overall planning process involved in integrated marketing communications (IMC) and its implementation. Initial planning is, of course, required before any message can be developed. It is essential to understand your market before you can begin to consider what you want to communicate, and how. In this chapter, we assume that this has been done, and look more specifically at the steps involved in the development of IMC content.

Regardless of the form, a message may take, or the medium in which it is delivered, the process for developing effective integrated marketing communication (IMC) messages is the same. It does *not* begin with a creative 'idea', but with a thorough understanding of the results from the initial planning stages. Although understanding the market and your target audience is essential, the critical first step in message development is an understanding of the communication strategy needed for positioning and to satisfy the communication objectives that have been selected. This means message development begins with positioning and the communication objective. With the communication strategy set, a creative brief is developed. Only now are we ready for the creative idea, and once this creative idea (or ideas) is fleshed out, it must be pre-tested.

Positioning

In Chapter 2, we looked at positioning; positioning decisions help inform our understanding of what is needed for message development. The discussion of brand awareness and brand attitude in relation to positioning bears directly on what the manager needs to know in talking about the brand. The link between the brand and category needs to answer the question 'What *is* it and what need does it satisfy?' and the link between the brand and its benefit provides the answer to 'What does it offer?' and why it is better than other brands. These links are the keys to identifying the correct brand awareness and brand attitude strategies and reflect what we might think about as a general model of positioning, as shown in Figure 9.1.

Positioning decisions provide a vital link between the communication objectives and the specific creative tactics used, which we will deal with in the next chapter.

After the positioning decisions have been agreed, a positioning statement should be written. In its simplest form, a positioning statement looks like this:

1   For _____ (the target audience)
2   _____ is the brand in the category
3   That offers _____ (benefit or benefits)

DOI: 10.4324/9781003169635-12

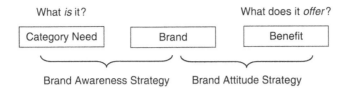

Figure 9.1 A general model of positioning.

In effect, a positioning statement outlines for a prospective consumer what the brand is, who it is for and what it offers (Percy and Rosenbaum-Elliot, 2021).

Benefit selection and focus

At the heart of the positioning statement is the benefit, and this is the key to message development. This benefit (or benefits) should be selected to help differentiate the brand from competition on an important purchase decision criteria, building a more positive brand attitude, leading to brand preference.

Specifically, in selecting a benefit for positioning, the manager should look for a potential benefit that is *important* to the target audience, that the target audience feels the brand either *delivers* now or could realistically deliver and, ideally, do it *better* than competing brands. What one is looking for here is the perception of *uniqueness* for the brand, and this must come from the way in which the benefit claim is made in the creative execution (Boulding et al., 1994).

A brand benefit may be expressed in terms of either an objective *attribute*, a subjective *characteristic* or an *emotion*. As an example, a benefit associated with a sports car might be related to the engine. One could create a message where the benefit claim talked about a 5.8-litre engine (an attribute), a 'powerful' engine (a subjective characteristic), or about it being 'exhilarating' (an emotion). However, the way in which a benefit is expressed in a message must be informed by the underlying motivation driving behaviour in the category.

Advert 9.1 for Monuskin provides a good example of the benefit being built around a subjective characteristic of the brand: 'Beautifully Natural', 'Naturally Beautiful'. As we shall see in the next chapter when we look at the tactics for facilitating learning from an advert, and how to deal with a benefit claim, this execution is very well done. It uses simple, short headlines that focus directly on the key benefit.

When the underlying motive is positive (transformational brand attitude strategies), the benefit claim should be built on a positive emotion. For products such as food, beverages, or fashion that are driven by a positive motive, the benefit should be a positive feeling associated with the brand. For example, this means creating sensual pleasure for food or sexual allure with fashion. The focus in the execution can be on the emotion alone, or perhaps associated with a subjective characteristic along the lines of 'our decadent flavours will leave you in ecstasy'. The emotion 'ecstasy' in this case is stimulated by the brand's 'decadent flavours'.

If the underlying motive is negative (informational brand attitude strategies), positive emotions are not appropriate as *benefits*. This does not mean that one should not create a positive emotional response to the message, only that the benefit claim should be built

Advert 9.1 Monuskin.

Table 9.1 Informational and transformational benefit focus options

---

Informational
- If dealing with an expert target audience, draw attention to a key *attribute*, otherwise
- Draw attention directly to a *subjective characteristic* of the brand, or
- Use an *attribute to support a subjective characteristic,* or
- Point out how a *problem or negative emotion can be eliminated because of the subjective characteristic* of the brand

Transformational
- Use a *subjective characteristic of the brand to draw attention to why you will experience a positive feeling* by using the brand, or
- Simply *create a positive feeling and link it to using the brand*

---

on either a subjective characteristic of the brand, an attribute supporting the subjective characteristic, or the subjective characteristic resolving a problem, or with an expert target audience, an attribute only focus. Such a focus is more in line with the need for the benefit to provide information that will help mediate the underlying negative motivation. For a cold remedy, for example, the benefit claim might be built around a subjective characteristic such as 'long-lasting relief', an attribute in support of the subjective characteristic such as 'our time-released capsules ensure long-lasting relief', or resolving a problem with the subjective characteristic, 'why take four capsules a day when one of ours gives you long-lasting relief?'

Of course, these illustrations are not meant to be an example of what the actual *creative* content of the message would be, but rather to provide a sense of the strategic possibilities associated with benefit focus in positioning. The point is that benefit selection must not only be based on an important, uniquely delivered benefit but also the appropriate motivation options for informational and transformational benefit focus. This is summarized in Table 9.1. The benefit focus for informational brand attitude strategies will be different from transformational brand attitude strategies, and these must be considered by the manager as part of positioning before moving on to setting communication objectives and specific brand attitude strategies. This means that the final question the manager must consider in terms of positioning is: 'What is the appropriate benefit focus?'

Communication objectives

Much goes into creating a successful IMC campaign but, perhaps the most important consideration is the communication objective. Communication objectives follow from the specific communication *effects* the manager is looking for as a result of the brand's marketing communication. All aspects of IMC work on the same basic communication effects: category need, brand awareness, brand attitude and brand purchase intention (Table 9.2).

It should be noted that while we use the term 'brand' in describing some of these communication effects, we are using the word in its broadest possible sense to include products, services, corporate identity – in short, whatever might be the beneficiary of marketing communication. Each of the four basic communication effects is briefly outlined next.

Table 9.2 The four basic communication effects

Category need	Target audience perception that a product or service is required to satisfy a need
Brand awareness	Target audience ability to recognize or recall the brand and associate it with the need
Brand attitude	Target audience overall evaluation of a brand, providing a reason for choice consistent with the underlying purchase motive
Brand purchase intention	Target audience's instruction to themselves to immediately respond to the message

Category need is the target audience's perception that they require a product or service to satisfy a need, and associating that need with a brand. In other words, they must 'be in the market' for the brand.

Brand awareness is the target audience's ability to recognize or recall the brand. As we saw in Chapter 4, in the case of recognition brand awareness, the potential consumer need only recognize the brand at the point-of-purchase; with recall brand awareness, they must recall or remember the brand name when the need for the product or service occurs.

Brand attitude refers to the target audience's overall evaluation of the product or service being offered in relation to its perceived ability to satisfy the reason they want it (the relevant motivation). It is important to remember that reasons for purchase or usage can differ at various times, even for the same individual. That is why it is important to always think about brand attitude in terms of the motivations that are likely to be driving behaviour when the target audience is 'in the market'.

Brand purchase intention is the target audience's instruction to themselves to purchase or use the brand. In other words, it is a commitment to take action, but it does *not* necessarily ensure actual purchase or use of the brand.

As one might gather, even from these brief descriptions, there is a lot involved with communication effects that must be considered in IMC planning. It is not enough to simply say you want people to like the brand or want people to use it more often. The manager must look carefully at what it will take to accomplish those ends, and what type of marketing communication will best do the job.

Next, we will summarize how the four communication effects are likely to translate into communication objectives for message development.

Category need

If there is little demand for a category, or people seem less aware of it, establishing or reminding people of it becomes a communication objective. You cannot really do much of a job advertising or promoting a specific brand of a new product until people have learned just what it was. Market share leaders can sometimes benefit from category-need advertising when category demand slackens. A good example of reminding people of a category need was when Campbell Soup ran a 'soup is good food' campaign in the United States. By stimulating the category need for soup, they generated differentially high sales for Campbell's because of their overwhelming share in the category.

And of course, all new product category introductions require category need as an objective. The need for the new product must be established before the brand can be seen as satisfying that need. With new product categories, advertising will be needed to link the brand to the new category, but it will not be easy to establish the category need. In its early stages, the IMC campaign will need to include communication options that will help build awareness of the new category – things like marketing public relations.

Brand awareness

Brand awareness is *always* an objective of any marketing communication programme, whether advertising or promotion. We know that based on how people make purchase decisions this awareness will occur through either recognition or recall. As we have seen, recognition brand awareness is when the brand is seen in the store and remembered from advertising or promotion. Recall brand awareness is when one must remember the brand or store name first, prior to buying or using a product (e.g., when deciding to have lunch at a fast food restaurant, or when an industrial buyer decides to call several suppliers for a quotation). A principal communication objective of all advertising is to create or maintain brand awareness.

Brand attitude

Brand attitude is also *always* a communication objective, and results from the information or 'feeling' imparted through a brand's marketing communication, consistent with the level of involvement associated with the purchase or usage decision and the underlying motivation driving choice. In message development, once the appropriate brand attitude strategy is identified using the Rossiter–Percy Grid, this will inform those creative tactics needed to optimize the likelihood of positive message processing.

Brand purchase intention

Brand (or trade) purchase intention is a communication objective when the primary thrust of the message is to *commit now* to buying the brand or using a service. Note that purchase-related behavioural intentions are also included in this communication objective, things like dealer visits, direct mail inquiries and referrals.

Creative brief

Once a brand's positioning and communication objectives are determined, the next step is to address how they can be best translated into an actual IMC campaign message that will effectively build and sustain that positioning for the brand in the market. This is the creative idea. But before work can begin on coming up with the creative ideas for implementing the communication and positioning strategy, this, along with all the planning to date, should be summarized in a creative brief.

It is the creative brief that ensures that the results of the strategic planning process inform message execution, and that everyone is on the same page. In fact, all the key people involved in the planning and execution of an IMC campaign should ideally be part of the development of a creative brief. This would include account executives, planners and creatives from the agency, as well as brand management from the company, or, whatever individuals in comparable positions are involved if the brand is not using a traditional advertising agency. The reason it is so important to include all of those playing a key role in the process is that once completed, the creative brief provides the consensus of how the message will be executed, and the benchmark against which the resulting advertising and promotion will be evaluated.

The creative brief format outlined in this section includes all the points that are essential to an effective creative execution. Many companies and advertising agencies have their own way of writing a creative brief, but most will in some fashion or other cover the ten key areas discussed here. Overall, one might think of a creative brief in three sections: one that helps define the task at hand, one that is principally concerned with the creative objectives, and one that is concerned with executional elements.

Task definition

The first four points of the creative brief deal with task definition: key market observation, source of business, customer barrier/insight and target audience. The purpose of these points is to help explain why the IMC programme is being put together. What is the brand hoping to accomplish; who in the market is being addressed with this creative; what do they already know, think, or feel about the brand; what is the message trying to affect? All of this information should be available from the marketing plan and strategic planning process. The four points that help define the specific task are as follows:

1   *Key market observation.* What one point can the brand make about the market that will help the creatives understand and believe in the rest of the brief? There is no need to be exhaustive, just provide the basics.
2   *Source of business.* Where, specifically, is the business expected to come from? One is not looking for general descriptions here, but specific sources (for example, current holders of long-term bonds, people unhappy with some particular aspect of their current brand, etc.).
3   *Consumer barrier/insight.* What one thing is known about the potential target audience that may need to be overcome, or that may help reach them? What do they know, or think they know about the brand or product category; how do they feel about it; how interested are they in it; how do they distinguish between different brands?
4   *Target audience.* What is the most vivid description that can be offered of the types of individuals to whom this communication will be directed? This description must go further than a simple listing of demographics or even lifestyle characteristics. It is important to provide enough information for the creatives to be able to picture in their mind's eye who they are addressing. Copywriters like to imagine they are talking directly to an individual, and specifically in their decision role (Kover, 1995).

Objectives and strategy

The next four points deal with communication objectives and strategy. What one is seeking to do here is help provide creatives with the best orientation possible, including the *one point* that, if communicated, will achieve the desired objective and also provide the evidence available to convince the target audience.

1   *Communication objectives and tasks.* What is the specific communications objective for this creative, and where does it fit within the total IMC programme? This is where to designate the primary objective (category need, brand awareness, brand attitude, brand purchase intention), and what communication tasks are to be accomplished.

2   *Brand attitude strategy.* What is known about the way consumers make decisions? Is the decision high or low involvement, and is the behaviour positively or negatively motivated? This positions the strategy into one of the four strategic quadrants of the Rossiter–Percy Grid.

3   *Benefit claim and support.* What is the *primary* consumer benefit and why? Identify the benefit claim that is most strongly associated with the relevant motivation, and provide the evidence that supports this choice. Anything that could be used in the communications to demonstrate or communicate the correctness of the benefit claim should be included. For example, if it is understood that consumer motivation is likely to centre on incomplete satisfaction, pointing out comparative advantages and how they should be presented might be appropriate.

4   *Desired consumer response.* What is it that the target audience should know, think, feel, or do as a result of the communication? This should be a brief summary of what is expected to happen.

Executional elements

The last two points in the creative brief deal with the actual execution, providing guidance on what sort of communication this should involve and what information must be included. These last two points are:

1   *Creative guidelines.* What tactics are appropriate for the type of brand awareness involved, and for the strategic quadrant chosen?

2   *Requirements / mandatory content.* What are the requirements, either creatively, legally or corporately, that must be included? Here, for example, is where the logo treatment is spelled out.

Now that we have detailed each of these points, there is one thing to always keep in mind when putting together a creative brief. It is important to create a balance between there being enough information for clear guidance and providing so much information that the creative people working on the assignment are placed in the position of working out their own communication priorities from the information provided. There are two areas where it is hard to give too much information – target market and support for the benefit claim. But for the rest, keep it to the bare essentials. There is a reason it is called a creative *brief*. It should be *complete* on one page (an example is shown in Table 9.3). If more detail is desired, creatives should be referred to the marketing plan and results of the strategic planning process.

With the creative brief in hand, it is time to develop creative ideas.

Creative idea

The primary task of a creative idea is to dramatize the key benefit claim. In other words, to bring the benefit (or benefits) identified in the positioning strategy to life. Rossiter and Percy (1997) have defined the creative idea basically as 'the choice of an interesting way to express the brand position in an advertising format'. In effect, an IMC message is built around the benefit. They go on to suggest that a creative idea may be defined more formally as: 'An attention-getting and catalytically relevant representation of the brand position, generated in a form that is detailed enough to be executed and tested, and (necessary in most cases) amenable to multiple executions'. Let us consider this in more detail.

Table 9.3 Creative brief example for disposable contact lenses

Product	Job	Date

Key market observations
Consumer research identifies dissatisfaction with the maintenance of contact lenses
Source of business
Current contact lens and prescription eyeglass wearers
Consumer insight
Residual concern over the idea of disposable lenses
Target audience
Adult contact lens and prescription eyeglass wearers; doctors and eye-care professionals
Communication objectives and tasks
Seed category need and build awareness and brand attitude that communicates to the target the advantages of disposable lenses
Brand attitude strategy
High-involvement informational brand strategy driven by problem solution and incomplete satisfaction motives
Benefit claim and support
Our disposable lenses are available. Support: no more solvents and cleaning
Desired consumer response
Accept the viability of disposable contact lenses and interest in looking into Acuvue lenses
Creative guidelines
Address potential concern over the idea of disposable lenses
Requirements/mandatory content
See your doctor or eye-care professional

To begin with, the creative idea must be attention-getting. This is obvious, of course. But, no matter how attention-getting the idea, it must not stray from the positioning strategy. Much advertising is very 'creative' and attention-getting, but not effective. Adherence to the positioning strategy is what helps ensure that a creative idea will lead to an effective execution. This is why Rossiter and Percy (1997) use the phrase 'catalytically relevant' along with attention-getting. It underscores the need for the creative idea to facilitate establishing a link between a brand's positioning strategy and the target audience's understanding of it. A catalyst increases the rate of chemical reactions, and a creative idea should 'accelerate' the target's understanding of the positioning, the link between the need and the brand, and the brand and the benefit.

There are four possible forms a creative idea may take: visual, key benefit claim, auditory, or postmodern. While these represent ways to develop a creative idea, they also reflect creative tactics that may be used in the final execution. Perhaps the most widely used form is a creative idea built upon a key visual. This is supported by Kroeber-Riel's (1993) pioneering work, where the key visual helps illustrate and reinforce the key benefit claim. While all IMC builds up a key benefit (or benefits) claim for positioning, it should be the primary focus for creative ideas when the message must be quickly processed, for example with posters. Auditory creative ideas incorporate unique music, jingles, or even a particular sound as the executional focus. A postmodern focus deals with something unpredictable and works best with younger target audiences who are likely to be most receptive to unconventional executions.

The creative idea must be detailed enough to enable a rough execution of it to be developed. The idea is *not* itself an advertisement or promotion, but the foundation for an execution or campaign. The creative idea must also be extendable, except in the rare case where the idea is used only once. This need for extendibility is what facilitates a consistent 'look and feel' for a campaign over time, something we deal with in the next chapter.

How many ideas are needed? The theory of random creativity suggests that the more ideas you come up with and test, the greater the likelihood of finding a 'winner'. Of course, there are time and budget constraints to be considered. Still, having several ideas to develop and test (preferably from more than one creative) will increase the odds of finding an idea that will work effectively.

The remote conveyor model

One way of coming up with potential creative ideas is to use a method that will identify elements associated with the benefit claim. One such theoretical framework for identifying effective ways to dramatize the benefit claim is the remote conveyor model (Rossiter, 1994). This model looks at three components: a conveyor, the product or service and the key benefit.

A conveyor is an executional element that is eye-catching, to attract and hold attention, but also one that initially seems to be unrelated to the product. This incongruity will excite some level of curiosity and the brain, being what it is, will try to make sense of it. What is this doing in the advertisement? The conveyor cannot be too remote, but rather just enough to initiate a 'search' of the execution for something that will resolve the inconsistency.

There are five essential properties to an effective conveyor. First, it must attract *reflexive* attention, not selective, because it seems out-of-place in the execution. Second, it must be quickly and correctly identified by the target audience. They must know what it is. Third, it must be initially seen as 'remote' from the brand. In other words, it should be highly unlikely that the conveyor and the brand would be associated in the real world, or even in the world of IMC where executions frequently indulge in fantasy of one sort or another. Fourth, once promoted, the association with the benefit should immediately become obvious. This is the hard part. Sometimes the benefit being conveyed will become clear after thinking about it for a moment. But more often a prompt in the headline or copy will be necessary to ensure the correct link to the benefit is made. Finally, there can be no conflicting association. The prompt should identify the desired benefit, and *not* lead to a negative or contradicting association.

We can summarize how the remote conveyor model works as follows. The conveyor attracts the attention of the target audience and arouses their curiosity because it doesn't seem to make any sense being there in an advertisement (or any other IMC message execution) for that product or service. They look for an 'answer', and are helped by the key benefit prompt, and the penny drops. Ah! The dilemma is resolved! Executions that use a conveyor communicate the key benefit indirectly, *purposefully* indirectly, in contrast to most IMC messages which directly deliver the benefit (Rossiter et al., 2018).

Candidate conveyors are best generated by 'brainstorming', by asking individuals for the first thing that comes to mind when prompted with the benefit claim, no matter how 'unconnected' or inappropriate it may seem. It helps here to direct the responses by asking for objects, animals, people and situations that come to mind when thinking about the benefit claim, again no matter how unrelated they may seem to the product or service. From the list generated, select those that have the least likely co-occurrence with the brand.

For each conveyor selected, 'back-test' it by asking a sample of the target audience for the first thing that comes to mind when they are cued by the conveyor. You are looking for those conveyors that elicit some aspect of the benefit – remember, the conveyors were originally 'brainstormed' from the benefit as a cue. The best conveyors, those that are most remote yet still elicit the benefit, are then worked into rough executions to be tested, just as we test the execution of any creative idea. Much more extensive discussions of the remote conveyor model, along with numerous examples, may be found in Rossiter and Percy (1997).

With the creative ideas in hand, this leads to the final stage of message development – pre-testing.

Pre-testing

We have made the point many times that what makes a message an advertisement rather than a promotion is strategic intent. Advertising has as its *primary* communication objective brand awareness and brand attitude in order to help the target audience 'turn toward' (*advertere*) the brand. Promotions have as their *primary* communication objective (along with brand awareness and attitude) brand purchase intention, looking for some kind of immediate response. Regardless of strategic intent, the execution of the message should be pre-tested, regardless of how that message is to be delivered: an in-store display, sales brochure, trade show banners, packaging, sponsorship logos; *any way* in which the message is delivered.

The reason is simple. The execution is meant to satisfy particular communication objectives, and a manager must be reasonably sure that it does so before investing in the production and delivery of the advertisement or promotion. There are two basic ways in which to pre-test executions: a management judgement test and target audience response pre-test. Each of these methods is discussed in the following sections.

Management Judgement Test

All advertisements and promotions should first be evaluated in rough form by managers, based on the creative brief, before they are brought to the finished form for pre-testing with the target audience. Basing the evaluation on the creative brief is critical. By focusing the evaluation on the objectives set out in the creative brief, the manager is forced to look at how well the creative execution conforms to the objective and creative strategy agreed on. It is not at all unusual for creative development to stray a long way from what was originally approved.

There is a series of basic questions to be addressed in a Management Judgement Test (see Table 9.4). The first is how likely is it that the target audience will easily understand that the message is addressed to them? This means, is the category need obvious? Next,

Table 9.4 Basic questions asked in a Management Judgement Test

1 How likely is it that the target audience will easily understand that the message is addressed to them?
2 Is the link between the brand and the need clear?
3 Does the overall message clearly and easily address the communication tasks set out in the creative brief?

the link between the brand and need must be clear. Third, does the overall message clearly and easily address the communication tasks set out in the creative brief? The manager must check that the creative tactics used for brand awareness are correct. If the brand awareness objective is recognition, is the package clearly shown as it will be experienced at the point-of-purchase? If recall is the objective, has the need–brand link been clearly established, in that order, and repeated? The manager must determine whether the creative tactics used for the brand attitude strategy are appropriate. We see when we discuss brand attitude creative tactics in Chapter 10 that there are specific creative tactics associated with the four quadrants of the Rossiter–Percy Grid. Then, are the benefit claim and support consistent with what was agreed on in the creative brief? If we are dealing with a promotion or direct response, is there a clear call to action? Finally, if specific creative guidelines or mandatory copy were required, was that done?

In effect, a Management Judgement Test gives the manager an opportunity to review the 'rough draft' of the intended advertising or promotion to ensure that it is likely to clearly communicate with the target audience, is consistent with the creative brief, and that the execution uses the appropriate creative tactics for the communication objectives.

Target audience response pre-test

All advertising and promotion should be pre-tested among a reasonably large sample of the target audience to ensure that the communication objectives are met. These should be *individual* interviews, using a single execution. Too often, focus groups are used to pre-test advertisements and promotions, but this is *totally inappropriate*.

When you see an advertisement or promotion somewhere, do you get a group of people together and talk about it? Hardly, yet this is what goes on in a focus group and this is why they are not a valid way of pre-testing. Communication is processed *individually*, so pre-testing must be done with individuals. Other problems with using focus groups to pre-test include overexposure of the test execution, and encouraging people to be 'critics' and study the material in detail. This is obviously not how marketing communication is processed in the real world.

In a pre-test, we want to measure the following and in this order: attention, learning (and acceptance of the message if high involvement), brand purchase intention, overall brand attitude, benefit claim delivery and brand awareness (see Table 9.5). Why this order? It is necessary to minimize the possibility of responses to some questions influencing the response to later questions. For example, overall brand attitude is measured before the specific content of the message (the benefit claims) is introduced so that the measure of brand attitude only reflects what is taken from exposure to the execution, and not after being 'reminded' by asking about specific benefits in the copy. People may have missed something, or be reminded of something not fully processed, which could then influence their overall brand attitude.

But why is brand awareness measured last when it is critical to effective communication? It is measured last in order to provide at least some time between exposure to the advertisement or promotion and the measure. This also means that the brand name should *never* be a part of any of the earlier questions. A good measure of brand awareness is difficult to obtain. Ideally, it would not be measured until a day after exposure, or even longer. This is because awareness of the brand is not 'needed' until a purchase decision is made, and then it must be appropriately linked in memory to the need through either recognition or recall, as we have seen (direct response, of course, is an exception).

Table 9.5 Order of measures for pre-testing

Processing responses
  1 Attention
  2 Learning
  3 Acceptance (if high involvement)
Communication effects
  1 Brand purchase intention
  2 Brand attitude
  3 Benefit claim belief
  4 Brand awareness

Unfortunately, conducting a re-interview later is expensive and, even if done on the Internet, can result in control problems and a significant drop in completion rates which affects reliability.

Attention

The first two measures in a pre-test should address how well the message is processed: attention and learning (plus acceptance for high-involvement strategies). By its very nature, a pre-test will ensure at least some attention to the test execution, because people are asked to look at it. However, one can measure how long someone 'looks' at the advertisement or promotion, and compare that with the time necessary for someone to reasonably process the message. Eye-tracking research has shown that it takes about 1.75 seconds to process an illustration in print advertising, and about a quarter of a second for each significant word in a headline or sub-heading (Kroeber-Riel, 1984). This would, of course, apply to print-like messages in Internet and social media advertising.

With information like this, it is possible to gain a sense of the minimum amount of time needed to process at least the basic components of a message. Using a timed portfolio test, where people are asked to look through a portfolio of advertisements and the time spent with the test execution recorded (relatively easy with Internet testing), one can compare the result with what is needed to minimally process the message. This will provide a reasonable idea of how well the execution attracts and holds attention. With commercials, of course, the timing is set. Here one must ensure that the exposure time on-screen is sufficient for processing important elements of the message. For example, research has shown that as the average screen time drops, so too does attention (MacLachlan and Logan, 1993).

Whether or not an attention measure is taken, all of the other measures are taken after attention is specifically drawn to the test execution. After this exposure, the advertisement or promotion is removed prior to questioning. But this means that all the subsequent measures reflect *full* attention. If a prior measure of attention is taken, it can be used to temper the other measures.

Learning and acceptance

The basic measures for learning and acceptance in the case of high-involvement strategies is the eliciting of 'cognitive responses'. This is nothing more than recording the answers to a general probe about what the advertisement or promotion is trying to communicate.

A typical question would be: 'Other than trying to convince you to buy their brand, what do you think the brand is trying to communicate?' What you are looking for here is playback of the key benefit claim(s), linked to the brand. For low-involvement products, this is all that is needed. But for high-involvement products, another step is required. For each thing mentioned, each cognitive response, the respondent is asked whether they consider it to be positive, negative or neutral. Here we are looking for evidence that the benefit claims have been 'learned', and linked to the brand and, in the high-involvement case, that the key benefit claim is seen as positive, implying acceptance of the claim as true.

Brand purchase intention

Attention and learning deal with how well a message is processed. The remaining measures deal with communication effects. Brand purchase intention is measured next, *before* brand attitude and specific response to the benefit claims. This is necessary to ensure that the response reflects only the recent exposure to the execution and has not been influenced by the attitude measures. Brand purchase intention measures will vary depending on the brand attitude strategy, and attention must be paid to how the question is asked and the time frame implied (Rossiter and Percy, 1997).

This is critical because we want the question to reflect as closely as possible how someone is thinking during the decision process. With new products or when trial is the action objective, the question should ask how likely one is to *try* the brand, not buy it. With frequently purchased products, the time frame should reflect this, along the lines of 'Next time you buy, how likely are you to buy the advertised brand?' But with high-involvement products, say a flat-screen TV, the question should be framed along the lines of 'If you were going to buy a new TV, how likely is it that you would consider the advertised brand?' As you can see, the wording of the intention and conditions for considering the purchase need to reflect as closely as possible the actual decision process.

The scales used must also be carefully considered. Just as we have seen with how the question is asked, there is also no 'one size fits all' scale for measuring brand purchase intention. Unfortunately, too often researchers use a standard likelihood scale regardless of the product or target audience. The brand attitude strategy guides scale selection. With low-involvement products with short purchase cycles, such as most fmcgs, Rossiter et al. (2018) have suggested using what they call a 'softer' brand preference measure which does not ask for a direct statement of purchase intent. Rather, ask for a relative preference: one brand I prefer, one of several I like, a so-so brand, a brand I don't like. They suggest using a relative scale because low-involvement brand attitude advertising has less emphasis on 'buying now'. Of course, this would *not* be an appropriate scale for a promotion or direct response advertisement where an immediate response is the objective. It would also be less appropriate when trial is the action objective, or where an extended purchase cycle is involved (e.g., with household cleaners). In these cases, the more traditional preference scale would be used: definitely try/buy, probably try/buy, might try/buy, will not try/buy.

With high-involvement brand attitude strategies, a more discriminating scale should be used, given the greater consideration involved in the purchase decision. A good example would be the 11-point Juster measure of purchase intent. This scale uses verbal description combined with percentages to indicate the degree of preference (Rossiter and Percy, 1997). In all cases, when measuring brand purchase intention, a *unipolar* scale should be used.

Brand attitude

Unlike brand purchase intention, where we are measuring the intention to try or buy the brand, with brand attitude we are looking at how favourably the brand is evaluated *relative to other brands*, regardless of purchase intent. Also, unlike brand purchase intention, measures of overall attitude use *bipolar* scales. As Rossiter (2011) points out, overall attitude is a quantitatively conditioned response, and therefore should be measured with a numerical answer scale, and, importantly, it should be measured with a *single item*. Regrettably, all too often researchers use multiple-item scales when attempting to measure overall attitude. This leads to trouble because the scales will more often than not be addressing different types of evaluations (Rossiter, 2011). As managers are trying to determine how well their brand performs in terms of satisfying a need, a simple Good–Bad bipolar scale will usually suffice.

Rossiter also makes the point that you need to consider how complex the brand and category are. For 'simple' products like most fmcgs, the scale should not exceed 5 points (−2, −1, 0, +1, +2, running bad to good) because people are not likely to be discriminating much when considering the brand (as we discussed with brand purchase intention). But with more 'complex' products, a larger 9-point or 11-point bipolar scale is more appropriate, reflecting the greater consideration given in evaluating the brand.

Benefit claim delivery

The key benefit claims made in an advertisement or promotion should be rated in terms of the perceived likelihood that the brand delivers the benefit. These ratings help provide a diagnostic understanding for the overall brand attitude measure. Here, the scales used should reflect the brand attitude strategy. For low-involvement/ informational advertisements, a simple 'yes–no' measure is all that is needed. The brand is seen as either delivering the benefit or not delivering it. Consumers are simply not likely to be involved enough to discriminate *degrees* of benefit delivery. With low-involvement/transformational advertisement, semantic differentials are recommended. These consist of bipolar adjectives separated by a 7-point interval scale. For each benefit, it may be necessary to use several semantic differentials to help improve the reliability. Recall from our discussion of transformational advertising that the benefit lies in the execution, in the 'feeling' elicited by it. This can be difficult to capture with a single semantic differential scale.

With high-involvement/informational strategies, unlike with low-involvement/ informational advertising, the degree of benefit delivery is important. Here, we want to use a scale that measures the *amount* of perceived benefit delivery: Do you think the brand is very reliable, moderately reliable, somewhat reliable, or not at all reliable? Measuring the benefit delivery for high-involvement/transformational advertising can be tricky. Depending on the benefit claims, because of high involvement, graduation of the benefit delivery is appropriate. This would certainly be the case with something like a luxury resort. But if the brand benefit is more of a 'feeling', as would be the case with a designer fragrance, then a semantic differential scale would make more sense. Given the nature of this type of advertising, where sometimes tangible or 'hard' benefits are needed in addition to the emotional arousal, both types of scales may be needed.

Brand awareness

Brand awareness is measured last in order to best reflect how it functions in the decision process. Awareness of a brand is not 'required' until the purchase decision is being made, either at the point-of-purchase for recognition awareness or when a need occurs requiring recall awareness of the brand. This all occurs well after exposure to the message (with the exception of direct response and some promotions). This means that ideally the brand awareness measure will be taken in a second interview a day, or even a week, or so later.

But, as we have noted, this can be a problem. One way around it is to create an artificial delay or distraction within the pre-test, after the earlier measures and before the brand awareness question. For example, a short filler task could be used. This will engage other memories and neural networks unrelated to the brand or product category. A simple distraction would be to collect demographic and other classification questions here, or a totally unrelated set of questions could be included.

Even with a delay like this, the measure of brand awareness is likely to vastly over-estimate the true level of brand awareness in memory resulting from exposure to the advertisement or promotion. After all, the pre-test specifically drew attention to the brand. However, at least for recognition awareness (which is the most troublesome to measure), a good way to help minimize this problem is to show a display with pictures of several competing brand packages and ask which of the brands would satisfy the appropriate category need, and record the order of mention. Remember, this is what brand awareness is all about, linking the brand to the need. When recall is the awareness objective, respondents are given the category need and asked for all the brands that come to mind that would satisfy that need. For example, suppose you wanted to go out to eat at a Mexican restaurant, what restaurants come to mind? Again, it is important to record the order of mention.

What we have outlined above provides a basic pre-test methodology that covers the essentials. However, pre-tests often cover more aspects of advertising or promotion, looking at the emotional response to the message, and addressing specific questions probing various aspects of the message or executional elements. Regardless, *all* pre-tests must be customized to the specific advertisement or promotion being evaluated. Although a standard format for pre-testing – along the lines we have discussed – makes sense, the actual wording and depth of the questioning will be unique to each test.

Social marketing communication

Social marketing communication is a special case of IMC. Everything we have been talking about in terms of message development, as well as the creative tactics to be introduced in the next chapter, will apply to social marketing, but the is much more involved. When dealing with most IMC campaigns we are looking to build awareness and positive brand attitude. But, with social marketing communication, we must effect a change in behaviour as well. What makes this so difficult is that when trying to change or modify unacceptable or undesirable social or personal behaviour, it will be necessary to find a motivation for the new behaviour that is at least as compelling as the motivation that is driving the socially undesirable or pathological behaviour.

To do this we must deal with the target audience differently. In addition to determining the target's attitude toward the behaviour we are trying to change, we must also deal with what Fishbein and Ajzen (1975) have called 'social norms' that reflect the influence of others on the target's behaviour.

Perhaps the leading model of behaviour change in social marketing is what is known as the 'stages of change model'. A good example is Andreasen's (1995) adaptation of the Transtheoretical Model of Change developed by Prochaska and DiClemente (1983). In this interpretation, there are four stages that lead to social behavioural change: pre-contemplative, contemplative, action, and maintenance. At the pre-contemplative stage, social marketing communication must raise awareness of the desired behavioural change, and begin to build interest in the values that are associated with the new behaviour. In the contemplative stage, you must begin to persuade and motivate the target audience to consider making the desired change. At the action stage, the task is to get the target to initiate the new behaviour, perhaps by providing an incentive. Finally, the maintenance stage is where you encourage a continuation of the new behaviour, perhaps by under-scoring the positive consequences of the new behaviour, or by reminding the target of the negative consequences of reverting back to the old behaviour.

Target audience

As social marketing communication addresses the four stages leading to behaviour change, note that in effect the target audience is 'changing'. In the social marketing literature, they talk about three groups: conformers, vacillation, and offenders. *Conformers* are those who are not engaged in the undesirable behaviour. *Vacillators* are those who may occasionally engage in the undesirable behaviour, or who may be thinking about it. *Offenders* are those who are engaged in pathological or undesirable behaviour, and to whom social marketing communication is initially addressed.

In relation to the four-step model of change, the conformers are the target audience for a maintenance message, while the vacillators and offenders will require a message keyed to the stage where they are currently. In effect, these last two groups become different target audiences depending upon the stage they are at, and will require a message that addresses the goals for that stage. The same person will become a part of a different target audience as they move through the stages of change.

In dealing with target audiences for social marketing communication, just as with the target audience for a product or service, *attitude* toward the undesirable behaviour is critical. As Rossiter et al. (2018) have pointed out, there is a world of difference between a conformer, or even a vacillator, who has a negative attitude toward the undesirable behaviour, compared with one who may be somewhat curious about it.

Communication strategy

In setting the communication strategy for social marketing communication, we begin with determining the target's attitude toward the behaviour at issue, but as we have noted, there is more. We must also account for the social norms associated with the behaviour by the target audience. To deal with this, an extended version of the Expecting-Value model introduced in Chapter 2 is used, following something Fishbein and Ajzen (2010) called the 'Theory of Reasoned Action'. This modified version begins with an attitude factor as before but adds a social or 'narrative' factor.

You will remember, that with the Expectancy-Value model, attitude toward an object is the summation of the beliefs about that object and the importance of these beliefs. When dealing with changing behaviour, rather than attitude toward an object we are looking at the attitude toward the behaviour we wish to change, where the belief that engaging in a particular behaviour will lead to consequences, and a person's evaluation of the outcome is summarized over the number of beliefs a person has about engaging in the behaviour. This may be expressed as follows:

$$A_b = \sum_{i=I}^{n} b_i e_i$$

where A_b is the personal attitude toward the behaviour; b_i is the belief that engaging in the behaviour leads to consequences; and e_i is the by person's evaluation of the outcome.

The normative factor that extends the model involves a similar equation, added to the altitude equation, as follows:

$$A_b = \sum_{i=I}^{n} b_i e_i + SN_b = \sum_{i=I}^{n} b_i m_i$$

where SN_b is the the 'social norm' or influence of others on a person's behaviour; b_i is a person's belief that a reference group or individual thinks they should or should not engage in the behaviour; and m_i is the felt motivation to comply with the reference group or individual (which is unipolar).

While the Theory of Reasoned Action model provides a good way to look at and understand the involved nature of trying to change behaviour, in social marketing communication changing an undesirable behaviour is a real challenge, especially when dealing with sociopathic behaviour or physiologically addictive behaviour. In fact, the model has proved difficult to use with addictive behaviour.

Adding to the general difficulty in applying the model to social marketing communication is finding the right message. As we mentioned earlier, the message must provide a motivation to change the behaviour that is at least as compelling as the motive driving the undesirable behaviour; and one that can counter any strong social norms supporting the undesirable behaviour for the target audience.

Many social marketing campaigns use a fear appeal, but one must be very careful in so doing. As McGuire (1985) pointed out long ago, as a drive state anxiety tends to increase the likelihood of a change in attitude, but as a cue, it will likely lead to avoidance of the message or an increase in counter-arguing the message. In other words, while raising anxiety toward an unfavourable behaviour can be persuasive, if it arouses too high a level of activity, you are unlikely to pay attention and process it. You have probably seen adverts that utilize such vivid images that you turn away.

What is needed is an execution that arouses some, but not too much, anxiety. Then, following Hovland et al.'s (1953) fear-driven model, the fear or anxiety is linked to the undesirable behaviour, but then it is removed by the message showing that by changing the behaviour the fear or anxiety will be avoided. This resolution is critical if social marketing communication to be successful (Rossiter and Thornton, 2004).

Charitable giving

Another aspect of social marketing communication deals with charitable giving. Research has shown that people are motivated to give to charities by experiencing what has been called a 'warm glow feeling' (Harbaugh et al., 2017). This helps to explain one of the anomalies of charitable behaviour. You may give even though you know your small contribution is unlikely to make much of a difference, but you give to experience that 'warm glow feeling'.

What appears to be critical in eliciting an altruistic motive is *seeing* others in need. But there is a caveat to this. It seems that when a very large problem is involved, or a large number of people are suffering, people are *less* likely to respond with contributions. This is because while it is easy to empathise with a single person or family who is suffering, where large numbers of people are involved it is difficult to believe your small contribution can make a difference. As a result, you are more likely to contribute to a cause when you can easily empathise or identify with a specific person who will benefit from your contribution.

This means that social marketing communication for encouraging charitable giving should make that 'warm glow feeling' as tangible as possible by providing a direct connection to an individual in need, or by motivating potential givers to feel they are a part of a community of givers. This means focusing on individuals in need and not on large groups who are in need. Personalize the suffering or tragedy.

Summary

The *process* for developing effective messages for IMC campaigns is the same, regardless of the form the message may take or the media used in delivering it. This process begins with a thorough understanding of the communication strategy for the brand, and this means specifically the positioning strategy and communication objectives. It is the positioning decisions that provide the important links between the brand and the awareness and brand attitude strategies. These decisions lead to a positioning statement outlining the benefit, which is key to message development. This could be a specific attribute of the product, a subjective characteristic of the brand, or an emotional response, alone or in some combination depending on the underlying motivation. This benefit must be seen by the target audience as important, something the brand delivers (or could deliver) and ideally delivers it better than other brands. How the message will focus on that benefit will be a function of the underlying motivation during purchase behaviour in the category.

The communication objective reflects the specific communication effects desired. Brand awareness and brand attitude are always communication objectives for every IMC message, and brand purchase intention is also always an objective for promotion. Category need may be an objective under certain circumstances, and brand purchase intention may sometimes, although not often, be an objective for advertising-like messages.

With this understanding of the communication strategy, the next step in message development is to outline this and other important considerations for the creation of the message in a creative brief. The creative brief is exactly that – *brief*. It should be complete on a single page, although support for the brief should be available at whatever depth and length is needed. Creative briefs take many forms; most will include sections on the task definition, background information on the market and target audience drawn from the marketing and communication plans, a section on the objectives and strategy, and a section detailing any specific requirements or creative guidelines called for by the brand.

With the creative brief as a foundation, those charged with the actual creation of the message execution must come up with a creative idea to uniquely and effectively dramatize the benefit. The remote conveyor model offers a way of helping creatives come up with a creative idea. Once the creative idea is given life in an actual rough execution, that execution must be tested to ensure it satisfies the objective outlined in the creative brief. A preliminary Management Judgement Test can provide a quick assessment of the likely effectiveness of the advertisement, promotion, or other IMC messages. Then, the execution must be pre-tested among a sample of the target audience. The pre-test will measure both how well it is processed as well as how effective it is in meeting the specific communication strategy.

With social marketing communication, a special case of IMC, while everything that goes into message development for brand advertising and promotion applies, much more is involved. Specifically, a social norm must be taken into account, the influence of relevant others on a decision to change an undesirable behaviour.

Review questions

1 Why does message development not begin with a creative idea?
2 Select a few advertisements and, based on the execution, write a positioning statement for the brand.
3 Discuss the links between benefit focus and brand purchase motivation.
4 Discuss why communication effects are the source of communication objectives.
5 Why are brand awareness and brand attitude always communication objectives?
6 Discuss the various forms that a creative idea may take.
7 Suppose you are tasked with developing a creative idea for a new brand of skin moisturizer. Come up with ideas for conveyors that might be used in advertisements.
8 What are the most important points to make in a creative brief?
9 Develop a creative brief for the introduction of a new 'healthier' carbonated soft drink.
10 Why is it important to pre-test message executions?
11 Pick an advertisement and use a Management Judgement Test to evaluate how likely it is to be an effective advertisement.
12 Why should brand awareness be the last thing measured in a pre-test?
13 How does social marketing communication differ from brand or service marketing communications?
14 In what ways is selecting a target audience for social marketing communication different from selecting a target audience for other IMC?
15 Discuss the Theory of Reasoned Action model and its application to social marketing communication.
16 What are the key considerations in social marketing communication for charitable contributions?

References

Andreasen, A. (1995) *Marketing Social Change*. San Francisco, CA: Josey-Bass Publishers.
Boulding, W., Lee, E., and Staelin, R. (1994) Mastering the mix: Do advertising, promotion and sales force activities lead to differentiation? *Journal of Marketing Research*, *31*(2), 159–172.

Fishbein, M. and Ajzen, J. (1975) *Beliefs, Attitude, Intention, and Behaviour: An Introduction to Theory and Research*. Reading, MA: Addison-Wesley.

Fishbein, M. and Ajzen, J. (2010) *Predicting and Changing Behaviour: The Reasoned Action Approach*. New York: Psychology Press.

Harbaugh, W.T., Mayo, V., and Burghart, D.R. (2017) Neural response to taxation and voluntary giving reveal motives for charitable donations. *Science, 316*, 1622–1625.

Hovland, C., Janis, I., and Kelley, H. (1953) *Communication and Persuasion: Psychological Studies of Opinion Change*. Newhaven, CT: Yale University Press.

Kover, A.J. (1995) Copywriters' implicit theories of communication: An exploration. *Journal of Consumer Research, 21(4)*, 596–611.

Kroeber-Riel, W. (1993) Effects of Emotional Pictorial Elements in Ads Analyzed by Means of Eye Movement Monitoring. In T. Kinneau (ed.), *Advances in Consumer Research*, XI. Ann Arbor, MI: Association for Consumer Research, pp. 591–597.

Kroeber-Riel, W. (1984) *Buldkommunikation*. Munich: Vahlen.

MacLachlan, J. and Logan, M. (1993) Camera shot length in TV commercials and their memorability and persuasiveness. *Journal of Advertising Research, 33(2)*, 7–61.

McGuire, W.J. (1985) Attitude and Altitude Change. In G. Lindsey and E. Armson (eds), *The Handbook of Social Psychology*. Reading, MA: Addison-Wesley Publishing, pp. 136–314.

Percy, L. and Rosenbaum-Elliott (2021) *Strategic Advertising Management*. Oxford: Oxford University Press.

Prochaska, J.O. and DiClemente, C.C. (1983) Stages and processes of self-change of smoking: toward and integrative model of change. *Journal of Consulting and Clinical Psychology, 51*, 390–395.

Rossiter, J.R. (1994) The RAM-Conveyor Theory of Creative Strengtheners in Ads. In P. Weinberg (ed.), *Festschrift fur Prof. Dr. Kroeber-Riel*. Munich: Vahlen, pp. 119–138.

Rossiter, J.R. (2011) *Measurement for the Social Sciences*. New York, NY: Springer.

Rossiter, J. R., Percy, L., and Bergkvist, L. (2018). *Marketing Communications: Objectives, Strategy, Tactics,*. London: Sage.

Rossiter, J.R. and Percy, L. (1997) *Advertising Communication and Promotion Management*. New York, NY: McGraw Hill.

Rossiter, J.R. and Thornton, J. (2004) Fear-pattern analysis supports the fear-driven model for anti-speeding road safety TV ads. *Psychology and Marketing, 21/11*, 945–960.

10 Creative execution

In Chapter 8, we looked at how marketing communication is processed and in Chapter 9, we examined the process for message development. Now we look at the creative tactics involved in executing the creative idea and how they are used in order to optimize the likelihood that a message will be processed. First, we discuss some general principles and creative tactics that reflect our understanding of how certain aspects of a message execution can significantly affect how well it will be processed. We address the ways in which the words and pictures used in an execution can maximize attention and learning. Research in psycholinguistics and visual imagery has yielded a great deal of knowledge of how the way in which something is said, or the characteristics and the images used in visual communication, can affect the likelihood that someone will pay attention and learn something from the message. We will be reviewing a number of these findings that have a direct bearing on marketing communication.

Following this, we look more specifically, at the creative tactics needed to address brand awareness and brand attitude objectives, and how consistency across different integrated marketing communication (IMC) executions will enhance the overall power of a brand's marketing communication.

Gaining attention

How much attention someone is likely to pay to marketing communication is a function of the way words and visual images (pictures and illustrations) are used in the execution. Additionally, for print, the size of the execution and its focus will influence the degree of attention paid, and for broadcast (both television and radio) as well as digital media, the length of the commercial. But attracting attention is only the first step. Executions must also *hold* attention so the message can be processed. In this section, we will be discussing some of the creative tactics that can help attract and hold attention (summarized in Table 10.1).

Unexpected elements

According to Myers (1994), one of the easiest ways to attract attention in print is to use letters in unexpected ways or by altering the spelling of words. A good example of this is the provocative logo for French Connection UK (FCUK). For commercials, the repetition of particular sounds can help draw attention to a brand name or slogan and reinforce it in memory.

DOI: 10.4324/9781003169635-13

Table 10.1 Creative tactics for gaining attention

---
* Unexpected elements
* Colour
* Larger pictures
* Correct placement in print
* Motive-dependent structure for commercials

The reason unexpected things attract attention is that people are accustomed to experiencing things in certain ways and when there is a departure from the norm, interest is aroused. People tend to notice changes in things that are out of the ordinary. If you were to hear someone say, 'you placed the em*phasis* on the wrong syll*able*', stressing the second syllable rather than the first in emphasis and syllable, your attention would be immediately drawn to what was said. In marketing communication, this can easily be done in the voice track by simply placing more emphasis on a particular word where it would not be expected.

Colour

For all print media, four-colour (i.e., full colour) attracts more attention than two-colour, which attracts more attention than black and white. This is true for both consumer as well as business and trade marketing communication. One sometimes hears arguments from marketing practitioners that black-and-white advertisements will attract attention because they 'stand out' from the clutter. However, there is nothing to support this idea. In fact, attention to black-and-white advertisements in consumer magazines is about 30 percent less than full-colour advertisements, and the advantage is even greater in newspapers. With business-to-business advertising, colour advertisements draw about 50 percent more attention than black and white (Rossiter et al., 2018).

Size of picture or illustration

In print advertising, the picture or illustration will draw most of the attention of a reader. For example, about 70 percent of the time spent looking at print advertisements is looking at the picture (Rossiter, 1999). Research has consistently found that the larger the picture size in an advertisement, the more it will be processed (cf. Franke et al., 2004). There is an old 'rule of thumb' in advertising that attention to a print advertisement will increase at a rate of about the square root of its size. This would mean that an advertisement with a picture or illustration four times larger than that in another advertisement should receive twice the attention (the square root of four being two).

Picture size is especially important for low-involvement transformational advertising where traditionally the picture is the most important element of the execution. But a key point to bear in mind is that when talking about picture size, we are referring to a picture or illustration with a single dominant focal point (Franke et al., 2004). In other words, a single picture, not several, making up the size and the visual content, and in that single picture, only one central image.

Print placement

While not strictly a creative tactic, where advertisements are placed within a magazine can have a significant effect on how much attention will be paid to them. Back cover placement will gain the highest attention, followed by the inside covers, and cover position in business-to-business publications will have very high-attention value (Rossiter et al., 2018). Paradoxically, having another advertisement on a facing page will *increase* attention slightly, while editorial content will significantly hurt attention to a nearby advertisement.

Format

With print advertising, the trend to smaller newspaper page size does not appear to have any effect on attention to advertisements within, nor does the page size of magazines impact the attention paid to an advertisement. Interestingly, the size of a banner advertisement on the Internet does not affect attention (Ahn and Edwards, 2002).

The length of commercials is directly related to attention. The longer the commercial, the greater the attention (Ritson, 2003). The number of cuts in a commercial does not seem to affect attention, even though as the number of cuts rises above the average of 13 per 30-second commercial, the level of *arousal* does increase. This is sometimes called 'fastcuts', where the scene changes on average every half-second, or even faster. While fastcuts are suitable for transformational commercials because they can increase the overall level of arousal during processing (Banks and Muehling, 2003), it is *not* appropriate for informational commercials because viewers will not be able to clearly understand the benefit claim, negatively affecting learning.

The key to *holding* attention with television commercials is a function of the pattern or structure of the execution. Communication for informationally driven commercials should use a *two-peaked pattern* where the category need is presented first, the brand is identified in between and the benefit provided is in the second peak. In this way, the target audience recognizes the need, associates the brand with that need, then 'stays tuned' to learn how the brand can satisfy that need. With transformationally driven commercials, the execution should reflect a *raising* pattern, beginning with brand identification and followed by a building of positive emotion, ending with a definite 'kick' (Rossiter and Percy, 1997).

Attention and Internet advertising

While online advertising continues to evolve, at least at this writing there are four main types: search adverts, display (which come in three forms), email adverts, and websites. In addition to the creative tactics just discussed, each of these types have very different attention probabilities.

Attention likelihood for search adverts, beyond the advert itself, will depend very much on where they were placed on the keyword entries; the higher on the page, the more likely it will be noted. There are three very different types of display adverts: banner, small print display adverts, and full-page print display adverts. Of these, full-page print display adverts are likely to attract full attention, with less than full screen between 20 percent and 30 percent; banner adverts around a 30 percent attention probability. Attention to video display adverts is very low, with some estimates as low as only 1 in every 20 clicked on and watched for more than 10 seconds.

In the early days of the Internet in the 1990s, emails enjoyed a large share of Internet advert spending, but now account for very little (e.g., only about 4 percent of US Internet advert spending). The attention probability for 'opt-in' adverts (those that users have not specifically 'opted-out' from receiving), however, is quite high .68 probability of being opened.

Website adverts are much more complex compared with other types of Internet advertising. The target audience will self-select to visit the website, so everyone is likely to be paying attention, at least to the 'home' page, but exploring the site will depend upon its ease of 'navigability'. You might think of websites in terms of direct response adverts and utilize high-involvement creative tactics. This could include using illustrations with a single dominant focal point to draw the reader into the more detailed copy. A detailed discussion of the attention probabilities for various media may be found in Rossiter et al. (2018, pp. 239–244).

Facilitating learning

It is, of course, not enough to simply pay attention to marketing communication – one must also 'learn' what it is trying to say. Critically, this means learning the brand and its primary benefit. There are a number of ways to facilitate learning based on the way words and pictures or illustrations are used within the creative execution. In this section, we review a number of ways in which attention to how words and pictures are used in an execution can increase the likelihood that someone will continue to process the message (after attending to it) and learn the brand and its benefit (summarized in Table 10.2).

Keep it simple

There is a large body of research that has found that using familiar words in familiar ways will facilitate learning (Paivio, 1971). The more complex or difficult a sentence, the greater the likelihood there will be difficulties in processing, and hence learning. This means avoiding passive sentences and long or complicated sentence structures. You should avoid the use of puns (verbal or visual) unless you are certain they will be *readily* understood by the target audience. The British are fond of using puns in advertising, but to be effective the point must be understood immediately.

The headline for a BMW advertisement reads: 'Bigger boots. More Welly'. What is the benefit here? In the UK 'welly' would be understood as short for wellington boots, which is the generic term for rubber boots. What associations are being activated from memory by the words 'boots' and 'welly'? How does this relate to 'bigger boots'? Does this reinforce the benefit of '1,395 litre of boot space' in the BMW, where 'this large, uncluttered space provides a variety of flexible storage options' (as detailed well into the copy)? One must be very careful with puns. If used, they must quickly be seen as conveying the 'real' meaning.

Table 10.2 Creative tactics for facilitating learning

- Keep it simple
  - avoid negatives
  - avoid passive constructions
  - avoid puns
- Headlines fewer than 6–7 words
- Product in use
- Use picture–word sequence
- Visual cuts in commercials consistent with brand attitude strategy

---

It is also a good idea to avoid using negatives. A great deal of research has been done that says it is more difficult to process negatives used in phrases or sentences. The problem is that to correctly understand a sentence using a negative requires two-step processing. One must first process the negative word, then 'reverse' the meaning. This is certainly not to say that one should never use negatives, but it does mean that one must be careful to ensure that the meaning is quickly and easily understood. In addition to the potential problem associated with two-step processing, when negatives such as 'not' are embedded in a sentence, it is easy for the eye to simply miss them unless one is carefully paying attention.

Use short headlines

Using short headlines is important because of the way people read. They do not read each word one at a time, but rather process *groups* of words. Those groups are made up of fewer than six or seven words, depending on their length (Wearing, 1973). Look at the following headline:

Just Beautiful Skin

The moment you glanced at the headline, you processed it at once. It was not necessary to 'read' the words, it was understood as a unit. On the other hand, with larger headlines the eye will initially only register a group of words, with perhaps taking meaning from a few scattered words near the edge of the group. Look at the following headline:

Confidence is Everything

But a Little Makeup Can't Hurt

To understand what it says requires one to be motivated to spend time processing it.

The implications of this for advertising are obvious. If someone is flicking through a magazine, each page will attract at least momentary attention in order to see if there is anything there worth holding their attention. But if there is a short headline, fewer than six or seven words, even with brief exposure, if the eye falls on the headline its content will be processed and communicated. Copy on posters and outdoor, as well as on packages, should also be short to ensure processing at a glance.

Product in use

Because of something known in psychology as associative learning, people are more likely to process and learn from an advert when they can make familiar associations with it. This is exactly what we see in Advert 10.1 for Meyer's. The visual with the benefit and product 'in use' are all likely to be linked to familiar associations in memory with washing and showering. The visuals, highlighted by the shower head, all reinforce the sense of using the products. The background is of a soft blue colour reflecting the package labels and provides an overall 'light' and pleasant feeling which will be associated with the brand, all reinforcing learning.

Advert 10.1 Meyer's.

Picture–word sequence

The order in which the eye attends to the pictures or illustrations and words in marketing communication will affect learning. In a study reported by Brainerd et al. (1997), it was found that when people confront a picture–word sequence rather than a word–picture sequence, learning increases. Contributing to this phenomenon could be the fact that pictures are known to have superiority over words in learning (Eyesenk, 1977; Bryce and Yalch, 1993). People tend to automatically engage with pictures, and they seem to elicit more elaboration from memory than words. Myers (1994) has made this point with a good example. If you were to read about a new soap that would make you beautiful, you would no doubt be a bit sceptical. But if you saw a picture of a beautiful woman holding a bar of that new soap, the image of the beautiful woman would help reinforce the claim and you would be more inclined to believe it.

But one must be careful not to take this idea of a picture–word sequence literally, at least for print, and this includes the Internet. It does *not* mean, for example, that a picture or illustration must be at the top of the page, with the headline and copy at the bottom. What it means is that the eye should be drawn to the picture or illustration first, then the headline. This is not a problem because the eye is more likely to be initially drawn to the visual. However, this can always be checked with eye-tracking.

This same idea also applies to television. When important points are to be made by people in a commercial, by voice-over or printed boards on screen, they should be immediately *preceded* by an appropriate visual element that elicits reinforcing memories that will help facilitate the processing of the verbal claims (Young and Robinson, 1992, 1999; Rossiter and Percy, 1997).

Pacing of commercials

In earlier our discussion of format and attention, we talked about the optimum patterns in commercials for gaining attention. Another aspect of this concerns the pacing, or the number of visual cuts in the execution. While the increase in arousal associated with more than the average of 13 cuts per 30 commercials may be good for transformational advertising where the emotional 'feeling' is so critical, it definitely is *not* for informational executions. With higher numbers of cuts only peripheral, executional content is likely to be learned. This is fine for transformational strategies where the benefit is in the emotional response to the execution itself. But with informational strategies, it is necessary to process and learn the content of the message, and this cannot happen when the number of visual cuts is much more than the average.

Interestingly, it is often argued that viewers today, and especially younger viewers of the so-called 'MTV-generation', are conditioned to fast-cut visuals. That may be true, but it does not mean they are processing much beyond sensual stimulation. In fact, at an MTV-rate of 20 or more cuts per 30 commercials, loss of attention among 19–34-year-olds is actually *greater* than among older adults (MacLachlan and Logan, 1993).

Music as a creative tactic

Music can be an effective creative tactic because of its close relationship to speech, and especially its ability to arouse emotions. The relationship between music and speech prosody is particularly strong. Speech prosody refers to the various aspects of speech, the way pitch moves up and down as we talk and the pace and loudness of our voice, the rhythm of our syllables, and the way we articulate words. Depending upon which aspect of speech prosody is involved, different primary emotions will be aroused: anger, fear, disgust, sadness, surprise, or joy. The impact of speech prosody on the arousal of primary emotions is similar across cultures (Balkwill and Thompson, 1999). The arousal of secondary emotions is more dependent upon the culture and the actual words used.

These speech prosody characteristics are the same as those we find in music. Happy-sounding speech tends to be faster, the same with happy-sounding music, while sad-sounding speech tends to be softer and lower in pitch, just as we find with sad-sounding music (Justin and Laukka, 2003). Another aspect of lower-sounding speech and music is that it tends to be associated with dominance and aggression. These associations are important to consider when using music in IMC. You probably don't want to use bright, happy-sounding music in a commercial for a pain reliever, or deep-sounding strings for a children's snack advert.

While both music and speech show the same basic characteristics of prosody, music goes much further in its ability to arouse emotion because it has the ability to si-multaneously reflect a blend of emotions. With its ability to vary the intensity and shading of basic emotions, it is able to express emotions that are richer and more nuanced, well beyond simply happy or sad feelings.

Musical timbre, the perceived sound quality, also affects emotional arousal. It has been known for sometime that music compiled in a minor key, for example, will be perceived as more serious or sad (Hermen, 1935). Timbre plays a significant role in musical memory. This is why we can quickly identify a song after only a few notes. Our ability to quickly identify sounds based on timbre is why it is so critical when using music in IMC that it is not at all similar to music used by another brand. Familiar or popular songs should also generally be avoided unless the lyrics are not easily remembered. Otherwise, you are more likely to mentally sing the lyrics rather than pay attention to the message (Allen, 2006).

Recall from Chapter 5 when we were discussing retail promotion we mentioned that music can have a significant effect on retail sales. For example, one study found that when the tempo of the music being played in a supermarket was varied between an 'easy listening' tempo of 60 beats per minute (bpm) and a 'rock' tempo of 120 bpm, sales were 38 percent higher with the 60-bpm tempo (Milliman, 1982). It has been suggested that the reason for this could be that resting heart rate of the average person is 60 bpm. It has also been shown that the content of music, as well as its tempo, can influence retail sales (North et al., 1999).

Nostalgia as a creative tactic

Sensory experiences from a person's past, such as smell and taste, as well as other more complex experiences can connect people with pleasant memories and be recalled in great detail. Products are often associated with these experiences and if so will result in a lasting preference for a brand. This same idea of nostalgic branding with the past, whether real or imagined, can provide the basis for an effective IMC strategy.

There are two types of nostalgia, personal and historical. Both can be used for an effective branding strategy. Personal nostalgia is linked to personal memories of past experiences and is likely to be idolized (Mueling, 2011). Historical nostalgia refers to a general feeling that things were better in the past.

Generally, we tend to hold more positive than negative memories, whatever the reality of the past might have been. When a brand is linked to the past it can trigger positive memories. In fact, fMRI studies have shown that positive memories activate reward centres in the brain and elicit positive emotional responses (Speer et al., 2014). Brands can utilize imagery and messages that will evoke a positive emotional response based upon those earlier experiences and memories, something known as *nostalgic bonding* (Loveland et al., 2010).

Nostalgia has also provided the basis for occasional periods of 'retro-marketing'. This can prove to be an effective marketing strategy because it taps into a general sense of historical nostalgia. Old brand names are often acquired for re-introduction, or held for future re-introduction. This is especially common in the whiskey and beer business. Pabst Brewing Company in the United States, which has brewed Pabst Blue Ribbon beer for many years, controls more than 70 beer brand names, including 30 dormant brands. They have been re-introducing several of these brands, brands that had not been marketed for many years (Schultz, 2016).

Specific creative tactics for brand awareness and brand attitude

In Chapter 4, we introduced brand awareness and brand attitude strategies. Now we are going to explore the creative tactics that should be used in developing executions in order to optimize the likelihood that they will be correctly processed to effectively implement the appropriate strategy. While we talk in terms of traditional advertising, it should be remembered that the same creative tactics apply to promotion-like messages (in terms of awareness and brand attitude) and also that it does not matter if it is a typical advertisement, brochure, in-store display, or package. These are the creative tactics necessary to ensure that brand awareness and brand attitude communication objectives are reached.

Brand awareness creative tactics

You will recall from our earlier discussion of brand awareness strategies that the correct brand awareness objective depends on the role awareness plays at the time the purchase decision is made. The brand will either be recognized at the point-of-purchase, re-minding the consumer of the need, or a need will come up and the brand must be recalled from memory prior to the actual purchase: recognition brand awareness versus recall brand awareness. The creative tactics involved will be different, depending on the specific brand awareness objective (see Table 10.3).

Brand recognition

With recognition brand awareness, the package (or a symbol or logo for the brand if that is how it is recognized at the point-of-purchase) must be *clearly* presented in the ex-ecution to ensure visual iconic learning (Kosslyn and Thompson, 2003). It is not enough to only show the product, unless the product is sold *without* a package. This can become a difficult creative problem when dealing with transformational products, where the package can easily get in the way of emotional presentation of the benefit. Nevertheless,

Table 10.3 Brand awareness creative tactics

Brand recognition	Package must be shown as it will appear at the point-of-purchase
Brand recall	Need must be linked to brand, in that order, and repeated

it is critical because that visual image of how the product will be recognized at the point-of-purchase must be stored in memory and linked to the appropriate need so that when it is seen in the store it will trigger that need.

Advert 10.2 for Fentimans pink grapefruit tonic water does an excellent job in avoiding this problem. There is obviously good package recognition, and the emotional benefit follows from the image of the 'product in use', the refreshing-looking drink side-by-side with the bottle. As we shall see shortly, with low-involvement transformational products like this, the benefit is in the execution, and it must be able to elicit a positive emotional response. The Fentimans advert does all of this. In this execution, we have strong package identification linked to the positive emotion aroused by the visual image of a drink. When you see the bottle in the store, you recognize it and that positive feeling associated with it, how good the drink looked, and because it is a low-involvement product with little or no risk in the trial, you give it a try.

If the package is not sufficiently exposed, there is every chance that one's marketing communication will not be associated with the brand, or even mistakenly linked to another brand. This is especially true for new product introductions, or when trying to reach new users. As a rule of thumb, the package should be attended to for two seconds if it is to be 'learned' and recognized later. This means being able to *hold* attention in print, and to be exposed for *at least* two seconds in a television or digital media commercial. In addition to visual recognition, you will remember from Chapter 4 that occasionally auditory recognition may be needed. The tactics are the same, except that the name must be *heard* as it will be heard during the sales process, and *repeated* to ensure exposure time.

Regardless of whether it is visual or auditory brand recognition, one must be sure that the category need is obvious. With established product categories, the appropriate need is usually understood. But with new products, or new brands in an established category, the need must be clearly evident. In either case, within the execution the *package* should trigger the need, not the other way around because it will be the package that is recognized first at the point-of-purchase and 'remind' the consumer of the need for the product.

As a footnote to the discussion of the creative tactics needed for effective recognition brand awareness, a study by Henderson and Cote (1999) identified four visual elements that significantly increase the likelihood that something will be recognized. First, there should be some sense of curvature. Second, generally, but not exactly, symmetrical. Third, some degree of repetition in the design. Fourth, that it represents some re-cognizable object. In designing packages and brand symbols or logos these points should be kept in mind, especially if recognition of brand awareness is involved.

Brand recall

With recall brand awareness, the need occurs first, and the brand must be recalled from memory. This means that the creative execution must establish in memory a link be-tween the need and the brand such that when the need arises, the brand name will come to mind as satisfying that need. The key is that the association is learned in that direction: need first, followed by brand (Nelson et al., 2003). This is generally done in the headline and repeated in the body copy. Because this is a more difficult learning process than that involved with recognition learning, this *association* must be repeated to ensure learning.

A visual could be used to establish the category need, but this is not always easy to do because the need must be immediately apparent. The visual would need to be im-mediately and correctly 'labelled' in the target audience's mind when they see it in the

Advert 10.2 Fentimans.

Source: © Fentimans Ltd.

advertisement because it is that verbal 'label' that is most likely to be used in working memory when the need actually occurs, not the image of the need. If you decide to go out to eat in a Chinese restaurant, you are likely to be thinking about Chinese food, not seeing visual images of Chinese food, although some images may follow. But the initial need is likely to be considered verbally. Advertising for a Chinese restaurant will want to associate the desire for Chinese food with the name of the restaurant: strategically, 'when you think about Chinese food, think about us'. This is the link that should be established (obviously much more creatively). While it is certainly appropriate to use strong visual images of Chinese food in the advertisement, this will primarily operate on brand attitude. The *need* should be labelled.

One way to help boost brand recall awareness is by using a celebrity presenter in the execution. However, the important thing to understand is whether the target audience easily recognizes the person, and that person is held in high regard by them. If they are famous and positively regarded in their eye, then research has shown that the visibility of the celebrity can be transferred to the brand (Holman and Hecker, 1993). That, however, is the key. The celebrity's visibility *must* be linked to the brand.

Brand attitude creative tactics

In Chapter 4, we briefly introduced the Rossiter–Percy Grid and pointed out how it helps define brand attitude strategy for marketing communication by looking at the level of involvement in a purchase decision and the underlying motivation that is driving behaviour in the brand's category. This results in four distinct quadrants defined in terms of low versus high involvement and negative (informational) versus positive (transformational) motives. The reason these considerations are so important is that each is directly related to the way in which a message will be processed, and that means that creative tactics needed to facilitate the processing of the message will differ for each quadrant (see Table 10.4).

The specific creative tactics associated with each quadrant of the grid are designed to optimize the likelihood of a person successfully processing the message. This means being able to communicate the benefit around which a brand is positioned within its marketing communication, and ensuring that the optimal emotional associations are triggered to facilitate message processing in working memory. We will first take a look at the creative tactics appropriate for the brand attitude strategy quadrants, and then review how emotion is handled within an execution to encourage processing.

Table 10.4 Brand attitude creative tactics

Low-involvement informational	Use one simple benefit, presented in the extreme
Low-involvement transformational	Emotionally authentic presentation in the execution becomes the benefit
High-involvement informational	Benefit must be consistent with the target audience's current attitude towards the brand and category, and without over-claiming
High-involvement transformational	Emotionally authentic presentation with which the target audience personally identifies

Low-involvement informational

This is the quadrant for low-involvement decisions involving negative motives. Because the decision is low involvement, one simple benefit in the message is enough. This benefit should be presented in the extreme because the target audience does not really need to believe the claim. All that is necessary is something Maloney (1962) has called 'curious disbelief'. This is a perfect description of what one is trying to accomplish with low-involving brand attitude strategies and especially low-involving informational marketing communication. One is looking for the consumer to think: 'I wonder if it can really do that? It would be great if it did!' Because it is a low-involvement decision, there is no risk in trying.

This is exactly what we have with the Deep Heat/Deep Freeze advert shown in Advert 10.3. The benefit should be clear, presented in a simple way, and immediately evident, and it is. The 'problems' to be solved are obvious in both cases, as is the solution: Deep Heat or Deep Freeze. Each half of the advert could effectively stand on its own, but together like this it adds synergy that helps build an even stronger positive attitude for the brands.

With informational messages, the target audience does not even need to like the execution. One of the classic examples of this was a long-running Charmin toilet tissue campaign in the US during the 1990s. In this series of commercials, women would attempt to squeeze packages of Charmin because it was 'squeezably soft', and every time they did, Mr Whipple, a store clerk, would appear and say 'Ladies, please don't squeeze the Charmin!' Research showed later that this was considered by consumers as one of the all-time most obnoxious commercials, but it nevertheless moved the brand to number one in the category (Freeman, 1999). How can such a thoroughly disliked campaign still be effective for the brand? By using such an extreme presentation, it also sharply focused on the benefit. When shopping, consumers were much more likely to see Charmin and wonder whether it really was that soft, rather than think about the obnoxious Mr Whipple.

BENEFIT CLAIM

In all marketing communication, how one deals with the benefit must be consistent with the underlying motivation. Informational versus transformational brand attitude strategies require different ways of supporting or drawing attention to the key benefit claim. When dealing with low-involvement informational brand attitude strategies, the focus is *directly* on the key benefit claim. This may be expressed with an attribute in support of a subjective characteristic of the brand, in terms of just the subjective characteristic, for example, 'fast acting', 'the latest technology', 'softer skin', etc.

This is exactly what we see in Advert 10.4 for Ivory. The focus on the benefit claim is directly on the subjective characteristic of the brand: it is 'full of gentle care, free of worries'. It is clearly presented and will be quickly and easily processed at a glance. Additionally, the key benefit of 'gentle' is on the package where it will be reinforced each time the product is used.

SOURCE CHARACTERISTIC

When dealing with low-involvement informational brand attitude strategies, the perceived source of the message must be seen as credible, and as an '*expert*'. We put the

Advert 10.3 Deep Heat/Deep Freeze.

Source: © Mentholatum.

Advert 10.4 Ivory.

word 'expert' in inverted commas because we are using it in its broadest sense here, not just in terms of technical expertise. For example, a mother is an 'expert' at getting children's clothes clean. When there are people in an advertisement, they will generally be seen as the source of the message, and, in this quadrant, should be perceived as an 'expert' in the product category. When there are no people, the company or brand itself will be seen as the source.

Low-involvement transformational

In this quadrant, we are dealing with low-involvement decisions, but the underlying motivation driving behaviour in the category is positive. The real key here is getting a positive emotional response to the execution because in a very real sense the brand benefit is in the execution itself. This requires a presentation of the benefit in an emotionally *authentic* way. If there are people in the advertisement, they must look real and natural, not posed. If they do not, the emotional response to them will not seem real.

The target audience must immediately connect emotionally with what they see, and the feeling they get in a very real sense becomes the benefit for the brand. At the point-of-purchase or when the brand decision is made, you want the consumer to re-experience that same positive feeling for the brand. Because it is a low-involvement decision, that should be enough to drive purchase. Only one benefit should be presented because the benefit is tied so closely to the emotional response. It would be impossible to process two independent emotional responses at the same time.

The advert for Cheerios shown in Advert 10.5 provides a good example of low-involvement transformational advertising 'Great tasting' is the key benefit claim, but it is the imagery that elicits the positive emotional benefit, a good feeling evoked by the friendly honeybee. But wait, you might be thinking, isn't the benefit 'heart healthy'? Not at all. That is a *category* benefit. If you are looking for heart-healthy food, the category cue, you now know that Honey Nut Cheerios provides a 'great tasting' heart-healthy option. With food and beverages, it is good taste that you want. This is handled very well in this execution.

Unlike low-involvement informational advertising, transformational advertising *must* be liked. Think about it. You may not need to believe that Häagen-Dazs ice cream will make you feel passionate or that a Wonderbra will make you sexy to enjoy the feeling that it just might. But you do have to have a positive response to the execution. Otherwise, how could you experience a positive emotional reaction? In effect, what is going on is that the target audience takes a positive emotional feeling stimulated by the execution and associates it in memory with the brand. This requires a complete positive experience with the message.

BENEFIT CLAIM

When dealing with positive motives, the benefit is the relevant *emotion*. One can either use the subjective characteristic of the brand in support of the 'feeling' you will get using the brand (e.g., 'tastes so great you'll think you are in heaven') or a pure expression of the positive emotion, usually visual. In the low-involvement transformational case, either focus on the emotional benefit is appropriate, again as we saw in the last chapter.

Advert 10.5 Cheerios.

The key source characteristic for transformational brand attitude strategies is attractiveness, and, for the low-involvement quadrant, the *likeability* component of attractiveness. This should be obvious given what we have just discussed. If there is only a
picture of the product, to elicit a positive emotional response you must instantly 'like'
what you see; if it is a person, they should not only appear 'real', but also likeable.

High-involvement informational

As we already know from Chapter 8, when dealing with high-involvement purchase
decisions it is necessary for the target audience to not only pay attention and learn
something from the message; they must also *accept* it. Perhaps the single most important
creative tactic for this quadrant is to make sure the message is consistent with the target
audience's current attitudes – both toward the product and the brand. Unlike with low-
involvement decisions, where the consumer is likely to suspend belief about the benefit
claim until trying the product, with a high-involvement decision too much is at risk.
The target audience must be convinced that the benefit claim (or claims) is true before
risking purchase.

In order to ensure that the message does not over-claim (which is not only acceptable
but also desirable with low-involvement decisions), it is essential to understand what the
consumer is or is not likely to believe. If the message over-claims, or is inconsistent with
the target audience's beliefs and attitudes, the consumer will counter-argue the message
and not accept it. Benefit claims should be made that fall within what Sherif and
Hovland (1961) call a person's latitude of acceptance, as discussed in Chapter 8. For all of
us, there are things we readily believe, and then there are grey areas where we are not
quite sure whether we do or not believe, but are open-minded (what Sheriff and
Hovland call the latitude of indifference). Beyond that, we reject the claim (our latitude
of rejection). The job of high-involvement informational marketing communication is
to ensure that the key benefit claim used in the message is at the *upper end* of the latitude
of acceptance (do not inadvertently underclaim), and that any other benefit claims used
in support also fall at the upper end, or within the latitude of indifference.

In terms of execution, the key benefit claim should be immediately apparent, in both
the headline and visual. Regardless of where the key benefit claim is placed within the
execution, it and any linked visual should be the first thing that confronts the target
audience's attention. It will attract their attention because it will be addressing something
important to them. If they are in the market, it will be this key benefit, communicated
through the headline and visual, that will encourage processing the entire message to see
what it is all about. It must 'hook' the target audience immediately, while the additional
benefit claims in the body copy will help convince them of the desirability of the brand.

With high-involvement advertising, the consumer must be convinced by the message
that the brand is likely to deliver the benefit. It must 'involve' the reader, and provide
support for why the benefit is likely to be true. But finding a good example of advertising for high-involvement informational strategies is never easy. The Savoir Beds advertisement shown in Advert 10.6 does an excellent job of this. It reminds you of how
much time you spend in bed and links the brand to a 'first-class' sleep. Support is
supplied by the visuals, all well-recognized symbols of luxury, and a reminder that the
brand has been marketed since 1905, reinforcing its credibility.

Advert 10.6 Savoir Beds.

Creative: Savoir Beds; photography: Dominic Blackmore.

BENEFIT CLAIM

The focus on the key benefit for high-involvement informational executions, as in the low-involvement case, will be to use an attribute in support of a subjective characteristic of the brand, brand, draw attention directly to a subjective characteristic of the brand that is seen as important by the target audience or to use the key benefit claim as the solution to a problem that is known to be important to the target audience. The focus on the other important benefits used in the copy should use specific attributes of the brand in support of the subjective characteristic: for example, 'with a 5.9-litre engine you have all the power you need' (the objective attribute, a 5.9-litre engine, supports the subjective characteristic of 'all the power you need').

SOURCE CHARACTERISTIC

Credibility is the key characteristic for the perceived source. As in the low-involvement informational case, the source must be seen as an *expert*, again as either a technical expert or as a 'user' expert. But because the message must be accepted, the additional credibility component of *objectivity* is also required.

High-involvement transformational

Just as with low-involvement transformational marketing communication, the execution here must be seen as emotionally authentic. But unlike high-involvement informational executions, even though the decision is high involvement the benefit claim should be expressed in the extreme. Here, you want to over-claim in the sense of communicating an intense and *personal* feeling. This is the key. When the target audience sees the execution, they must think, 'Yes, that is what *I* want'.

It must be 'real' to the individual, not necessarily in the sense of reality but in terms of their wishes, dreams or desires. Most four-wheel-drive trucks, for example, are purchased by men who never drive them off-road. But they want to experience the 'feeling' of masculine adventure portrayed in the advertising for such vehicles. Women who see glamorous images portrayed in advertising for high-fashion perfume purchase it to experience the 'feeling' that is elicited by the imagery in the advertisement. In neither case is the image in the advertising likely to reflect their reality, but it is nevertheless 'real' for them. High-involvement transformational advertising must elicit such highly authentic emotional responses. Identifying personally with the image is, in effect, their acceptance of the key benefit claim.

Advert 10.7 for the Indian Ocean does just that. The beautiful setting evokes a strong positive emotional response, and this is clearly linked to the brand. The product visual will also contribute to this, and be linked to the brand. When considering outdoor furniture, this positive emotional association in memory will be experienced again. The inclusion of 'SALE' at the top of the advert does not get in the way of the message, but merely reflects the addition of brand purchase intention as an objective to the already well-executed brand awareness and brand attitude objectives.

When people look at adverts they are unconsciously reacting to the visual environment depicted. Appleton (1996) has shown that views to the horizon, as we see here, will evoke a feeling of opportunity. This will help reinforce the positive emotional response to the advert, even for those not in the market for outdoor furniture.

Because the decision is high involvement, for some transformationally driven purchase decisions some information may also be needed. This will not be the case for high-imagery products like fashion or jewellery, but could be for such things as a cruise holiday. In an IMC sense, for such cases the strong imagery may be conveyed via television with the same imagery reflected in print, along with some functional

BALHAM - HARRODS - HAMPSTEAD
0208 675 4808
www.indian-ocean.co.uk

INSPIRATIONAL OUTDOOR FURNITURE

Advert 10.7 Indian Ocean.

support benefit to help facilitate message acceptance. Just as with high-involvement informational executions, the key benefit (here in terms of the strong emotionally arousing imagery) must be noticed first, attracting attention via a sense of, 'They are talking directly to me'. That will lead them into whatever *brief* copy might be needed. Ideally, this copy will direct them to a website, toll-free number or retail location for more detailed information. Wherever they might be directed, the information there must be consistent with the emotional response aroused by the original message.

BENEFIT CLAIM

In high-involvement transformational executions, as with low-involvement transformational, the benefit focus will be either a subjective characteristic in support of the positive emotion, or simply the emotion. If some additional information is needed to help with the acceptance of the message, present either a straight expression of a subjective characteristic or use the specific attribute in support of a subjective characteristic.

SOURCE CHARACTERISTICS

As with low-involvement transformational strategies, the key source characteristic here is attractiveness, which means the source should be likable. But in this case, it must also be seen as *similar* to the target audience in their perceived emotional state. This is what helps the target audience personally identify with the message. The perceived source either implies the way they wish to see themselves (e.g., someone who wears Chanel perfume if only the package is shown), or the people in the execution reflect their perceived image of themselves using the brand. Again, their 'similarity' is unlikely to reflect reality, but rather the 'feeling' they wish to experience. How Louis Vuitton successfully dealt with this is discussed in the following box.

Eliciting the correct emotional response

In Chapter 8, we discussed the important role emotion plays in the processing of marketing communication. To help facilitate the correct emotional association with the key benefit, the emotional response to an execution must be consistent with the underlying motivation involved. Depending on whether it is a positive or negative emotion that is driving behaviour, the nondeclarative emotional memory associated with the category need will differ. In fact, given the nature of how we experience life, the emotions associated with satisfying a behavioural motivation will follow a sequence or change in emotional response, and marketing communication should reflect this (see Figure 10.1).

The idea of a sequence of emotions being involved in the processing of marketing communication was first introduced by Rossiter and Percy (1987) and is based on Hammond's (1970) re-conceptualization of Mower's theoretical work in the area. Mower (1960) looked at how unlearned emotional states relate to motivating behaviour in terms of a simple pleasure–pain dichotomy. Hammond then built on this idea, considering the relationship between emotion and motivation in terms of

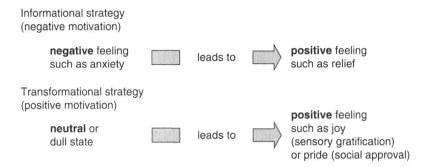

Informational strategy
(negative motivation)

negative feeling   leads to   **positive** feeling
such as anxiety   such as relief

Transformational strategy
(positive motivation)

                                                positive feeling
neutral or   leads to   such as joy
dull state   (sensory gratification)
                                                or pride (social approval)

Figure 10.1 Emotional response sequence.

approach and avoidance behaviour. When people find themselves in a 'painful' situation, as it increases, fear is excited; as the situation decreases, it is inhibited, and
one feels relief. On the other hand, when someone is experiencing 'pleasure', as it
increases hope is excited, but if it decreases that hope is inhibited and they feel
disappointment.

Louis Vuitton and celebrity sources

Since 2007, Louis Vuitton, a part of the LVMH luxury goods conglomerate, has
featured more than a dozen famous people in their handbag advertisements. This
list has included Andre Agassi with Steffi Graf, Catherine Deneuve, Sean Connery,
Buzz Aldrin, Mikhail Baryshnikov, Pelé, Angelina Jolie, and, for 2012,
Muhammad Ali. Mikhail Gorbachev was the brand's first famous face, back in
2007. He was seated in the back seat of a limousine with a remnant of the Berlin
Wall visible outside the window. On the seat beside him was a Louis Vuitton
Keepall 50 bag.

While not many people may realize it, Louis Vuitton began as a French luggage
maker in the 19th century. Given this heritage, the company sees the central
message of their marketing as travel and journeys, with a Louis Vuitton bag a part
of any great trip. Their advertisements have featured what might be considered
iconic individuals whose lives might be seen as extraordinary journeys. Yves
Carcelle, Louis Vuitton's chairman and chief executive believes, 'We are a very
special brand. We are the only one bound with travel'.

The idea for the campaign came from Antoine Arnault, the son of LVMH
chairman Bernard Arnault. The original list of 'icons' was compiled from a
meeting of Louis Vuitton executives, where they offered up their own heroes.
Known at the company as the 'Core Values' campaign, it stands out from most
high-fashion advertising because it features very accomplished people, and not
people likely to be seen endorsing any other product.

Source: *The Wall Street* Journal, 7 June 2012

This distinction has a direct bearing on what creative tactics should be used in marketing communication because it implies that different tactics will be necessary, depending on whether positive or negative motivations are involved. The emotional portrayal of the motivation in an execution must not only be consistent with the motivation driving behaviour but it should also reflect the *sequence* of emotions involved in the elicitory behaviour driven by positive motivations as positive feelings are increased, and in the inhibitory behaviour resulting from negative motivations as negative feelings are decreased, leading to a positive feeling.

All of this is actually a lot simpler than it may seem from this brief theoretical discussion. If we think about informational brand attitude strategies, the negative motivations involve solving or avoiding a problem of some kind – addressing a particular need. There will be negative emotions like fear or anxiety associated with the category need, and the brand as the solution will 'solve' the problem. In doing so, using the brand changes the negative feelings associated with the problem to a positive emotion like relief. For years, Michelin tyres has run television commercials that begin with a situation fraught with fear and anxiety, such as a woman with a baby in a car driving at night in a storm. Having built this fearful situation, it is then resolved by reminding us that with Michelin tyres, they will be safe (relief).

It is a sequence of emotions that parallels the emotional experience that should be reflected in marketing communication. The same thing applies to transformational brand attitude strategies. Moving from a neutral, or dull, state advertising for expensive chocolate should excite a feeling of joy or happiness at the prospect of eating some (sensory gratification), or with social approval, beginning from a feeling of perhaps shame or apprehension; being motivated to buy jewellery for a wife or girlfriend, or a sports car for yourself, to excite within yourself feelings of pride or being flattered.

In terms of creative execution, for informational brand attitude strategies, the emotional response will follow *indirectly* from an evaluation of the benefit claim. The negative emotion associated with the category need should be initiated first in the sequence, underscoring the feelings associated with the problem to be solved or avoided. Then, move the target audience to a positive emotional response linked to the brand's benefit as the solution.

With transformational brand attitude strategies, as we have seen, the emotional response will follow *directly* from executional elements within the advertising. In print, the emotional association with the need is necessarily assumed in most cases, with a strong feeling elicited by the emotional authenticity of the imagery used, providing a sense of the positive emotional consequences of using the brand. With television, especially when social approval is the underlying motive, it will be possible to establish the prior neutral or negative feelings that are resolved by the brand and replaced with positive emotions.

Logos, slogans, and taglines

With *logos,* while they may evolve over time, they should remain easily identified with the brand. Only when a brand is being repositioned should a new logo be considered. If a new logo is created, it is critical that it be unique to the brand and will not be confused with another brand's logo. Over time, just as we shall see with campaign consistency in the next section, the ideal logo will be one that by itself is linked to the brand, without the need for the actual brand name, excellent examples of just that are the Apple and Nike logos.

It is important to point out that slogans and taglines are *not* the same thing. Of the two, *slogans* are more flexible and about the product. They are used throughout all IMC media: adverts, packaging, point-of-purchase material; *all* media. *Taglines* on the other hand, tend to be more likely about the company, and are used more sparingly. They are more likely to be used in corporate communications and for brand building. In 2020, Jack Daniel's introduced a new tagline, 'Make it Count', which they said reflects the spirit of 'Mr. Jack', founder of Jack Daniel's. Both slogans and taglines, but especially slogans, should reflect the category need and the brand's key benefit, as with BMW's long-running slogan 'The Ultimate Driving Machine'.

Consistency in IMC executions

One of the most important, and often most difficult, tasks for IMC is ensuring consistency in executions within and across the different types of marketing communication a brand is using, as well as over time. *Everything* connected with an IMC campaign should have a similar 'look and feel'. That means everything from advertisements, to direct mail, to collateral, to packaging, to posters, to the sides of delivery trucks, to business cards and letterheads – everything.

The target audience should be able to immediately identify any execution within a campaign, and over time, as belonging to the brand. This is an important part of a brand's identity, and the more consistent the executions, the more readily brand awareness and communicating the brand benefit will be achieved. Yet it is surprising how many marketers do not seem to understand this. Too often a brand's advertising changes completely within a campaign, and it is not at all unusual for a brand's promotions to have nothing visually in common with its advertising (or in terms of the benefit). But consistency in execution does *not* mean that everything must look exactly the same. It is a 'feeling' that ties everything together, and this evolves over time. In fact, some variation in execution is essential to maintain attention and interest, and to help forestall wearout. Consistency within an IMC campaign, and over time, is important for brand awareness. When the look and feel of a brand's execution is consistent over time, that alone 'triggers' the brand in memory, along with the appropriate link to the need. In fact, just this 'look' or 'feel' can be enough, without even mentioning the brand name itself.

The long-running campaign for Silk Cut tobacco in the United Kingdom (up until all tobacco advertising was banned in the early 2000s) was one of the best examples of what we are talking about. For years, the brand's advertising never included the brand name. The advertisements were always some variation of scarlet silk and a 'cut'. Of course, it took many years of advertising following this 'look' *with* the brand name to seed the association in memory before it could be dropped from the advertising. We are not advocating that one's goal should necessarily be to reach a point where the brand name is no longer used (after all, there are always new people entering the market), only that it reaches the point where the target audience would know it was the brand advertising even if the brand name was not used.

Jack Daniel's has maintained just such a consistent 'look and feel' over the years as we can see in Advert 10.8. The underlying benefit of 'great taste' following from the cave spring water is presented with compelling authentic emotional imagery, consistent with

Advert 10.8 Jack Daniel's.

Source: © The Jack Daniel's trademarks appear courtesy of Jack Daniel's Properties, Inc. Jack Daniel's is a registered trademark of Jack Daniel's Properties, Inc.

the long history of Jack Daniel's advertising. This image will be firmly linked in memory with Jack Daniel's.

Unfortunately, too often advertising for different brands of fashion products, cosmetics and beverages (among others) affect the same image. One look through a women's fashion magazine is enough to illustrate the point. But no matter how well executed the emotional presentation is, if it is similar to another brand then both brands are in effect offering the *same benefit*. One can experience that same positive feeling with either brand.

The key to consistency is the *visual* feel. This is because the visual memory for the imagery associated with the brand actually elicits faster brand identification than the brand name itself. Studies have found that a consistent look and feel provides a faster trigger than the actual brand name or logo because visual memories are superior to those for encoded verbal stimuli such as words. This may be because over half of the brain's cortex is used for processing visual images. Eye-tracking studies of print adverts consistently show that around 70 percent of the time spent looking at an advert is spent with the visuals.

Consistency also helps in building brand attitude. The key here is to make sure that this visual look and feel is linked to the primary benefit being communicated. When the visual imagery is also associated in memory with the benefit, or if the associations reinforce the nature of the benefit, the consistency over time will ensure communication of the brand and its benefit with even a brief glance.

Visual look must be unique

The reasons for a consistent look among all the parts of an IMC campaign argue for its uniqueness. If there is any chance that the target audience may confuse the brand's marketing communication with a competitor's, the problem is obvious. Yet there is an incredible similarity between competitive brands' advertising. Pick up any magazine and you will see how similar the look and feel of advertising for competing brands is. This is especially true of retail, bank, car, fashion and cosmetic advertising.

What are needed are *unique* executions that have the same look and feel, and over time become firmly associated in memory with the brand. If competitors copy a brand's 'look' after it is firmly associated with that brand, misattribution is likely to occur, and the competitor's similar-looking advertising will merely reinforce the brand that 'owns' the look. Because of the nature of memory, once a brand is associated with a particular look or feel, any time that imagery is encountered it will stimulate associations with the brand. Good IMC planning can help ensure a unique and consistent look and feel for all brand's marketing communication.

Audio branding

In addition to the obvious need for visual and thematic consistency over time, music can be used to provide consistency within an IMC campaign. This is often referred to as 'audio branding'. A good example of this is AXA, a financial service group operating in some 56 countries. They created a library of specially composed music that could be mixed-and-matched by their many groups and agencies around the world. But the key is using an 'audio logo' for all their marketing communication (Hayzlett, 2014).

Summary

In this chapter, we have explored a number of creative tactics that may be used in marketing communication in order to facilitate message processing. These tactics are based on work by psychologists in psycholinguistics and visual imaging that has revealed ways in which the written word and pictures should be used in communication to increase the likelihood of it being positively processed. Specific tactics to help attract and hold attention include using unexpected elements in print and visual, colour rather than black-and-white illustrations, larger pictures where possible, attention to placement in media and format. We also looked specifically at a number of attention factors associated with the Internet.

Perhaps the most important creative tactic for facilitating learning is to keep everything simple. This is at the heart of all learning. Use familiar words and simple sentences, avoiding compound sentences and inverted clauses, passive constructions, puns and negatives. Headlines should be held to less than six to seven words so they may be fully processed at a glance without the need to 'read' them. In television commercials, the pacing is important, minimizing the number of visual cuts, especially for informationally driven strategies.

Music can be used as an important creative tactic in IMC, especially its ability to arouse emotions. There is a close connection between music prosody and speech prosody. Both personal and historical nostalgia can also be used as an effective creative tactic.

It was pointed out that different brand awareness and brand attitude strategies require different creative tactics. Recognition brand awareness requires a clear visual of the package as it will appear at the point-of-purchase. Recall brand awareness requires establishing a link between the need and the brand, in that order, and repeated within the execution. This is necessary so that when the need occurs, it will be linked in memory with the brand, and the brand will come to mind as satisfying that need.

Brand attitude creative tactics are dependent on the brand attitude strategy as indicated by the Rossiter–Percy Grid. Each quadrant demands particular creative tactics in order to accommodate the processing requirements associated with the involvement and motivation driving brand choice. With low-involvement informational messages, the key is to use one simple benefit, presented in the extreme. For low-involvement transformational messages, the critical creative consideration is the emotional authenticity of the execution, because this in effect becomes the benefit. Because of the risk involved, high-involvement informational messages must be believed and accepted. This means the message must present an initial benefit claim in the headline and visual that is consistent with the target audience's existing beliefs about the brand in relation to the benefit, and presented at the upper level of acceptance, careful not to over-claim. High-involvement transformational messages, like low-involvement transformational, must also be seen as emotionally authentic, but additionally, the target audience must personally identify with that feeling. In all of this, eliciting the correct emotional response is critical.

Logos, slogans, and taglines each can play a role in the creative execution of IMC, but have specific uses. Importantly, slogans and taglines are not the same thing.

One of the most important creative considerations for IMC is the need for consistency across messages and over time. This consistency does not require a 'cookie-cutter' approach where everything looks exactly like everything else, but rather a look and feel that is clearly associated with the brand. The key to this consistent look is the visual feel, and this requires a unique visual look.

Review questions

1 What are the key creative tactics for gaining attention?
2 Discuss the attention likelihoods for IMC adverts.
3 Find examples of advertising that is likely to hold attention and discuss why.
4 What is the key to facilitating learning in marketing communication?
5 Identify advertisements that do a good job of facilitating learning and ones that do not, and discuss why.
6 What is the relationship between music and speech, and why is this important to understand in executing creative?
7 What role does music timbre play in creative execution?
8 Discuss nostalgia as a creative tactic.
9 What is the fundamental difference in the creative tactics needed for recognition versus recall brand awareness?
10 Find examples of advertisements that you feel do a good job establishing the category need – brand awareness links needed for recall brand awareness.
11 What is the key difference in the way the benefit is presented in informational versus transformational executions?
12 Find good examples of advertisements for each of the four quadrants of the Rossiter–Percy Grid and discuss why you feel they are good executions.
13 Why are the characteristics of a source used in marketing communication important for its effectiveness?
14 Why would it be inappropriate to use the head of a company as a spokesperson for a high-involvement product?
15 Find examples of advertisements where the benefit focus is executed correctly and examples where it is not, and discuss why.
16 Discuss the importance of eliciting the correct emotional sequence in marketing communication.
17 Identify advertisements that you feel do a good job in presenting the correct emotional sequence for the motivation involved and discuss why.
18 What is the difference between a slogan and a tagline?
19 How should logos be used in IMC?
20 Why is consistency in IMC executions so important?

References

Ahn, E. and Edwards, S.M. (2002) Does size really matter? Brand attitude versus click-through in response to banner Ads. *Proceedings of the 2002 Conference of the American Academy of Advertising*, 8–9.

Allen, D. (2006) Effects of pop-music in advertising on attention and memory. *Journal of Advertising Research*, 46/4, 434–444.

Appleton, J. (1996) *The experience of landscapes* revised edition. Chiehester: John Wiley and Sons.

Balkwill, L.L. and Thompson, W.F. (1999) A cross-cultural investigation of the perception of emotion in music: psychological and cultural cues. *Music Perception: and Interdisciplinary Journal*, 17/1 Fall, 43–64.

Banks, P.D. and Muehling (2003) The effects of television commercial pacing on viewers attention and memory. *Journal of Marketing Communication, 9(1)*, 17–28.

Brainerd, C.J., Desrochers, A. and Howe, M.L. (1997) Stages of learning analysis of picture–word effects in associative memory. *Journal of Experimental Psychology: Human Learning and Memory, 7(1)*, 1–14.

Bryce, W.J. and Yalch, R.F. (1993) Hearing versus seeing: A comparison of learning of spoken and pictorial information in television advertising. *Journal of Current Issues and Research in Advertising, 15(1)*, 1–20.

Eyesenk, M.W. (1977) *Human Memory: Theory, Research, and Individual Difference*. Oxford: Pergamon.

Franke, G.R., Huhmann, B.A. and Mothersbaugh, D.L. (2004) Information content and consumer readership of print ads: A comparison of search and experience products. *Journal of the Academy of Marketing Science, 32(1)*, 20–31.

Freeman, L. (1999) Wisk rings in a new ad generation. *Advertising Age*, 19 September, *1*, 91.

Hammond, L.J. (1970) Conditioned Emotional States. In P. Black (ed.), *Physiological Correlates of Emotion*. New York: Academic Press, Chapter 12, pp. 245–260.

Hayzlett, J. (2014) The language of audio-branding. *Marketing News*, 18 June.

Henderson, P.W. and Cote, J.A. (1999) Guidelines for selecting or modifying logos. *Journal of Marketing, 62(2)*, 14–30.

Hermen, K. (1935) The affective characteristics of major and minor modes in music. *American Journal of Psychology, 47/1*, 103–118.

Holman, R.H. and Hecker, S. (1993) Advertising impact: Creative elements affecting brand recall. *Current Issues and Research in Advertising, 6(1)*, 157–172.

Justin, P. and Laukka, P. (2003) Communication of emotions in vocal expressions and music performance: different channels, same codes?. *Psychological Bulletin, 129/5*, 770–814.

Kosslyn, S.M. and Thompson, W.L. (2003) When is early visual cortex activated during visual mental imagery? *Psychological Bulletin, 129(5)*, 723–746.

Loveland, K.E., Smeesters, D. and Mandel, N. (2010) Still preoccupied with 1995: The need to belong and preference for nostalgic products. *Journal of Consumer Research, 37*.

MacLachlan, J. and Logan, M. (1993) Commercial shot length in TV commercials and their memorability and persuasiveness. *Journal of Advertising Research, 33/2*, 7–16.

Maloney, J.C. (1962) Curiosity versus disbelief in advertising. *Journal of Advertising Research, 2/2*, 2–9.

Milliman, R.E. (1982) Using background music to effect the behaviour of supermarket shoppers. *Journal of Marketing, 46/3*, 869.

Mower, U.H. (1960) *Learning Theory and Behaviour*. New York: Wiley.

Mueling, D.D. (2011) The relative influence of advertising-evolved personal and historical nostalgia thoughts on consumer's bran attitudes. *Journal of Marketing Communication, 19(2)*, 98–113.

Myers, G. (1994) *Words in Ads*. London: Arnold.

Nelson, D.L., McEvoy, C.L. and Pointer, L. (2003) Spreading activation or spooky action at a distance? *Journal of Experimental Psychology: Learning, Memory, and Cognition, 29(1)*, 42–52.

North, A.C., Hargreaves, D.J. and McKendrick, J. (1999) The influence of in-store music on wine selections. *Journal of Applied Psychology, 82/2*, 271–276.

Paivio, A. (1971) *Image and Verbal Processing*. New York: Holt, Rinehart, & Winston.

Ritson, M. (2003) *What Do People Really Do During TV Commercials?* Working Paper. London: London Business School.

Rossiter, J.R. (1999) The increase in magazine ad readership. *Journal of Advertising Research, 29/5*, 35–39.

Rossiter, J.R. and Percy, L. (1987) *Advertising and Promotion Management*. New York: McGraw-Hill.

Rossiter, J.R. and Percy, L. (1997) *Advertising Communication and Promotion Management*. New York: McGraw-Hill.

Rossiter, J.R., Percy, L. and Berkvist, L. (2018) *Marketing Communication*. London: Sage Publications.

Schultz, E.J. (2016) Pabst bets on nostalgia. *Advertising Age*, 22 August, *18*.

Sherif, M. and Hovland, C.I. (1961) *Social Judgement*. New Haven, CT: Yale University Press.

Speer, M.E., Bhanji, J.P., and Delgado, M.R. (2014) Saving the past: Positive memories evoke value representations in the striation. *Neurons, 84*, 19 November, 1–10.

Wearing, A.J. (1973) The recall of sentences of varying length. *Australian Journal of Psychology, 25(2)*, 155–161.

Young, C.E. and Robinson, M. (1992) Visual connectedness and persuasion. *Journal of Advertising Research, 32/2*, 51–59.

Young, C.E. and Robinson, M. (1999) Video rhythms and recall. *Journal of Advertising Research, 29/3*, 22–25.

Part IV

The IMC Plan

Up to this point, we have dealt with various aspects of IMC. The role of IMC in building brands and its contribution to corporate communication goals has been considered. The distinction between traditional advertising and promotion has been discussed, along with various ways of delivering IMC messages. How messages are processed was introduced to gain a better idea of what is required of an IMC message if it is to be successful. We looked at message development and how to execute the message in order to increase the likelihood it will be processed and lead to a positive decision for the brand. Now it is time to put it all together.

In Part IV we address the IMC plan and its implementation. There are a number of key considerations a manager must take into account as the planning process begins, and these are dealt with in Chapter 11. To develop an effective IMC plan, it is important to begin with a review of the marketing plan because that will provide an overview of the brand and its marketing objectives. This is an essential foundation because IMC must support the marketing plan. With the review completed the manager must look at cultural considerations, and then consider various conditions in the market that could inform the mix of advertising and promotion, as well as if direct marketing should be considered. It is also important to have an appreciation of the strengths and weaknesses of advertising-like messages versus promotion-like messages, and how they may be best used together in meeting the overall marketing communication objectives for a brand. Each has particular strengths in terms of specific communication objectives, and these must be considered.

The specific steps involved in the planning process are addressed in Chapter 12. It begins with target audience selection and gaining an understanding of how they go about making decisions in the category. This is often overlooked but is critical because it helps identify where in the decision process marketing communication is likely to have a positive effect on brand choice. The next step deals with the key consideration of how the brand should be positioned within the message, and selection of the benefit to be used as the basis for the benefit claim in the message. Then, the communication objectives must be set. While brand awareness and brand attitude are always objectives, the manager must decide if category need should also be addressed, and if short-term brand purchase intention may also be needed. With the communication objectives set, one can then put together a set of media options that are compatible with those objectives.

Once the planning process is complete, the manager has all of the information needed to finalize and implement an IMC plan. Chapter 13 deals with how this information is used to make the decisions required in finalizing the IMC plan, and the steps necessary to implement it. Finalizing a plan requires coordinating marketing communication efforts

DOI: 10.4324/9781003169635-14

aimed at identifying a number of touch points in the decision process. By its very nature, this almost always means there are a number of communication tasks involved. The planning process will have identified many potential opportunities for positively affecting the brand purchase decision. Because budgets rarely are large enough to afford addressing all of the opportunities, deciding what will be essential to accomplish, and then how to make the best use of the remaining budget, is the most important aspect of finalizing the IMC plan. The finalized plan will include various media options that are appropriate for the communication tasks that are to be addressed. Then, a budget must be set.

To implement the plan, the manager must decide how to allocate the available budget in terms of media selection. Specifically, decisions must be made about what should be the primary versus the secondary media used for each communication task, and a media plan developed. With this plan implemented, it remains to track the campaign in the market in order to determine how effective it is in satisfying the communication strategy and driving sales.

11 Planning considerations

In this chapter we look at some of the considerations a manager must take into account in developing an IMC plan. Before a manager can begin to think of specific marketing communication issues, it is important to carefully analyse what is known about the market. This means that the first step in the IMC strategic planning process is to outline the relevant market issues that are likely to affect a brand's communications. The best source of information will be the marketing plan, as all marketing communication efforts should support the marketing plan. (If for some reason a marketing plan is not available, answers to the questions posed below will need to be based on the best-available management judgement.) Something that needs to be considered at this stage are cultural issues.

Another question that may come up in reviewing the marketing plan is whether to include direct marketing in the IMC plan. We will be considering the role of direct marketing in IMC. The marketing plan will also indicate various characteristics of the brand's market that should be considered in formulating the plan. With this foundation, we look at the role of advertising messages and promotion messages in the mix. Communication objectives are important here (beyond the obvious reasons) because the appropriateness of using advertising and promotion in the IMC plan will be a function of the communication objective selected, and the role advertising versus promotion will play in the mix will be a function of not only these objectives, but also the specific market credentials.

Reviewing the marketing plan

The first consideration in strategic planning for IMC is to review the marketing plan to understand the market in general and where a brand fits relative to its competition. What is it about the brand, company or service that might bear upon what is said to the target audience? There are at least six broad questions that a manager should answer before beginning to think specifically about the IMC plan (see Table 11.1).

What is being marketed? The manager should write out a description of the brand so that anyone will immediately understand what it is and what specific need it satisfies. Taking time to focus attention like this on the details of a brand often enables the manager to see it in a clearer light. This is also important, because it is just this information that will serve as a background for the people who will be creating and executing the brand's marketing communication.

DOI: 10.4324/9781003169635-15

Table 11.1 Marketing background questions

Key consideration	Question
Product description	What is being marketed?
Market assessment	What is known about the market where the brand competes?
Competitive evaluation	What is known about major competitors?
Source of business	Where will sales and usage come from?
Marketing objective	What are the brand's marketing objectives?
Marketing communication	How is marketing communication expected to contribute to the marketing objective?

What is known about the market where the brand competes? This is information that must be current. If it comes from a marketing plan, one must be sure nothing has occurred since it was written that could possibly be outdated. What one is looking for here is knowledge of the market that is going to influence how successful the brand is likely to be. Is the market growing, are there new entries, have there been recent innovations, bad publicity? While enough information must be provided for a good understanding of the market, the description should be simple and highlight only the most relevant points.

What is known about the market where the brand competes? What are the key claims made in the category? What are the creative strategies being used; what types of executional approaches and themes? Here it is helpful to collect actual examples. Something else to consider here is an evaluation of the media tactics being used by competitors. What is their mix of marketing communication options and how do they use them? All of this provides a picture of the communications environment within which the IMC programme will operate.

Where will sales and usage come from? The manager needs to look at this question both in terms of competitive brands and the consumer. Again, this reflects the increasing complexity of markets. To what extent is the brand looking to make inroads against key competitors? Will the brand compete outside the category? Where will customers or users of the brand come from? What, if anything, will they be giving up? Will they be changing their behaviour patterns? This is the first step toward defining a target audience (which is dealt with in detail in the next chapter), and begins to hint at how a better understanding of the target will lead to the most suitable IMC options to reach them.

What are the brand's marketing objectives? This should include not only a general overview of the marketing objective, but specific share or financial goals as well. When available, the marketing plan should provide these figures. Otherwise, it is important to estimate the financial expectations for the brand. If the IMC programme is successful, what will happen? This is critical because it will provide a realistic idea of how much marketing money can reasonably be made available for the marketing communication programme.

How is marketing communication expected to contribute to the marketing objective? As we now know from the previous chapters, the answer is much more than 'increase sales'. It is likely that marketing communication will be expected to make a number of contributions towards meeting the marketing objectives. This is where the manager begins to get an idea of how much will be expected from the IMC programme, and the extent to which multiple messages and different types of marketing communication might be required.

Global cultural considerations

When dealing with IMC campaigns that will run in multiple countries, or worldwide, it is critical to understand how each country's culture is likely to inform how the message will be received and processed; and importantly, how creative tactics may need to be adapted for particular cultural groups. Even within a single country or region there may be cultural considerations that will need to be taken into account.

An understanding of the cultural considerations needed for IMC is built upon language, ethnicity, religion, and family, and this forms the foundation of cultural values. Perhaps the most widely acknowledged dimensions of cultural values are those of Hofstede (1984). Based upon thirty years of research in seventy-two countries and twenty languages, he identified four dimensions of cultural values,: power distance, individualism versus collectivism, masculinity versus femininity, and uncertainty avoidance. Later, he added a fifth dimension, long-term orientation (Hofstede, 1991).

Power distance: this dimension describes cultures where there is a clear and accepted inequality in how organizations and society at large are ordered.

Individualism versus collectivism: most Western cultures tend to focus on the individuals and their immediate family, while Asian and Latin American cultures tend to be more collectivist, with people belonging to in-groups that look after themselves in exchange for loyalty.

Masculinity versus femininity: regardless of gender, most Anglo-Saxon cultures tend to exhibit more traditional masculine traits such as achievement and success, while Scandinavian cultures, for example, exhibit more feminine traits such as caring for others and quality of life.

Uncertainty avoidance: in some cultures people are fine with uncertainty, while in others people feel threatened by uncertainty and ambiguity, and try to avoid it.

Long-term orientation: some cultures, such as Asian, tend to have a programmatic future-oriented view of things while others focus more on conventional historic or short-term goals.

In addition to Hofstede's five dimensions, a number of other cultural dimensions have been proposed by researchers in the field, such as Hall (1976) and Trompenaar and Hampden-Turner (1997).

Global cultural groupings

Using the cultural value dimensions, researchers have identified ten groups of countries that are similar in terms of cultural values (Livermore, 2013), and these are summarized in Table 11.2. But it is important to remember that while the countries representing each grouping tend to be similar in their cultural values, some are better fits than others. This is especially true of the Confucian Asian groups. While Japan and China share many cultural values such as collectivism, there are some sharp differences, such as uncertainty avoidance, which is much higher in Japan than in China.

IMC must take the cultural values of its target market into consideration when developing creative messages, and this means both verbal and visual elements. A good example of what can happen when you do not is what happened to Nike in 2019. They

Table 11.2 Global cultural groupings

Cultural Group	Representative Countries	Key Cultural Values
Anglo	UK, US, Australia	Individualism
Nordic	Denmark, Finland, Iceland, Norway, Sweden	Very Individualistic
Germanic	Austria, Switzerland, Netherlands, Germany	Punctuality
Eastern European Central Asian	Poland, Russia, Albania, Greece	Collectivist
Latin European	Italy, France, Portugal, Belgium, Israel	Paternalistic and Collectivist
Latin American	Brazil, Argentina, Mexico, Ecuador	Uncertainty avoidance and Particularism
Confucian Asian	China, Japan, Korea, Singapore	Collectivism and Long-term orientation
South Asian	India, Pakistan, Thailand, Malaysia, Cambodia, Philippines	Very high power distance and Uncertainty avoidance
Sub-Saharan African	Nigeria, South Africa	Very collectivist
Arab	Countries from Monaco across North Africa to the Persian Gulf	High on being versus doing and Very Short-term oriented

Source: Adapted from D. Livermore (2013) Customs of the World: Using Cultural Intelligence to Adapt to Wherever You Are. (Chantilly, VA, The Teaching Company).

were accused of 'blasphemy' for the apparent similarity between their stylized AirMax logo and what was thought to resemble the word Allah in Arabic. Adding to the perceived insult, the logo was on the sole of the shoe, and showing the sole of a shoe is considered very disrespectful.

One of the most extensive surveys of how advertising between cultural groupings differ and reflect their cultural values was conducted by deMooj (1998). She did a content analysis of advertising from countries around the globe and found that the advertising 'style' of a country reflected its cultural values. She also noted that because advertising is an expression of culture, the symbols and imagery used may even reinforce cultural values. Examples would include how the sensual and erotic style of much French advertising would never work in Germany where the style of advertising reflects a need for structure and facts, indirectness is a strong part of Japanese advertising, while Italian advertising is collectivist and strongly masculine, and Dutch advertising reflects their feminine culture. DeMooij's research shows how cultural values are reflected in the ways in which the message is constructed and executed. This is very important because cultural values will inform how an IMC message is processed.

The role of direct marketing in IMC

One of the decisions to be made early in IMC planning is whether to use direct marketing as a part of the campaign. Direct marketing, while it is generally thought about in terms of delivering a promotion-like message because it is usually looking for a specific,

Table 11.3 Basic characteristics of direct marketing

Accountability	Tracking response to control content and cost
Effect a response	Objective is an immediate response to the message
Interactive process	Feedback helps modify future messages
More efficient targeting	Database helps target specific individuals or groups
Database	Used to identify target audience and track response

short-term response, is much more than that. The key is that, regardless of the medium used to deliver the message, the target audience is database driven, as we discuss later.

When most people think about direct marketing they think of direct mail. In fact, many marketers assume that they are the same. But direct mail is only one part of direct marketing, and while it is an important part, it is not even the largest in terms of the money spent on direct marketing. In one sense, it probably does not matter what is meant by direct marketing. But as Schultz (1995a) has pointed out, what someone means when they say direct marketing may have absolutely no relationship to what others think is direct marketing. This is always a danger when terms are used loosely, and doubly so in IMC planning.

Consumers are unlikely to know or care what marketers call the messages they send, or the way they deliver them. But if managers are to be disciplined in their planning, they must. In fact, consumers think that nearly all the marketing communication they are exposed to is 'advertising'. This means everything from bumper stickers, to coupons to refunds (Schultz, 1995a). But for effective IMC planning, there must be an agreement on what is meant by such things as advertising and promotion (as already seen in earlier chapters), and what it means to include direct marketing as a part of an IMC programme.

The basic characteristics of direct marketing (see Table 11.3) are briefly described below, with the exception of the database which was discussed in some depth back in Chapter 7.

Accountability. Accountability is a key issue in direct marketing. While all marketing communication should be cost-effective, direct marketing is tightly controlled because of its dependence on a database. With appropriate models, direct marketing offers the manager not only the opportunity to predict and measure responses, but also the ability to determine the actual costs associated with particular responses. Because of the database, managers can continually purge and update files to maximize the cost-effectiveness of their direct marketing programmes.

Effect a response. The point has already been made many times that all forms of marketing communications must address brand awareness and brand attitude. But the primary job of direct marketing is to stimulate the target receiver to take some kind of action now: place an order, use a service or make an enquiry. In this way, it reflects the primary communication objectives of promotion-like messages.

Interactive process. All direct marketing is interactive in the sense that the response to a message becomes new information to be recorded in the database. This new information is then used in developing new messages to be used in future direct marketing efforts. When telemarketing or the internet are involved, there is an opportunity for modifying the message during contact.

More efficient targeting. As the primary goal of direct marketing is a response of some kind, the effort must be highly targeted. One is looking for an individual, or relatively small group of similar people, likely to respond favourably to the brand's message. Even when mass media are used for direct marketing, an effort should be made to target as specific an audience as possible.

For direct marketing to be profitable several conditions must be met (Rossiter et al., 2018) to). To begin with, there must be a substantial number of actual or potential customers in the database. Secondly, there needs to be a realistic chance of either reducing switching behaviour or increasing usage of the brand. It is also important to consider whether the expected profit from the campaign will be greater than the expected profit from using the same marketing expenditure on other IMC programs. Finally, the database must be difficult for competitors to duplicate and go after your customers.

Difference between direct marketing and traditional advertising

There are a number of ways that direct marketing differs from traditional advertising and several are detailed in Table 11.4. Perhaps the most important difference between direct marketing and traditional advertising is that rather than trying to stimulate brand purchase intention using brand attitude through multiple exposures to the message, direct marketing usually makes only one attempt to generate a response. As we have already discussed, while brand purchase intention is rarely a specific objective for advertising, it is always an objective with direct marketing. The target audience is always asked to do something, and do it now.

Another difference is the personal nature of direct marketing. Because the target audience can be tightly targeted, direct marketing rarely addresses a mass audience. One speaks directly to members of the target audience about their particular needs, *and never in the third person*. The focus of direct marketing is also generally on existing customers (Reichheld, 1996).

Distribution is also considered in a much different light. With direct marketing, distribution itself can become an important brand benefit (for example, not sold in stores). Direct marketing also uses the delivery medium (direct mail, telemarketing, broadcast) *as the marketplace*, whereas with traditional advertising distribution is used to define the marketplace. For example, direct marketing is the only way many companies and others distribute their products.

In terms of communication objectives, while both brand awareness and brand attitude must be objectives, advertising will be more strongly oriented towards brand attitude goals while direct marketing clearly means to stimulate immediate brand purchase intention, the same as promotion. Yet just as we saw that promotion can and should help support brand equity, direct marketing, too, can help build brand equity.

Table 11.4 Differences between direct marketing and traditional advertising

	Direct marketing	*Traditional advertising*
Message delivery	Single exposure	Multiple exposures
Target audience	Individual	Mass
Distribution	The delivery medium serves as the marketplace	Distribution is used to define the marketplace
Primary communication objective	Brand purchase intention	Brand awareness and brand attitude
Accountability	Direct	Indirect

One final difference is related to the issue of accountability in direct marketing and databases. In a very real sense, direct marketing may be seen as 'interactive'. Based on information about the target audience, a specific message is tailored to it which in its turn repays the marketer with new information about the target market, either through a purchase response or request for information. All of this is tracked and measured, providing a record of a programme's effectiveness. One, of course, tracks and measures the effects of advertising, but the accountability is not nearly as tight (although continuous tracking programmes for advertising have made significant gains in measuring response to advertising).

In many ways, direct marketing is much like personal selling (Tapp, 1998). Before the 'sales call', one gathers as much information as possible about the customer. With direct marketing, this is found in the database. Like personal selling, direct marketing communicates directly to individuals, and the message can be tailored for them.

When to use direct marketing

Direct marketing can be an important part of IMC planning. But one must remember that it is only *one* way to deliver marketing communication. Although it has become an increasingly used tool, this does not mean that direct marketing need be a part of any particular IMC campaign, only that it should be considered when appropriate. Direct marketing is not appropriate for every type of product or service. In fact, it is rarely a good way of marketing most fast-moving consumer goods (fmcg). While direct marketing can be effective for some low-involvement products, its primary use is with high-involvement products.

This does *not* mean that consumer-packaged goods marketers do not use marketing communications tools that may look like they are part of a direct marketing campaign. This is where the definition is important. Does the inclusion of an 800 number in advertising constitute direct marketing? Probably not, in most cases. What about direct mail coupons? Again, probably not. As we have seen, direct marketing is a way of delivering a message that asks for an immediate response, is highly targeted, but importantly, is based on a database. An 800 number in an advertisement is probably a convenience for enquiry, not the primary objective of the marketing communication, and the mass mailing of coupons is not highly targeted. When considering the use of direct marketing in IMC planning, it should be within the bounds of its definition.

There are three questions a manager must ask when thinking about using direct marketing in an IMC programme (see Table 11.5). First, does direct marketing make sense – are there situations where a direct response is desirable, and is all or part of the target audience concentrated and easily identifiable? This would certainly be the case, for example, with customers for military aircraft or some specialized manufacturing equipment. But what about consumer markets? As we have just noted, the *key* is likely to be whether or not the purchase decision is high involvement.

Table 11.5 Questions to answer when considering direct marketing

- Does direct marketing make sense given the brand and its communication strategy?
- Is a good database available for identifying the target audience?
- What is the best way to deliver the message?

Table 11.6 Strengths of basic direct marketing

Media	Strength
Direct mail	Greatest flexibility
Telemarketing	Provides immediate feedback
Mass media	More broadly based audience
Interactive	Largely self-selecting

Again, this does *not* mean that direct marketing is never appropriate for low-involvement products. But it does mean that one should take a closer look if marketing low-involvement products, *and apply the definition*. Of course, we are also assuming these low-involvement products are available through traditional mass merchandising chains of distribution. Many catalogue and other marketers deal with low-involvement products, but direct marketing is their *only* (or primary) means of distribution. These marketers, if they indeed only distribute through direct marketing, are not involved with IMC.

If direct marketing does make sense, the second question that must be asked is whether there is a good database available for the target market? If direct marketing has been a part of previous marketing programmes, a list is probably available. Many businesses retain customer and prospect lists. If not, lists of businesses and consumers are often available to rent, covering almost any product category or selected demographic group. If nothing satisfactory is available, consideration could be given to developing custom lists. This, of course, would only work if there were time to develop the list.

As the definition implies, a database is required for direct marketing. To underscore the importance of a database in direct marketing, it has been suggested that the quality of the list used accounts for 40 percent of the effectiveness of a direct marketing effort, compared to the headline or primary thrust of the message, which accounts for another 40 percent and the remainder of the message, which accounts for only 20 percent (Lamons, 1992). Without a good list, direct marketing is unlikely to be effective.

The third question to ask is: How do I deliver the message? There are four media to choose from: direct mail, telemarketing, mass media and interactive digital media. As a rule, only *one* form of media will be used in direct marketing when it is part of an IMC programme. Messages in other media in an IMC programme may play a secondary role by alerting the target market to the direct marketing efforts, but the nature and cost of direct marketing usually dictates a single, primary medium for delivering the message. An exception would be when different segments of the market are more easily reached by one medium over another. The strengths of each of these four basic media for different direct marketing tasks are highlighted in Table 11.6.

Market characteristics that influence IMC effectiveness

In a very interesting study conducted a number of years ago, senior marketing executives from large companies that manufacture nondurable consumer goods were interviewed (Strang, 1980). Among other things, they were asked whether they felt different market scenarios would be likely to increase the importance of either advertising over promotion, promotion over advertising, or have no effect. While we must bear in mind that these are packaged goods marketers, the results nevertheless provide a valuable insight into how marketers actually allocate their marketing budget in communication planning, especially in relation to the product lifecycle, an idea introduced many years ago by Dean (1950).

One of the points made by the Strang study is that marketers feel advertising and promotion have different strengths relative to a brand's position in the product life-cycle: introduction, growth, maturity or decline. For example, advertising is more important than promotion earlier in a product's lifecycle (especially in the 'growth' stage), and that promotion is more important late in the product's life (especially in the decline stage). Although this reflects a relative use of advertising and promotion in IMC during the product lifecycle, there are absolute cost considerations here as well (Farris and Buzzell, 1979).

This, of course, fits nicely with our understanding of the overall strength of advertising versus promotion, which we discuss below. It is essential to build and nurture brand equity as a product grows, and this is what brand attitude, advertising's strength, is all about. A product in decline is often being phased out, and while managers want the product to move through the pipeline, they are not interested in any real investment in the brand. The tactical strength of promotion to stimulate brand purchase intention fits this need well.

There are a number of other market characteristics that seem to call for different advertising versus promotion strategies, and four key areas are discussed next.

Product differentiation

If a product or service is truly different from competition in the mind of the target audience, and (importantly) that difference is seen as meaningful, there is a strong reason to advertise that difference. On the other hand, if the target audience perceives all brands in the category as more or less the same, then at least in the short term promotion will make more sense than advertising. Why do we emphasize the short term? Because in the long term, one would hope to create at least a meaningful perceptual, if not actual, difference for the brand with advertising. It must be remembered that when we talk about differentiated brands, we are talking about *perceived* differences. Whether the difference is 'real' or not is beside the point if the target audience believes it is real.

Two general characteristics that should be considered are price and quality. In both cases, when consumers perceive a difference, it calls for attention to how one uses advertising and promotion. If a brand is seen as significantly higher in price than other major competitors, advertising is *more* important than promotion. At first this may seem counter-intuitive, but on reflection you will see that it really isn't. Yes, a price promotion will make a higher-priced brand *temporarily* more price competitive, but it does nothing to justify its regular price in the long term. Advertising, through brand attitude, can build brand equity and provide a reason for why a higher price is justified.

Once again, one must be alert to perceptions. For example, consumers say they 'know' some brands of frozen prepared foods are *much* more expensive than others. But how much, and is the difference really that significant? Interestingly, the actual price of more expensive brands is often not that much higher (no more than a few pence more), but the *perception* is that 'quality' brands are much higher priced. Under such circumstances if you are the manager of one of the 'quality' brands seen as more expensive, it makes no sense to decry this misconception of a significantly higher price, and to try to convince people that for only a little more you get a much better product. Consumers already believe it is better. Advertising must reinforce this perception, along the lines of 'naturally it costs more – good quality is expensive'. If a brand is seen as being of higher quality than its major competitor, it makes sense to advertise and reinforce the perception. If a brand is in fact of lower quality than its major competitors (not too low, of course), promotion will often help overcome a reluctance on the part of the target audience to 'trade down'.

In general, one can say that when a brand is perceived to be positioned differently from major competitors, advertising is more important than promotion in IMC planning.

Market position

If a product or service is frequently purchased or used, advertising is more important in the IMC mix than promotion. There are many reasons for this, but again they centre on the need to continually reinforce a positive brand attitude under circumstances where the opportunity for brand switching is high. Promotions, of course, may be used tactically, but without a strong brand equity all promotions really do is 'steal' usage. This is a problem underscored by the 'cola wars' between Coke and Pepsi. While continuing to advertise heavily, they nonetheless have turned more and more to using price promotion. As a result, it is not unusual for the leading brand in a market at any one time to be the one with the best price promotion. If taken to an extreme, this can lead to brand suicide because in effect it is telling consumers not to pay attention to the brand's advertising, but to make their brand choice based only on price.

It also makes more sense to advertise than to use extensive promotion when a brand has a clear market share advantage. Once again, it is the brand attitude strength of advertising that nurtures the brand equity sustaining market share advantage.

With a strong market position through either frequent purchase or high market share advantage, advertising will be more important than promotion in IMC planning.

Poor performance

When a brand finds itself struggling, promotion becomes more important than advertising. When what is needed is help *now*, the more immediate sales results from promotion make sense. This flows naturally from promotion's strength – driving brand purchase intention. Although this is unlikely to provide a long-term solution to the problem, it is definitely a way to accelerate sales in the short run. This in turn should help increase cash flow and enable a return to the marketing plan. A corollary to this is when a brand is in danger of losing distribution (which can be a natural consequence of a disappointing sales performance) or having trouble building distribution. This is a perfect time to use trade promotion.

When brand performance, either at the store or trade level, is faltering or not up to expectation, promotion will assume more importance than advertising in IMC planning.

Competitive activity

Not surprisingly, when competitors cut advertising and increase promotion, most brands will follow suit for fear of losing sales. If competitors increase spending on advertising while cutting back on promotion, again most brands will do the same. This may make sense as a short-term tactical move; however, the actions of competitors should not necessarily guide one's own marketing communication strategy. Each brand must take a careful look at its own situation, and respond in its own best interest.

As noted above, a high-priced brand may indeed increase its advertising expenditures (correctly) to help nurture a strong positive attitude toward the brand in the face of aggressive pricing strategies by competitors. But a 'price' brand should probably not increase its advertising expenditure, and may wish to counter with even deeper, short-run price promotions. The point here is that each situation must be looked at within the context of a brand's marketing objectives and its position in relationship to major competitors.

In recent years, at least for consumer packaged goods, there has been a strong increase in market share for private label product. Private label remains a small proportion of any market, but its share can rival the share of many individual brands in a category. Where private label is a significant factor, it makes sense to increase *advertising* activity, *not* try to compete on price with promotion. More often than not, this will take the form of stressing 'quality' or some other aspect of brand equity. Unfortunately, as scanning data continue to show, as shares increase for private label brands too often companies turn to price promotion rather than attempting to reinforce the equity value in their brand.

What we are talking about here are traditional private label brands. We do not mean 'branded' private label products. These better-quality private label products (in fact often of comparable quality with national brands and actually made by them) must be considered like any other lower-priced competitor. The actual price differences are generally not that great, and they are being marketed much like any other widely distributed brand, including the use of advertising.

How should competitive activity be treated in IMC planning? Managers must look at each situation and respond with increased advertising or promotion in the best interests of their brand regardless of what major competitors may be doing. This usually means a short-term tactical response, increasing advertising or promotion when competitors increase theirs, but this need not be a blind response. When a private label is a serious competitor, increased emphasis on advertising is usually called for.

Overall, we have seen that various market conditions will direct the strategic and tactical use of advertising and promotion. Managers cannot afford to think of advertising or promotion as independent means of marketing communication. Each has particular strengths, and within each there are particular types of advertising or promotion that may be used singly or in combination to address various situations in the market. It is not a question of 'should we use advertising or promotion', but rather 'should we *emphasize* advertising or promotion' in IMC planning. The market considerations discussed and their impact on IMC planning are summarized in Table 11.7.

Table 11.7 Market characteristic impact on advertising versus promotion emphasis in IMC

Market characteristic	IMC planning emphasis
Product differentiation	Advertising
Market position	
High brand share	Advertising
Frequently purchased product	Advertising
Poor brand performance	
Slow sales	Promotion
Distribution problems	Promotion to trade
Competitive activity	
Increase in spending	Analyse competitive situation carefully and respond accordingly
Strong private label	Advertising

Relative advertising versus promotion strengths

Traditional advertising makes its strongest contribution to brand awareness and brand attitude. Traditional promotion makes its strongest contribution to brand purchase intention. Nevertheless, promotions must still contribute to both brand awareness and brand attitude. Even though brand attitude is not a particular strength of promotion, the best promotion offers will be those that have a positive effect on brand attitude. This was recognized many years ago by Prentice (1977), a marketing practitioner, who called them *consumer franchise building* promotion offers. In other words, the promotion works well beyond its short-term tactical goal of immediate purchase, also helping contribute to positive brand attitude and building strong brand equity.

One should also bear in mind that promotion alone, as well as advertising, can actually create all of the communication effects. Store brands and so-called 'price brands' are marketed successfully without advertising by using point-of-purchase promotion. Although there is now a trend towards advertising private label and store brands, even when store brands are only promoted at the point-of-purchase, promotion must stimulate awareness and build at least a tentatively positive attitude for the product.

Promotion, just like advertising, works through successful message processing and either can satisfy all the communication objectives. But as we have seen, the whole idea of IMC is to approach one's marketing communication tasks with an open mind, and to explore all marketing communication options in order to maximize the brand message to the target audience. The relative strengths of advertising and promotion (see Figure 11.1) are discussed next for each of the four communication effects.

Communication objective	Relative strength	
	Weak	Strong
Category need		
Advertising		
Promotion		
Brand awareness		
Advertising		
Promotion		
Brand attitude		
Advertising		
Promotion[1]		
Brand purchase intention		
Advertising Promotion		
Promotion		

[1] This assumes a 'consumer franchise building' promotion addressing brand attitude and consistent with the advertising message. Otherwise, it would be weak.

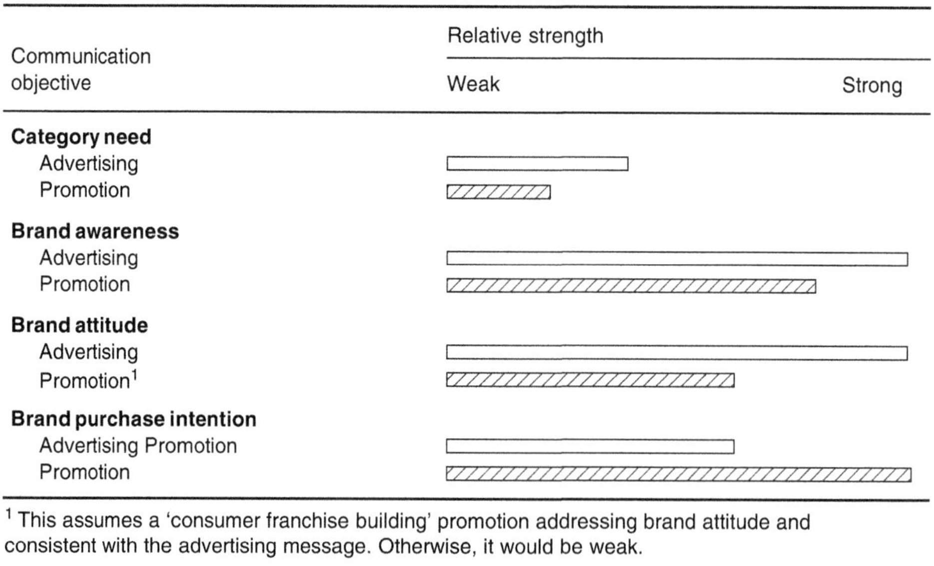

Figure 11.1 Relative strengths of advertising and promotion.

Category need

Category need, for most product categories, originates mainly from market changes (for new categories) and arises from a person's usual or temporary circumstances (for new and existing categories). Advertising can have some effect on category need by stimulating a perceived need. However, this is more a matter of suggesting the category need. If there is not an underlying motive to be tapped, 'selling' this need will be all but impossible. Only rarely can advertising create a motivation as such. Rather, it positions the category as a better way of meeting an existing motivation. In the case of mini vans, it was the motivation of incomplete satisfaction with alternatives for family transportation.

Various forms of promotion can help accelerate category need, making it occur earlier, although usually only to a fairly minor degree. This is one of the reasons why couponing and other price promotions are almost always a part of new consumer product introductions, and why direct marketing as a means of delivering a very targeted promotion can play such an important role in the introduction of an innovative service or product for a business. *Accelerate* is the key term here. None of this sells the category need so much as it attempts to speed it up.

Overall, both the advertising and promotion components of IMC have, in general, only a relatively minor influence on category need (as we see in Figure 11.1). Again, this is only a general effect, for one may find specific instances of successfully selling or accelerating category need with either advertising or promotion.

Brand awareness

Brand awareness is one of the strengths of advertising. However, almost any form of marketing communication can and should contribute to brand awareness, at least to some extent. New product introductions, for example, when brand awareness is a major objective, typically use several marketing communication options.

Promotion offers help prospective buyers consider new brands and reconsider existing brands. They can achieve this by drawing reflexive attention to the brand (for example, a point-of-purchase display or a sample pack) and by producing selective attention (for example, price-off or coupons promising extra value). Various promotions and most messages (whether promotion or advertising) delivered through direct marketing are primarily useful for increasing brand recognition (or initial cognition for previously unfamiliar brands) at the point-of-purchase or at the point-of-decision rather than stimulating brand recall prior to purchase (although this is possible). As a result, promotion and direct marketing are less often an option when brand recall is involved.

Brand attitude

Building brand attitude has historically been the province of advertising. However, as already pointed out, all marketing communications should help build positive brand attitude. In the case of promotion, because it is aimed primarily at causing a short-term increase in sales, for competitive or inventory moving reasons, without regard to brand attitude, their execution is often weak in this regard. But the ideal communication should always help create longer-term communication effects, and this is especially true for promotion, where it is important to seat this long-term effect in order to maximize full-value purchases when the promotion is withdrawn.

Consumer Franchise Building promotions as described by Prentice (1977) – or as we consider them, any promotion that pays attention to consistently reinforcing a brand's equity – will contribute to inducing full-price purchases by working, like advertising, on brand attitude (for example, free samples). Promotion too often does not help build brand attitude, concentrating only on brand purchase intention. This is a mistake. There should always be some reinforcement of brand attitude, consistent with the overall brand attitude communication strategy.

Chuck Mittelstadt (1993), a long-time consultant to the Interpublic Group of Companies (the group that owns McCann and other major advertising agencies and media companies), has offered an interesting observation on this subject. He points out that years ago, image-building promotions were the norm. Among others, there were such classic promotions as the Pillsbury bake-off and the launch of White Rain hair care products, which date back to well over 50 years ago. The Pillsbury bake-off he sees as a classic example of IMC. Advertising in many media linked to the promotion, in-store merchandising, events, and sponsorship, were all involved. Women were encouraged to contribute recipes and baked goods, all made with Pillsbury flour. The bake-off created an image of well-crafted quality products and constant innovation. As a result, this promotion was a major contributor to the Pillsbury brand image.

For the introduction of White Rain, a young woman (consistent with the demographics of the target audience) dressed in a white raincoat and white boots and holding a white umbrella was used as the most prominent element on the package. Models dressed in the same fashion were used to dispense free samples. They used white raincoats and umbrellas as premiums and as point-of-purchase displays. The advertising spokeswoman was dressed the same, and the copy stressed the widely accepted folklore on the softness of rainwater. Here we have a good example of a consistent IMC programme.

The launch of Elizabeth Arden's Curious perfume in Sweden offers another excellent example of a consistent message using both advertising and promotion together in an effective IMC programme. The benefit claim for the new perfume was 'Curious – do you dare?' This is an emotionally charged line, exactly what is needed for transformational messages. It was enhanced by linking the brand with Britney Spears, providing at the time a strong source with whom the young women making up the target audience could identify. Note, too, that she reflects the appropriate source characteristics needed for transformational executions: both the likability and similarity components of attractiveness.

Complementing the introductory advertising, 'do you dare' promotions were run in *Elle* and *Cosmopolitan*, live competitions on radio to 'sing like Britney' were conducted, and samples of the product were offered at outdoor sites. Here we have an IMC campaign where the promotions are directly linked to the overall benefit, and consistent with the advertising in look and feel. The results of the launch significantly exceeded sales targets.

Unfortunately, too often today many package goods brand managers lean too heavily on short-term price promotions to help reach sales objectives without attention to brand attitude, and are injuring long-term brand equity. The proof of this may be seen in the overwhelming allotment of promotion dollars given to the trade, where half the money is kept by the trade and the rest usually passed along to consumers through price-off 'specials'. As Mittelstadt (1993) put it, somewhere along the line marketers took a short cut into price promotions as a way of life, and a lot of brands are now paying dearly for it.

Brand purchase intention

Brand purchase intention has historically been the communication strength of the promotion component of IMC. With the exception of retail advertising and other direct response advertising, most advertising does not deal directly with brand purchase intention. However, all promotion, and most messages delivered through direct marketing and channels marketing, are aimed at moving sales forward immediately (too often, as noted above, regardless of their longer-term consequences), and they achieve this by stimulating immediate brand purchase intentions. More particularly, promotions stimulate intentions to buy now, or to buy more than usual. Additionally, there are the many purchase-related intentions for consumer durables and industrial products such as intention to visit showrooms, call for a sales demonstration and so forth.

Advantages of using advertising and promotion together

We have noted that more and more money is spent today in marketing communication areas outside traditional advertising, in fact, about three to one. However, for most marketing communication problems, advertising will almost always be central to a brand's marketing communications planning.

What is it about using advertising and promotion together that offers advantages relative to using only advertising or promotion alone? We have already discussed the fact that advertising and promotion have different strengths in relation to communication objectives. But the critical communication objective for the joint effectiveness of advertising and promotion is advertising's *prior* establishment of a strong brand attitude, which is the main link to brand equity.

Schultz (1995b), while perhaps not going quite so far as this, has talked about the role advertising has to play in IMC, stating that 'image advertising is a critical ingredient in any marketing and communications programme'. He goes on to talk about the need to 'protect or build the perceptual value of the brand'. To our way of thinking, this is just another way of talking about brand equity, and the communication strength of advertising – brand attitude. People may approach the matter differently, and use different words, but there is no doubt that advertising must almost always play a crucial role in IMC planning.

The key to this importance lies in the fact that when advertising has been effective in generating a strong brand attitude that has led to a strong brand equity, all of a brand's promotional efforts will be that much more effective. There are two fundamental reasons for this:

1 When the target audience holds strong favourable attitudes toward a brand, it means that when the brand does use promotions, the target audience will see them as much better value.
2 When the target audience holds strong favourable attitudes toward a brand, then if competitors offer promotions the target audience will be less likely to respond to them.

If one thinks about it, this makes sense. The more someone likes a product or service, the less likely they will be to switch because of a promotion. When the brand offers its own promotion, they will think that much better of it, *and* it will tend to reinforce their already positive brand attitude.

Before leaving the impression that advertising, in creating a favourable brand attitude, may be all that is needed, there is something else to consider. Regardless of how favourable brand attitude may be, it is unlikely that everyone in the market buys or uses that brand exclusively. It is also unlikely that any core market is ever dominated by totally brand loyal customers. What brand attitude is working on is maintaining a dominant share of favourable brand switchers. Of course, it also holds brand loyal customers, but in today's markets consumers switch among various competitive alternatives. Unfortunately, this phenomenon of declining loyalty is being accelerated by an over-reliance on promotion, especially price promotion, to attract switchers. We have already referred to the cola wars. In one major supermarket chain, over 80 percent of all Coke and Pepsi sales were price-off deals. The leading brand was simply the brand on special offer that day.

This does not change anything we have just discussed about the critical importance of advertising. It only underscores the fact that it is advertising and promotion working together that will create the most effective IMC programmes. Without effective advertising, it is unlikely that a brand will maintain its equity over time. However, this must be coupled with appropriate tactical use of promotion. One of the best ways to understand how this strategy of combining advertising and promotion optimizes IMC planning is by looking at something Moran (1978) has called the 'ratchet effect'.

The advertising and promotion 'ratchet effect'

The notion of a 'ratchet effect' rests on the idea that when advertising is used in combination with promotion, it increases the value of a brand's promotion while minimizing the effect of competitor promotions. As mentioned earlier, promotions tend to 'steal' sales, especially from existing customers. The promotion, more often than not, will accelerate an already planned purchase by customers, or attract a switcher to the brand for this purchase only. The hope, of course, is that the promotion will increase the number of purchases of the brand by switchers. In other words, encourage them to 'switch-to-us' more often. If someone is using (for example) coupons as the key to switching, *without* a coupon or other price promotion, it is unlikely they will 'switch' to a brand. The price promotion will attract a switcher, but without advertising support, what reason would there be to continue buying at the regular price? There would be nothing to nurture a positive brand attitude.

When running a promotion, it should generate higher than normal levels of sales. But with promotion alone, without adequate prior and ongoing advertising, once the promotion is over sales levels will dip below average levels until the product purchased on promotion has been exhausted, and customers are 'back' in the market. Switchers are back on their normal switching pattern and loyal customers have used up the product they stocked up on while it was on promotion. This effect is illustrated in Figure 11.2.

However, when advertising and promotion are used effectively together, the effect of promotion on top of prior advertising is to *increase* the rate of growth stimulated by advertising alone. Remember, of course, that this rate of growth may be flat or even declining. There is no guarantee that advertising alone will stimulate sales growth. The point is that the *combination* of advertising and promotion should improve overall market performance when it is part of a good IMC programme.

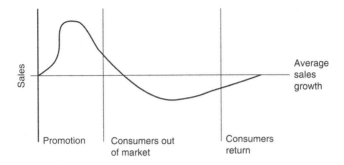

Figure 11.2 Effect of promotion alone without advertising.

This is what Moran (1978) has described as the *ratchet effect*. Because of prior advertising, there is a positive brand attitude. When the brand is promoted, loyal customers' favourable brand attitude is reinforced. Switchers attracted by the promotion will be more likely to continue purchasing or using the brand on a more regular basis after the promotion is withdrawn *because* of the advertising's positive brand attitude effect. This means the regular customer base grows, and the average sales level 'ratchets' up. This 'ratchet effect' is illustrated in Figure 11.3.

All of this assumes, of course, that the combination of advertising and promotion is cost-effective and the IMC campaign has been well conceived and truly *integrated*. One must be alert to the fact that price promotion has the potential of actually increasing prices at the consumer level. There are major costs tied to promotions, beyond the obvious. Uneven production runs and distribution add costs. Carrying extra inventory costs the trade money. Tracking promotions can absorb a lot of brand marketing overhead. In-store pricing and re-pricing add costs. Without careful planning, all of this could eventually lead to significant price differentials.

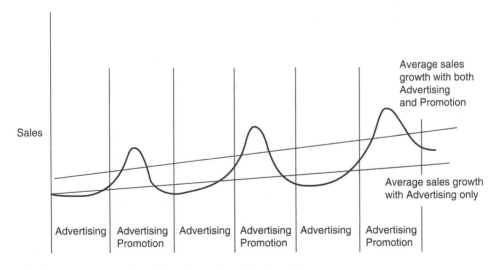

Figure 11.3 Moran's ratchet effect: advertising with promotion.

The impact of demand elasticity

At the heart of consumer response to the interaction between advertising and promotion is the economist's notion of demand elasticity. Again, this is a point made by Moran (1978). Understanding the relationship between a brand's demand and its competitor brand's demand elasticities is an important part of IMC planning. Specifically, in Moran's terms, one needs to be concerned with 'upside' and 'downside' elasticities. We especially like his ideas here because they focus the manager's thinking on the relationship between advertising and promotion in effecting sales, not simply the overall price elasticity of a brand.

Upside elasticity refers to the sales increases resulting from a price cut or promotion; downside elasticity to the sales decline resulting from a price increase. While these definitions reflect a brand's action regarding pricing strategy, it is important to understand that a brand's *competitors'* pricing strategy will directly affect the demand elasticity of the brand – both upside and downside. Competitors' price increases in effect cut the price of those brands that do not raise their price. Aggressive price-cutting or promotion by competitors in effect raises the price of brands that do not.

The ongoing market dynamic, especially in a time of heavy price-oriented promotion, underscores the need for effective advertising in most IMC programmes. Our discussion of positive brand attitude and brand equity illustrates how effective prior advertising creates a more fertile ground for long-term sales benefit from promotion. We also discussed how effective prior advertising helps lessen the impact of competitor promotion. In other words, relative to competitors, effective advertising will generate *high* upside elasticity and *low* downside elasticity.

A brand's upside and downside elasticities will depend to a large extent on its current brand equity (unfortunately, an elusive concept to measure). As a result, to the extent that a brand's promotional activities contribute to brand attitude, and reinforce brand equity, they will make advertising's job easier. Brand equity-oriented promotions act just like advertising, increasing upside demand elasticity and reducing downside demand elasticity. As a result, with the exception of short-term tactical promotion, all IMC should aim for positive demand elasticity.

We are not suggesting that a firmly calibrated calculation of demand elasticities must be a part of IMC planning, only that it is important to *think* about it. We know, for example, that frequent or heavy price promotion on its own can negatively affect brand attitude. Managers must think about where their brands stand in terms of target audience brand attitude versus attitude toward major competitors, the brand's pricing strategy versus competition, and how one is allocating marketing monies versus competitors. This, along with what we have been discussing, should greatly help understanding of the interdependence of advertising and promotion in successful IMC planning.

Summary

The first step in the IMC planning process is a careful review of the marketing plan. This is what provides the necessary background for understanding a brand's overall marketing objectives, which the IMC programme will support. Beyond these marketing objectives and how marketing communication is expected to support them, key issues to address in this review are the specifics of the brand itself and the market within which it will compete, with special emphasis on its competition. Finally, the marketing plan will outline where sales are expected to come from. In addition, at this time cultural considerations should be taken into account.

Direct marketing is like traditional promotion in that its objective is an immediate response and the results can be measured directly. But it is not promotion. Direct marketing may utilize both promotion and advertising. For direct marketing to be profitable there must be a large number of customers and potential customers in the database, a realistic chance of working, a likelihood of generating more profit than using the money on other programs, and the database must be difficult for competitors to duplicate.

Direct marketing differs from advertising not only in terms of seeking an immediate response, but in using a single exposure rather than multiple exposures, addressing a highly targeted rather than more broadly-based target audience, and using its delivery system as the marketplace instead of using the distribution chain to define the marketplace. A strong database is critical for effective direct marketing.

Managers need to address three questions in considering the use of direct marketing as part of an IMC programme: Does it make sense given the brand and its communication strategy? Is a good database available to identify the target audience? If it fits within the brand's overall communication strategy and a good database is available, what is the best medium to deliver the message?

Certain characteristics of the market at any particular time will inform whether advertising or promotion should be emphasized. If the brand is really different from competitors in terms of a meaningful benefit, advertising should be emphasized. Frequently purchased brands and brands with a high market share call for an advertising emphasis, while poor performance calls for promotion as a tactic in the short-term. When competitors increase their marketing communication, the manager should carefully access the situation and respond with advertising or promotion accordingly. If there is a strong private label presence in the market, use advertising and do not try to compete on price with promotion.

Both advertising and promotion may be used for any communication objective, owing to the nature of their particular strengths and weaknesses; depending on the communication objective one or the other will be more appropriate. Marketing communication can only contribute partially to category need. Advertising can help stimulate the need, and promotion can help accelerate the need, but more will be needed through such things as public relations and word-of-mouth. Brand awareness is a traditional strength of advertising, but promotion should also make a contribution. Brand attitude is the primary job of advertising, although all promotion should help reinforce the benefit claim. The real strength of promotion is brand purchase intention.

The manager should look at both advertising and promotion, and how they can be used together to optimize the overall effectiveness of the IMC plan. As Moran (1978) described it, the optimum use of advertising and promotion together will create a 'ratchet effect' where the short-term gain from promotion is more likely to be held and built on by the long-term effects of advertising. This means that a good IMC plan optimally utilizing advertising and promotion together where appropriate will be more effective than using only advertising, and certainly more effective than only using promotion.

Review questions

1 Why is it important to review the marketing plan at the start of the IMC planning process?
2 What key cultural considerations are important for IMC campaign?

3 Why is it important to understand global cultural grouping in IMC planning?
4 How would you define direct marketing?
5 In what ways is direct marketing similar, and in what ways different, from other ways of delivering advertising and promotion?
6 Why is accountability necessary for direct marketing?
7 How can certain characteristics of a brand's market influence how advertising and promotion should be used in an IMC programme?
8 Why should an advertised brand not try to compete with price brands or store brands?
9 What are the traditional strengths of advertising versus promotion, and why?
10 What is meant by a 'consumer franchise building' promotion, and why is this important?
11 Find examples of promotions that are well integrated with the brand's advertising.
12 What is the advantage of using advertising and promotion together in IMC?
13 Discuss demand elasticity and what it means to IMC planning.

References

Dean, J. (1950) Pricing policies for new products. *Harvard Business Review, 28*(6), 45–53.

deMooj, M. (1998) *Global Marketing and Advertising: Understanding Cultural Paradoxes.* London: Sage, pp. 72–88.

Farris, P.W. and Buzzell, R.D. (1979) Why advertising and promotion costs vary: Some cross-sectional analyses. *Journal of Marketing, 43*(4), 112–122.

Hall, E. (1976) *Beyond Culture.* New York: Doubleday.

Hofstede, G.H. (1984) *Culture's Consequences: International Differences in Work-related Values.* Beverly Hills: Sage, pp. 32–33.

Hofstede, G.H. (1991) *Cultures and Organizations: Software of the Mind.* New York: McGraw-Hill.

Lamons, B. (1992) Creativity is important to direct marketing too. *Marketing News,* 7 December, *10.*

Livermore, D. (2013) *Customs of the World; Using Cultural Intelligence to Adapt Wherever You Are.* Chantilly, VA: The Teaching Company.

Mittelstadt, C.A. (1993) The coming era of image-building brand promotions, lecture given at Yale University, 3 March.

Moran, W.T. (1978) Insights From Pricing Research. In E.B. Bailey (ed.), *Pricing Practices and Strategies.* New York: The Conference Board, pp. 7–13.

Prentice, R.M. (1977) How to split your marketing funds between advertising and promotion. *Advertising Age,* 10 January, *41.*

Reichheld, F.F. (1996) *The Loyalty Effect.* Cambridge, MA: Harvard Business School Press.

Rossiter, J.R., Percy, L., Bergkvist L. (2018) *Marketing Communications: Objectives, Strategies, Tactics.* London: Sage Publications, Ltd.

Schultz, D.E. (1995a) What is direct marketing? *Journal of Direct Marketing, 9*(2), 5–9.

Schultz, D.E. (1995b) Traditional advertising has role to play in IMC. *Marketing News,* 28 August, *18.*

Strang, R.A. (1980) *The Promotion Planning Process.* New York: Praeger.

Tapp, A. (1998) *Principles of Direct and Database Marketing.* London: Financial Times Management Pitman.

Trompenaar, F. and Hampden-Turner, C. (1997) *Riding the Waves of Culture: Understanding Diversity in Global Business.* Maidenhead: McGraw-Hill.

12 The IMC planning process

In this chapter we look at the specific steps involved in the strategic planning process for IMC. But before a manager can begin to think of specific marketing communications issues, it is important to carefully analyse what is known about the market. This means that the first step in the IMC strategic planning process is to review the marketing plan, as we saw in the last chapter. After a review of the marketing plan, it is time to begin the five-step strategic planning process introduced in Chapter 1. First, target audience action objectives will need to be carefully considered. Most markets have multiple target groups, and as a result, there may be a number of communication objectives required to reach them. In fact, it is for this reason that a brand needs more than one level of communication, occasioning the necessity for IMC. After identifying the appropriate target audience, it will be time to think about overall marketing communication strategy. This begins at the second step in the strategic planning process by considering how purchase decisions are made in the category. Then the manager must optimize message development to facilitate that process, which involves steps three and four, establishing the positioning and setting communication objectives. Finally, in step five, the manager must decide how to best deliver the message. We now look at each of these three areas in some detail.

Selecting a target audience

Once the manager has thought through the market, it is time to take the first step in the strategic planning process and focus more on whom it is that should be addressed with marketing communications. When thinking about the target audience, one must look beyond traditional demographic considerations. While they are perhaps the most familiar way of thinking about the target audience, demographics more properly define a *target market,* not a target audience. This is a critical distinction. While demographics can provide a useful description of a market for a brand, you must look *within* that group for a target audience. It must be selected in terms of brand buyer groups because they provide the best indication of attitude toward a brand. It is also important to 'think ahead'. What type of person will be important to the future of the business? In this stage of the planning process there are four quadrants that should be addressed (see Table 12.1).

DOI: 10.4324/9781003169635-16

Table 12.1 Key questions in target audience selection

- What are the relevant target buyer groups?
- What are the action objectives?
- What is the target group's demographic, lifestyle and psychographic profile?
- How is the trade involved?

What are the relevant target buyer groups?

While one always hopes that business will be broadly based, realistically one must set a primary objective concentrating on either existing customers or non-customers, which will involve repeat purchase of the brand or trial.

Following a useful designation of buyer groups introduced by Rossiter and Percy (1987), one may think about customers in terms of being either brand loyals (BL) or favourable brand switchers (FBS). Some customers buy a brand almost exclusively, others buy the brand along with others in the category. Non-customers, too, may be loyal to one brand (OBL, other brand loyals) or switch among other brands (OBS, other brand switchers), or they may not buy any brands in the category now, offering potential for the future (NCU, non-category users).

It is useful to consider the potential target audience in these terms because it *reflects* brand attitude. Ideally, one would select a target audience in terms of their attitudes. Unfortunately, it is not possible to find people profiled in terms of their attitudes in media buying databases. However, brand purchase behaviour is available. Although not a perfect substitute, these buyer groups do reflect a certain degree of brand attitude. BL and OBL should have strong positive attitudes towards the brands they buy. FBS and OBS too will hold generally positive attitudes toward the brands they buy. Interestingly, most consumers actually prefer two or three brands in a category, primarily for variety or because of slightly different end uses (vanTripp et al., 1996). Brand attitudes, however, cannot be inferred for NCU. They may indeed have rejected the brands in the category, or they may simply see such products as inappropriate for them at the time (for example, baby products if you do not have a baby).

Communication strategies will differ significantly, depending on which of these target groups is selected, and could differ within groups of customers or non-customers. If the target is primarily BL or FBS who use the brand along with competitors, promotional tactics would clearly differ between these two groups. The brand is looking to retain BL, but to increase the frequency with which the brand is purchased by FBS. Among non-customers OBL would be difficult to attract. On the other hand, those who switch among several brands (but not the company's) are at least behaviourally susceptible to trying the brand because they already buy several brands, and should be open to trial promotions. It is important to think about various alternative buyer groups and to place the primary communications effort where it makes the most sense.

In making the decision, it is important to think beyond the expected purchase and use of the brand by the target group selected. There are cost considerations involved. If trial is the objective, the cost will necessarily be greater than it will be for protecting or increasing current usage. And while the cost for targeting new users who switch among brands, but not yours (OBS) will be higher, it will not be nearly as high as going after regular users of other brands (OBL). It is important for the manager to consider the *value* of reaching a target audience. What will be the cost of the media needed be relative to the increase in most sales if you do?

What are the action objectives?

Once the relevant target audience buyer group has been selected, the next step is to set specific action objectives. All action objectives are some form of either trial or repeat purchase, and may be looked at in terms of pre-purchase behaviour, purchase behaviour, and post-purchase behaviour. Pre-purchase action objectives are needed primarily when IMC is being used to get the target audience to do something to facilitate purchase, like visit a website, sample the product, or encourage a store visit.

For most campaigns, however, you are looking at either stimulating trial or repeat purchase, depending upon the relevant buyer group or groups selected. Trial or retrial should be the action objectives for NCU and OBS, but rarely OBL. Because of the difficulty in trying to convince OBL to try your brand, they are generally too costly to pursue. Repeat purchase, which can mean continuing to buy, buy more often, or buy greater quantities, should be the action objective for FBS and BL. Beyond the trial and repeat purchase action objectives associated with pre-purchase and purchase behaviour, there may be the potential to encourage post-purchase behaviour as well. A frequently used post-purchase action is to offer incentives for customer referrals.

One final point should be made here. Action objectives are more than just trial or repeat purchase objectives for a brand's target audience. Specific, realistic trial and repeat purchase *goals* should be sales. In other words, quantitatively specific objectives should be set, as well as for a specific brand period.

What are the target groups' profiles?

Once selected, target audiences have traditionally been described in demographic terms: women, 18–34 years, with some university training. Sometimes efforts have been made to include so-called 'psychographic' or lifestyle descriptions (Antonides and van Raaij, 1998). All of this is important, but it is not enough. While this provides useful background for creatives in developing the message, one must understand the target audience(s) in terms of behaviour and attitude, but also in terms of patterns that are relevant to communication and media strategies. This means how they now behave or are likely to behave in relationship to the brand and competition, what their differing information needs or motivations might be, and how they 'use' various media. This is important information for IMC strategy, and should be gained through research and regularly updated.

How is the trade involved?

It is important to think about the trade in the broadest possible terms, including all those who are involved in the distribution and sale of the brand without necessarily buying, stocking or using it themselves. What one needs to think about here is whether people not directly concerned with the purchase and use of the brand might nevertheless be an important part of the target audience. For example, one may need to pre-sell a new product to distribution channels or inform possible sources of recommendations about the brand (for example, doctors or consultants). Where the trade might fit should be considered when thinking about how purchase and brand decisions are made, which we cover next.

In selecting the target audience, at this point the manager is identifying the primary target for the brand. As we see in the next section, in determining how decisions are made in the category this selection will be refined, looking at the roles played by the primary target group at different points in the decision process, as well as secondary targets that may be involved.

Determining how decisions are made

If IMC is to positively affect brand purchase, it is essential to understand just how purchases in the category are made by the target audience, and this is what is involved at step two in the strategic planning process. In consumer behaviour, decisions are often described in terms of need arousal leading to consideration, then action. Although this does provide a general idea of how decisions are made, for IMC planning purposes, it is not specific enough. A good way to look at how brand purchase decisions are made has been offered by Rossiter and Percy (1997) with something they call a behavioural sequence model (BSM). A generic BSM is illustrated in Figure 12.1.

It asks five fundamental questions: What are the stages consumers go through in making a decision? Who is involved in the decision and what roles do they play? Where do the stages occur? What is the timing? How is it likely to occur? This results in a chart that identifies where members of the target audience are taking action or making decisions that will ultimately affect purchases. Each of these questions is addressed next.

What stages do consumers go through?

A BSM first asks the manager to think about the major decision stages a brand's target audience goes through prior, during and following actual purchase or use of a product or service. A generic decision model may be built on the general consumer behaviour model mentioned above: need arousal, brand consideration, purchase, and usage. Notice that *usage* is included as part of the purchase decision here because it provides an opportunity to communicate with the consumer in anticipation of future purchase or use. Also, it helps reinforce the purchase decision. It has been found, for example, that people continue to pay attention to advertising for brands that have been purchased (Ehrlich et al., 1957). Additionally, especially for high-involvement decisions, attending to advertising for the brand purchased reduces dissonance as Festinger (1957) pointed out in his theory of cognitive dissonance.

The generic model of decision stages can be useful, and can be adapted to almost any situation, but always remember that the *best* model is the one that comes closest to how decisions are actually made in the brand's specific category. For example, in many

	Decision stages			
Consideration at each stage	Need arousal	Brand consideration	Purchase	Usage
Who is involved and what role(s) do they play?				
Where do the stages occur?				
What is the timing?				
How is it likely to occur?				

Figure 12.1 Generic BSM.

Figure 12.2 Decision stages involved in a lamp purchase.

business situations, distribution or trade hurdles must be surmounted before there is any thought of need arousal in the target audience. Other decisions may be even more complicated, or quite simple. The idea is to capture the essence of the decision process, and use this as the basis for planning. Qualitative research can be helpful here in providing specific details unique to particular categories.

Two examples will help illustrate this. First, consider a retailer that has a chain of lamp stores. A hypothetical model of the decision stages involved in a lamp purchase, might be as follows. The first stage in the decision to buy a new lamp probably involves a decision to redecorate. One of the most popular ways to redecorate is to buy a new lamp. These two stages would constitute *need arousal*. Next, one must decide *where* to shop for the lamp, shop the store (or stores) and make a choice. These three steps would be a modification of *brand consideration*. Once the lamp has been chosen, the *purchase* is made and the lamp is taken home and *used*. The decisions stages would then be: decide to redecorate → consider new lamp → look for places to buy lamp → shop → select lamp → purchase → replace old lamp with new (see Figure 12.2). It should be apparent just how helpful this discipline can be for IMC planning. Even with a simple example such as this, you can see how thinking about the decision process suggests a number of possible ways to communicate with potential lamp purchasers. The most obvious insight here is that a lamp purchase is unlikely to take place outside the context of 'redecorating' (and research has indeed suggested this). This means that to interest people in lamps, one must first awaken an interest in redecorating or changing the look of a room.

As a second example, consider a manufacturer of commercial kitchen equipment that is distributed through restaurant supply companies. How does a restaurant supply company go about deciding what items and brands they will distribute? A probable decision model might begin with looking out for better items to stock in order to maintain a competitive edge. This could lead to an awareness of a potential new line or item to stock. These two stages would correspond to *need arousal* in the generic model. Once interest is aroused, the new item will then be compared with what is now carried; the *brand consideration* stage. If the evaluation is positive, it will be ordered and added to inventory; *purchase*. Once stocked, sales will be monitored, and if positive, the item or line will be reordered. These last two stages would correspond to the generic model's *usage* stage. The decision stages for a restaurant supply company then might be: monitor new items → identify potential items to carry → compare with current items stocked → if positive, add to stock → monitor sales → if good, reorder.

Here is a good example of where the decision process suggests it might make sense to pay a lot of attention to the *usage* stages. An important question for a manufacturer of a new kitchen product would be: how much end-user 'pull' would be necessary to ensure sufficient sales for their customer, the restaurant supply company, to reorder? If initial sales are expected to be slow, it might make sense to offer a reorder incentive. These are the kinds of questions a good understanding of the stages in a decision process stimulates.

Who is involved and what roles do they play?

Once the specific stages of the decision process have been established, it is important to understand the roles individual members of the potential target audience are likely to play at each stage. Those who study consumer behaviour identify five potential decision roles involved in making a decision: initiator, influencer, decider, purchaser and user (see Table 12.2). Let us consider as an example the roles that might be involved in a simplified illustration of a cruise holiday decision, using the four generic decision stages.

What role or roles are most likely to be involved during the *need arousal* stage? As those who play the role of an initiator in the decision get the whole process started, it is the initiators that will be included under *need arousal* in the BSM model. This could include family members, friends who have been on a cruise, potential cruisers, travel agents and cruise fairs. Notice that the trade is considered here in terms of travel agents and cruise fairs. As influencers recommend and deciders choose what to do, both roles will be influential during the *brand consideration* stage of the decision process. The influencers may include family members, friends who have been on a cruise, and travel agents. The decider is either an individual adult potential cruiser or a couple. The actual *purchase* is made by the purchaser, who is likely to be an individual adult potential cruiser, while the *usage* stage is experienced by all those who go on the cruise.

These roles will inform how message content is processed at particular stages. In the early stages when you are trying to generate awareness and interest in the brand, the messages will be addressing the target in their role as initiator and influencer. Here, the information provided in, or feelings aroused by, the creative execution must be consistent with the underlying motivation driving the decision. In considering alternative brands and making a choice the message is addressing the target in their roles as decider and purchaser. Here the message must create either a tentatively favourable attitude that leads to an interaction to try (yielding in McGuire's sense) in a low-involvement decision, or be accepted in the high-involvement case. When this intention is acted upon, the target is the role of user.

In most cases, especially with low-involvement products, all the roles will be played by the same person. But, this may be a good point to deal with the issue of individual versus group decisions. It is certainly true that many family decisions are made through a husband/wife or family consensus, and many business purchase decisions are the result of a group effort. However, when it comes to IMC, we are interested in the *individual* and the role they are playing in the overall decision process. Communication efforts must first persuade the individual *prior* to their participation in any group decision. So, while many actual decisions are the result of group action, specific advertising or promotion must address individuals in the roles they are playing in the decision process.

This is why understanding the roles people play in the decision process can lead to messages in an IMC campaign addressed to specific target segments. McDonald's understood

Table 12.2 Decision roles

Initiator	Proposes the purchase or usage
Influencer	Recommends (or discourages) the purchase or use
Decider	Actually makes the choice
Purchaser	Actually makes the purchase
User	Uses the product or service

the importance of mothers being both influencer and decider when it comes to what fast-food restaurants the family visits. Recognizing the concern over child obesity, and to help overcome potential negative associations with fat content in much fast food, McDonald's in Sweden ran a series of inserts in magazines oriented towards mothers and specifically addressing their role as influencers and deciders in matters of family health and eating habits, positioned to build more positive brand attitude through increasing trust in McDonald's food.

This provides a good example of what is known as a *creative target*. From the target audience selected, the manager must determine who the key role player is in the decision process. When developing an IMC execution, most creatives will imagine themselves talking to a particular individual about the brand, and this should be the person playing the key decision role, the person who must be positively influenced by the message if it is to be successful; the creative target.

Where do the stages occur?

Locating opportunities for marketing communication is vital to successful IMC, and a BSM can help pinpoint likely places. In fact, as one considers a BSM, the first thing one notices is that different stages in the decision process occur at different times and, as a result, where individuals may be reached as they play their role at each stage can certainly vary. There are exceptions, of course. For example, a shopper could be given a sample of a new cookie to taste, along with a coupon. They like it, and decide to buy some. They see the special end-aisle display, pick up a box, open it, and enjoy a few while they finish shopping. In this case, all of the stages occur at one location – the store. However, this is not likely to be the case very often. Because potential locations can vary widely under different circumstances, unusual media might be appropriate.

Building on situation theory (Belk, 1975) in buyer behaviour and Foxall's (1992) work on selling and consumption situations in marketing, Rossiter and Percy (1987) offer four points for marketing communications managers to consider for each location identified:

1 *How accessible is the location to marketing communication?* This could range from no accessibility to too much, in the sense of a lot of clutter from other marketing communication or competition from other things.
2 *How many role-players are present?* Is the message directed to an individual or are several people participating at this stage of the decision at that location?
3 *How much time pressure exists?* This could range from none to a great deal and the greater the time pressure the less opportunity there will be to process the message. The difference between relaxing at home and dashing in and out of a store will seriously affect the likelihood of a message being processed.
4 *What is the physical and emotional state of the individual?* Certain personality states can seriously affect message processing. For example, is someone in a doctor's waiting room there for a routine check-up and feeling relaxed (assuming they haven't been kept waiting too long) or because of symptoms of a serious illness and therefore upset and anxious?

As you can see, it is important to think about what is going on at each location where part of the decision is made. Some locations are going to be better than others as a potential place to reach the target audience.

What is the timing?

The timing of decision stages should reflect the general purchase cycle or pattern for the category. Understanding when each stage of the decision process occurs, and the relationship between the stages, is important for media scheduling. Obvious examples would be seasonal decisions such as back-to-school shopping or holiday purchases. But understanding the timing of even such routine behaviour as meal planning is important.

A good example of this is the decision process for choosing a dessert. Obviously, for the average day, what to buy and serve for dessert is a low-involvement decision. Most dessert decisions are made *after the meal*. This means that whatever is to be served must be in inventory, and even more importantly, *must be ready to serve*. This is no problem for such things as cookies, ice cream and fruit. But what if you are selling cake mix or something like Jell-O brand gelatin? If all you do is 'sell' the end product, all you will do is move the product from the store shelf to the pantry shelf. This will *not* move it from the pantry to the table. For a cake or Jell-O to be served for dessert it must have been made some time *before dinner*. This suggests advertising to homemakers in the morning to make the dessert so it will be ready *after* dinner.

This example underscores the fact that even the simplest seeming decision process can have hidden traps if it is not fully understood. This is also why we talk about both purchase *and* usage in the decision stages.

How is each stage likely to occur?

The last thing to consider in the BSM is *how* each of the stages is likely to occur. What is it that arouses need? How is the target audience likely to go about getting information? What are they likely to be doing at the point-of-purchase? In what way will the product or service be used? These are questions managers will want to have answers to prior to thinking about message development and delivery.

The usefulness of the BSM for IMC planning is that it forces the manager to think about what is likely to be going on when various stages of a decision occur, and this will provide a perspective on marketing communication options that are likely to be effective under those circumstances. Figure 12.3 illustrates a BSM for a cruise holiday using the generic decision stages. An actual BSM for a cruise vacation would require many more specific stages, but this will provide an example of how everything fits together.

Establishing brand positioning

For effective IMC, awareness of a brand must be quickly and easily linked in memory with the category need, reflecting the way in which the brand choice decision is made. This requires a positioning where the need for the product reflects how the target audience perceives that need. This is not always so straightforward as it may seem. The manager must know how the consumer refers to the need that products in the category satisfy, which is a function of how they define the market.

This is the answer to the 'What is it?' question posed in the general model of positioning introduced back in Chapter 9, and informs brand awareness strategy. For example, is a household cleaner brand seen as a general cleaner, or as a heavy-duty cleaner? Is a television made by Bang & Olufsen simply a television or is it seen as part of a home entertainment system? These differences are critical, because they inform how the brand

	Decision stages			
	Need arousal	Brand consideration	Purchase	Usage
Considerations at each stage				
Decision roles involved	Family members, friends who have been on a cruise, potential cruiser as *Initiator* Travel agents and cruise 'fairs' as *Initiator*	Family members, friends who have been on cruise, and potential cruiser as *Influencer* Individual adult potential cruiser or couple as *Decider* Travel agents as *Influencer*	Individual adult potential cruiser as *Purchaser*	All adults traveling on cruise as *Users*
Where stage is likely to occur	At home, travel agent's office or cruise consumers At office for travel agent or cruise 'fair' operator	At home, talking with friends, travel agent's office or cruise 'fair' for consumers At office, trade shows or actual cruises for travel agents or cruise fair operators	At home or travel agent's office	On cruise
Timing of stage	Special trip or vacation holiday planning, or word-of-mouth	3–6 months following need arousal	Shortly after completing information search and evaluation	1–3 months after purchase
How it is likely to occur	Looking for something special	Ask, call, write for brochure, visit cruise 'fair', talk with experienced cruiser of travel agent	Call or visit travel agent	Enjoy cruise

Figure 12.3 BSM for cruise holiday.

is stored in memory. Long ago in his classic article 'Marketing Myopia', Levitt (1960) pointed out the need to understand a brand's market in terms of how the *consumer* sees it. This is what establishes the true competitive set.

If a brand is seen as a heavy-duty cleaner, its marketing communication should position it as such, linking the brand to heavy-duty cleaning needs and *not* to general household cleaning. If the brand talked about itself in terms of a household cleaner, it would be inconsistent with how the target audience sees the brand, and unlikely to tap into the relevant associations in memory. This assumes, of course, that the brand is not trying to *re-position* itself as a more general household cleaner. The question the manager must answer here is: How does the target audience think about the brand?

Ramlösa offers an excellent example of this. Some years ago, they wanted to introduce a line of taste-varied waters to challenge LOKA, who dominated the market at that time, especially among young women. Unfortunately, consumers perceived the brand as something for older, more serious people. Clearly, the brand needed to be re-positioned in the consumer's mind. They did this by running a saturation campaign emulating a movie launch or rock concert announcement, using outdoor media in a unique way. After only three weeks, Ramlösa had passed LOKA in the scented waters category.

If a brand is centrally positioned, the benefit to the category are assumed, and must be reinforced. If a user-oriented positioning is adopted, the benefit is subsumed by an identification with brand usage. In all other cases, which again is most of the time, the manager must select the benefit most likely to maximize positive brand attitude in differentiating the brand from competitors in the eyes of the target audience, and to determine the best way in which to focus on that benefit with the executions. The benefit selection will provide the basis for the benefit claim made about the brand in its marketing communication. In effect, it will let the consumer know what the brand offers and why they should want it. This is the answer to the 'What does it offer?' question asked in the general model of positioning, laying the foundation for building positive brand attitude.

Setting communication objectives

In earlier chapters, we talked about the four basic communication effects of category need, brand awareness, brand attitude and brand purchase intention, and saw in Chapter 9 how communication objectives follow directly from them. As these are the possible effects of marketing communication, the manager must establish the importance of each to the overall communications strategy. As already emphasized, an important point to remember is that communication effects result from all forms of marketing communication. In other words, regardless of which type of marketing communication is considered, it will have the ability to stimulate any of the major communication effects. However, as we have seen, all types of marketing communication are not necessarily equally effective in creating particular effects.

Communication objectives are quite simply the communication *effects* one is looking for. Next, we will summarize how the four communication effects are likely to translate into communication objectives in the IMC plan.

Category need

The first consideration in establishing the communication objective for an IMC campaign is to determine whether there is a 'need' for the product. This may seem a strange question to ask, for why would there be a product if there were no need for it? But that is not the point. There are times when demand in a category is weak, as we noted in Chapter 9 in our discussion of communication objectives in message development. If that is the case, the manager must decide if one of the objectives should be to include 'selling' the category along with the brand. Obviously, this can only make sense if the brand has a competitive share of the market. The key to successfully implementing a category need communication objective is to ensure a strong link between the need for the product and the brand as the best 'solution' in satisfying that need. Category need will almost always be a communication objective for new and newly developing product categories.

Brand awareness

Brand awareness is *always* a communication objective. As we have seen in our discussions of brand awareness, there are two different brand awareness strategies: recognition and recall. When the purchase decision is made at the point-of-purchase, this calls for a recognition brand awareness strategy, where seeing the brand in the store reminds the target of the 'need' for the brand that was aroused by the IMC campaign. This is almost always the objective for low-involvement strategies. If the purchase decision occurs prior to actual purchase (for example, when deciding on what restaurant to go to), then a recall brand awareness strategy is called for.

Brand awareness is usually seen as a traditional strength of advertising, as pointed out in the last chapter, however, promotion can make a significant contribution. Generally, promotion is best utilized for increasing brand recognition. Merchandising promotions do this by drawing more attention to a brand at the point-of-purchase (for example, with coupons or special displays).

Brand attitude

Brand attitude, too, is *always* a communication objective, again as we have discussed. What is meant by brand attitude is the information or feeling the brand wishes to impart through its marketing communication. Information about a brand or emotional associations with it that are transmitted by consistent advertising over time build brand equity.

We have dealt with brand attitude a great deal in this book because it is really at the heart of marketing communication. Strategies for implementing the brand attitude objective are derived from one of the four quadrants of the Rossiter–Percy Grid. Reviewing, the manager must consider whether the target audience sees the purchase of a brand as low or high risk (involvement), and whether the underlying motivation to buy or use the brand is positive or negative. Where the brand falls in relation to this will determine the appropriate brand attitude strategy:

1   Low-involvement informational is the strategy for products or services that involve little or no risk, and where the underlying motivation for behaviour in the category is one of the three negative motives (you may want to look back at Table 4.2 to refresh your memory of these motives). Typical examples would include pain relievers, detergents and routinely purchased industrial products.
2   Low-involvement transformational is the strategy for products or services that involve little or no risk, but where the underlying motivation in the category is positive. Typical examples would include most food products, soft drinks and beer.

3   High-involvement informational is the strategy for products or services where the decision involves risk (either in terms of price or for psycho-social reasons), and where the underlying behaviour is negatively motivated. Typical examples would include financial investments, insurance, heavy-duty household goods, and new industrial products.

4   High-involvement transformational is the strategy for products or services where the decision involves risk, and where the underlying behaviour is positively motivated. Typical examples would include high-fashion clothing or cosmetics, cars and corporate image.

Whereas traditionally one thinks of advertising for building brand attitude, as suggested in the last chapter, the best promotions will also work on building brand attitude. While the immediate aim of a promotion is a short-term increase in sales, they can also create more long-term communication effects, maximizing full-value purchase once the promotion is withdrawn. For example, free trial periods or free samples help create a positive feeling for a brand, as do coupons seen as a small gift from the manufacturer. Promotions can also provide useful information to ensure a continued favourable attitude after trial as well; for example, with such things as regional training programmes for businesses, cookbooks and on-package usage suggestions.

Brand purchase intention

Brand purchase intention becomes a communication objective when the goal is an *immediate* response. As we have seen, this is rarely the case for advertising, but it is always the objective for promotion, even if there is no incentive involved.

Along with brand awareness, stimulation of brand purchase intention is the real strength of promotion. All promotions are aimed at 'moving sales forward' immediately, and they do this by stimulating immediate brand purchase intentions, or other purchase-related intentions such as a visit to a showroom or a call for a sales demonstration. For consumer target audiences, the potential power of promotion is underscored by research that has shown that purchase intention can be influenced at the point-of-purchase in about two out of every three supermarket decisions (Haven, 1995).

Matching media options

The fifth step in the strategic planning process involves identifying appropriate media options for delivering the brand's message. IMC media strategy is not a simple matter of finding media that reach the target audience, or satisfying particular reach and frequency objectives. This is important to media planning, but it is *not* the first step. In considering the wide range of media options available for delivering IMC messages, the critical concern is to first identify those media that will facilitate the type of processing necessary to satisfy the communication objectives.

There are three areas in which media differ that will have a direct bearing on this: the ability to effectively deliver visual content, the time available to process the message and the ability to deliver high frequency (the number of times the target audience will be exposed to a message through a particular media). Each of these media characteristics has particular significance for both brand awareness and brand attitude strategy, as we see below. Additionally, managers must also consider media options in terms of the size and type of their business. This too will inform what IMC media options will make the most sense given the markets within which they operate.

In this section, we will be addressing three questions the manager should consider in developing an IMC media strategy. What media options are appropriate for recognition versus recall brand awareness strategies? What media options help facilitate the brand attitude strategy? From this set of media options, what media make the most sense, given the size and type of business?

Appropriate media for brand awareness

Visual content and frequency are issues for brand awareness processing. When the brand awareness strategy is *recognition*, one must be able to see the package. This means that almost any visual media should do, but not radio. Newspaper, while able to show a package, should be considered with caution because of potential limitations in colour reproduction. If correct colour is essential for brand package recognition (for example, because of similarity of package colour among brands in the category), newspaper may not be a good option. An exception to these restrictions for recognition awareness would be where brand recognition is verbal, not visual. This could be the case for companies that rely on telemarketing, where the target audience must recognize the brand name when they hear it.

When a recall brand awareness strategy is used, frequency is a concern. Media selected must be able to deliver a high frequency to seed the category need–brand name link in memory. Certain media like monthly magazines and direct mail have obvious frequency limitations. Posters have potential frequency limitations, unless they are positioned in an area of high target audience traffic.

A good example of using IMC to build the link between category need and the brand for recall brand awareness is a campaign that ran in Sweden several years ago for Apoteket. Integrating advertising and public relations, a bus tour was carried out across Sweden to educate people about pain (the category need), providing booklets about pain and how to avoid it. The bus tour was supported with advertising and public relations in local newspapers and radio announcing when the bus would be stopping in various towns and cities. As a result of the tour, when people experienced pain, Apoteket seen as the way to alleviate that pain, and as someone caring and in a position to determine the best medical care for them.

Appropriate media for brand attitude

The four brand attitude strategies that follow from the Rossiter–Percy Grid are a function of the level of involvement in the decision and the underlying motivation driving behaviour, as we have seen. If the brand attitude is *low-involvement informational*, almost any media will work because these are the easiest messages to process, needing only to communicate a single, simply-presented benefit that is easily grasped, not requiring repeated exposure. There may, however, be creative constraints that might limit media choice. This would be the case, for example, if the product must be demonstrated in order to effectively communicate its benefit. For *low-involvement transformational* strategies, good visual content capability is critical, and high frequency is needed to build the positive effect associated with the benefit.

Table 12.3 Appropriate media for brand attitude strategies

Mass media options	Brand attitude strategy			
	Low-involvement informational	*Low-involvement transformational*	*High-involvement informational*	*High-involvement transformational*
Television	Yes	Yes	No	Yes
Radio	Yes	No	No	No
Newspaper	Yes	Colour limitation	Yes	Colour limitation
Magazines	Yes	Frequency limitation	Yes	Yes
Posters	Yes	Frequency limitation	Processing time limitation	Yes
Digital media	Yes	Yes	Yes	Yes
Direct mail	Yes	Frequency limitation	Yes	Yes

When the brand attitude strategy is *high-involvement informational*, the key requirement is enough time to process and consider the message, since it must be accepted. This means that media like radio, television and streaming digital video, if there is no option to replay the advertisement, should not be considered because the target audience is not able to control the pace at which they process the message. For *high-involvement transformational* strategies, it is important to ensure the ability to provide strong visual content. For some products falling in this category, especially high-priced luxury goods, a strong visual image will immediately stimulate a strong emotional response and positive attitude (if the target audience identifies with the image), and higher frequency may not be necessary. But this is something the manager must carefully consider, based on research.

A number of IMC media options appropriate for brand attitude strategies are summarized in Table 12.3. An important consideration in putting together the media strategy is to remember that while one medium may be appropriate for brand awareness, it may not be appropriate for the brand attitude strategy. This does *not* mean that it should not be used, but it does mean that the manager must keep firmly in mind that the message may be building brand awareness but not doing much for brand attitude. In such a case, make sure to also use appropriate brand attitude media. A good example here would be high-involvement informational strategies. Broadcast is inappropriate for this brand attitude strategy, but could be perfect for brand awareness. The brand might use television to build awareness and introduce the key benefit, while delivering a more detailed message in print where there is more time to process.

Appropriate media for the size and type of business

Depending on the size of a business and its market, the primary media used will be different. Rossiter and colleagues (2018) have made this important point, and define four groups to consider: large-audience advertisers including both business-to-business and consumer, small-audience local retail advertisers, small-audience business-to-business advertisers, and direct-response advertisers.

Most marketers with large audiences will select from among appropriate major mass media for the brand awareness and brand attitude strategies. These will include television, digital media, radio, newspapers, magazines and posters. Notice that we are talking about large *audiences* or markets, not necessarily large businesses. Airbus is a big company, but with few potential buyers. Small-audience local retailers will not usually use mass media because of the expense and wasted coverage. Unless there are enough stores in an area covered by local mass media, it makes no sense. Rather, they are more likely to use local print and direct mail, as well as event marketing and sponsorships, and digital media, especially social media such as Facebook, as discussed in the box nearby. Whatever media are used, however, they must be appropriate for the communication objective. Small-audience, business-to-business marketers will be likely to use print almost exclusively as their primary medium, especially trade publications and direct mail.

Facebook fees and small business

Many small businesses are upset with being asked to pay a fee to reach a larger percentage of their Facebook fan base. According to Facebook, the average business post only reaches about 16 percent of its fans, something that surprises many small businesses that rely on it as their main vehicle for marketing. Under a change in the fee structure, businesses are asked to pay anywhere from US$ 5.00 to hundreds of US dollars in order to 'promote' their posts if they want more fans to see it. The fee varies with how many fans the business wants to reach.

Small businesses, especially, were drawn to Facebook because it was free to join and had a massive user base, enabling them to keep their marketing costs low. Some, in fact, use their business page in place of a company website. Facebook is not alone in adding fees for businesses. But having to pay for social media, or to pay to increase their reach to a meaningful level, could put small businesses at a distinct disadvantage compared to larger businesses.

Source: *The Wall Street Journal*, 11 October 2012

Direct-response businesses tend to use direct marketing and, as discussed in Chapter 11, this primarily means direct mail and telemarketing. But some direct-response is not database driven and, as such, is not direct marketing. These businesses will be likely to use telemarketing and print, or even television and digital media. But direct-response advertising is different from traditional advertising in that its primary communication objective is brand purchase intention and *immediate* response. This means there is no time to build brand awareness, and very little time to build positive brand attitude for all but low-involvement informational strategies. In using television, say to demonstrate a product (especially a high-involvement product), the message will require more than 30 to 60 seconds. In fact, it is not unusual for direct-response marketers to use a *30-minute* television 'programme', so-called infomercials. The rules for effective processing still hold, but the medium is used differently.

Summary

Once the marketing plan has been reviewed, the actual IMC planning begins with target audience selection. This will have been informed by what the marketing plan has to say about where the brand is looking for business. While demographics are often used in selecting a target audience, this is not appropriate. Demographics define a target market, not a target audience. Nevertheless, they are useful for profiling a target audience. When selecting the target audience it is important to consider the value of reaching them relative to the cost. Once the target audience has been selected, the next step is to set action objectives, and associate them with specific goals. If trial is the action objective, brand switchers who switch among other brands (OBS) are the key buyer group because they already exhibit switching behaviour and will be the easiest group to attract. Those loyal to other brands (OBL) or non-categories users (NCU) offer potential for trial, but are much more difficult to attract. If increased repeat purchase is the action objective, brand switchers who include the brand in their set (FBS) will be encouraged to select the brand more often; BL will be encouraged to buy more, or more often.

Having identified the target audience, it is important to gain an understanding of how they go about making purchase decisions in the category. The BSM is a good way of looking at this, identifying the stages involved in the decision and, for each stage, who is involved and the roles they play, where it is likely to occur, the timing and how it happens. The key role player in the decision process becomes the creative target, the person who must be positively influenced if the campaign is to be successful. With the target audience selected and an understanding of how they make purchase decisions in the category, it is time to begin planning message development.

The first step in message development is to determine the appropriate positioning for the brand within its marketing communication. For most brands, this will mean a differentiated positioning rather than a central positioning, which is only appropriate if the brand is seen as delivering on all of the benefits associated with the category. It will also almost always mean a benefit-oriented rather than user-oriented positioning, which is only appropriate for specific market niches or when social approval is the motivation involved. Once these two basic issues are addressed, a benefit must be selected around which to base the message.

Having positioned the brand, the next step is to set the communication objectives. These objectives are selected from the set of four communication effects: category need, brand awareness, brand attitude and brand purchase intention. Brand awareness and brand attitude will always be objectives, and must reflect the type of awareness needed (recognition or recall) and the appropriate strategic brand attitude quadrant of the Rossiter–Percy Grid.

After the message development section of the plan is complete, the final step in the IMC planning process is to identify an appropriate set of media options that are consistent with the communication objectives.

Review questions

1   What are the important considerations in target audience selection?
2   What are some of the cost implications in target audience selection?
3   Discuss target audience action objectives.
4   Why is it important in IMC planning to understand how the target audience goes about making brand decisions?
5   What are the decision stages likely to be in choosing a mobile phone?
6   What is a creative target?
7   Why is it important in IMC planning to understand the roles people play in the purchase decision process?

8   Discuss the importance of positioning in IMC planning.

9   Find examples of advertising where the brand is well positioned and examples where it is not and discuss why.

10 Find an example of advertising that has category need as a communication objective.

11 What is the key to selecting media for the IMC plan?

12 Discuss the criteria for making media selection decisions for the different brand attitude communication objectives associated with the Rossiter–Percy Grid.

13 Why is it important to look at the size and type of business in selecting the primary media for an IMC plan?

14 Contrast the use of traditional against digital media for different sizes and types of business.

References

Antonides, G. and van Raaij, W.I. (1998) *Consumer Behaviour: A European Perspective*. Chichester: John Wiley and Sons.

Belk, R.W. (1975) Situational variables and consumer behaviour. *Journal of Consumer Research*, 2(*3*), 157–164.

Ehrlich, D., Guttman, I., Schönbach, P. and Mills, J. (1957) Postdecision exposure to relevant information. *Journal of Abnormal and Social Psychology*, *54*(*1*), 98–102.

Festinger, L. (1957) *A Theory of Cognitive Dissonance*. Stanford: Stanford University Press.

Foxall, G.R. (1992) The consumer situation: An integrative model for research in marketing. *Journal of Marketing Management*, 8(*4*), 383–404.

Haven, L. (1995) Point of purchase, marketers getting with program. *Advertising Age*, 23 October.

Levitt, T. (1960) Marketing myopia. *Harvard Business Review*, *38* (July–August), 45–56.

Rossiter, J.R. and Percy, L. (1987) *Advertising and Promotion Management*. New York: McGraw-Hill.

Rossiter, J.R. and Percy, L. (1997) *Advertising Communication and Promotion Management*. New York: McGraw-Hill.

Rossiter, J.R., Percy, L. and Bergkvist L. (2018) *Marketing Communications: Objectives, Strategies, Tactics*. London: Sage Publications, Ltd.

vanTripp, H.C.M., Hogen, W.D. and Inman, J.J. (1996) Product category-level explanations for true variety seeking behaviour. *Journal of Marketing Research*, *33*(*3*), 281–292.

13 Finalizing and implementing the IMC plan

The planning process discussed in the last two chapters yields all the information needed to put together the IMC plan. The overall context for the plan is provided by the brand's marketing plan, the target audience is identified, and an understanding of how they make brand decisions established. The creative positioning and objectives are determined, and a set of media options consistent with those objectives identified. Now it is time to put it all together.

In this chapter, we look at how the knowledge gained through the IMC strategic planning process is used in finalizing a plan for the actual IMC campaign, and how to implement it. Finalizing a plan requires identifying the touch points in the decision process where marketing communication is likely to have the most significant effect on a brand decision, the communication tasks required at each of these touch points, and media appropriate for accomplishing these tasks. Once this is determined and the plan detailed, it is time to implement the plan. Creative is executed to meet the communication objectives, and the appropriate media selected to optimize the delivery of the message. The manager is then in position to deliver an effective IMC campaign for the brand, but the job is not complete. The campaign must be tracked.

Finalizing the plan

Once the strategic planning process is complete, the manager can begin finalizing a plan for implementing an IMC campaign. Based on the understanding of how purchase decisions are made in the category, in conjunction with target audience action objectives and the communication strategy, the manager must decide whether the brand's marketing communication goals:

1 can be satisfied with a *single* message directed at one primary target audience, using one primary type of marketing communication (for example, advertising, direct-mail, brochures, etc.), or
2 if a number of communication tasks should be considered, directed at one primary target, but to different roles in the decision process; different messages to different targets; and/or using various types of marketing communication directed to different times or places in the decision process.

If the brand's communication objective can be satisfied by a single message and one primary medium based on what was learned from the strategic planning process, the manager can proceed directly to selecting the most appropriate medium.

DOI: 10.4324/9781003169635-17

It is important to understand that even if all that is necessary is a single message delivered through one primary medium, this is still IMC. If a brand has gone through a strategic planning process such as the one described in Chapter 12, and all potential options were considered, but in the end one message delivered to the target audience through one primary medium satisfies the brand's communication objective, we would argue this is still an IMC programme. It only means that, at this particular point in time, this is all that is needed. Of course, this is rarely the case, but it underscores the importance of seeing IMC as a *planning process*. IMC is an ongoing process. Market dynamics could change, and different messages in other media might become necessary. The brand will be ready to respond to these changes because the manager has been through an IMC planning process.

When a more detailed plan is required, which again is almost all the time, it will be necessary to first determine the important places in the decision process where marketing communication can be most effective, second establish the communication tasks needed at each of these points, and finally select the appropriate media to deliver the message.

Identifying where IMC can have an impact

In the last chapter, a behavioural sequence model was introduced, underscoring the need to understand consumer brand decisions as a *process* involving multiple stages with, potentially, several people involved and playing different roles in that process. Using a consumer decision model like the behavioural sequence model (BSM) makes it possible to organize all the available knowledge of how brand choices are made in a category into a usable form for strategically integrated communication planning. An effective IMC plan can only be achieved if it is based on the decision process for a brand.

This understanding is extremely valuable because the manager must be able to identify those places in the decision process where marketing communication can have a positive impact on brand choice. One might think about these places where marketing communication may influence the brand decision as touch points. It will be these *touch points* that provide the framework for the IMC plan.

Many of those who are interested in IMC have pointed out the importance of a solid understanding of the consumer in the effective implementation of IMC programmes. In fact, it is important to look carefully at how consumers behave and see the world *before* it is possible to develop an effective IMC plan. The BSM is an ideal way of gaining this insight. It is indeed this insight into the consumer, more than anything else, which will help identify the touch points for effectively implementing an IMC programme.

In order to help pull this together and demonstrate how one goes about identifying the important touch points in a decision process, consider the hypothesized BSM shown in Figure 13.1 for an IT system. Suppose a company is marketing an innovative new IT system to improve alignment between technology initiatives and business goals, and has developed this BSM of how companies go about deciding on introducing a new IT system into their operations. Given this understanding of the decision process, what does it suggest about how best to positively affect the decision with marketing communication? Let us think through this process, which is in effect what a manager would be doing in finalizing an IMC plan. It is obvious that in the real world this would be a complex decision process, with multiple potential target audiences, but for this example we use only the generic decision stages. As we look at the BSM, there is no doubt that more than a single message in one medium will be needed. Can one really imagine that a

Decision stages			
Need arousal	Brand consideration	Purchase	Usage
Users of current system/managers as **initiator**	Users/managers as **influencers**	Manager or purchasing agent as **purchaser**	Users/manager as **user**
Dealers or outside consultants as initiator	Dealers or outside consultants as **influencers** Manager as **decider** Senior management as **decider**		

Figure 13.1 Decision roles for a hypothesized BSM for an IT system.

single advertising campaign, let alone a single promotion of some kind, would be able to do the job? Of course not.

Looking at the *need arousal* stage, we see that a number of people might be involved. At the simplest level, the users of the current system in an initiator role might be complaining about their current system. On the other hand, the manager in charge may be dissatisfied as a result of seeing or hearing about better alternatives. The need of the users or managers may be aroused without marketing communication if they are unhappy with what they are using, but if a brand wishes to help stimulate need, some form of marketing communication will be required. As it is a *new* IT system being marketed, it will be necessary to communicate with both those involved as initiators within a company and those in the trade, which will be asked to carry and sell the new system. At the very least there will be two target audiences participating at the need arousal stage who must be aware of the new system, and begin to form a positive attitude towards it.

Once initial interest has been aroused, at the brand evaluation stage the potential user and the trade will begin to form attitudes about the various alternative IT systems available. The same individuals who were involved as initiators will probably fill the role of influencer as well, but others could also play a part. Consultants may be called in, and at some point during the evaluation, senior management will become involved. At this stage, managers and senior management will assume the role of decider.

Does it make sense to use the same message for everyone involved? While the message to the trade (both consultants and distributors), users and managers should be basically the same (and certainly reflect the same look and feel), the medium of delivery will likely vary. Messages to senior management will certainly be different. Management is not interested in the technical aspects of the system, but they are interested in 'value' issues. There would appear to be a number of different marketing communication opportunities at this stage in the decision process. Additionally, if the brand does not already have a database in place, it would be a good time to begin. If there is one, it should be updated during this stage.

At the *purchase* stage the manager, or perhaps a purchasing agent, will be involved in the actual purchase. What message, if any, might we wish to deliver at this stage that differs from earlier material? The trade may wish to follow-up with an incentive promotion; the brand may wish to send direct mail to those the trade has indicated have shown interest in the new system. But in reality, with a high-involvement purchase like this, if there has been senior management approval of the choice, there will be no opportunity to change the decision as there might be with a low-involvement purchase at a retail store.

Finally, what should be done during the *usage* stage? At the very least, it would make sense to do something to reinforce the manager's choice of the new system. Some form of direct mail would be appropriate, but so too would general advertising that reinforces overall brand image. This positioning affects not only the manager, but also those who are actually using the new system.

Even using only the four generic decision stages in this example, one can see that there are a number of potential touch points where marketing communication can help inform brand choice. The task of the manager is to now identify the communication tasks that will be necessary to address these touch points, and then to set priorities in terms of what is essential for brand success, and what else might be helpful. Then, from this set of communication tasks, the manager determines what will be affordable given the budget. In other words, the foundation has been late for an effective IMC plan.

Identifying communication tasks and media options

The important touch points in the decision process reflect where marketing communication will have the best opportunity to positively influence the decision in favour of a brand. The manager must next consider the communication tasks necessary for each touch point. This means identifying the relevant target audience at each stage in the decision process and what marketing communication is expected to accomplish at each stage. Finally, in the development of the IMC plan, the manager must identify what appropriate media options are available to deliver the message.

Communication tasks

At each touch point in the decision process there may be a number of potential target audience roles involved. These must be carefully considered, and those most likely to be responsive to marketing communication at that point identified. The manager must also decide exactly what is required of marketing communication at each touch point to positively influence the decision process. Together, these decisions identify the communication tasks required.

Target audience. What specific members of the target audience should be addressed at each stage, and what roles are they playing? It would be rare indeed for all the potential target audience members in all their roles to be included. This is where the manager must begin making choices. Which target audience members in what roles are critical? These become the primary target audiences at that stage. One may also identify a secondary or even tertiary audience in the event that there is enough in the budget to consider them after all the primary target audiences for each stage are addressed.

Communication objectives. Next, the manager needs to translate the appropriate communication effects into specific communication objectives for each stage. For example, brand awareness is always an objective, but what kind (recall versus recognition); and is it necessary to raise or simply maintain the awareness? With brand attitude, is it necessary to educate the target audience? Does the message at that point need to interest the target audience in the brand, stimulate enquiry, give them a good feeling, or underscore a unique feature? Should brand purchase intention be a commitment to call and make a reservation or place an order, or to ask for more information? Should the target audience request the brand specifically, say from an investment broker or health care provider, or pick the brand on their next visit to the store?

What is needed here is a clear, concise interpretation of the proper communication effects required to meet the overall communication objectives for the IMC campaign. This can be a very involved process, drawing together all the knowledge and understanding that came out of the strategic planning process. To illustrate, let us look at just some of the possible communication tasks associated with each stage of the generic decision model.

What communication effects are likely to be relevant to need arousal? This is the stage when someone begins to think about possible purchase or usage of a brand, so raising brand awareness will be a primary objective. An initial favourable brand attitude will also be needed, especially for low-involvement decisions. It is clearly not enough for people to simply be aware of a brand at this initial stage. Some tentatively positive attitude will also be required if the brand is to remain a contender in the decision process. But the manager must also consider category need here. It may not be necessary, but one should always ask if the target audience is both experienced *and* active in the category.

At the brand evaluation stage, one must be concerned with both brand attitude and brand purchase intention effects. For low-involvement decisions, the tentatively favourable brand attitude built during need arousal must be reinforced, providing again what Maloney (1962) called 'curious disbelief', and leading to a positive intention to try. For high-involvement decisions, it is essential that enough appropriate information is provided at this stage because the target audience must be both informed *and* convinced. If dealing with positive motives, one must be concerned with nurturing the appropriate feelings as well. Authentically reflecting the emotion involved in decision processes involving positive motives implies more than just a favourable attitude. A positive intention to buy or use the brand is needed, and this will follow from a favourable evaluation owing to the correct emotional associations.

But deciding to choose a brand does not guarantee it will actually be purchased or used. So, at the actual purchase stage it will be necessary to ensure that the positive brand attitude is reinforced, and that the brand purchase intention is actually carried out. During usage, messages should help continue reinforcing brand attitude and encourage repurchase or continued use of the brand. All these decision stage–communication effects relationships are summarized in Table 13.1.

Table 13.1 Decision stage–communication effect relationship

Decision stage	Communication effect
Need arousal	• Consideration of category need • Raise brand awareness • Tentative brand attitude
Brand consideration	• Build positive brand attitude • Convincing benefit claim for high-involvement strategies • Establish authentic emotional link for transformational strategies
Purchase	• Reinforce positive brand attitude • Ensure positive brand purchase intention
Usage	• Reinforce positive brand attitude • Encourage repeat brand purchase intention

Media options

Once the manager has determined the communication tasks, it is necessary to identify appropriate media options for delivering the message at each touch point in order to accomplish the task, and any processing requirements associated with it. This is where the manager specifies exactly what media options are available to reach the target audience, consistent with the primary communication objective for the task. How can recognition awareness be sustained? Should print advertising, billboards or coupons be used? Will video advertising or direct mail be appropriate? To facilitate purchase, should the brand use in-store banners or special displays? What about incentive promotions? This may be a good place to point out that if multiple media are used in an IMC campaign, it is done because of the specific appropriateness of the various media to the communication tasks, *not* from any sense of 'synergy' (Dijkstra, 2002).

IMC planning worksheet

The touch points identify those stages in the decision process where IMC can positively affect the brand decision, communication tasks establish what marketing communication must accomplish at each of those points, and media options are selected that are appropriate for those tasks. A good way of summarizing this is with an IMC planning worksheet as shown in Figure 13.2.

The first column lists the touch points that were identified from a BSM or some other model of the consumer decision process for the category. In the next two columns, the specific target audiences and their role, and the communication objectives making up the communication tasks, are listed for each touch point. The last column provides those media options appropriate for the corresponding communication tasks. Summarized in this way, the manager may objectively review the various communication tasks likely to positively influence the brand decision along with appropriate media options for each, and consider what would best fit the brand's overall objective and budget.

To illustrate what we have been discussing, let us consider what might have been involved in the development of the IMC plan when disposable contact lenses were introduced. This is a particularly good case to consider because it involves a somewhat complex decision process where both the patient as consumer and their doctor or eye-care professional are involved. Figure 13.3 offers an overview of the eyeglass lens decision process, and illustrates the interrelationship between patient and doctor considerations. This model reflects what was learned from a BSM, and from it come the

Touch points for decision stages	Communication tasks		Media options
	Target audience	Communication objectives	

Figure 13.2 IMC planning worksheet.

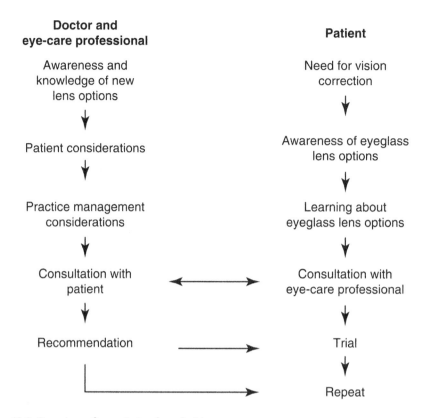

Figure 13.3 Overview of prescription lens decision process.

significant touch points. You can see that both the patient and doctor are involved together in making the decision to use disposable contact lenses, and this will clearly require a carefully planned IMC programme.

Using the IMC planning worksheet just described, the manager can summarize the communication tasks and media options available for each touch point, as we see in Figure 13.4 for patients and Figure 13.5 for doctors. What these worksheets suggest for the IMC plan is discussed below.

Looking at the first touch point for patients, *Awareness of need and options*, although family members and friends could play an important role as initiators and influencers, the primary target audience will be those who currently wear prescription eyeglasses or contact lenses and the action objective trial. At this first touch point in the decision process, category need must be initiated. If only one brand was initially available, creating awareness and initial interest in disposable contact lenses will correspond to brand awareness and initial brand attitude. The best way of accomplishing these communication objectives will be with advertising in broadcast, digital media and print. For the doctor's role in the *patient's* decision, it will be necessary to build brand awareness along with a clinical understanding of its performance in order to stimulate interest in looking more deeply into them. Obviously, the doctor must feel comfortable in bringing disposable contact lenses to the attention of their patients or recommending them. Much of this initial awareness and attitude will follow from the patient advertising, but must be

Touch points	Communication tasks		Media options
	Target audience	Communication objectives	
Awareness of need and options	Current prescription eyeglass and contact lens users as initiators and influencers Doctor and eye-care professional as initiator and influencer	Create awareness of disposable contact lenses Build brand awareness and initial brand attitude	Broadcast, digital and print advertising Direct mail to doctors, advertising in professional journals, professional conferences
Learning about options	Current prescription eyeglass and contact lens users as influencers and deciders	Strengthen brand awareness Build brand attitude by providing information to convince	Print and digital advertising Point-of-purchase (for doctor's office) Direct mail Internet
Consultation and decision	Current prescription eyeglass and contact lens users as influencers and deciders Doctors and eye-care professionals as influencers	Strengthen positive brand attitude Stimulate brand purchase intention	Point-of-purchase (for doctor's office) Incentive promotions via direct mail, point-of-purchase or Internet
Usage and reinforcement	Current prescription eyeglass and contact lens users as users and influencers	Brand purchase intention Maintain brand attitude	Broadcast, digital and print advertising Direct mail

Figure 13.4 Patient IMC planning worksheet.

reinforced by more targeted communication through advertising in professional journals, direct mail and at professional conferences.

At the *Learning about Options* touch point, the most logical point for the patient to seek information about disposable contact lenses is from their doctor or eye-care professional. This will require providing them with brochures or other merchandising material not only for point-of-purchase (the doctor's or eye-care professional's office), but also for possible inclusion as statement stuffers or self-contained mailers for the doctor to send to patients. Additionally, ongoing advertising, especially print and some digital media such as the internet where there is more time to process because this is likely to be a high involvement decision, will continue to build brand awareness and attitude. Toll-free numbers and the internet also offer opportunities to provide more information.

To facilitate the actual purchase at the *Consultation and decision* touch point, the patient must consult with the doctor and try the product. Again, this will require good point-of-purchase material at the doctor's or eye care professional's office, and possibly a promotion to reinforce positive brand attitude and purchase intention. At the final patient touch point, *Usage and reinforcement*, it will be necessary to reinforce confidence in the

Touch points	Communication tasks		Media options
	Target audience	Communication objectives	
Awareness of needs and options	Doctor and eye-care professional as initiator and influencer Sales force as initiator and influencer	Create awareness of disposable contact lenses Build brand awareness and initial brand attitude	Broadcast, digital and print advertising (to patients) Professional journals, direct mail, professional conferences Sales force collateral and merchandising kits
Learning about options	Doctor and eye-care professional as influencer and decider	Build positive attitude for both disposable contact lenses and brand	Professional journals Professional conferences Direct mail
Practice management considerations	Doctor and eye-care professional as influencer and decider Sales force as influencer	Build positive brand attitude Link brand to practice	Point-of-purchase merchandising programme Joint programme through channels marketing
Acquisition and review	Doctor and eye-care professional as purchaser, user and influencer	Build positive brand purchase intention Reinforce positive brand attitude	Incentive promotions Direct mail Professional journals Patient advertising in television, digital media and print

Figure 13.5 Doctor and eye-care professional IMC planning worksheet.

decision, building and sustaining positive category and brand attitude, and the action objective changes to repeat purchase. Here, advertising with television, digital media and print can reassure the patient, and give them the comfort of feeling part of a much wider group of users than may actually be the case. Direct mail can also help reinforce the decision, perhaps also including an incentive to continue using.

Now that we have considered the patient along with the doctor's participation in their decision, let us briefly look at the two touch points dealing specifically with the doctor and the eye-care professional, where it is important to reinforce for them the positive business side of the decision. At the *Practice management consideration* stage, independent of satisfying the patient's needs, doctors must be attentive to the impact of what they dispense in their practice. A key concern, of course, is patient demand. A programme to acquaint them with the patient IMC support can address this issue. Additionally, educating them regarding the brand's potential contribution to their business practice can be accomplished through merchandising programmes, direct mail, sales calls and professional seminars. Positive brand attitude can also be built by using some form of channels or tactical marketing to specifically associate the practice with the brand. At the last touch point, *Acquisition and review*, promotion incentives can be offered to stimulate brand purchase intention, along with continued reinforcement of brand attitude using patient and trade advertising in television, digital media and print.

This example not only underscores the often-complex nature of the decision process, but also how many communication tasks can be involved in putting together an effective IMC plan. The IMC planning worksheet offers the manager a good way of looking at all the options available. It suggests what will be needed to meet communication objectives, and the media options that can be used. In effect, it provides an outline for completing the IMC plan.

This does *not* mean that the manager now has the 'answer'. What is provided is a summary of the best reading of everything known coming out of the strategic planning process, and what the brand hopes to accomplish with its marketing communication programme. If the budget was large enough, it would be possible to proceed directly to implementing everything outlined in the worksheet. Unfortunately, that is rarely the case. Realistic budget constraints will no doubt limit what may be accomplished. But using the worksheet as a guide, it will be possible to make more efficient *and* effective decisions on which communication tasks to implement in order to most effectively drive brand success. It will be these decisions that inform the final IMC plan.

Implementing the plan

Once the communication tasks required have been identified and the IMC plan completed, it must be implemented. This means creating the advertising and promotion called for, and determining how best to deliver it. In previous chapters, we have considered what is necessary to create effective marketing communication. Now we must look at how best to deliver it.

Selecting the best media options

In developing the plan, the manager includes all the media options appropriate for each communication task that satisfy the necessary processing requirements. To implement the plan, it is now necessary to select the *best* media options from that set, and develop a media plan. This will require the manager to identify a primary medium for each task, along with potential secondary media that might be appropriate. Once this has been done, the difficult task of allocating the available budget to the various communication tasks must be dealt with. It is beyond the scope of this book to go into the details of media planning. However, we would like to offer one last planning worksheet to help visualize what is required in allocating the IMC media budget.

Before dealing specifically with these issues, we should look more broadly at media allocation for advertising versus promotion messages. The IMC planning worksheet helped identify whom the brand wanted to reach, and with what type of marketing communication, in order to satisfy the communication objective. This all bears significantly on IMC media strategy. Depending on the communication tasks, either advertising, promotion, or both, could be appropriate.

Although mass media for advertising is often the best way to satisfy many communication tasks, when it is *not* the best solution, it is unlikely to figure in the media strategy at all. Of course, this is not a hard and fast rule, but it is a good rule of thumb. The reason for this lies in the general reach objectives of advertising and promotion. As we have seen, most of the time promotions are aimed at a more highly targeted audience or a narrow reach. Given the broad-based reach of mass media, it is unlikely to be efficient in support of a more narrowly-based target audience.

Yet as we have seen, many promotions simply are not very efficient *without* corresponding or prior advertising support. This can be a problem. But the key here is that with things like specialized print media, local radio, and certain digital media, mass media can be adapted to more targeted audiences and a narrower reach. When broad-based, mass markets are not the target, for effective IMC media planning the manager must begin to think of media options in a more narrow way. A good example of this is illustrated in the discussion of interactive billboards in the box below.

Media for advertising

Almost any medium can serve as a means of delivering advertising; those traditionally considered are mass media such as television, digital, radio, newspapers and magazines, and outdoor. As noted in the last chapter, when looking at the effectiveness of individual media in meeting brand awareness and brand attitude communication objectives – as a group – these mass media tend to be more effective in satisfying brand awareness objectives than the more narrowly targeted media typically used for promotion.

Interactive billboards and posters

Billboards and posters are one of the world's oldest forms of advertising, dating back to antiquity. Now, new technology will enable people to interact with billboards and posters at bus stops, train stations, airports and ferries. Initially, the technology was used as a way of distributing wireless applications or ringtones for smartphones, but marketers saw it as a way to distribute video adverts and promotions, and even to sell products or services.

Telecom SA's Orange ran a campaign using 300 posters in London and New York for its ON wireless application. All one needed to do was hold a smartphone near the poster and download the app over Wi-Fi or by sending a text to them. The advertiser pays only when someone interacts with the advert, much like the internet. Nokia ran an interactive poster campaign in the US, UK, South Africa and Australia to promote their Ovi app store, and reported good results. The poster read 'Get apps and much more for your Nokia, turn on your Blue-tooth now', and displayed a Nokia phone and icons of apps for Facebook, Foursquare, Angry Birds and other programmes. Over 1.5 million people interacted with the poster over the ten weeks the campaign ran, and tens of millions of people saw it.

Source: *The Wall Street Journal*, 4 February 2011

The *best* overall media is television (Barlow and Papaziou, 1980) although some users of only digital media can often be as effective. It is the best way for achieving any of the communication objectives. It has been shown in study after study that when television is compared with other mass media such as radio or magazines, and even digital media, messages delivered by television do a better job driving sales. There are several reasons for this. To begin with, television employs words and pictures, movement and sounds. Radio offers words and sound, but no pictures or movement. Magazines offer words and pictures, but no movement or sound. Digital media has several potential problems, as we have seen. Television offers high reach, and can combine it with high-effective frequency. This is very difficult for either radio or magazines. Newspapers generally have the same problems as magazines.

Does this mean one should always consider television when selecting media for advertising? The general answer is yes. However, for many reasons television may not be a viable choice. Nevertheless, when possible, television should be the medium of choice for mass advertising, *except* for high-involvement, informational strategies.

Media for promotion

Are there such things as promotion media? Of course, only they are not usually thought about in terms of media. But in IMC planning it is important to think of any way in which an advertising or promotion message can be delivered as a medium within the overall media strategy. Promotion media would of course include mass media (as a group), but also such things as direct mail, FSIs (free standing inserts), point-of-purchase, along with mobile and the internet. Again, each of these vehicles could be (and often all are) used for advertising, but with the exception of mass media, the others are primary means of delivering a promotion. The best media for delivering the six consumer promotions introduced in Chapter 5 are discussed below (see Table 13.2).

COUPONS

There are many ways of delivering coupons, but the most effective are direct mail and FSIs, and through the internet and mobile. Direct mail and new media offer greater flexibility in targeting, but FSIs are about half the cost. Coupons may also be offered at the point-of-purchase.

Table 13.2 Media for basic consumer incentive promotions

Promotion	Media options
Trial promotions	
Coupons	Direct mail
	FSIs
	Internet and mobile
Sampling	Point-of-purchase
	Direct mail
Refunds and rebates	Mass media
	Point-of-purchase
	FSIs
Repeat purchase promotions	
Loyalty and reward programs and loading devices	Direct mail
	Point-of-purchase
Premiums	Mass media
	Direct mail
	Point-of-purchase
Sweepstakes, games and contests	Mass media
	Point-of-purchase

SAMPLING

The two best ways of delivering samples are at the point-of-purchase or with direct mail. Sampling in-store or at a central location is perhaps the least expensive way of sampling, and for many products it is the only effective way. Direct mail is somewhat limited by the type of sample one can mail, but with a good mailing list it has the advantage of being able to better target delivery.

REFUNDS AND REBATES

The primary medium for a refund or rebate promotion is mass media. The reason for this is that refunds and rebates must be 'announced' and explained. This is ideally done with advertising. The next most likely means of handling a refund or rebate would be at the point-of-purchase or through an FSI.

LOYALTY AND REWARD PROGRAMS AND LOADING DEVICES

Depending on the specific promotion, direct mail or point-of-purchase are the most likely media for both loyalty and reward programs and loading devices. Loyalty and reward programs are perhaps best suited to direct mail, while most loading promotions are best delivered at the point-of-purchase. Loyalty and reward programs as well as loading devices do not necessarily require advertising; it is often useful to include mass media announcements or explanations of the programme, especially if they are aimed at a broad-based target audience.

PREMIUMS

Much like refunds or rebates, to be successful a premium promotion will generally re-quire mass media advertising to generate awareness and interest. This is especially true if the premium is aimed at a broad-based target audience. More narrowly targeted pre-mium promotions use direct mail or point-of-purchase. Point-of-purchase can provide a good recognition cue for a brand's advertising, if well done, by including specific ele-ments from the advertising (Keller, 1987). Regardless of the primary medium, any premium promotion will also want to use in-store merchandising.

SWEEPSTAKES, GAMES AND CONTESTS

Again, here is a situation where mass media are going to be required to announce and explain the promotion, unless it is aimed at a more targeted audience where direct mail will work. As with premiums, point-of-purchase display will generally be needed.

Selecting primary and secondary media

In the last chapter, we saw that the media selected for an IMC programme must be able to facilitate the processing requirements of the communication objectives (visual con-tent, time to process and frequency). The principal difference between primary and secondary media in an IMC campaign is that primary media must be able to satisfy *all* a brand's communication objectives while secondary media are selected to boost a particular communication effect, or reinforce specific tactical concerns.

In effect, the primary media selected should be the most effective option, or options, and capable of doing at least an adequate job on their own without using additional media (always assuming that the budget is sufficient). The key consideration in selecting primary media is that they address the combined requirements of both the brand awareness and the brand attitude objective. For most brands, one primary medium is sufficient. However, for some very large advertisers with diverse target audiences it may be necessary to include one or two additional primary media in order to reach all of the target audience, some of whom may not be reached, or reached with enough frequency, by the main primary medium.

Secondary media are used in IMC programmes for three reasons (Rossiter and Percy, 1997). First, there may be important segments or niches that are not effectively reached by the primary medium. Second, it may be that one or more of the communication objectives would be more effectively satisfied with another medium. For example, while print should be the primary medium for a high-involvement informational product because of the need for sufficient time to process the message, television would do a better job of driving up awareness. This would be especially true with a new product introduction. Third, there could be specific tactical reasons for including other media at certain times during a campaign. Promotion, for example, as we have just seen, will likely use a secondary medium other than the primary medium carrying the advertising.

Overall, the selection of primary media and secondary media is a function of the size and type of advertiser, and the brand awareness and brand attitude objectives. The goal is to achieve total target audience reach at an effective frequency.

Next, we shall briefly review the primary and secondary media likely to be selected for the four basic types of advertising addressed in Chapter 4: consumer advertising, retail advertising, business-to-business (B2B) advertising and corporate image advertising. While these are not hard and fast rules, they do reflect the general nature of the media appropriate for meeting overall IMC objectives.

Consumer advertising

For most widely distributed consumer products, the primary medium will be television or digital media video. This is because they are generally the overall best media for generating exposure and facilitating the processing of the message (except, of course, for high-involvement informational messages).

They are the best media for driving awareness because of their intrusive nature and ability to sustain attention, and because of their dynamic nature (for example pictures, movement, seen and spoken words, music) they). They are also the strongest media for building brand attitude.

A wide variety of secondary media are used to boost reach and provide support for specific communication objectives. For example, in a classic study Grass and Wallace (1974) showed that print, when used as a secondary medium, can increase image transfer for a brand by using key visual elements from television.

Retail advertising

Most retail advertising has two jobs. It must advertise the store itself (image advertising) as well as the products it sells (brand advertising). The primary medium is likely to differ, depending on the job. Retail store image advertising requires brand *recall* as well, and short-term brand purchase intention (visiting the store). This means that any local, high-frequency media could be considered for the primary medium (for example, digital media or local broadcast and newspaper), which may then be supplemented by appropriate secondary media.

Retail product advertising takes two forms: advertising for the store's own products, or re-advertising other brands the store carries. The primary media used will vary, depending on the specific characteristics of the retailer and its market. Again, because of the wide range of brands a retailer is likely to carry, newspapers are often a good primary medium for re-advertising, as well as some digital media. This is because, at the strategic level, when advertising products they carry, they rely on the fact the advertised product is supported by consumer advertising. In advertising or promoting a store's own products, local television and newspapers along with new media can be effective.

B2B advertising

The key factors in selecting primary media for B2B advertisers are the size of the target market and the decision-makers involved (the target audience itself). With a small target audience, fewer than 100 decision-makers, it is unlikely that any mass-media-based advertising would make sense. Personal selling should be all that is necessary, backed up with collateral material (brochures or pamphlets) for the sales call. As the target audience size increases, the reach of particular IMC options will help determine what is appropriate. Generally speaking, this will mean specialized print media. Trade publications will serve as the primary medium for lower-level decision-makers in the target audience, with direct mail or relevant business magazines for upper-level decision-makers. To the extent that any secondary media are needed, it is likely to simply be more targeted uses of other specialized print media, although highly targeted use of digital media is playing an increasing role.

As with most things, there are exceptions. If a company's target market is potentially very large, mass media would make sense. International carriers such as DHL or UPS, for example, use television advertising because of its broad reach. Their target would include anyone responsible for shipping at any company with shipping needs. Think of advertising you have seen for them; it is addressing individuals in their role as someone responsible for deciding how things are to be shipped.

Corporate image advertising

With corporate image advertising, the primary medium will vary with the size of the company. For smaller companies, or those with very localized target audiences, beyond the carryover from the company's product-oriented marketing communication (primarily stimulated through logo or slogan associations), local public relations and sponsorships can be effective. Larger companies and medium sized companies with large target audiences should be looking to drive *recognition* of the company name, and to build positive attitudes towards the firm. This means the primary medium should be television, digital, or print, with secondary media as appropriate.

Recall from Chapter 3 that in addition to corporate image, corporate *identity* is an important part of IMC. All companies must address their identity through IMC options appropriate for relevant internal and external communication, and public relations should be used whenever there is a positive story worth relating. As Rossiter and Percy (1997) pointed out long ago, it is incredible how many companies use corporate image advertising while ignoring the image-transmitting aspects of direct-contact media. As they put it, this is like a large packaged goods brand running a great advertising campaign that is offset at the point-of-purchase by a terrible package.

Allocating the media budget

Once the primary and secondary media are selected, the last step in finalizing a media plan to implement an IMC campaign is to determine how to allocate the media budget. Just as the IMC planning worksheet provides the manager with an opportunity to summarize the critical considerations necessary for developing the IMC plan, we can also use a worksheet to help organize the information needed to optimize the allocation of the media budget. Figure 13.6 illustrates what this might look like for the patient part of the disposable contact lens case discussed earlier. What it does is bring together the various communication tasks that are to be accomplished and the various media options that will be needed to get the job done. This information comes directly from the IMC planning worksheet, and it looks at those media options in terms of primary and secondary options. Across the top, we have filled in the communication tasks that were identified, and under each the various media options that were selected as appropriate for each task. *Specific* media should be included here (for example, Facebook, newspaper, brochures, etc.), but for our example we are using general types of media. In this example, television advertising has been chosen as primary media for all but the task strengthening brand attitude and building brand purchase intention, reinforced by various secondary media. Because the communication tasks reflect what needs to be done at the various stages of the decision process, it also serves as a timeline.

What the worksheet shows is that the brand should continue to be using television advertising as the primary medium to stimulate category, brand awareness and attitude for disposable contact lenses. Additionally, a number of secondary media have more specific roles for particular communications tasks. Television would do a good job in satisfying all the communications tasks; but because this is a high-involvement informational decision, we know additional information will be needed to convince the patient, with time to process it. This is where newspapers and magazines can play a role, along with point-of-

	Communication tasks				
	Generate Category Awareness	Build Brand Awareness, Initial Brand Attitude	Strengthen Brand Awareness, Build Brand Attitude	Strengthen Brand Attitude, Build Brand Purchase Intention	Act on Brand Purchase Intention, Maintain Brand Attitude
Primary Media	Television	Television	Television	Direct Mail	Direct Mail Television
Secondary Media	Digital Print	Digital Print	Digital Print P-O-P Direct Mail	Digital Print P-O-P	Digital Print Direct Mail

Figure 13.6 Media allocation worksheet for implementing patient IMC plan.

purchase merchandising material such as brochures and posters, direct mail and some digital media, especially the internet. All the secondary media provide an opportunity for delivering both advertising and incentive promotions (if and where needed).

Not shown here because this is the patient worksheet, advertising to the doctor or eye-care professional will also find its way to the patient during consultation. For example, it will inform the doctor's recommendation and it may include such things as flip-charts for the doctor to use in explaining disposable contact lenses. This, of course, underscores the importance of consistency for everything in the IMC campaign.

Looking at the summary worksheet, the manager now knows what is needed in order to accomplish the communication tasks in terms of primary and secondary media, and it only remains to set priorities and allocate the budget. The boxes in the worksheet would, of course, contain media costs for each task. One of the real advantages of using a worksheet like this is that it permits the manager to see at a glance where and, importantly, *why* the budget is being spent. If adjustments must be made, for example, because there is simply not enough money to deal with all the communication tasks, or if budget cuts are needed over the course of the campaign, any adjustments can easily be considered within the context of the overall IMC programme.

Setting the IMC budget

In setting the overall budget for an IMC campaign, the media to be used will no doubt constitute the major share. But, there will also be costs associated with the production of the advertising and other merchandising material: any costs associated with implementing promotions, as well as the cost of the research to pre-test the adverts and promotions, and to track the campaign (which we consider in the next section).

When setting the IMC budget, something called 'adverlasticity' must be considered (Rossiter et al., 2018). This is the expected increase in sales that follow, say, a 10 percent increase in spending on the campaign. In other words, the manager must consider the likely return from increased sales versus the cost of achieving it. This of course assumes *effective* marketing communication. This can become especially tricky with promotions. Depending upon the margins involved, it can often require a significant increase in unit sales to offset the lost revenue from the reduced price. Although it may not make budgeting sense, a promotion may nonetheless have a sound tactical reason for being implemented, such as encouraging future full-price purchases.

While it is fairly easy to estimate promotion, production, and research costs, estimating the media budget for implementing the media plan is more difficult. Using something like the media allocations worksheet, the manager will know what media to use in order to satisfy all of the campaign's communication tasks, and satisfy the brand's sales goals. It will be necessary to work backwards from the sales goal to arrive at the media budget necessary to achieve it. Then, the difficult task of optimizing the media allocation within this budget will follow. Rarely will you be able to fund all of the media identified to satisfy the communication tasks.

Most companies use some variation of the task method for setting the media budget. The task method reflects the Communication Response Sequence introduced in Chapter 8, along with a few additions. Recall that the Communication Response Sequence identifies the steps required for marketing communication to be effective: exposure to the message, successful processing of it leading to the desired communication effect, resulting in target audience action.

Table 13.3 The task method for setting the media budget

1 Set sales goals for brand.
2 Determine the number of purchases required to reach that goal.
3 Establish how many members of the target audience must become aware of the IMC campaign in order to successfully process the message through action.
4 Determine how much effective reach will be required to accomplish this.
5 Select the appropriate reach pattern from the media plan and estimate the number of insertions necessary to generate that reach at the minimum effective frequency.
6 Determine what this will cost to implement.

Applying the task method, you begin by setting sales goals for the brand, and then estimate how many purchases will be required to reach that goal. This will require having good purchase data for the target audience. To reach that many purchases with the IMC campaign, you need to estimate how many members of the target audience must become aware of the IMC campaign in order to successfully process the message. Then, determine what effective reach will be required to achieve it. With this in hand you select the appropriate reach pattern from the media plan and estimate the number of insertions that will be necessary to generate that reach at a minimum effective frequency. Finally, determine what this will cost to implement. The task method is summarized in Table 13.3. The media budget is now set, and to determine the overall campaign budget, add to it the costs for creative production and research.

Tracking IMC campaigns

To ensure an IMC campaign is working, as well as to effectively manage it, it is essential to track it in the market. This involves much more than simply monitoring sales. Sales depend on many things beyond IMC: things such as distribution, price and changes in the economy, to say nothing of competitor activity. It is important for a manager to understand the extent to which IMC is 'working', and *causally* contributing to sales. This means both how the overall campaign is working as well as the individual components. Because we are looking at campaign effectiveness within the overall market for the product or service, we are also interested in monitoring any marketing or other economic activity that may influence target audience behaviour. This means looking at competitor behaviour as well as trade activity. It is essential for the manager to have a good understanding of what is going on in the market.

While keeping an eye on the market is important, effective tracking requires a survey of consumers. There are three basic methods for tracking consumer response to an IMC campaign. The first is using a *panel* where the *same* people are interviewed at various stages over the campaign. The second involves interviewing *separate* samples of the target audience at various stages over the course of the campaign. The third, and the method considered to be the best, is *continuous* tracking. With continuous tracking, small random samples of the target audience are interviewed on a daily or weekly basis, and periodically (say every four weeks) looked at using moving averages of the results.

Tracking measures

In Chapter 8 we began our discussion of message processing by looking at something we called the *consumer response sequence*. Tracking must deal with each of the four steps in the consumer response sequence: exposure, processing, communication effects and target audience action. All but the first, exposure, are dealt with in the consumer tracking survey. This is because exposure is a *media measure*, and should be expressed as a rate or level of media activity for the time period of the survey. Nevertheless, the manager must look at the level of IMC media input and relate it to results of the consumer survey and to sales. If there has been a heavy media schedule during a period, yet the results of the survey and sales do not reflect this, a careful analysis of the consumer survey results should be able to pinpoint the problem.

Processing measures

Actual processing of the campaign, of course, cannot be measured directly because it is an *immediate* response to the message. Because of this, processing must be measured *indirectly*, by using self-reported measures of attention. The assumption here is that at least some processing must have occurred if someone is able to remember an advertisement or other IMC message when asked about it.

There are a number of ways of doing this. You can ask whether an advertisement or other IMC message is recognized, or recalled with either a brand or category cue. With a brand cue, people are shown a list of brands and asked if they have seen or heard any advertising or other marketing communication lately for any of them. This provides a measure of *claimed* recall – the number of people who think they have seen the message. But this is not enough. You should go on and ask them to describe the advertising in as much detail as possible. If the description is consistent with the executions, this provides what is called *proven* recall – you can be certain that they did indeed process the advertising. Coding the content of the descriptions can also provide a good indication of just what was processed.

Perhaps the best measure of processing is category-prompted recall. Here, people are asked what marketing communication they remember for a specific category of product or service. If you are marketing, for example, bottled water, you would ask what advertising or other marketing communication people remember seeing or hearing for bottled water (the category), and to describe it. If the brand is not mentioned, you ask what the brand was. What you are looking for, of course, is a good description of the execution, linked to the brand. Category cued recall measures should be taken separately for each medium of interest used in the campaign.

Communication effects measures

These measures will be exactly the same as those used in the pre-test (which we discussed in Chapter 9). However, there is one important difference in the order in which the questions are asked. Recall that in a pre-test, the brand awareness questions are asked last in order to 'distance' the response from the forced exposure to test execution. But in tracking, they are asked first. There is obviously no need to delay the question because there will have been plenty of time since exposure. If the message has worked, brand awareness will be the first step necessary before there is any target audience action.

Target audience action measures

For an IMC campaign to be effective, the net result of all the messages delivered must satisfy the overall communication objectives and lead to the desired target audience action. If brand purchase or usage is the desired action, you ask what brands in the category were purchased, or services used, in the period surveyed. If the desired action was a specific non-purchase related behaviour, for example, a social marketing campaign aimed at binge drinking, ask about that. For fmcg markets, when the desired action is almost always sales, scanner technologies are often used.

Managing the campaign with tracking

The most important aspect of tracking is that it enables the manager to 'manage' the campaign by monitoring how well it is doing, and why. The consumer tracking survey is full of important tracking and diagnostic information. But equally important, and what helps provide context for the tracking results, is the ongoing audit of what is happening in the market. The manager must be alert to any significant change in the market or economy generally, and competitor activity specifically. Have there been new products or line exclusions introduced that compete with your brand? Has there been a shift in competitive advertising strategy, or an increase in media budgets? Have there been aggressive competitor promotions during the tracking period? It should be obvious that such things could have an effect on a brand's tracking results.

The tracking results can be of significant help in managing the campaign in many areas, but three are especially important. Attention data can help fine-tune media plans by adjusting reach and frequency to increase effective reach if the results are weak. The processing measures can be used to adjust the IMC mix. Individual executions within a medium, or the medium itself, may or may not be pulling their weight. Over time, the processing measures will also help alert the manager to potential 'wearout', even if the overall strategy remains the correct one. There are three areas of potential creative wearout to consider: attention, learning (owing to interference) and overexposure.

Attention wearout

Diminished attention to a message that has been seen or heard a number of times is a common problem, especially with print media (and that would include non-video messages in digital media). If the attention measures are seen to decline over time, one way of addressing the problem is to introduce slightly different executions of the strategy, always with attention to maintaining a consistent look and feel (as discussed in Chapter 10).

Learning or interference wearout

Results that show a decline in learning suggest that the problem could be caused by interference. Of course, measures of learning will also slip if attention falls. But learning, or interference, wearout usually occurs in response to a significant change in competitor's media schedule or message. It is also important to realize that with a new IMC campaign, a major surge or 'interference' picked up in a tracking survey could be caused by the brand's own earlier campaigns. Sutherland and Sylvester (2000) provide a number of examples of this from tracking studies, still the best book on tracking. The answer to interference wearout, whether caused by competitors or one's own previous campaigns, is to increase the media budget to build exposure for the brand's message.

Overexposure wearout

It is also possible for a message to be overexposed; it is unlikely with print executions, but it can be a problem with broadcast, especially television (and again this includes video on digital media). With low-involvement brand attitude, for informational strategies it doesn't really matter if some negative attitude builds through overexposure. Recall that people do not need to 'like' this type of message for it to be effective. But if it is transformational, the execution should be pulled at once because a positive 'feeling' is required for this type of message to be effective. If the brand attitude strategy is high-involvement, the best course is to introduce new variations on the execution, minimizing those points identified by the tracking measures.

Summary

The IMC plan is created out of the planning process. The target audience has been identified and an understanding of how they go about making decisions established. This understanding helps the manager identify those places in the process where marketing communication is most likely to have a positive effect on the decision, something we call touch points. The overall communication objectives that were established in the planning phase inform specific communication tasks that must be accomplished at each touch point in order to achieve that positive effect on the decision. Media options must then be selected that are compatible with the communication objectives and appropriate processing requirements in order to deliver the message.

In putting the plan together, it is helpful to look at the component parts in a way in which an assessment of all the options available may be considered. An IMC planning worksheet is one way of getting at this, where for each touch point identified, the specific target audience and communication objectives associated with the communication tasks needed, along with the media options appropriate to deliver the message, are summarized. The ability to consider all the opportunities to positively affect the brand purchase decision with a worksheet like this simplifies the manager's task in putting together the final plan. It enables the manager to optimize the IMC programme for selecting those communication tasks that are essential, and then to decide what trade-offs must be made among the remaining opportunities because it is rare that the budget will be large enough to accommodate everything.

The next step in finalizing the plan is to select the best media for delivering the message. The IMC plan identifies the set of media options appropriate for each communication task, and now the manager must select the primary and secondary media that will best accomplish the job. But just as the manager must in almost all cases make trade-offs among the communication tasks, in the same way it is unlikely that every appropriate medium can be used. Trade-offs will be necessary because of budget constraints. Again, a worksheet can provide a useful way of summarizing the options a manager must consider in order to more easily evaluate those options and make the best media budget allocation decision.

The last step in implementing the plan is to set the budget. This will require identifying the cost of such things as creative production and necessary research, and determining a media budget. Together, this will establish the overall IMC budget for the campaign. Most companies will use some form of the task method in determining a media budget. With this in hand, the final selection of primary and secondary media can be made, and the plan implemented.

Once the plan has been implemented, it is critical to track its effect in the market. In addition to monitoring what is going on in the market, it is important to track consumer response to the campaign. The best way of doing this is with continuous tracking, where small random samples of the target audience are interviewed daily or weekly and, with moving averages, analysed periodically. Measures of both how well the campaign messages have been processed and purchase behaviour should be taken, and measures taken to address any wearout issues identified.

Review questions

1 How does the manager go about identifying touch points for the IMC plan?
2 How does an IMC planning worksheet help the manager in finalizing the IMC plan?
3 In Figure 12.2 (from the last chapter) the decision stages for a lamp purchase were illustrated. What are the important touch points likely to be?
4 Complete an IMC planning worksheet for these touch points.
5 What is necessary to implement the IMC plan?
6 What are the important criteria in media selection for the final IMC plan?
7 How do secondary media contribute to the effectiveness of the IMC plan?
8 How can a media budget allocation worksheet help the manager implement the IMC plan?
9 What are some of the important considerations in setting an IMC budget?
10 How does the task method work in determining the media budget?
11 Why is it important to track an IMC campaign?
12 Discuss wearout and its causes.

References

Barlow, W.E. and Papaziou, E. (1980) *The Media Book*. New York, NY: The Media Book, Inc.

Dijkstra, M. (2002) *An Experimental Investigation of Energy Effects in Multiple-Media Advertising Campaigns*. The Netherlands: Tilburg University, Published PhD. Thesis.

Grass, R.C. and Wallace, W.H. (1974) Advertising communication: Print vs. TV. *Journal of Advertising Research*, *14(5)*, 19–23.

Keller, K.L. (1987) Memory factors in advertising: The effect of advertising retrieval cues on brand evaluation. *Journal of Consumer Research*, *14(3)*, 316–333.

Maloney, J.C. (1962) Curiosity versus disbelief in advertising. *Journal of Advertising Research*, *2(2)*, 2–8.

Rossiter, J.R. and Percy, L. (1997) *Advertising Communication and Promotion Management*. New York, NY: McGraw-Hill.

Rossiter, J.R., Percy, L. and Bergkvist L. (2018) *Marketing Communications: Objectives, Strategies, Tactics*. London: Sage Publications, Ltd.

Sutherland, M. and Sylvester, A.K. (2000) *Advertising and the Mind of the Consumer*. St. Leonards, NSW, Australia: Allen & Unwin.

Glossary

Acceptance   A response in processing a message where the receiver believes the benefit claim to be true, and necessary for high-involvement brand attitude strategies.

Adblocking   The use of apps and other software to avoid advertising on traditional broadcast and digital media.

Advertere   The Latin root of the word advertising, roughly translated as 'to turn toward'.

Allowance promotion   Any incentive promotion for the trade where a monetary allowance is given in return for stocking or promoting a brand and achieving specific performance or purchase requirements.

Assimilation-contrast theory   Sherif and Hovland's idea that someone's current attitudes provide a point of reference in any attempt to persuade, where a person assimilates positions close to their own and rejects position significantly different from their own.

Attention   Necessary first step in processing a message, central to perception and consciousness.

Attitude   A relative concept that reflects those things people believe weighted by how important they are to them.

Attribute   The objective characteristics of something, for example, '25 percent fewer calories'.

Audiobranding   The use of music, usually proprietary, to help provide consistency and uniqueness to a campaign.

Awareness-trial-reinforcement (ATR)   A low-involvement model of purchase behaviour introduced by Ehrenberg, where awareness is followed by a tentatively favourable attitude leading to trial, after which a final attitude is formed.

Behavioural sequence model (BSM)   A model of buyer behaviour built on the stages involved in brand choice, identifying touch points where marketing communication is likely to positively affect the decision.

Benefit   What a brand offers in terms of attributes, subjective characteristics, and emotional stimulation.

Benefit focus   How the benefit is used in an execution, consistent with the underlying motive driving behaviour in the category.

Bottom-up processing   The direct response to a stimulus without integration with one's knowledge and assumptions about it.

Brand attitude   A communication effect that is always a communication objective, reflecting a link between a brand and its benefit.

Brand awareness A communication effect that is always a communication objective, reflecting the link in memory between the brand and the need it fulfils (category need).

Brand line All of the products that are marketed under a single brand name.

Brand portfolio A company's brands and those linked through alliance that are considered together in the formation of business strategy.

Brand purchase intention A communication effect that is the primary communication objective for promotion.

Brand salience More than just awareness of a brand, it follows from correctly linking the brand in memory with the appropriate need.

Branded content Also known as 'native advertising' or sponsored content, it is what drives content marketing.

Branding strategy The management of brand–product relationships, especially in terms of the indication of their origin (for example, a standalone brand or linked in some way to a parent brand).

Buzz marketing A formalized attempt to create favourable word-of-mouth for a brand.

Campaign tracking A survey among the target audience to determine how well an overall campaign and its individual IMC elements are working and causally contributing to sales.

Central position Usually the positioning strategy for market leaders, when the brand is seen as delivering all the main benefits associated with the product category.

Channel marketing The term used to describe all levels of marketing communication to the retail trade, combining co-op advertising and tactical marketing.

Cognitive response A term used in psychology to describe a response based on conscious knowledge or assumptions.

Communication effect One of the four possible responses to marketing communication from which communication objectives are selected: category need, brand awareness, brand attitude, and brand purchase intention.

Communication objective The communication effects that are targeted by the message execution, and must always include brand awareness and brand attitude.

Communication response sequence The sequence of steps necessary for marketing communication to be effective: exposure to the message, processing of the message, achieving the desired communication effect, and the desired target audience action.

Communication strategy Setting the overall communication objectives and selecting the appropriate brand awareness and brand attitude strategy consistent with how the target audience makes decisions.

Communication tasks What marketing communication is expected to accomplish at each important touch point in the decision process.

Consciousness The act of focusing mental resources onto something, becoming aware of what is attended to, and being able to tell others about it.

Conscious processing Utilization of declarative or explicit memory in the processing of a message.

Consumer franchise-building promotion (CFB) An idea first introduced by Prentice recognizing the need for effective promotion to not only stimulate immediate target audience action, but also to contribute to long-term positive brand attitude.

Content marketing Where a brand creates 'content' of some kind, such as entertaining articles or short videos, that is to be shared through digital media.

Co-op advertising   Retail advertising where both the marketer and retailer cooperate in a part of the marketing communication.

Corporate advertising   Advertising for the company as a corporate brand rather than a specific brand from its portfolio.

Corporate brand   A term used by companies to describe the organization itself as a brand.

Corporate identity   The visual and verbal symbols used by a company to set itself apart from other companies so that the consumer can readily identify it.

Corporate image   The set of emotions and beliefs held about a company.

Corporate reputation   Values such as honesty and integrity associated with a company and evoked by its image.

Corporate story   A comprehensive narrative about a company, including such things as its mission statement and history.

Coupon   A certificate redeemable at retail for a specific price reduction on a brand.

Creative brief   A one-page document summarizing the strategic direction for a brand's marketing communication used to guide the development of creative executions.

Creative idea   An interesting way of presenting the brand positioning in an attention-getting way.

Database   A collection of information about a target market available for use (usually on computer), interactive and necessary for direct marketing.

Decision roles   The part(s) a person plays in the decision process, as initiator, influencer, decider, purchaser, and/or user.

Decision stages   The important steps involved in making a brand choice, forming the foundation of the behavioural sequence model.

Declarative memory   Conscious or explicit memory, for information that can be consciously recalled as words or visual images.

Differentiated positioning   The positioning strategy for most brands, based on a benefit that is seen by the consumer as giving the brand an advantage over competitors.

Direct mail   A medium for delivering messages by post (or private letter distributors), often used for promotions.

Direct marketing   Marketing technique targeted towards specific target audiences based on a database, bypassing traditional distribution channels.

Downside elasticity   When sales decline as a result of a price increase.

Duchenne smile   Named for the nineteenth-century French anatomist Duchenne de Boulogne, it is a form of smile believed to occur spontaneously and only during the experience of true enjoyment.

Embodiment   The bodily state, such as facial expression, posture, or tone of voice that occurs in response to an emotional stimulus, and the later use of that emotional response.

Emotion   A coordinated change in the body at several levels in response to a stimulus; for example, in processing marketing communication, especially the subjective feelings linked to it in conscious memory.

Emotional sequence   The desired portrayal of emotion in marketing communication, reflecting the motivation involved: negative to mildly positive for informational brand attitude strategies and neutral to strongly positive for transformational brand attitude strategies.

Encoding specificity   Tulving's notion that in order to successfully retrieve something from memory, there must be a match between how information is originally encoded and how it is available when being retrieved from memory.

Endorser branding strategy   A sub-branding strategy where the parent brand serves as the guarantor for a brand, but less directly linked than with a source branding strategy.

Episodic memory   Memories for a specific event, and part of declarative memory.

Event marketing   Brand or company sponsorship of a single event such as a concert or sporting event.

Expectancy-value model   Generally considered the best model of attitude, it considers a person's attitude towards something to be the summation of everything believed about it weighted by how important each of those beliefs are to them.

Experiential marketing   Utilizing limited-run, pop-up, Instagramable events, actively engaging people with a brand.

Explicit memory   Information that is consciously understood to have been recalled from memory.

Feeling   Often considered a synonym for emotion; it is not, but does reflect the subjective feeling component of emotion, which is that part of an emotion that can be felt with the aid of consciousness.

fmcg   A term standing for 'fast moving consumer goods'.

fMRI   The abbreviation for functional magnetic resonance imaging, a neuroimaging procedure.

Frequency   The average number of times one member of a target audience has the opportunity of seeing or hearing a message within a given time period, usually four weeks.

FSI   The abbreviation typically used for 'free-standing inserts', marketing communication inserted in a print medium, but not bound into it.

Hierarchical partitioning   Looking at a market in terms of the order in which consumers use characteristics of the product or market in making decisions.

Hierarchy-of-effects   The general high-involvement decision model where awareness is followed by learning *and* acceptance that leads to a positive attitude before action is taken.

High involvement   Where there is a perceived risk in making a brand or product choice, either economic or psychological, and full acceptance of the message is required before action is taken.

Implicit memory   Defined by Schacter as that part of memory that facilitates the performance of a task without conscious or intentional recollections (for example, typing).

Information processing paradigm   McGuire's model of the steps required in processing a message in order to achieve attitude change: the message must be presented, attended to, comprehended, yielded to, that intention retained and then acted upon.

Informational brand attitude strategy   Those strategies from the Rossiter–Percy Grid dealing with negatively motivated brand decisions.

Inoculation theory   An idea originally suggested by Janis and his colleagues in the 1950s, and developed by McGuire, it posits that the stronger your beliefs about something, the more likely you are to avoid exposure to opposition arguments.

Involvement   Perceived risk attached to making a brand or product decision, and a determinate of brand attitude strategy.

Latitude of acceptance   Following Sherif and Hovland's assimilation-contrast theory, one's area of agreement with a message, an understanding of which is required for high-involvement brand attitude strategies.

Latitude of indifference   Following Sherif and Hovland's assimilation-contrast theory, information in a message that one neither agrees nor disagrees with, and a potential level to pitch high-involvement messages in order to initiate attitude change.

Latitude of rejection   Following Sherif and Hovland's assimilation-contrast theory, message content not consistent with one's existing beliefs, and therefore not likely to be believed.

Learning   An essential step in the processing of all marketing communication; it is the acquisition of information from a message with or without conscious effort – the result of long-term potentiation.

Loading device   An incentive promotional technique for encouraging larger than normal purchase quantities to effectively remove the target from the market in the short term; for example, with bonus packs.

Long-term potentiation (LTP)   The neural basis of learning following repeated stimulation of a neuron's dendritic spine leaving it more responsive to additional input of the same type.

Low involvement   Where there is no perceived risk in making a brand or product choice, and where only a tentatively favourable attitude is necessary for action to be taken.

Loyalty and reward programmes   An incentive promotion technique designed to reward and retain loyal customers, perhaps the most familiar example being frequent-flier programmes.

Marketing plan   An outline of the goals and objectives set for a brand, and how to reach them, which must form the foundation for the IMC strategic planning process.

Marketing public relations   The term introduced by Harris to describe public relations activities in support of marketing objectives.

Media vehicles   The specific publications, programmes, events, etc. through which marketing communication messages (both advertising and promotion) are delivered.

Memory   Representations in the brain of learning; physical records of our experiences encoded within our neural system.

Mere exposure   A term associated with Zajonc and his colleagues that reflects an unconscious affective memory, independent of declarative memory, a result of priming.

Message processing   The steps necessary for effective communication, involving attention, learning, acceptance (in high-involvement cases), and emotion.

Minimum effective frequency   The number of exposures necessary to ensure effective processing of a message at least once.

Mobile marketing   Using mobile communication sources such as mobile phones for delivery of marketing communication, with the potential for interactive response.

Motivation   The innate or acquired drive that underlies behaviour, negatively originated (to solve or avoid a problem) or positively originated (for sensory gratification or social approval), and a determinate of brand attitude strategy.

Neural network   A collection of neurons that learn and organize themselves through a synaptic learning rule advanced by Hebb and leading to long-term potentiation (LTP) in the brain.

Neuroimaging   A way of identifying those areas of the brain active under particular circumstances (such as making a choice between brands of soft drinks), measured by such procedures as PET scans (positron emission tomography) and fMRI (functional magnetic resonance imaging).

Nondeclarative memory   Unconscious memory that results from experience and leads to a change of behaviour (for example, learning to ride a bicycle) but not as recollection.

Partitioning   Looking at markets according to how consumers group products in relationship to various category characteristics or benefits.

Permission marketing   Where prior permission is granted for a marketer to send text messages on mobile phones, emails, or messages via other personal media.

Personal selling   Any direct contact with consumers in an effort to communicate a brand's message, either face-to-face or by telephone.

PET scan   Positron emission tomography, one of the first methods used for neuroimaging studies.

Point-of-purchase (p-o-p)   Retailer promotion often provided by the marketer as part of a co-op or tactical marketing programme, it gives visual prominence for a brand and may or may not include an incentive.

Positioning   Locating a brand in a consumer's mind through marketing communication in terms of the need it is seen as satisfying (what it is) and its benefit (what it offers).

Preconsciousness   That part of the brain where all possibilities for awareness that have been unconsciously attended to wait while the conscious mind is occupied.

Premium   An incentive promotion that is offered free or at reduced price with purchase of a brand, and which should have a logical link to the product.

Pre-testing   Using a management judgement test and/or audience response to evaluate an advertisement or promotion's ability to satisfy its communication objective prior to exposure in the market.

Price-elasticity of a brand   How a brand responds to price cuts and price increases.

Primary media   The medium that does the best job of delivering all the communication objectives in an IMC campaign.

Product line   A group of products within a product category that are closely related to each other.

Product placement   More appropriately brand placement; it is the inclusion of a brand in entertainment vehicles such as television shows, movies, and video games, in a conspicuous fashion in the expectation of raising brand awareness and brand attitude through association with a celebrity or situation; a practice raising ethical concern.

Product portfolio   The range of products offered by a company.

Programmatic buying   The use of automated systems to buy and place media rather than through direct contact with media representation.

Promovere   The Latin root of the word promotion, which roughly translates to 'move forward or advance'.

Publicity   Often used as a synonym for public relations, it is more than public relations, including sources outside of the company.

Public relations (PR)   Activities paid for by a company to generate positive publicity about the company or a brand.

Ratchet effect   Moran's idea that using advertising and promotion together, as appropriate, produces stronger results than either alone by 'ratcheting up' the effects of advertising with occasional promotion coupled by retaining more customers attracted by the promotion through the effects of the advertising.

Reach   The percentage of the target audience that is exposed to a message within a given time period, usually four weeks.

Recall brand awareness   The brand awareness strategy needed when the purchase decision relies on the category need bringing to mind brands to satisfy that need.

Recognition brand awareness   The brand awareness strategy needed when the purchase decision relies on recognizing the brand at the point-of-purchase, stimulating or reminding of category need.

Refunds and rebates   An incentive promotion technique where a set amount of money is refunded to buyers upon submitting proof of purchase.

Refutational strategy   A creative strategy used when there is a well-known objection to a product, where the objection is acknowledged first and then countered.

Remote conveyor model   A theoretical framework for identifying an effective way to dramatize a benefit claim using an eye-catching element that initially seems unrelated to the product but, with prompting, becomes obvious.

Repeat-purchase action objective   When the marketing focus is on existing customers, communication is aimed at increasing the rate of repeat purchase.

Retail promotion   Promotions initiated by the retailer for the store itself, or specific brands, or promotions provided by marketers and delivered through the retailer.

Rossiter–Percy Grid   A four-cell grid that highlights the need for different creative tactics for the four types of brand attitude strategy, based on the different processing requirements associated with the level of involvement in the purchase decision (high versus low) and whether the motivation driving behaviour in the category is positive or negative (transformational versus informational strategies).

Sales promotion   The traditional way of referring to promotion, generally associated with an incentive.

Sample   An incentive promotion technique designed to provide the consumer with an opportunity to try the product prior to a purchase.

Secondary media   Media used to reinforce a specific communication effect that is an objective of the IMC campaign.

Semantic memory   That part of declarative (i.e. conscious) memory containing knowledge and assumptions unconnected with specific experiences (episodic memory).

Social marketing communication   Different from most marketing communication in that it is looking to effect a change in undesirable or pathological behaviour.

Social media   A group of internet-based applications where individuals act as both content creator and receiver.

Source branding strategy   A sub-branding strategy where the parent brand is directly linked to the sub-brand in its branding and marketing communication, associating its identity with the brand.

Sponsorships   An arrangement where a brand provides financial support for an athlete, team, charity, or such in return for publicity associated with that support.

Stakeholders   A term describing all those groups with an interest in a company, both inside and outside of an organization, including consumers, investors, trade, and employees.

Stand–alone brand Brands that do not include a parent source or endorser as part of their branding strategy.

Strategic planning process The five-step process involved in developing the communication strategy for IMC: target audience identification, determining how they make brand decisions, positioning, establishing the communication objectives, and identifying appropriate media to deliver the message.

Sub-brand A brand name linked with a parent brand either directly through a source branding strategy or secondarily through an endorser strategy.

Subliminal processing Stimuli processed below the threshold of consciousness that can never be made conscious.

Sweepstakes Along with contests and games, an incentive promotion technique designed to create excitement for a brand.

Tactical marketing Grew out of a desire for more control over co-op monies, providing programmes tailored to specific retailer's needs but maintaining control over content and timing.

Target audience The specific segment of a brand's target market identified in the strategic planning process to receive advertising and/or promotion.

Telemarketing Personal selling using the telephone.

Theory of reasoned action The extended version of the expectancy-value model that adds a social norm component.

Top-down processing The use of knowledge and assumptions in the processing of a stimulus, for example, marketing communications.

Touch points Those places in the decision process where marketing communication is likely to have a positive effect.

Trade promotion Incentives offered to retailers and distributors to encourage them to stock or promote a brand.

Trade show An event where products from a particular industry or related industries are exhibited and demonstrated.

Transformational brand attitude strategy Those strategies from the Rossiter–Percy Grid dealing with positively motivated brand decisions.

Transtheoretical model of change A stage of change model developed by Prochaska and Di Clemente.

Trial action objective When the marketing focus is on attracting new customers, and communication is aimed at stimulating trial.

Unconscious processing Processing of information at a subconscious level as part of implicit or nondeclarative memory.

Up-side elasticity When prices are cut and sales go up.

User-oriented positioning Where the focus is on the user of the brand, not the product, and the target audience represents a specific segment or the underlying motivation is social approval (although a benefit positioning is also appropriate in these cases).

Index